Thinking of Grad

Kaplan can take you

Take a Kaplan Course or Take Your Chances.

Our live classes offer the most comprehensive test preparation available, combining expert instructors, superior materials, and the smartest technology to provide proven results. With more than 185 centers worldwide, we offer courses for the LSAT, GRE, GMAT, MCAT*, and more. Kaplan can help you get the score you need to get into the school of your choice.

For more information, call:

1-800-KAP-TEST.

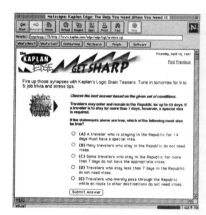

The Kaplan Edge: Hot Tips Via Email!

Looking to get a competitive edge in school or at work? Sign up for the Kaplan Edge, a fun, FREE email service. Each day you'll get emailed a math, logic, or English brain teaser, grad school or career trivia, academic reminders, plus regular stress-relief tips and a word-a-day vocabulary booster.

Finally, a fun and easy way to train your brain. Visit **www.kaplan.com** to subscribe now!

Yes! Please send me more information on Kaplan services and products!

❑ Yes, I plan to attend grad school.

I'm interested in receiving information on (circle one): (courses) (books & software) (KapLoan)

Please Print

Name: _____

Address: _____

City: _____ State: _____ Zip: _____

Phone: _____ E-Mail: _____

Graduation Date: _____ circle: (high school) (college)

Computer: (Mac) (Windows) (No Computer)

I plan to take the: (circle one) (GRE) (GMAT) (LSAT) (MCAT)

My first-choice school is: _____

*All test names are trademarks of their respective owners, which neither sponsor nor endorse this product.

Mac is a registered trademark of Apple Computers Inc. Windows is a registered trademark of Microsoft Corporation.

639.0021

Everything you need to help you get into grad school.

Score higher. Kaplan's test prep **software** and **books** provide realistic practice exams and strategic insights to maximize your performance on the day of the test.

Develop an effective application campaign. Our graduate admissions guides offer key admissions and financial aid information, insider's advice, and more.

The latest in educational innovation: Kaplan's Roadtrip software for the GRE/GMAT/LSAT.* On CD-ROM for Mac and Windows.

Getting Into Medical
School 1997–98

Getting Into Law School
1997–98

Getting Into Business
School 1997–98

Getting Into Graduate
School 1997–98

GRE 1997–98

GMAT 1997–98

NCLEX* 1997–98

MCAT* 1997–98

MCAT Comprehensive Review
1997–98

LSAT 1997–98

Pass Life's Other Tests
Whether you want to make the most of your college career or need help launching your real-world career, Kaplan can help.

*GRE, GMAT, MCAT, LSAT and NCLEX are registered trademarks of their respective owners and do not endorse or sponsor this product.

This Book Was

Donated To _____

Sandra Drake

Family

Date: *May 1998*

The Yale Daily News

Guide to

Internships

1998

Kaplan Books
Published by Kaplan Educational Centers and Simon & Schuster
1230 Avenue of the Americas
New York, NY 10020
Copyright © 1997, by Kaplan Educational Centers

For bulk sales to schools, colleges, and universities, please contact Renee Nemire, Simon & Schuster Markets, 1633 Broadway, 8th Floor, New York, NY 10019.

Project Editor: Doreen Beauregard
Cover Design: Suzanne Noli
Interior Design: gumption design
Production Editor: Maude Spekes
Assistant Managing Editor: Brent Gallenberger
Managing Editor: Kiernan McGuire
Executive Editor: Del Franz

Special thanks to Sumi Wong and Linda Volpano

Manufactured in the United States of America
Published simultaneously in Canada

September 1997
10 9 8 7 6 5 4 3 2 1

ISBN 0-684-84170-3
ISSN 1093-1414

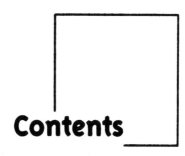

Contents

About the Authors... vi

Preface.. vii

Chapter One: Résumes, Cover Letters, and Interviews
by Kalpana Srinivasan and Erin White........................ 1

**Chapter Two: The Intern-Net: Going Online in
Your Internship Search** *by Shawn Bayern* 29

Chapter Three: Print Journalism *by Noah Kotch*.................. 45

Chapter Four: Broadcast Journalism *by Julie Hirschfeld* 85

Chapter Five: Business *by Danny Weiss* 113

Chapter Six: Technology *by Chris Grosso* 159

Chapter Seven: Science Research *by Melissa Lee*............... 179

Chapter Eight: Performing Arts *by Kate Merkel-Hess* 205

Chapter Nine: Museums and Galleries *by Bettina Lerner* 249

Chapter Ten: Entertainment *by Yen-Wen Cheong* 265

Chapter Eleven: Politics and Government *by Matt Terry* 283

Chapter Twelve: Advocacy *by Duncan Levin* 307

Chapter Thirteen: Public Service *by Sara Schwebel* 335

Chapter Fourteen: Interning Abroad *by Nicole Itano* 373

Chapter Fifteen: How to Make the Most of Your Internship
by Stacy Atlas 387

Indexes

Index of Companies Offering Internships 399

Geographic Index of Companies Offering Internships 405

A Special Note for International Students 413

About the Authors

Stacy Atlas of Orange, Connecticut, is an American studies major. She served as the city editor for the *Yale Daily News* in the 1996–1997 year.

Shawn Bayern is a computer science major from Laurel Hollow, New York. He was one of the *Yale Daily News*'s first online editors and specialized in handling the paper's Web site.

Yen-wen Cheong of New York, New York, was one of the 1996–1997 news desk co-editors at the *Yale Daily News*. She is a history major.

Chris Grosso is a former managing editor of the *Yale Daily News*. He earned his Yale degree in computer science and history.

Kate Merkel-Hess, a native of Iowa City, Iowa, reports for the *Yale Daily News*. She is majoring in east Asian studies, with an emphasis on China.

Julie Hirschfeld of New York, New York, majored in ethics, politics, and economics while at Yale. She was a *Yale Daily News* news editor in 1995–1996.

Nicole Itano comes from Boulder, Colorado, and is a reporter for the *Yale Daily News*. She plans to graduate with a degree in history.

Noah Kotch, originally of Raleigh, North Carolina, majored in classics while at Yale. He was the *Yale Daily News*'s editor-in-chief in 1995–1996.

Melissa S. Lee of New York, New York, was a *Yale Daily News* photo editor in 1995–1996. She graduated from Yale with a degree in biology and history of science/history of medicine.

Bettina Lerner of New York, New York, double majored at Yale in art history and French. She is now a graduate student in Yale's French Department.

Duncan Levin hails from New York, New York, and studied psychology at Yale. He was the executive editor of the *Yale Daily News* in 1995–1996.

Marc Lindemann of Port Washington, New York, was a news desk co-editor at the *Yale Daily News* in 1996–1997. He plans to graduate from Yale with a B.A. in history and humanities and an M.A. in history.

Sara Schwebel is a history major originally from Columbus, Ohio. In the 1996–1997 academic year, she served as the arts and living editor for the *Yale Daily News*.

Kalpana Srinivasan hails from Oak Brook, Illinois. She graduated from Yale with a B.A. in ethics, politics, and economics and comparative literature (that's two majors unbelievably). She served as the managing editor of the *Yale Daily News* during the 1995–1996 academic year.

Jason Tepperman of Boca Raton, Florida, served as the editorial editor of the *Yale Daily News* in 1996–1997. He pursued a double major in computer science and ethics, politics, and economics at Yale.

Matt Terry of Sandwich, Massachusetts, is a reporter for the *Yale Daily News*. He plans to double major in history and international studies at Yale.

Danny Weiss of East Meadow, New York, studied political science at Yale and reported for the *Yale Daily News*.

Erin White is a Westport, Connecticut resident. She reports for the *Yale Daily News* and is a history major.

Preface

Internships have become a key element of the competitive student's résumé. As the number of college graduates in America has increased, it has become increasingly difficult for students to distinguish themselves in the job market. Internships help students accentuate their skills and strengths, and serve as test runs to see how students might function in the workplace. Internships offer opportunities for students to challenge themselves and expand their horizons, and for future employers to get well-rounded and experienced entry-level employees.

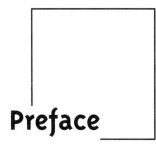

Aside from adding some extra hands to their staff, companies benefit in other ways from hiring interns. According to Andrew E. Schwartz, president of A.E. Schwartz & Associates, a management-training and professional-development organization for businesses based in Watertown, Massachusetts, internships can help prep students for the work force and ease the transition into regular postgraduate employment. "Many job applicants want a job but often do not have the prerequisite experience, experience they can only have by getting a job. Managers who take the chance and hire them may have to spend considerable time and effort training them, only to find the new recruits unsuitable or unhappy with the jobs," says Schwartz. "One way around this problem for many organizations is an internship program. For students and recent graduates, such programs provide working experience that otherwise would never be supplied to someone interested in a specific field."

At some places, the internship functions as a trial period and comes with a full-time job offer upon completion. Using this arrangement gives companies the first crack at some of the most qualified recent grads, since many students accept job offers from their internship employers over other offers. "Companies do summer internships to hire people. They want someone who is interested in their company and industry. This is not just a summer job," says Margaret Dinneny, the vice president of candidate services at Crimson & Brown Associates, which specializes in diversity recruitment. The group offers an internship referral service which collects students' résumés and forwards them to the appropriate companies. "Companies, when they are hiring interns, are looking for people who are going to come back to them. This is your chance to show what you can do on a permanent basis," says Dinneny.

Internships can reveal a lot about prospective job candidates. Beyond transcripts, GPAs, and teacher recommendations, internships provide employers with insight about students: their hands-on skills, their ability to translate academic performance into work performance, how they handle unexpected work situations. George Bunn, former general counsel for the Arms Control and Disarmament Agency and a member of the board of directors for the Arms Control Association, a nonpartisan group providing information on arms control to policy makers and the public, recommends internships for students serious about planning a career in government or public policy. "As an academic with a long background in U.S. government, I advise students to get experience in Washington before going on to graduate school or to academic or business employment in foreign affairs. I believe it impossible for students to understand how the U.S. government works on foreign affairs these days without some time in Washington, 'on the firing line,' " says Bunn. The Arms Control Association offers annual internships.

In some fields, internships are almost a prerequisite for landing that first job. In other areas, the internship may not be preparation for a job in the same field. But the internship still gives an employer a sense that a candidate is more than "book smart" and has something to offer the company.

For students, internships at the very least provide insights into the working world. At the most, they can lead to full-time positions with competitive companies. Some offer students a chance to work in big cities with experts in their field. Others offer students a chance to do the same work as full-time employees. Still others provide interns with chances to travel and to meet famous people. "In sum, an internship is a great experience for students and recent grads because it offers them the opportunity to try new things, learn a lot about the working world, and really stretch the limits of creativity," says one Washington, D.C., intern coordinator.

Internships benefit just about everyone involved (even bad internships can be good learning experiences). And the number of available internships is growing. There are plenty of resources to help you find internships, including books, Internet sites, career counselors. This book itself contains information on thousands of internship positions. But what good is knowing about available internships if you don't know how to get picked for them?

This book is meant to be a "start to finish" guide. Many internship positions are very competitive, with hundreds of applicants for only a few coveted positions. This book offers suggestions and recommendations on how to find the internships you want as well as how to make yourself a strong applicant. The first couple of chapters deal with general internship information: résumé writing, networking, interviewing, and using the Internet to find internships. The following chapters give you the specifics about internships in various fields (because applying for an internship in investment banking is different from applying for an internship in the performing arts) with advice on how to highlight your skills, increase your experience, and present yourself as a more competitive candidate. These chapters also provide insider tips from students who have been through the internship mill. They'll tell you what worked for them, and what they would do differently if they could start over. Advice from employers and career counselors supplement the student suggestions on how to be a top-rate applicant.

When it comes to internships, think ahead. If you discover an internship position that you would like to have in a couple of years, find out what you need to become eligible and what experience previous students in that position have had. Then, when the time is right, you'll have what it takes to get that internship.

Finally, make use of some of the resources described in this guide to hunt down internships (the Internet, for example) or to create your own. The worst thing you can do is be passive and expect opportunities to fall into your lap. You need to be creative, determined, and resourceful in order to create an effective internship game plan.

Applying for internships can be frustrating, time consuming, and sometimes disappointing. But in the end. it will open doors and expand horizons in ways you might never have guessed. Good luck, and keep at it.

—Kalpana Srinivasan

Résumés, Cover Letters, and Interviews

by Kalpana Srinivasan and Erin White

It's February, and you've decided that this summer, you're going to turn in the old lawnmower and burger flipper in favor of something new: a briefcase, a reporter's notebook, a stage prop, a computer. In short, you want a summer internship. You want to get started on the long, winding path you will call your career. You're pretty pleased with yourself for making such a wise decision; you are on your way. But before you become too smug, you suddenly realize that *it's February*! While some summer internships have late and rolling deadlines, you want to make all the right moves, and being late in the game is not one of them.

The first rule in the world of internships is to start looking early, whether you're looking for a summer internship or one that takes place during the academic year. Some people barely finish their summer internships before whipping out cover letters and résumés for the following summer. By mid-fall, some students may have already applied to a dozen places. If you start considering a summer internship in late winter, you're falling behind in the internship hunt.

Consider early on what kind of work you would like to do and in what field. The Washington Center for Internships and Academic Seminars, which places candidates from around the country in Washington, D.C., internships, advises that planning is a critical stage of the process. Before you start anything, you should know yourself and what you want to do. What is important to you— money, status, advancement, recognition, independence? Assess your skills and experience so that you can clearly define them on your résumé.

The Washington Center
for Internships

One option for finding an internship is using an internship placement service. This is what a couple of former interns have to say about The Washington Center for Internships and Academic Seminars:

"My internship search began when I was accepted into The Washington Center program. This program helped me look for internships in my field. They matched me up with at least five companies and gave me the opportunity to conduct phone interviews with the companies. In addition, these companies received a copy of my résumé as well as other documents about me from The Washington Center. I obtained an internship with The Widmeyer-Baker Group by interviewing with someone within the company, along with sending them some portfolio samples."

"With the help of The Washington Center, I not only had an outstanding experience as an intern, I also participated in two of its academic seminars and returned the following year to serve as a program assistant for a third seminar. I was fortunate enough to be able to narrow my [internship] choices down to just two: CNN and the television program *America's Most Wanted*. Wanting so badly to be a journalist, I was tempted to choose CNN immediately, but my supervisor really took the time to explain the pros and cons of each option, and my ultimate decision was *America's Most Wanted*. In January of '96 I did return to Washington to serve as an assistant for a two-week seminar called "Leadership 2000: Within the Independent Sector," which is one of several short-term seminars The Washington Center offers. That gave me the opportunity to have another Washington experience and reestablish contacts made at *America's Most Wanted*. Consequently, I am writing this from my office at *America's Most Wanted: America Fights Back*, where I hold the position of office coordinator."

For more information about The Washington Center, contact them at 1101 14th Street NW, Suite 500, Washington, D.C. 20005, (202) 336-7600/(800) 486-8921, fax (202) 336-7609.

That Oh-So-Important First Impression

Once you've decided which companies you want to work with, you must make them want you. Application requirements vary. Some require you to type a formal application, some require transcripts, some require recommendations, and some require just a résumé. But they all contribute to a first impression.

"Communication skills, written and oral, are very important. Make time to take that extra writing class or speech class; it will be well worth it," advises Darrell M. Ayers, the Intern Program Coordinator at the John F. Kennedy Center for the Performing Arts. Since the Center takes interns from across the country, many candidates do not have the opportunity to interview in person. Instead, they are represented by their applications, so they better be good. "The written information you send and how you communicate on the phone are what sells you," Ayers says. You owe it to yourself, then, to make sure the application package you put together reflects well on you, and shows what sets you apart from everyone else.

Your Résumé

Résumés may seem like a standard, no-big-deal part of your application. While résumé formats are pretty standard (there are only so many ways to jazz up a résumé without being tacky), it's the content that should be special. Your résumé is, in most cases, the first impression you give to a company. When internship coordinators look at your résumé, they generally will look for the basics (courses, major, GPA, skills, etcetera) as well as a neat, clean, easy-to-read format. At the same time, they'll be looking for what sets you apart and what strengths you have to offer.

Here are a few suggestions for résumé writing, from the top down.

Name and Address

You would think that everyone would agree on how to write the name and address, but they don't. Some say to spell out the whole state name and never abbreviate. Some say to put parentheses around your area code, and others abhor it. The common sense approach says it doesn't matter. Is the heading neat and appropriate looking? Will an intern coordinator know how to get in touch with you? That's all that really matters.

Here's a good way to do it. Put your name centered at the top in bold, capital letters. Put the rest of the heading in lower case, and not in bold. On the line beneath your name, write your street address. On the next line, write your city, state, and zip code. On the final line, write your phone number. Include your E-mail address if you have one.

If your home address is different from your college address—and if you think an intern coordinator may need to know both—you can include both addresses by placing one to the left and one to the right, under your centered name.

Objective

Some people include on their résumés an objective, which states in one line what they are looking for in an internship or what they hope to achieve through an internship. An objective is not a necessary part of a résumé and may take up precious space. Showing is better than telling. Highlighting your experience and interests might better serve the same purpose as an objective.

There are two schools of thought on the objective. Some consider it to be too broad or meaningless, or, if written very specifically, too limiting. Others like objectives, because they help identify where a person might fit in.

The decision to include or exclude an objective is a personal one, but in the interest of space, think about what, if anything, an objective adds to your résumé. Perhaps you are really interested in working at a certain company and would be happy in any one of several different departments within the company. An objective may put you in a pigeonhole, not allowing the scope you need to be considered for different kinds of positions. On the other hand, if you're focusing on a very specific internship position, and can clearly match the requirements of the job with the statement in your objective, go for it. Also, if there are a variety of internships that you're interested in, you could create a few versions of your résumé with different objectives to match.

Scannable Résumés:
DOs and DON'Ts

Many companies now electronically scan the résumés that they want
to keep on file. But the process can be tricky; unusual typefaces or
layouts might make a résumé unscannable.

DOs
- Use 8.5 x 11-inch paper only
- Use standard typefaces such as Times Roman, Universal, Futura,
  Optima, New Century Schoolbook, and Courier
- Use a point size between 10 and 14 points (but avoid 10-point
  Times Roman)

DON'Ts
- Don't fold or staple your résumé.
- Don't use atypical formats, such as multiple columns.
- Don't use colored paper; stick with white or beige.
- Don't use italics, underlines, shadows, or reversed type.
- Don't use extended or condensed spacing.

Education

Put your educational background in reverse chronological order, and include
your major. You may also want to point out areas of concentration or focus
in your studies, published works, and special honors, specifically those that
pertain to the field in which you want to work.

Regarding your GPA: some employers will be more interested in your
grades than others. But as one intern coordinator points out, if you have
good grades, there's no reason to hide them. If you think your GPA may
work against you, leave it off, but be prepared to answer questions about
academic work in an interview. In general, internship coordinators will
want to know about your academic performance in order to measure your
work ethic and skills.

Work Experience

This also should be in reverse chronological order, listing the starting/ending dates and places of your employment and a description of the work you did. These descriptions are the place for you to highlight your experience and skills. Don't go into a detailed description of the organizations for which you've worked; instead, focus on what your responsibilities—and preferably accomplishments—have been. Use industry-specific jargon to show off your familiarity with the field in which you aim to work. Avoid personal pronouns and full sentences (not, "I developed a reliable spreadsheet system to aid the reporters," but "Developed reliable spreadsheet system to aid reporters.")

The following is a list of strong résumé words to choose from in describing your work experience:

achieved	directed
acted	diversified
administered	edited
advised	eliminated
analyzed	established
arranged	exceeded
assisted	expanded
automated	facilitated
balanced	forecast
budgeted	handled
changed	helped
collected	honed
composed	implemented
conducted	improved
confirmed	initiated
consolidated	innovated
continued	installed
controlled	interfaced
converted	introduced
counseled	joined
created	launched
demonstrated	lectured
designed	led
developed	lessened

maintained	reengineered
managed	reported
negotiated	represented
obtained	researched
organized	restructured
outlined	revised
performed	revived
positioned	saved
prepared	scheduled
presented	selected
produced	specialized
promoted	strengthened
provided	succeeded
purchased	supervised
raised	targeted
realigned	taught
recommended	trained
reconciled	turned around
recruited	utilized
reduced	wrote

Room permitting, include all of your employment experience (except, of course, any jobs that you left after a couple of weeks), even the jobs that may not specifically apply to your field. A complete list will indicate the breadth of your work experience, and your flexibility in different work environments.

Skills

Computer skills are vital in today's workplace, so don't forget to list any software applications you are familiar with, any programming skills you may have, and the extent of your experience using the Internet. Employers are also generally interested in your proficiency in foreign languages.

Honors/Awards/Extracurriculars/Hobbies

Here's another shot at rounding yourself out as a candidate. Do you ride horses, white-water raft, paint mosaics? Were you involved with your school's ballroom dance team, bowling league, or singing group? Did you

Would a Functional Résumé Format Function for You?

Not everyone uses the traditional chronological résumé format; some opt for the "functional" format. A functional format organizes your experience by type (see the sample résumé of "Tasha Manycareer" in Figure 1). This format is helpful for people who have a variety of relatively unconnected work experiences, or who want to emphasize skills not used in recent jobs. It's also handy for people who have gaps in their work history—and for that reason, it can seem suspicious to some employers. But since students aren't really expected to have a solid "work history," you might consider this option.

receive special honors for your ability to analyze Greek epics, your skill in swimming, or your perfect GPA? Such details might jump start the conversation in an interview. They also add a little life to a flat piece of paper—showing you as the multidimensional creature you really are. Warning: It's not a good idea to pad your résumé with activities that your roommate (and not yourself) participated in. You never know when an internship coordinator may actually ask you about your stint as the world chess champion.

Résumé Design

A résumé is not exactly the place to let your interest in cubist art flourish. Résumé design should be neat, readable, and graphically appealing. Figures 1, 2, and 3 show sample résumés for your reference.

A simple résumé design can be created on a word processor or using word processing software on a computer. It could even be done on a good typewriter. As long as you can type and use the spacebar, you should be able to handle this. For the more graphically inclined, desktop publishing software (such as QuarkXPress and PageMaker) allows you to play around with typefaces, point sizes, and spatial elements. (Just don't go overboard or use elaborate typefaces. *Simple* and *legible* are the keywords here.) It also makes it easy to redesign your résumé in the future.

Figure 1

TASHA MANYCAREER
120 South End Ave., #2A
New York, NY
(212) 555-1212

Education

Columbia University, New York, NY
Degree: M.S., Journalism, 1996
Awards: James A. Wechsler Scholarship for local reporting

Swarthmore College, Swarthmore, PA
Degree: B.A., English, 1993

Teaching

The Maryville School, New York, NY, English Teacher   1993-95
Taught British, American, and Advanced Placement Literature, writing, drama, and debate.

Tutor for the SAT   1993-1995
Provided advanced instruction in vocabulary, reading, and math.

Broadcasting

WBAI Radio, New York, NY, Intern   Spring 1995
Reported and edited three-minute stories for on-air broadcast.

Writing and Editing

Vermont Opinion, Woodstock, VT, Feature Writer   Summer 1992
Wrote articles including "The Connecticut River: New England's Lifeline."

New Jersey Magazine, Morris, NJ. Editorial Intern Summer 1991
Edited, checked facts, wrote pieces including "Great Weekends in NJ."

College Literary Magazine, Senior Editor   1991-92
Coordinated publicity and distribution, edited, and directed graphic design.

The College News, Staff member, writer   1990-92
Reported, edited.

References

Available upon request.

Figure 2

Sarah Smiley

P.O. Box 4365   143 Lane 101
Collegiate Mailroom   Blase Road
Bridgeview, GA 39850   Warm Beach, FL 20987
814-436-0157 (H)   415-834-9283
electronic mail: ssmiley@collegiate.edu

EDUCATION

1995-present	Collegiate College Bridgeview, GA Drama Major
1991-1995	Private Academy Private, FL

EXTRACURRICULAR ACTIVITIES

1995-present   College Dramatic Association
                     Producer for "Identity Crisis" and "Wet Cement"
                     Stage Manager for "All in the Timing"
                     Assistant Properties Manager of "Sweeney Todd," the
                     major fall musical

1993-1995   High School Dramatic Club
                     Proctor; managed the theater's maintenance and business.
                     Lights Designer for "The Inner Circle"
                     Technical Crew for "Grease"
                                   "Once Upon a Mattress"
                                   "Fifth of July"
                                   (major fall musicals)

1991-1993   Key Club, School Chapter
                     Community Service Organizer
                     Salvation Service; took care of abandoned babies
                     Veteran's Hospital Children's Cancer Ward; visited young
                     cancer patients and threw parties for them

PROFESSIONAL EMPLOYMENT

Sept. 1993   PRIVATE ACADEMY DRAMA DEPARTMENT PROCTOR. Head of
to Feb 1995   the student drama society, managing the budget and
                     administration. Also in charge of the committee deciding on
                     student play proposals.

HONORS

June 1995   Inducted into the Cum Laude Society, Phillips Exeter Academy
                     Chapter. High Honors

REFERENCES

Available on request

Figure 3

GORDON P. EVANS
14980 East Ave.
Clear Lake, NY 11756
(516) 555-1212

EDUCATION

Cornell University, _Ithaca, NY_
Degree: B.A., Video Production, expected 1997
GPA 3.75

EXPERIENCE

Summer 1996   **MTV, New York, NY** _Production Assistant_
• Achieved status as #1-requested production assistant.
• Placed casting calls, recorded casting-session notes, placed ads for casting calls, and logged shoots.

Summer 1994   **WABC-TV, New York, NY,** _Booking Intern_
• Averted hurricane-related delays to morning shows by making advance, alternative travel plans for guests, achieving 100 percent guest presence the morning of a major hurricane.
• Assisted booking producers in current news trends by reading over 10 daily publications and press wires and by providing liaison with agents and celebrities.

Summer 1994   **Exponential Media, Queens, NY,** _Video Production Intern_
• Served as the first intern to edit a full-length documentary program.
• Wrote award-winning radio commercial script.

1994-96   **Blockbuster Video, Syosset NY** _Assistant Manager_
• Earned promotion from Sales Associate to Assistant Manager after one month by providing reliable and consistent customer service.
• Designed inventory strategy resulting in a 30 percent increase in classic movie rentals.

ACTIVITIES

1995-96   **Cornell Radio Station,** _Weekend Newscaster_

1994-95   **Cornell Video Production Department,** _Lab Assistant_

SKILLS   Computer skills include mastery of Avid editing system.

For most internship applicants, a one-page résumé will suffice. Any more than that gets long-winded and may turn off employers who are looking for a concise and accurate description of your background.

Again, if you are applying for different kinds of internships, you may need to come up with a few different versions of your résumé. For example, if you were applying for internships in science and public policy, one version of your résumé would highlight scientific research and course work and the other would emphasize experience and course work in public policy.

Finally, once you're happy with the content and design of your résumé, don't send out any copies until you've proofread. Proof it once, twice, and have someone else look at it a third time. Sloppy grammar and spelling won't impress anyone.

References

Some applications may require you to provide references, so be ready to approach a few people who know you or your work well and would be willing to vouch for you. These people might include a professor for whom you did research, a colleague who knows your work well, or most likely a supervisor from a previous job or internship.

First, make sure they feel comfortable about providing a recommendation. They may feel they are not the best choice for the job. In that case, consider finding another person. If someone seems only lukewarm when talking to you, chances are that person is not going to provide a glowing picture of you to a potential employer. People who are not very familiar with you and your work or whom you haven't talked to for a long time may also be poor choices. You don't want a vague reference. ("I knew Linda when she took my class three years ago but I don't remember her that well.") Someone who taught you an introductory course many years ago may not be able to say much about your skills and personal development. Similarly, a supervisor from your job several summers ago will have less insight than someone who has worked with you recently and can attest to the strengths you suggest in your résumé.

Consider what the intern coordinator will be most interested in: your specific accomplishments in the field, your ability to interact with other people, and your motivation and drive to succeed. Discuss these elements with your reference writers so that they have some basic guidelines. For example, if you are applying to a company that is looking for young, ambitious self-starters, try to convey this to your reference writers: "This company has asked me to include some references from people who are familiar with my abilities and who also know my character. They are interested in how I handle challenges or new situations and how I approach independent projects." Depending on your relationship with your reference writers, you could be more direct and explain specifically what you think they want in an intern. At any rate, try to avoid reference writers who might be too general and lump you in with all the other "hard-working, bright, personable" applicants out there.

Even if you aren't required to include recommendations with your application, it's a good idea to touch base with a few people so that you can offer them as references.

Get Organized

Once you have your résumé and references in order, you can set up an internship file. Make a checklist of all the places you are applying to, all the contact info, the deadlines, and the needed application materials. You should call or write companies to make sure you have all the necessary information, forms, etcetera. Take care of the paperwork as early as possible, ordering necessary transcripts and filling out forms. With that in place, you can begin completing applications and composing cover letters.

The Letter That Covers It All

The cover letter, like the résumé, seems pretty standard. (See the sample letter in Figure 4.) But it stays with your file, and to a potential employer, it's like "hearing" your voice on paper.

Cover letter formats vary more than résumé formats. Some people take a narrative approach, telling how they became involved in the field, what experiences they've had, what they've learned. Their passions, convictions, their darkest dreams, and brightest hopes. Cover letters can become pretty stirring. But before you begin to write beautiful prose, think about these basic questions: Why are you interested in this particular internship? What makes you qualified to intern at this company? What do you have to offer to the company, and what do you hope to achieve as an intern? What do you think you will gain from this internship? How will this apply to your future?

These important questions will drive you away from the form-letter mentality. This is your chance to sell yourself to a company, and you want to be as convincing as possible. This demands a little legwork. What does the company specialize in, what are they known for, what are the features of their internship program? And how do all of these relate to you? If you don't know enough about the company or group, you won't be able to explain your reasons for applying there.

Demonstrating your knowledge of the company shows potential employers that you've done your homework. But it also shows that on the basis of what you know about the internship and what you know of your own interests, you have found a good match. An internship might offer a lot of hands-on experience or chances to work with an expert mentor or opportunities to improve your interpersonal and communication skills. Any of these would be good reasons for wanting an internship. You want to not only make yourself stand out as a candidate, but also show why a company stands out for you.

The Smithsonian Museum in Washington, D.C., offers hundreds of internships in various fields. Applicants are asked to supply a 500- to 1,000-word essay on why they are seeking an internship and what they hope to do while they are there. That essay, in many ways, functions like a cover letter, says Elena Mayberry, the intern services coordinator. But she stresses that cover letters and essays are *not* just writing samples to test whether you can formulate an articulate sentence. "I need to know more about the person than whether they can go through a creative writing exercise." Elena says the essays are meant to show applicants' strengths and interests and show whether they are right for the position. The essay reveals "where we fit into your life and where you fit into ours," she says. "Sometimes I get the essay in the form of a cover letter. Frankly, I don't care if it's in the form of a poem. Fine, be creative, but tell me about you; give me clues."

Keeping all of these factors in mind, you can start writing individualized, one-page cover letters or answering essay questions. You may be able to

Figure 4

December 1, 1997

Ann Spin
Assistant Managing Editor
The Downtown Times
P.O. Box 15779
Downtown, CA 95864

Dear Ms. Spin,

As a junior pursuing a career in newspaper journalism, I am very interested in interning at the *Downtown Times*. I have chosen a career in daily newspaper journalism because of the opportunities for constant exploration and the power to effect change that it affords journalists. I believe a summer at your publication will only further my experiences and knowledge in the field.

I am looking for an internship that will allow me to build on my experience as editor of my campus paper, and also as an intern at the *Local Register* and a stringer for the *Town Crier*. John Carter and Lisa Lee, two former *Downtown Times* interns, have highly recommended your program to me.

I've never been to California, or, for that matter, spent any amount of time on the West Coast, but I would relish the chance to get to know the *Downtown* area. I also hear that your program teaches its interns a lot about hands-on reporting, and gives them the opportunity to write some really interesting stories. The program sounds exciting, and I'd love to take part in it. I think the *Downtown Times* is really one of the most ambitious papers I've seen.

After I graduate, I hope to be one of the lucky few to find employment in the newspaper industry, and go from there. Ideally, I would like to end up making a career covering politics somewhere for a major newspaper like yours.

This summer, I would most like to write for your state or national desks, but I could also perform well on your metro and business desks. Thank you very much for your consideration.

Sincerely,

Jean Fisher

create a template that contains some basic information, like descriptions of your past experience. From there, you can tailor your cover letters to each company. As one intern coordinator says, in the computer age, there is no excuse for not customizing your cover letter for a specific opportunity.

"The most important thing is to tailor your cover letter and résumé; students often have one generic résumé, and this can be really detrimental. If they have something in their portfolio specific to the job they are applying for, they should highlight it," says Margaret Dinneny, vice president of candidate services at Crimson & Brown Associates, which specializes in diversity recruitment.

Internship coordinators want to know that this experience is more than a way to kill time. "Bring out in your cover letter why you are applying to that company," Dinneny says. She adds that doing research is key, because it "reflects your understanding of the company—not just its history but what's going on in the company now and what you can add to that." For example, you may read the *Wall Street Journal* or business sections of other papers to track the latest achievements of the company in which you are interested. Where are they making new acquisitions, what new areas are they targeting, what are some new strategies they are using? This reveals interest not only in the company but in the industry as a whole.

The cover letter is the perfect place for you to carve out your hypothetical niche in the company. For example, in your cover letter to a marketing company that recently opened an office in the Pacific Rim, you might mention your own interest in this area, any pertinent geographic or language study you may have done, or your willingness to travel and be on the cutting edge of the field. This isn't to suggest that you should lie about proficiency in Mandarin, but if there is a match between your personal interests and the company's, the cover letter is a great place to highlight it.

Most of all, show yourself to be a self-starter. How are you going to make this internship a part of your life? How will it help you in the broad sense to learn, or what horizons do you hope to expand? How will a summer in a museum internship influence your plans to study art history as a graduate student? What new frontiers do you hope to explore doing research at a science institution? According to James L. Ward, intern coordinator at the North Carolina Botanical Garden, "Beyond the basic knowledge of plant culture and identification *the* most important qualifications of a successful applicant are enthusiasm to be an important part of the staff, a willingness to be a 'self-starter,' and the ability to find valuable opportunities in basic gardening tasks. Secondly, the more pertinent the experiences available (here) are to the applicants' goals, the better."

And for your own sake, you want to make clear what you hope to gain from the internship. If you are serious about doing hands-on work and not baby-sitting the phone or fax, you need to make this known. You may eliminate some jobs that you wouldn't have been interested in anyway.

The Interview

Be Confident

Confidence is the most obvious and most important quality to display during an interview, but it's often the most elusive. How do you "be confident"?

Having some substance to back up your style is one way. It's much easier to be confident if you know what you're talking about. The key? Research, research, and more research. Use the Internet, run a search on LEXIS-NEXIS, read the newspaper, and get a copy of the company's annual report, for starters. Talk with employees, interns, other people in the field, and people who have interviewed for similar positions. Look for information not just about the company, but the field as well. To set yourself apart from other candidates, you should be able to talk about the things that matter to your interviewers and to their colleagues—not just about yourself and why you would like the internship.

Once you have the information, practice delivering it. Jot down a list of questions you anticipate, and prepare answers. Ask other people for potential questions. See if your school's career services office offers mock interviews. If not, ask friends to interview you and tape it. Although verbal feedback on your performance is better than nothing, you can often recognize your flaws more quickly by watching yourself in action. "I found out that I said *uh* too much," says a George Washington University student of his mock interview.

Interviews Gone Bad

An aspiring magazine writer recalls two internship interviews best forgotten:

"I was interviewing to work at *Seventeen* magazine, and I had an interview with the daughter of a TV celebrity that went terribly. She had been out sick and was so disorganized that she had barely seen my résumé. She began by reading that I went to Yale, and was very impressed because she had gone to Brown and had always wanted to transfer to Yale. She had never even tried to transfer because she thought it was impossible. Needless to say she hadn't noticed that I had transferred to Yale. I thought it would be dishonest not to mention it (since it was right there on my résumé). It all went downhill from there.

"Then I interviewed at *Rolling Stone*. I was so excited that I brought everything with me: clips, copies of our campus paper, the previous magazines I had worked for. The interviewer, who had begun as an intern, spent the entire interview telling me how overqualified I was for the position of faxing and clipping newspapers all day long. I spent the interview trying to convince him that I really wanted to be there and do that, after I had all but told him I would be bored out of my wits. At least I got a great tour of the place before I left."

All those clichés about body language—a firm handshake, eye contact, a warm smile, an open posture—really do make a difference. Even if you're not completely confident, body language can help you fake it.

Also, don't shoot yourself in the foot by being overly modest. "It's a problem especially with female applicants. I get so many women that come in and say, 'I don't want to brag about myself.' And I say, 'Well this is an interview; that's what you're supposed to do,'" says an employment coordinator for a large newspaper. "Don't be arrogant, but you've earned these things—you should talk about them."

Although it's never possible to be too prepared, be careful about sounding too rehearsed. If you're so polished you have to fake spontaneity, do it. "Even if you've heard a question 20 times before, you can still say, 'Oh, that's an interesting question,' or 'Hmm, that's a tough one,' or 'Hmm, let me think about that one,'" says one recruitment director.

What to Wear

Err on the side of overdressing. Even if you are dressed nicer than anyone else in the office, your appearance will show that you are serious and enthusiastic about the job, and that you are savvy enough not to underdress. How do you know what the office dress standard is? One Brown University student suggests getting the company's brochure, if it has one. Brochures usually depict workplace scenes and picture employees dressed in attire the company considers exemplary. Another way to find out what to wear is to ask employees or former employees.

If you're a woman, wear pants if you prefer, but be aware that some interviewers still consider pants inappropriate business attire for a woman.

Handling the "Tell Me About Yourself" Question

Some interviewees hate this open-ended question because they don't know where to begin. But almost every interviewer will ask it, so you should come prepared with an answer. This question is your golden chance to tell your interviewer exactly why you are a uniquely qualified candidate without having to frame your responses according to his or her questions.

Before the interview, think of four or five personal characteristics you want to convey to the interviewer and then pick personal anecdotes to illustrate them. Want to show him you are responsible, can work with other people, and are willing to take risks? Tell him about the organization you manage, the team you play on, and the white-water rafting trip you took. "I've interviewed for a lot of political internships and they expect things like, 'I got to work for Senator so-and-so and I got to take a picture with him,' " says a Brown University student. "But if you can throw out, 'I went to Mexico and I went bungee jumping,' that's something not a lot of people have done, and people remember me by that. That helped me get the Clinton/Gore internship."

The Art of Schmoozing,
Part One

Making connections can be a critical career move at any stage of the game. When you first start your internship hunt, try to make as many acquaintances in your field of interest as possible. Start by calling employees and human resource coordinators at companies in which you are interested. Make sure to keep track of everyone you talk to, where they work, and what they do. As you meet people, discuss with them your interests and seek out advice. Most people are more than happy to share their wisdom and knowledge.

If you already know people in the industry, either friends, alumni, or former co-workers, now is the time to solicit their opinions and help. Where would they suggest looking for jobs? What kind of work environment do they think would match your goals? Who are the right people you should be talking to?

Once you have laid this groundwork, start using those connections. Suppose you once had an informational interview with a metro editor at a newspaper during which she told you about her job and experience. If you now decide to apply for an internship at that newspaper, be sure to mention your meeting with her: "On a visit to the *City News,* I had the opportunity to meet with the metro editor, Veronica Bullet. Based on our conversation, the *City News* seems like a great place to work and to gain hands-on experience in journalism."

If in the course of networking someone recommends that you contact a specific person, be sure to mention who referred you when you do get in touch: "Jane Avery suggested I call you because I am interested in health care consulting. She mentioned that you have an extensive background in this field, particularly in consulting for HMOs, and I would love to hear more about your experiences in this area." It's always helpful and impressive when you know about the areas of expertise of the people you contact. It gives them an incentive to return your call or letter if they know how they might be able to help or enlighten you. Again, getting people to talk about what they do for a living is not all that difficult if you come across as interested and enthusiastic.

Many students find alumni connections to be extremely useful. Check with your school's career services office or alumni office to find the names of alumni who have either interned or are working at the places in which you are interested. Then call or write them. If they are former interns of the company, this is a great chance to find out what it's like to intern there and what kinds of experiences you can expect. Often, former interns have a hand in recruiting new interns. At the very least, they might be willing to pass your name through the appropriate channels, and let internship coordinators know that you went to the same school. That alone can be valuable. If the company had one good experience with a student from School X, chances are it would be willing to gamble on another one.

All of these networking efforts share one major goal: to make your cover letter/application/interview stand out in the minds of intern recruiters. Your cover letter will stand out if it refers to an employee you know or an experience you had with the company. Your comments and questions seem more personal when they come with a reference from someone else in the industry.

Even less glitzy accomplishments can help set you apart if you present them in the right way. "I use student organizations to show that I'm not just a boring business student—I talk about being a musician, that I play intramural sports," says a George Washington University student.

Picking a "Weakness"

You know it's coming: "What's your biggest weakness?" Despite this question's seeming invitation to dishonesty, most interviewers ask it, if only to gauge how much you know about interviewing. If you are prepared and experienced, you will have an answer ready. The key is to make it not seem like a stock answer. "It is not a good idea to belt out that answer immediately after the question is asked," says a Princeton University student. "It should seem like you had to think for a few seconds to come up with your biggest flaw."

One "weakness" interviewers say to avoid is claiming to be a perfectionist. One recruitment director says she and a colleague once interviewed 12 consecutive applicants, and asked each to name a weakness. "Eleven of the 12 said, 'perfectionist.' You know, the first couple people you can believe, but. . . ."

You should also avoid anything that is too much of a weakness. If you are interviewing for a proofreading internship, don't say you have problems with accuracy. Avoid weaknesses that portray you as inflexible or unable to work with people, because employers prize these skills. "Don't ever say you have a conflict with your supervisor—that's probably the worst thing," says one employment coordinator. "That shows an interviewer you can't get along with people. We know there are horrible bosses out there who are impossible to get along with, but we don't want to hear that in an interview." Instead, she suggests, say something like, "In my overzealousness I bite off more than I can chew; I don't delegate enough; I take all of the responsibility."

The key is to find something that is actually a weakness of yours, albeit not one that will eliminate you from candidacy, and show that you are aware of this weakness and have worked to overcome it. Interviewers say that describing how you are tackling your weakness can be even more important than the weakness itself. Talk about workshops you have attended, goals you have set for yourself, self-analytical conversations you have had with mentors or peers—just make sure to give details so interviewers can recognize the sincerity of your self-improvement efforts.

Dealing with Your Lack of Experience

Many students fear that their lack of practical experience in the field for which they are interviewing will hurt them. True, someone with pertinent experience will probably have an advantage. But just because you don't have experience per se doesn't mean you don't have skills and interests that appeal to employers.

Talk about your involvement with extracurricular organizations to show interviewers that you can work with people. If you've attained leadership positions, use them to demonstrate your leadership abilities. Discuss relevant books and articles you've read or pertinent courses you've taken to demonstrate your interest in the field.

Past work experience, even if it seems unrelated, can also be a plus if framed in the right way. "Make a correlation between what you've done in the past and what you could do for us. Like, if the only job you've ever had was at McDonald's, OK, but say, 'I learned how to deal with people, how to deal with angry customers . . . ,' " one employment coordinator says.

If It's Not Going Well

If the interview is going badly, the worst thing you can do is sit there and fret about how badly it's going. If you're off on a tangent or don't feel like you're presenting yourself well, don't be afraid to stop and say so to get the interview going in the right direction. "I think you just need to be honest. If things are just going horribly, you can say, 'Things are getting off track here, what you really want to know about me is this,' " says one recruitment director.

The Stress Interview

It's every interviewee's worst nightmare: the stress interview. If you're not familiar with the term, a stress interview is a deliberate attempt by the interviewer to make the interviewee feel uncomfortable. It is supposed to measure a candidate's reaction to pressure and hostility. There are several ways to deal with a stress interview, but the most important thing to remember is to keep your cool. Interviewees who lose their nerve fail the test.

"There are two schools of thought on the stress interview. One is to ignore the fact that you're interviewer is tapping his pencil, looking out the window, or yelling at you. The other thing to do is to call them on it—'I'm noticing you're tapping your pencil. . . .' This is obviously for the person with a lot of chutzpa," says an interviewer at a Washington, D.C., nonprofit organization.

A student at Massachusetts Institute of Technology says he took the chutzpa route and found that it worked well in a particularly high-pressure stress interview. "He starts out by asking me a question about my last job. In mid-sentence, he cuts me off, laughing. This continued for over an hour, the room getting hotter, him flip-flopping madly between technical and touchy-feely questions, never letting me finish my answer, racing to the whiteboard and back, starting chit-chat and then cutting it off with insane laughter. Finally he said, 'You don't seem to be doing well on the technical stuff. Just how did you get the GPA you got at MIT and not know the answers to these simple questions?' The real answer was that he wasn't even giving me space to think, but I replied cockily, 'Well, sir, my high school English teacher always told us that grades don't measure how much you learned, but how much you lost.' This triggered bouts of insane laughter from him and probably won him over. But at the end I was sweat drenched and completely worn out. I found out later that he often reduces people to tears as part of his interview technique, and that me being cocky with him was probably the best defense mechanism there was."

Phone Interviews

An in-person interview is generally better than one conducted over the phone, but sometimes logistics make phone interviews your only option. Since you cannot use facial expressions and body language to convey emotion over the phone, you must rely more heavily on vocal intonation. Think about keeping your enthusiasm and energy level higher than you would in an in-person interview. "Somebody who face to face might just seem calm and competent could just sound incredibly low-energy on the phone," says one interviewer.

Also, on the phone, it's harder to gauge how the interviewer is reacting to your questions. To compensate, one interviewer suggests taking time at the end of the interview to ask if you have gotten certain points across. If you really want to stress your leadership skills, ask your interviewer if he or she has gained a strong sense of your leadership abilities. If not, expand upon what you said earlier and hammer home your strengths.

One upside to a phone interview (besides not having to dress up) is the fact that you can use notes. Keep your résumé in front of you for quick reference. Have research notes handy, as well as possible answers to anticipated questions.

What to Do at the End

When you reach the end of an interview, make sure you feel like you've made the impression you wanted to make. If you're uncertain, don't feel bashful about asking if you can clarify or elaborate on certain points. Also, the interviewer is bound to ask you if you have any questions. Never say no. Come to the interview with questions ready, and not just with ones about what you would be paid and when you would start. Ask questions that let you show off your research and interest. For example, a Brown University student had been reading newspapers to prepare for a Department of State internship interview. During the interview, he asked questions about the proliferation of weapons in the former Soviet Republics and the expansion of NATO.

The Follow-up

When you leave the interview, whether it went horribly or splendidly, it's over—but you're not done. The follow-up letter is a crucial part of the interview, and in a close-call situation, it can sometimes sway the employer your way. As soon as you get home, write a short letter thanking the interviewer and briefly noting some aspects of your conversation. "The thank-you note is important for an extended phone interview and critical for an in-person interview. I tend to think a handwritten note is nicer. The key is that it's prompt—you write it when you get home," one recruiter says.

Some interviewers prefer handwritten notes; others consider typed letters to be more professional. Use the tone of the interview and the personality of the interviewer to determine the most appropriate format.

Learn from Your Mistakes

If you don't get the internship, don't be afraid to ask your interviewer why. A great way to improve is to ask interviewers what you did wrong and what you did well. Most will be happy to give you feedback. Even if they won't, you have nothing to lose by asking.

Internship Etiquette

Ms. Manners might have her own suggestions, but here's some advice on gracefully handling various issues that might arise in the course of your interview and internship.

Sending Thank-You Notes
Most people agree that thank-you notes are a must. This lets a potential employer know that you remember what you learned during the interview. You might mention someone you met or some topic that came up during the interview to show you were paying attention. This will help distinguish you from the other candidates.

If you are going to find out soon after your interview whether you've been chosen, you may want to wait on the thank-you note until you know for sure. "I would feel pretty stupid putting a glowing thank-you note in the mail in the morning and finding out that afternoon I didn't get the job," says one intern. Even if you don't get the internship, you could still send a note thanking the company for showing you around and telling them you will keep in touch in the future.

You could also phone in your thank-you note, and even phone the people with whom you'll be working (assuming you got the position). This lets co-workers know that you remember their names and what they do. If you think a phone call might be awkward, you could also use E-mail, which has the added benefit of showing off your familiarity with technology. It also saves you the hassle of trying to track down busy people.

Answering Questions About Your GPA
Making excuses about your GPA in an interview is not a great idea. First of all, defensive behavior may lead employers to think you have something to hide or are embarrassed about the work you've done. Self-confidence is a key component of the interview; you don't want potential employers thinking they have uncovered your weak point. If your GPA is on the low side, and if they ask for specifics about your grades, you should be willing to discuss the matter. But don't offer information like, "Well, my cat died that semester, which is why my performance in advance physics was not

up to par." Your interviewers will probably follow your lead: if you seem to have no problem and are comfortable with your grades, they will probably follow suit. If you get flustered about it, they will sense something is wrong.

One more reason to go easy on your GPA: the person interviewing you may have had a similar GPA! You don't want to step on any toes by saying that you think your 3.0 sucks, only to find out that your interviewer graduated quite happily with a 2.8. Better to play it safe and assume it's not an issue unless someone makes it one.

Handling the Corporate Luncheon

If your interview takes place over lunch or dinner, go easy on the food and booze! Sure, this is a free meal, but you want them to think you are interested in the job, *not* the food they are willing to buy you. Order something simple and not messy (so you may want to skip on the crab shells you have to crack open yourself). Don't fill your mouth with so much grilled panini that you can't get a word in edgewise. You might even want to have a little snack before your meeting, so your ravenous appetite want get the better of you.

Some companies will even offer you drinks or hold information sessions for potential interns at bars. Again, remember that this is valuable opportunity for you! While the other applicants might be sitting in the corner getting tipsy over mai-tais and vodka tonics, you could be chatting it up with major company officials and selling yourself. Even if you already have the job, this is a good time to make connections, meet people, and impress them with your skills. Sure, you may want to help yourself to some social cocktails. But getting sloshed is a good way to humiliate yourself in front of company officials as well as a wasted opportunity. Moderation at these social events is a good thing.

Asking for Business Cards

Business cards are an intern's dream. In most cases, if your employers plan to give you business cards, they will tell you ahead of time. If they don't bring it up or you work at a low-budget place, you probably aren't going to get any. One way to broach the issue (and an important thing to know anyway) is to ask your supervisor how you should identify yourself to people outside the association. For example, if you are doing research on a legal case and are interviewing involved parties, should you tell them you are merely the summer intern? Probably not. In most cases, if you have to work with people outside your office, then you are considered an employee (albeit temporary) and not an intern. In any case, this may inspire your employers to think about how outside people should address you and reach you, and business cards may suddenly seem like a good idea. But this is not an issue to be pressed.

The Intern-Net: Going Online in Your Internship Search

by Shawn Bayern

Even if you've never used the Internet (or even a computer) before, modern technology can help you find information about companies, communicate with them, and even publish your résumé for the world to see. You may be surprised at how easy, productive, and fun using the Internet can be. And, familiarity with computers and the Internet will probably be important to whatever career you choose, so it's a good idea to get those skills under your belt now.

If you're a computer novice, our discussion of the basics of the Internet and the World Wide Web will help get you started. We'll walk you through the crucial steps toward taking advantage of the resources the Internet provides—includes publishing your own résumé on the Web. If you already have online experience, our guide to internship-oriented Web sites will help you begin your research, and you can build off of our résumé HTML script when designing your own.

The Basics: Exactly What Is the Internet?

The Internet (sometimes called the Net) is a huge network of computers. Using a computer that's hooked up to the Internet (through a modem usually), you can send and receive letters, documents, sound clips, pictures, video, and other types of information to and from other people and companies that have Internet connections.

The Web

The World Wide Web (often called just the Web) is a big part of the Internet. Most of the sites you'll visit on the Net are Web sites. Usually, navigating the Web involves using "browser" software, such as Netscape Navigator, Microsoft Internet Explorer, or Lynx, to access files that are stored on computers all over the network.

Addresses

You get to a site by typing its URL (Uniform Resource Locator) into your browser. URLs are usually called *addresses*. Addresses of Web sites usually take the following form:

http://www.somecompany.com

The *.com* at the end usually indicates a commercial site. Educational institutions usually have addresses ending in *.edu*; nonprofit companies' addresses usually end in *.org*; and government addresses end in *.gov*.

What's on a Web Site?

When you go to a Web site, you can view text and graphics (and sometimes hear sounds) mixed together on a page. The first page that greets you when you visit a site is called the *home page*. If a site has more than one page, which most do, those pages are linked together so that you can jump back and forth between pages. For example, on a company's home page, you might see the words *About our company* (probably underlined) and there might be a small graphic right next to the words. By clicking on those words or on the accompanying graphic, you would jump to another page in the company's Web site, probably containing basic information about the company. These words or pictures that you click on are called *links* because they link one page to another. They can also link you to other Web sites.

By following the links, you can navigate the Web and find what you're looking for. Links might also lead you to things you weren't specifically looking for, but still find helpful. For example, many newspapers list their classified ads on their Web sites. Often, when you go to the page where the job ads are, you'll find links to other Web sites that are great for job hunting—or to sites that specialize in career counseling, résumé building, etcetera.

One reason that the Web has become so popular is the fact that it's easy for people to publish their _own_ Web sites. It would be virtually impossible for you to publish your résumé in the _New York Times_ or as a commercial during the evening news, but you're only a few steps away from being able to publish it on the Web.

Another great feature of the Web is that almost all of it is free! Aside from the cost of your computer and modem, of course, and whatever service charge you may have to pay to your college or Internet service provider to get and stay online, most Web sites can be visited for free.

Great, So How Do I Actually Use It?

First, a general word of advice: if you know how to contact your college's computer-support personnel (or have a friend who's Internet savvy), most of the steps involved with learning how to use and publish things on the Internet will be much easier. The Internet is a large network, and it involves many different types of computers: Macintoshes, PCs, UNIX systems, VAXes, etcetera. There is therefore no one, uniform way to use the Internet. Even an expert, when faced with an entirely new computer system, will be forced to sit down and learn about it. This learning process will be much easier if your college has good computer-support services and if you know how to get help when you need it.

Get Connected

The first step in going online is to get your computer hooked up to the Net or to find a computer that's already hooked up. If you have an network card or a modem on your personal computer, then you can continue your search for internships without even leaving your room. You'll have to choose an Internet provider (it's like choosing a phone company, although there are usually more to choose from). Ask around to find out what provider offers the best service for a reasonable monthly fee. Usually, you can choose from varying fees for varying amounts of online time, or pay one fee for unlimited usage. The provider may also charge you an initial "setup" fee. The provider will send you a browser (such as Netscape) as well as software that will allow your modem to connect to the Net.

If you don't have a computer and modem, then find a computer that is already hooked up to the Net: a friend's machine, a public computer at your college or public library, even a machine at one of those Internet cafes. So ask around; say you're looking for a "computer connected to the Internet."

Get on the Browser

Once you have access to an Internet-connected computer, the next step is to get on the browser software. Netscape Navigator and Microsoft Internet Explorer are the two most common browsers for modern PCs and Macintoshes, but these two browsers rely on connections to the Internet of a certain quality. If you're using a public computer at your school, it might have a text-only connection to the Internet. If this is the case, then you might not be able to use Netscape or Internet Explorer.

First, find out what type of connection the computer you're using has. A good question to ask your college's computer-support people is, "Does it run Netscape or Internet Explorer?" If it doesn't, then it's probably using a text-only connection. For text-based connections, Lynx is a popular browser; it can be run by typing *lynx* (or, on your system, perhaps www) at the prompt.

But sophisticated connections are pretty standard these days, so the rest of our discussion will assume that you're using either Netscape or Internet Explorer. If you have a text-only connection and have to use a browser such as Lynx, you will still be able to follow the discussion and access the Web, but the following differences might be important to you:

- In Lynx, you can't "click on" a link in order to follow it. You'll probably have to use the arrow keys and the ENTER key. Help should be available from within Lynx by pressing the H key; use the arrow keys to navigate through help, and press ENTER on the option that you want to read more about. In Lynx, the left arrow means "return to the page that I looked at last."
- You cannot view graphics directly with a text-only connection. Therefore, some Web sites may be difficult to navigate if their navigation relies on graphics.

When you start up the browser, you will often be taken directly to a home page for your college or for some other organization (perhaps the company that created your browser). You're now online.

If you already know the address of the site that you want to visit (let's say it's http://altavista.digital.com), simply move the mouse to the white box at the top of the screen (to the right of the word _location:_ or _address:_ or URL:) and enter the address of the page you want, exactly as you have it written down. You need every colon, every slash, every period. You should not enter any spaces in the middle of an address. So, for the example above, you would enter:

http://altavista.digital.com

exactly like that. (To enter an address in Lynx, you must press G and then type in the address.) If you don't have a specific Web site in mind, then start out by using one of the search engines that will search the Net for you, such as Yahoo or Excite. (See the section later in this chapter on using search engines.)

Once you're in a site, if you want to go back to the last page you were on, press the Back button toward the upper-left corner of your browser. This feature is very convenient if you ever click on the wrong link or if you want to return to a useful list.

Now That I Can Navigate the Web, What's Out There?

What's out there? Quite a lot. And it can be overwhelming at first, because there is no general structure for the information on the Web. There is no master directory, no index of absolutely everything, no single company that runs the whole Web. The Web is decentralized, and that may take some getting used to. But practice will show you which is the best search engine for you and what is the best way to word your searches to get exactly what you want. You'll find some favorite sites (which your browser will allow you to "bookmark" for fast, easy access in the future), that will probably link you to other helpful sites, and so on, and so on. . . .

Some Useful Job and Internship Sites

You may find the following sites particularly useful for finding information about jobs and internships. (In the next section, we'll explain how to find more job-related sites — or how to track down info on a particular company.)

http://www.jobtrak.com

JOBTRAK has a national internship database as well as listings targeted at individual campuses. (To get to the school-related databases, you may need to get a password from your school's career center. Or you may have to access JOBTRAK through "pathway access," which your school's career center may be able to tell you more about. First try to gain access and see what happens.)

You can get to the national database as a link from the school-related databases or by selecting "A Sample JOBTRAK University (password test)" as your school, pressing the "Access Job Listings" button, and then selecting "JOBTRAK National Internship Database" from the resulting page. You can search the databases by "type of work," "geographic location," "keyword," "company name," and "date."

JOBTRAK also has job search tips, a guide to graduate schools, and a service through which you can post your résumé on the JOBTRAK site. (This is different from putting your résumé on your own Web page, which we'll discuss later. It may help to do both.) Through JOBTRAK, you can also access a calendar of career fairs, a list of sites for undergraduate and graduate students, and "The Riley Guide," an acclaimed guide for using the Internet to help with job searches, written by Margaret F. Riley.

http://www.tripod.com/work/internships

Tripod provides a searchable copy of the *National Directory of Internships* (published by the National Society of Experiential Education). You can search for internships by field of study and/or location, or by keyword. You can also browse the directory by location or field of study.

http://www.4work.com

While this site's scope goes beyond just internships, it has an internship database that you can search by keyword. This site also has a free service called "Job Alert!" that allows you to enter a personal profile (remember to check off the box for internships, because this service also covers full-time positions, volunteer work, and "youth/part-time/seasonal" work). It then tries to match your profile with the needs of the employers who use the service. It will send you E-mail if it finds a match.

http://www.jobsource.com

This site offers a list of internships and part-time jobs as a link from its home page.

http://www.daily.umn.edu/~mckinney

A self-admittedly "humble but growing" list of places where students may be able to get journalism internships, this site contains the names and addresses of several daily newspapers (organized by state), a handful of magazines, and a radio station. It also has anonymously written reviews of some of these internships. While it's not exactly a comprehensive list, perhaps you would like to hear what other (albeit anonymous) students have to say about their experiences. Every bit of information can help, and this is a good example of how the Web can provide small, focused lists in addition to massive indexes.

Also, check with your school's career counselors. They may be able to recommend some good internship-related Web sites.

Using Search Engines and Directories on the Net

What if you want to go beyond the sites listed above? What if you're looking for a particular company's Web site, or if you're looking for an unusual type of internship?

While there is no master directory or index of the Internet, there are search engines that can perform "intelligent" searches for you. To get to a search engine, press Netscape's "Net Search" button or the Internet Explorer's "Search" button. (If you can't find these buttons on your browsers, they may be turned off. Go to the "View" menu in Internet Explorer and choose "Toolbar," or the "Options" menu in Netscape and choose "Show Directory Buttons," to turn the buttons on.) The browser will then bring up a search engine, or even several to choose from. The search engine presents you with an empty box in which you type what you want to find—*internships,* maybe, or *job ads,* or the name of the company in which you're interested. Then click on the word *Find* or *Search,* and the search engine goes to work, presenting you with a list of sites that might interest you. You'll probably get far more than you can use, depending on how general your search terms were. Scroll through the list, and click on the link to any site that looks like what you want. Generally, the most likely hits are at the top of the list, so try those first.

Search engines usually provide tips on how to word your searches effectively, so that you don't get a lot of useless information. It's worth taking a minute to learn these tips.

There are also online directories of various kinds that will make using the Web easier. Below are a few details on some of the most helpful search engines and directories.

http://altavista.digital.com

AltaVista Search is a well-known search engine. It's "Help" page gives a more complete description of its interface that we can give here, but one useful method is to surround your search term with quotation marks. Thus, if you enter "Proctor & Gamble," including the quote marks, into the AltaVista searcher, you'll get a list of sites that contain that entire phrase, not just the individual words *Proctor and Gamble.* This is one of the easiest ways to find the Web sites of companies and individuals.

http://www.yahoo.com

Another staple of the Internet, Yahoo differs from AltaVista in that it provides a hierarchical "directory" of the Internet, organized into top-level categories such as "Arts and Humanities," "Business and Economy," and "Education." You may search Yahoo's directory, which is another convenient way of finding specific companies or types of companies.

Find "Summer Intern Program"

A query on "summer intern program" in AltaVista turned up about 500 sites. Following are a few of them. Each of these sites has information about the organization's summer internship programs:

GTE: http://info.gte.com/career/jobs/sip/sippast.html
INSTITUTE OF GOVERNMENT:
http://ncinfo.iog.unc.edu/interns/index.html
LDEO: http://www.ldeo.columbia.edu/dallas/abbott_app.html
MAPCO: http://www.mapcoinc.com/intern.html
KOHN: http://www.jvs.org/kohn.htm
THE FLORIDA TIMES-UNION:
http://www.times-union.com/inside/summer97interns.htm

Some of these sites may be outdated, which is often a problem when doing research on the Net. Nonetheless, the sites may give you valuable information, like addresses to write to for more information. You could modify the search term to narrow down or even expand the results. For example, changing the query to "intern program" (with the quotes) yielded about 3,000 sites.

Like Switchboard below, Yahoo also provides a "yellow pages" directory through which you can find businesses. You can access this service through a link at the top of Yahoo's home page.

http://www.switchboard.com

Essentially a gigantic phone book, Switchboard allows you to search for businesses by either category and location, name, or name and location. You can get the phone number and address of a business, and even a map of the area in which it's located. Switchboard also lets you search for people.

Other popular search engines include:

- http://www.lycos.com
- http://www.hotbot.com

- http://www.infoseek.com
- http://www.excite.com

Putting Your Résumé Online

Just as there is no uniform way to access the Internet, there's no uniform set of instructions for putting your résumé online. The details vary from school to school and from computer system to computer system.

Our discussion will therefore assume that you have find out from your school or your Internet provide how to put up a page on the Web. Not all Internet providers offer you space to post your own Web page, so ask this question when you're shopping around for a provider. (A good question to ask your college's computer services people would be, "Can I put my Web page online through this school? And what will its address be once I put it up?") Once you have this information, you will need to have a basic knowledge of how to use a computer (or help from someone else who does). No expertise is required, but you'll have to know how to create a file, edit a file, and follow your school's or provider's instructions for putting the file online.

Web pages are constructed with a simple (though perhaps intimidating-looking) language called HTML. HTML is not very complicated, though it can look strange at first sight. The "language" essentially involves interspersing instructions surrounded by brackets (<>) among the text on a page. These bracketed instructions are called *tags*, and they instruct the computer how to display a page on screen—what color background and type to use, where the text (and graphics) should appear, what size they should be, etcetera. Therefore, an HTML script is in many ways similar to a plain text file of your résumé, except that it has a few extra instructions included for the computer.

In this section, we'll present a simple HTML script to create a text-only Web page that displays a résumé, and we'll note how you can use this script to fit your needs. For more information on HTML, you may wish to refer to "The Beginner's Guide to HTML," which is available at:

http://www.ncsa.uiuc.edu/general/internet/www/htmlprimer.html

Or check out the page at Netscape called "Creating Net Sites":

http://home.netscape.com/home/how-to-create-web-services.html

Sample HTML Script for a Résumé

```
<HTML>
<HEAD>
<TITLE>
Joshua Adam Davis
</TITLE>
</HEAD>

<BODY BGCOLOR="#FFFFFF">

<H1>
Joshua Adam Davis
</H1>
Campus address: 123 Dorm Street, College Town, NY
12345<BR>
Permanent address: 456 Main Street, Home Town, NY
23456<BR>
E-mail address:
<A HREF="mailto:my-email-address@college.edu">
  my-email-address@college.edu
</A>
<HR>

<DL>

<DT> <H2> Education </H2>
  <DD>
  <B>Example University, College Town, NY</B><BR>
  B.A. expected 2001<BR>
  Major: English
  <P>

  <B>Example High School, Some Town, NY</B><BR>
  Graduated with Honors
```

```
    <P>

<DT> <H2> Work Experience </H2>
  <DD>
  <B>Example College Student Council</B><BR>
    <I>Treasurer: September 1998 - September 1999</I><BR>
Managed the funds of the student council, which amounted
to $40,000. Advised council on appropriations to student
groups. Prepared reports for college administration.
    <P>


  <B>The Weekly News</B><BR>
    <I>News Editor: October 1997 - October 1998</I><BR>
Responsible for the activities of the News Desk at Example
University's largest student-run newspaper.
    <P>


    <I>Beat Reporter: October 1996 - October 1997</I><BR>
Wrote three or four stories each week covering the affairs
of Example University's Office of the President.
    <P>


  <B>Local Investment Bank</B><BR>
    <I>Staff Assistant: June 1996 - August 1996</I><BR>
Helped manage office.  Answered telephone.  Ordered
supplies.
    <P>


<DT> <H2> Other Skills </H2>
   <DD>
   <UL>
   <LI> Proficient in Portuguese, Hebrew
<LI> Familiar with Microsoft Word, Microsoft Excel, and
WordPerfect.
   </UL>


</DL>
```

```
<!- OPTIONAL: ->
<HR>
<A HREF="http://www.my.page/">
   Return to my home page
</A>
<!- ----- ->

</BODY>
</HTML>
```

This résumé has a simple, straightforward design (see Figure 1). It is formatted nicely, but it uses no advanced Web features such as graphics, a fancy background, and multiple colors. In most cases, you wouldn't print out a résumé on bright pink paper and include a picture of yourself with it, so why do the equivalent online? Simplicity of design makes your résumé look professional, and it makes it easier and faster for potential readers to access.

To use this HTML script, type it in (using any word processing program) exactly as it appears above, substituting your name and information in place of Joshua's. As you type, keep in mind that spacing is usually irrelevant in HTML; it doesn't matter where the lines break, or how many spaces or tabs appear between words. In general, the browser ignores the spacing.

It is important that you enter the tags—such as <H2>—precisely as they appear. Make sure, for example, to leave the <BR> at the end of the lines where it appears; this tag tells the browser to start a new line. (Since HTML ignores spacing, simply pressing return won't do it.)

As you insert your E-mail address, if you have one, into this résumé, be sure to include your address twice: once between the quotation marks and once on its own line. Leave the phrase "mailto:" in the line, as it appears in the sample résumé; insert your own E-mail address directly after the colon. If you don't have an E-mail address, then don't enter the four lines starting with "E-mail address:" and ending with </A>.

If your information is similar enough to the sample information on this résumé, you may need to make very few modifications except for the content. However, you may not have exactly three organizations that you want to list under "Work Experience," for example, or you may have two different

Figure 1

Joshua Adam Davis

Campus address: 123 Dorm Street, College Town, NY 12345
Permanent address: 456 Main Street, Home Town, NY 23456
E-mail address: my-email-address@college.edu

Education

Example University, College Town, NY
B.A. expected 2001
Major: English

Example High School, Some Town, NY
Graduated with Honors

Work Experience

Example College Student Council
Treasurer: September 1998 - September 1999
Managed the funds of the student council, which amounted to $40,000.
Advised council on appropriations to student groups. Prepared reports
for college administration.

The Weekly News
News Editor: October 1997 - October 1998
Responsible for the activities of the News Desk at Example
University's largest student-run newspaper.

Beat Reporter: October 1996 - October 1997
Wrote three or four stories each week covering the affairs of Example
University's Office of the President.

Local Investment Bank
Staff Assistant: June 1996 - August 1996
Helped manage office. Answered telephone. Ordered supplies.

Other Skills

- Proficient in Portuguese, Hebrew
- Familiar with Microsoft Word, Microsoft Excel, and WordPerfect.

Return to my home page

positions that you want to list for the second organization. If you want to make such modifications, you need to understand a little more about HTML. The guides mentioned above, as well as this discussion, will help you.

On this résumé, the basic "block" of information is a heading (such as "Work Experience") constructed as follows:

```
<DT> <H2> Work Experience </H2>
  <DD>
  <B>Organization Name</B><BR>
    <I>Position: Start Date - End Date</I><BR>
Your description goes here; it takes as much space as it
needs, with no tags like <BR> at the end of each line.
It's followed only by the P tag coming up ...
    <P>
```

Therefore, to add a new heading—for instance, "Travel Experience"—you could pattern it after this block. If the line containing the "position" is not appropriate (that is, if you don't need an extra line providing information but want to launch directly into a description), then simply erase it. If the description is unneeded, you can erase it, too. (But leave the <P> tag.)

To add an organization that you worked for—including mention of one position that you held and a description of that position—simply go to the place in the file where you want it to appear (directly following either a <P> or a <DD>) and add the lines starting with:

```
<B>Organization Name</B><BR>
```

and ending with a <P>, as above. To add a new position for an organization, simply insert the position starting with:

```
<I>Position: Start Date - End Date</I><BR>
```

and ending with a <P>. (Insert these lines directly after a <P>.)

To delete an organization, erase the line starting with the organization name and ending with the final <P> before the next organization's name. To delete a position, erase the lines starting with the position's name and ending with the next `<P>`. (Always add or erase the `<B>`, `</B>`, `<I>`, and `</I>` tags along with the words that they surround. In other words, don't just erase an organization's name: erase the surrounding tags as well.)

One other thing to note is the list of skills at the bottom of this résumé, which is laid out as a bulleted list. The tag `<UL>` begins a bulleted list in which each bulleted item is introduced by the tag `<LI>`. You can use this technique anywhere in your résumé that calls for a bulleted list; just make sure that the list ends with the final `</UL>` tag. If it doesn't, the lines following the list in your résumé will be indented too much.

The segment at the end of this résumé that adds a link to your home page may be convenient for people who want to find out more about you. Of course, if you don't have any Web pages other than this one with your résumé on it, or if you would rather not link your home page to your résumé page, leave out the lines that are marked as "optional."

By getting access to the Net and learning how to use browsers such as Netscape, you'll open up new avenues in your hunt for an internship. And posting your résumé online might improve your chances of getting the job you want. Happy surfing!

Print Journalism

3

by Noah Kotch

A career as a print journalist is one of the most wonderful—and frustrating—careers you can consider. Jobs are amazingly hard to get, the pay isn't good, but there are few other lines of work that offer as much excitement.

The first thing to realize about print journalism is just how competitive the industry's job market actually is. With the explosions of cable news, the Internet, and the decline of reading skills in children, Americans are reading less. Newspaper readership is relatively stagnant, and the classic, family-owned newspaper is going the way of the dinosaur, replaced by corporate ownership with a keen eye for the bottom line. Magazines are relying less on paid staff writers and more on a few, big-shot writers or freelancers. And both newspapers and magazines are printing shorter stories, bigger photographs, and more advertisements. Still, the surviving publications are no less influential, perhaps more so, and believe it or not, the quality of the copy that does get printed might be the best ever.

During their twenties, newspaper reporters will jump from paper to paper, often staying in one job for only a few months. I have a friend who bounced from the *Connecticut Post* to the *Associated Press* to the *Palm Beach Post* to the *Charlotte Observer* in two years. It is very unlikely you will get a job at a top newspaper or magazine right after graduation, unless you can take advantage of affirmative action programs. Many entry-level jobs might seem demeaning to someone with a college degree (writing obituaries and compiling community calendars, for example). So if you are picky about where you will work or what you're willing to do when you're just starting out, do not choose print journalism as a career.

That being said, getting a leg up in the business is pretty tough. If you are seriously considering a career in print journalism, you need to pile up experience, early, including internship experience. The key is to amass as much writing experience as possible. Until your senior year, it does not matter that much where you get your experience. It just matters that you have written a lot. Most newspapers and magazines offer internships. Some don't pay, offering academic credit instead. A few will pay as high as $800 a week.

What Matters (and What Doesn't)

You may be relieved (or chagrined) to learn that employers in publishing do not care very much about your grades or your coursework—unless you have specialized in a specific subject about which you wish to write. They care about where you went to school, but most of all, they care about your skill and experience as a reporter and a writer.

Journalism school is not the necessity you might think it is. Some newspapers and magazines actually prefer students who did not attend journalism school. And it isn't necessary to spend all that money on J-school if you gain the experience you need in college. In journalism, you advance not by the strength of your graduate degree but by your connections and your abilities.

Still, many people choose to attend journalism school if they decide too late in their undergraduate careers that they want to become print reporters. J-school offers the chances you might have missed to do summer internships, to make connections, and to get a feel for the industry. J-school might be worthwhile if you're lacking writing experience—and if you can afford it.

Fluency in a foreign language can be a big plus—for instance, knowing some Spanish is helpful to anyone who wants to work in an urban setting, especially in the Southwest. Graduate-level specialization in a particular field—law, for example—can help you land a reporting job covering that field.

If you are a freshman or sophomore and you haven't joined your college newspaper or magazine yet, do it. And get start doing summer internships as soon as possible. College newspaper work can open the door to that first newspaper internship, usually at a small to mid-sized newspaper. While it may

Riding Through Bertha

Summer in North Carolina is hurricane season, and it's standard practice at one large newspaper there to give one of their interns a laptop and a cell phone and send them out into a hurricane. I was one of those lucky interns. With Hurricane Bertha approaching, I drove to the coast and checked into a hotel—my first real "business trip," I told myself, and my most frightening. The next morning, my editor called me and told me they had found me the last hotel room available near Myrtle Beach, and that I should drive there as fast as I could before the storm broke. I did, but the storm broke more quickly than expected, and I found myself the only car on a lonely coastal road, with branches flying and the rain squirting into my car windows. It was undoubtedly the worst drive I'd ever had to make, and when I finally slid into Myrtle Beach, my windshield was cracked and my door was dented. But I had seen a hurricane strike firsthand, and the next two days—spent wandering through damaged towns and sitting through press conferences with emergency officials—proved terrifically exciting. Scrounging for food, borrowing cash, speeding from damage site to damage site with a photographer, and trying to file from my hotel room, with the phone lines going in and out, made me feel almost like a foreign correspondent. And the passages I wrote describing the ride through the storm ran prominently in the paper the next day. I figured only a newspaper reporter could get such a ground-level view of a big storm, and the experience sealed my decision to stay in journalism.

—Yale senior

be tough to intern with a small, local paper while your friends are interning with more high-profile organizations, you will almost certainly have more responsibility than they will. And you'll get that vital writing experience.

Stringing

A great source of writing experience is "stringing" or freelancing—plus, you can do it during the school year. The _New York Times,_ for instance, has stringers on many college campuses; it pays them $20 an hour for leg work, and up to $200 a story. Stringing for the *Times* offers you a glimpse into the workings of the highest tier of the Fourth Estate. I started stringing for the *Times* from Yale during my sophomore year; by my senior year, I was regularly working full days for them. I loved doing it, but I would not recommend stringing for the *Times* unless you're located within the New York metro area. Also, you have to deal with the fact that you don't get a byline as a *Times* stringer; your hard work is credited to "By the *New York Times*." Also, be aware that there is a glass ceiling: the *Times* almost never hires stringers for staff positions until they have gone and worked somewhere else.

A better company for which to string is the Associated Press, the great news god, which can keep a stringer anywhere busy. But many newspapers employ stringers. So contact a big daily nearby and ask if they would consider some freelanced articles. Over time, you can turn yourself into a valuable stringer. And you might be able to segue your stringer experience into an internship.

Magazines and Weeklies

Magazine internships are generally not as competitive as newspaper internships. One reason for this is the fact that many of them don't pay. A second reason is the fact that magazine interns tend to write little and do fact checking, odd jobs, and clerical work instead.

Some news magazines like to use their interns for special projects. *U.S. News and World Report,* for instance, has low-paid interns work on its special college issues (*U.S. News,* by the way, has a good record of hiring interns.) A *U.S. News* intern usually ends up with a very short piece in the college issue and a longer piece or two in the special edition on colleges sold as a supplement in the fall. *Business Week* often has paid interns work on its business schools issue, and will sometimes give interns lengthy, bylined articles by the end of the summer.

One of the more competitive magazine internship programs is at the *New Republic,* which hires summer and fall interns for a pittance but gives them a chance to write signed pieces and connects them to a valuable journalistic

48

Interning with Aperture

Aperture (a photography publisher) distinguished itself by its structured Work-Scholar Program, in which interns work in specific departments under specific guidance for an extended period of time. My own interest in photography and publishing, as well as my English literature studies, led me to the decision that Aperture would provide a unique opportunity to participate in the production of high-quality books of and about photography. I was given the opportunity to learn, ask questions, and significantly, head my own projects. The vice president of production and the production manager were excellent mentors—supportive, instructive, and above all, dedicated to working at Aperture.

—Meredith Hinshaw

network. The *Washington Monthly* does not pay its interns at all, but offers them similar valuable connections. The *National Journal* pays its interns, runs a well-regarded program, and often hires interns as reporters. The *Nation* pays very little and offers few chances for a piece with a byline.

Overall, magazines tend to be less discriminating in selecting interns. Their editors will take you seriously even if you've written only for college publications, and don't expect the often unattainable experience that good newspaper programs require. Magazine internships are not the best way to segue into a newspaper internship the following summer, but if you want to work in magazines after graduation, they are a terrific option.

"Alternative" weekly newspapers are also an interesting option, especially if you want to work for one after graduation. The mother of these publications is the *Village Voice*. One Yale graduate who interned at the *Voice* said she gleaned a lot from her experience and had a chance to see all aspects of the operation. "I was working for the executive editor, Richard Goldstein, so I think I was in a fortunate position because he's involved in so many different activities: editing articles, laying out the magazine, writing columns," says the former intern. "I would do a lot of research for his columns. We went through a Nexis workshop prior to the internship. As with many internships, there was a lot of dead time. We spent some time just flipping through magazines and newspapers looking for topics for him to write about. In general, the *Voice* is a great place to be. It's not as outlandish as it used to be, but it is still considered a left-wing, radical paper. And there was a lot of encouragement for us to pitch our own story ideas."

Business Reporting

Business reporting is one of the few growing fields in print journalism. If you're interested in business, you might want to aim for this field. Some newspapers specifically choose business desk interns who have no prior experience in business, but the majority prefer interns who know the field.

Editing

If you are interested in editing more than writing, consider your options in editing for newspapers or book and magazine publishers. Unlike writing internships, editing internships usually don't require a lot of writing samples. But you should have some samples that reveal thoughtful, articulate, and clean writing. This collection can include papers written for classes, short pieces of nonfiction or fiction, magazine-length pieces, or published columns. Your samples should reflect the fact that you can handle working with complicated text—your own or someone else's.

Publishing companies generally ask for a few select writing samples, a résumé, and a cover letter. Your cover letter should stress any course work in English composition, any writing courses, and any classes for which you have written significant and involved essays. Aside from that, you want to highlight any editing you have done for publications or for individuals.

Responsibilities in publishing internships vary. One Yale graduate interned with Grolier, a popular reference publisher in Danbury, Connecticut. Her duties consisted of editing the text of contributors to Grolier's encyclopedia-style books. "You'd be surprised how many people can't write to save their lives," she says. She spent most of her time monitoring the writing for stylistic errors and trying to polish it. She was also able to write some pieces herself. She said the key to her publishing internship was experience and skill in writing.

The Business of Books

Heading into my last year in Columbia University's M.F.A. program in fiction writing, I wanted to use my final student summer for experimentation, to look at career possibilities beyond those I had already experienced. So with a love for books and a desire to understand more about the business that produces them, I decided to pursue internships in publishing.

I was right about liking editorial best—the opportunity to make choices, the direct contact with books, the chance to work with and help authors—all of this appealed to me greatly. I also got to work with two terrific editors, both of whom trusted me enough to read and report on manuscripts, compose letters, and carry out some special assignments. I created an online quiz to help with the promotion of one book, and I researched the names, addresses, and telephone numbers of every major league baseball announcer to help promote another book. Projects like these helped me to see how interrelated the different departments were, and how crucial each department truly was. Editorial worked closely with publicity, which worked closely with sales, which worked closely with subsidiary rights, which worked closely with editorial.

—Kevin Roth

If you are serious about a career in publishing, you might consider taking Radcliffe's six-week-long summer publishing course. Of course, this course costs money and takes up precious internship time, but participants say it can open doors in the publishing world.

Finding a Position and Applying

Start out by making a list of internship programs for which you think you are qualified. Newspaper programs tend to be more competitive than magazine programs, since most magazines use their interns only for fact-checking and writing briefs. Some newspapers let their interns write stories, and give them a surprising amount of independence. Therefore, no matter what field of print journalism you end up in, it's probably a better idea to intern for newspapers, where you will get a chance to compile writing clips that will impress future employers.

If you are applying to newspaper programs, you will have to apply to a lot of them. If you have never interned before, you should aim for smaller newspapers, which tend to accept people with only college newspaper experience. Even if it's a poor-quality newspaper, don't worry—as long as they will let you write a lot. Lists of newspaper internships are available online. The best list I have seen comes from the journalism school at the University of Missouri. (See the chapter on the "Intern-net" for more information about online searching.) Another resource is *Editor and Publisher*, an annual directory that lists daily newspapers nationally and internationally.

For summer internships, start planning at the beginning of the fall. Most newspaper program deadlines are usually between November 1 and January 1, with a few programs holding later deadlines. Magazines tend to have deadlines between January and March. A typical application to a print journalism internship program consists of a one-page cover letter, a résumé, and several writing samples.

The readers of the applications tend to be senior-level editors (such as assistant managing editors), a sign of how seriously publications take their internship programs. So the writing samples you submit should come from past internships or freelance work. If you don't have these yet, then clips from your college newspaper experience will do.

Most programs will contact finalists within two months of the deadline. If you do not hear from someone by then, you're probably out of the running, although it never hurts to call and find out. If you receive an offer and have to give your answer immediately, but are holding out for an offer from another organization, give that organization a call. Sometimes a newspaper or magazine will make an offer early if you've received another offer from a comparable program.

Use Connections, and Think "Local"

You are more likely to get an internship if you have a connection. Many school newspapers have connections to newspapers in the "real world." For instance, many students go from the *Daily Tar Heel* at the University of North Carolina to the *St. Petersburg Times* in Florida. You should also try the newspapers that are geographically closest to your school, as well as your hometown newspaper. I've tried both approaches over two years, and they've both worked.

I interned for the *New Haven Register* after my sophomore year. Not only did a get to sit through meetings where dour editors announced the latest hiring freeze (typical in newsrooms these days), I also spent six weeks helping cover a high-tension trial in Hartford, where I met several top New Haven drug dealers. I reported on the Special Olympics World Games, murders, small-town mayoral campaigns—in short, the basics of being a reporter. It was necessary—and terrific—experience.

The following summer, I went home to work for the *News & Observer* in Raleigh, North Carolina. I was fortunate to live near one of the best regional newspapers in the country, and I don't think I would have been picked for the internship had I not been from the area. At the *News & Observer,* I got to do more advance work than I did in New Haven, covering state government and politics. It's a terrific program that gives a lot of responsibility to its interns, and I recommend it highly to aspiring newspaper journalists.

Selecting Your Writing Samples

The key component of your print journalism internship application is your set of "clips," or writing samples. These are photocopies of anything you've had printed in any publication. Ideally, the entire article should be laid out neatly on one 8.5 × 11-inch sheet of white paper (I often use both sides of the sheet if I have an article that continues onto another page). Longer, magazine-style articles can require more than one sheet of paper. Don't put more than one clip on a sheet of paper.

Select your best clips for your internship applications. Newspapers and magazines sometimes request five to 20 clips, but usually the number is between eight and ten. Your choice of clips should be geared toward the program to which you are applying and the kind of person you think will be reading your application. For example, if you are applying for a metro reporting internship, send work that shows you can cover crime, courts, and schools. If you are applying to a political magazine, send in a trenchant opinion piece you wrote for your college newspaper on some substantial topic.

Some students find it helpful to meet with an experienced journalist to go over which clips to submit—their selections may surprise you! I made mistakes in clip selection for awhile during my senior year, when I submitted too many weighty articles and too few pieces that showed I could cover the fish-fries and swim meets that are standard intern fare. I met with a journalist who chose an entirely different set of clips, one that reflected a diversity of writing, and I soon found myself doing much better in the internship hunt.

Your résumé is also important. List all applicable experience in writing, emphasizing the publications for which you've written. Editors seem to care little about academic achievements. They look for experience. Also be sure to note any fluency in a foreign language, as well as experience in doing research on the Internet (which is a big plus).

Beyond Graduation

You should continue interning through the summer after your senior year. Then you can start looking for a full-time job. Many newspapers see their internship programs as part of the hiring process, especially for female and minority students. Your chances of getting a permanent job at a publication increase greatly if you intern there. In some cases, graduating seniors are forced to choose between interning at a large publication unlikely to hire them at the end and interning at a smaller publication that does tend to hire interns. The choices they make depend on the risks they're willing to take, and how badly they want to start their careers at major publications.

Many newspapers offer short-term reporting jobs to graduating seniors. Such temporary positions don't include benefits and generally don't lead to job offers when they're over. But these programs, which usually last one or two years, are good for developing reporting skills. The best-known two-year programs are at the *Philadelphia Inquirer* and the *Baltimore Sun*. Newspapers such as the *Chicago Tribune*, *Newsday*, the *Providence Journal-Bulletin*, the *New York Times*, and the *Washington Post* offer year-long positions, but often these positions require a year or so of reporting experience. *The*

Associated Press offers nine-month reporting positions that sometimes do turn into permanent jobs.

Summer Programs with Good Reputations

The following list of news organizations is very unofficial, but represents what the staff at the _Yale Daily News_ has long considered to be the best newspaper internship programs. They are all very competitive. (An asterisk indicates newspapers that have been known to hire interns after they graduate.) In no particular order, they are:

- _Wall Street Journal_*, nationwide
- _Washington Post_, Washington D.C.
- _Dallas Morning News_, Dallas, Texas
- _Boston Globe_ (graduating seniors cannot apply), Boston, Massachusetts
- _News & Observer_*, Raleigh, North Carolina
- _Oregonian_, Portland, Oregon
- _St. Petersburg Times_*, St. Petersburg, Florida
- _Times-Picayune_*, New Orleans, Louisiana
- _Associated Press_* (minority only), nationwide
- _New York Times_, New York, New York
- _Seattle Times_, Seattle, Washington

The following is a list of well-established magazine internship programs:

- _New Republic_ (very low pay)
- _Washington Monthly_ (no pay)
- _Newsweek_
- _Time_
- _Business Week_

Although many people may try to discourage you from going into print journalism because of the stiff competition and tough market these days, that's all the more incentive for you to pursue an internship if you really want to make it. In an industry in which practice makes perfect, the more hands-on work you do, the better.

Anchorage Daily News

P.O. Box 149001
Anchorage, AK 99514-9001
Phone: (800) 478-4200

Position: Intern

Department: Human Resources

No. of Positions Offered Annually: 4

Description: Internships available in the following areas: reporting, photography, copy editing and art. Interns attend weekly "Lunch and Learn" sessions on newspapering issues and practices.

Qualifications: Members of minority groups and women are encouraged to apply. Applicants should have published work from school or other publications and should have been trained in the basics of journalism. Photography and reporting interns must have reliable transportation. Applicants are encouraged to submit their material early.

Salary: $9.35/hour

Position Dates: Summer

Position Location: Anchorage, AK

Average No. of Applicants Annually: 150-200

Potential for Job Placement: N/A

Application Process: Send résumé, cover letter and at least six samples of best work. Photo applicants should submit a slide portfolio of about 20 slides.

Deadline: November 15

Contact: Internship Coordinator

Aperture Foundation

20 East 23rd Street
New York, NY 10010
Phone: (212) 505-5555
Fax: (212) 979-7759

Position: Work-Scholar

Department: Various

No. of Positions Offered Annually: 26

Description: Work-scholar program is designed to offer individuals of special promise an opportunity to learn through involvement with a nonprofit organization devoted to photography and the visual arts. Positions available in the following departments: Editorial, Production, Development, Circulation, Marketing, Publicity, Foreign Rights, Director's Office, Burden Gallery, Traveling Exhibition and the Paul Strand Archive (located in Millerton, New York). Internship is a full-time commitment and must be at least six months in duration.

Qualifications: Work-Scholars are selected on the basis of their interest and experience in photography, publishing and the visual arts, the ability to contribute significantly, and openness to gaining meaningful experience from the program. Skills such as typing, computer knowledge, copy editing, design, printing, business management, sales and marketing and print preparation will enhance a candidate's application.

Salary: $250/month

Position Dates: Year round

Position Location: Millerton, NY; New York, NY

Average No. of Applicants Annually: 500

Potential for Job Placement: Possible

Application Process: Send résumé, cover letter and two short writing samples.

Deadline: Rolling

Contact: Internship Coordinator

Beacon Press

25 Beacon Street
Boston, MA 02108
Phone: (617) 742-2110
Fax: (617) 723-3097

Position: Intern

Department: Various

No. of Positions Offered Annually: 48

Description: In an effort to diversify the book publishing industry, Beacon Press has created an educational, hands-on internship for people of color. Therefore 24 of the 48 positions are reserved for people of color. Positions available in Editorial, Marketing, Production, Business, Publicity and Administration.

Qualifications: Strong clerical skills a plus.

Salary: Unpaid

Position Dates: Fall, Spring and Summer

Position Location: Boston, MA

Average No. of Applicants Annually: 200

Potential for Job Placement: Yes

Application Process: Application to be completed.

Deadline: September 15 for Fall; January 10 for Spring; April 1 for Summer.

Contact: Sharon Rice

Birmingham News

P.O. Box 2553
Birmingham, AL 35202
Phone: (205) 325-2111
Fax: (205) 325-2283

Position: Intern

Department: News, Sports

No. of Positions Offered Annually: 6

Description: Internship positions available in news and sports reporting. Internship emphasizes practical experience and the intern is expected to perform as a beginning reporter. Summer internships last 12 weeks and Fall internships last 16 weeks. Interns will have the opportunity to work for the newspaper with the largest circulation daily in Alabama.

Qualifications: Applicants are expected to have completed substantial course work in journalism, to have written for campus or other publications, and to have maintained a GPA of at least 3.0 in college course work.

Salary: $325/week

Position Dates: Fall and Summer

Position Location: Birmingham, AL

Average No. of Applicants Annually: 150

Potential for Job Placement:

Application Process: Send résumé, cover letter, and eight to ten clips.

Deadline: April 1 for Fall; January 15 for Summer.

Contact: Carol Nunnelley

The Blade

541 North Superior Street
Toledo, OH 43660
Phone: (419) 245-6000

Position: Reporting Intern

Department: N/A

No. of Positions Offered Annually: 4

Description: Intern will perform general
assignment work on City Desk and other
news desks as opportunities arise.
Internship is a full-time commitment (37.5
hours per week) .

Qualifications: N/A

Salary: $430/week

Position Dates: Summer

Position Location: Toledo, OH

Average No. of Applicants Annually:
300

Potential for Job Placement: Possible

Application Process: Send résumé, cover
letter and three writing samples.

Deadline: November 1

Contact: Frank L. Craig

The Bulletin

1526 Northwest Hill Street
Bend, OR 97701
Phone: (541) 382-1811

Position: Intern

Department: Various

No. of Positions Offered Annually: 1

Description: Intern works on general
assignments and provides vacation relief for
reporting staff.

Qualifications: Applicants generally must
have made substantial progress toward a
degree in the field and have significant
experience with a campus or community
daily paper to be competitive.

Salary: $1,500

Position Dates: Summer

Position Location: Bend, OR

Average No. of Applicants Annually:
150

Potential for Job Placement: N/A

Application Process: Send résumé, cover
letter, six to ten clips and three to four
references with phone numbers.

Deadline: March 15

Contact: Steven K. Bagwell

Center for Investigative Reporting

500 Howard Street, Suite 206
San Francisco, CA 94105
Phone: (415) 543-1200
Fax: (415) 543-8311

Position: Reporting Intern

Department: N/A

No. of Positions Offered Annually: 6-8

Description: Interns usually follow a major project from idea to publication or broadcast, assisting with research and contributing to final stories with sidebars or other reporting. Interns do most of their research using data banks, by phone and through personal interviews. Current projects include investigations into the environment, public health, personal safety and public trust issues.

Qualifications: Applicants should have strong writing ability, research experience and interest in public policy and reporting. Published work is not a prerequisite and both students and nonstudents are encouraged to apply.

Salary: $150/month

Position Dates: Two sessions, each six months in duration. Session One begins January 15; Session Two begins June 15.

Position Location: San Francisco, CA

Average No. of Applicants Annually: 100

Potential for Job Placement: Possible

Application Process: Send résumé, cover letter, and writing samples.

Deadline: December 1 for Session One; May 1 for Session Two.

Contact: Internship Coordinator

Central Newspapers, Inc.

P.O. Box 145
Indianapolis, IN 46206-0145
Phone: (317) 633-9224
Fax: (317) 630-9549

Position: Fellow

Department: Fellowship Program

No. of Positions Offered Annually: 20

Description: Summer fellowship competition for those earning their bachelor's degrees during the August—June period preceding the fellowship. Fellowship lasts ten weeks and fellows will work at one of the newspapers owned by Central Newspapers in Indianapolis or Phoenix.

Qualifications: N/A

Salary: $4,725 (stipend)

Position Dates: Summer

Position Location: Indianapolis, IN; Phoenix, AZ

Average No. of Applicants Annually: 130

Potential for Job Placement: Possible

Application Process: Application to be completed.

Deadline: March 1

Contact: Russ Pulliam

Charlesbridge Publishing

85 Main Street
Watertown, MA 02172
Phone: (617) 926-0329
Fax: (617) 926-5720

Position: School Editorial Division Intern

Department: N/A

No. of Positions Offered Annually: 9-12

Description: Intern will work as an editorial assistant and will be assigned projects working in conjunction with an editor. The School Division publishes educational materials for students and teachers.

Qualifications: Applicant should possess strong written communication skills and a background in English and education. Familiarity with Macintosh computers a plus.

Salary: Unpaid

Position Dates: Fall, Spring and Summer

Position Location: Watertown, MA

Average No. of Applicants Annually: 50-75

Potential for Job Placement: Possible

Application Process: Send résumé, cover letter and writing samples.

Deadline: One month prior to desired start date.

Contact: Susan Shapero

Chilton

201 King of Prussia Road
Radnor, PA 19089-0193
Phone: (610) 964-4221
Fax: (610) 964-2928

Position: Intern

Department: Human Resources

No. of Positions Offered Annually: 19

Description: Positions available in the following areas: Editorial, Marketing, Information Systems, Marketing Research and Human Resources. Internships are typically 10–12 weeks in duration. Interns are expected to work 10–15 hours per week. Internships are Unpaid and students must therefore receive academic credit for their work. Interns will have the opportunity to work for one of America's largest and most diverse business-press publishers. Positions available in Radnor, PA, New York City and Carol Stream, IL. Additional information can be found at http://www.chilton.net.

Qualifications:

Salary: Unpaid

Position Dates: Fall, Spring and Summer

Position Location: Carol Stream, IL; New York, NY; Radnor, PA

Average No. of Applicants Annually:

Potential for Job Placement:

Application Process: Send résumé and cover letter stating dates of availability and area of interest.

Deadline: Rolling

Contact: Andrea Clark (E-mail: aclark chilton.net)

Connecticut Magazine

789 Reservoir Avenue
Bridgeport, CT 06606
Phone: (203) 374-3388
Fax: (203) 371-0318

Position: Editorial Intern

Department: N/A

No. of Positions Offered Annually: 5-10

Description: Duties include: providing seasonal help on particular guides, composing letters to and returning manuscripts and queries from freelance writers, answering phones, fact checking, copy editing, proofreading, cross-indexing articles from back issues and compiling mechanicals.

Qualifications: Applicant should be detail oriented and a self-starter who is interested in publishing, well read and has a good command of the English language.

Salary: Unpaid

Position Dates: Fall, Spring and Summer

Position Location: Bridgeport, CT

Average No. of Applicants Annually: N/A

Potential for Job Placement: N/A

Application Process: Send résumé, cover letter and sample of written material. Interview is desirable but not mandatory.

Deadline: One to three months prior to desired start date.

Contact: Alison Cicchetti

David R. Godine, Publisher

P.O. Box 9103
Lincoln, MA 01773
Phone: (617) 259-0700
Fax: (617) 259-9198

Position: Editorial/Publicity Intern

Department: Publicity Department

No. of Positions Offered Annually: 9-15

Description: Duties include correspondence with book reviewers, entering of books for award competitions, database maintenance, coordination of author events and evaluation of unsolicited manuscripts.

Qualifications: Applicants should have a GPA of at least 3.5. Most interns are recent college graduates, though some have been college juniors or seniors. English or communications background or experience helpful but not required.

Salary: Unpaid

Position Dates: Fall, Spring and Summer

Position Location: Lincoln, MA

Average No. of Applicants Annually: 50

Potential for Job Placement: Minimal

Application Process: Send résumé and cover letter. In-person interview preferred but not required.

Deadline: August 1 for Fall; December 1 for Spring; May 1 for Summer.

Contact: Lissa Warren

David R. Godine, Publisher

P.O. Box 9103
Lincoln, MA 01773
Phone: (617) 259-0700
Fax: (617) 259-9198

Position: Sales/Marketing Intern

Department: Publicity Department

No. of Positions Offered Annually: 9-15

Description: Duties include correspondence with cataloguers, libraries and bookstores, database maintenance and creation of sales materials for the representative force.

Qualifications: Applicants must have a GPA of at least 3.5. Most interns are recent college graduates, though some have been college juniors or seniors. Business background or experience helpful.

Salary: Unpaid

Position Dates: Fall, Spring and Summer

Position Location: Lincoln, MA

Average No. of Applicants Annually: 50

Potential for Job Placement: Minimal

Application Process: Send résumé and cover letter. In-person interview preferred but not required.

Deadline: August 1 for Fall; December 1 for Spring; May 1 for Summer.

Contact: Lissa Warren

Denver Post

1560 Broadway
Denver, CO 80202
Phone: (303) 337-2500

Position: Intern

Department: N/A

No. of Positions Offered Annually: 3

Description: The 10-week program has positions available in reporting, copy editing, graphics and photography.

Qualifications: Applicant must have completed his/her junior year in college. Minority students are encouraged to apply.

Salary: $400/week

Position Dates: Summer

Position Location: Denver, CO

Average No. of Applicants Annually: 300

Potential for Job Placement: N/A

Application Process: Send résumé, cover letter, list of three references and clips.

Deadline: December 1

Contact: Jeanette M. Chavez

Detroit Free Press

321 West Lafayette
Detroit, MI 48226
Phone: (312) 222-6490
Fax: (312) 222-5981

Position: Intern

Department: Recruiting and Development

No. of Positions Offered Annually: 13-16

Description: Internship positions available in the following departments: Editing, Graphics, Design, Photography, City Desk, Features Desk, Business Desk, Sports Desk, Entertainment Desk and Editorials Desk.

Qualifications: N/A

Salary: $485/week

Position Dates: Summer

Position Location: Detroit, MI

Average No. of Applicants Annually: 300

Potential for Job Placement: N/A

Application Process: Send résumé, cover letter, six work samples, a four-page autobiographical essay, three references, and a letter explaining why a Free Press internship is desired.

Deadline: December 1

Contact: Joe Grimm

Dow Jones Newspaper Fund

P.O. Box 300
Princeton, NJ 08543-0300
Phone: (609) 452-2820
Fax: (609) 520-5804

Position: Business Reporting Intern

Department: N/A

No. of Positions Offered Annually: 12

Description: All interns selected for this program will spend the summer working as business reporters at daily newspapers. Before beginning work, all interns attend a pre-internship training seminar paid for by the Dow Jones Newspaper Fund.

Qualifications: Applicants must be minority students attending college full time who are of sophomore or junior standing at time of application. Sincere interest in a newspaper career and previous work on a campus newspaper or other publication helpful. Journalism major not required.

Salary: Salary varies depending on hiring newspaper.

Position Dates: Summer

Position Location: Nationwide

Average No. of Applicants Annually: 75-100

Potential for Job Placement: Yes

Application Process: Application to be completed.

Deadline: November 1

Contact: Jan Maressa/Linda Waller (E-mail: newsfund@dowjones.com)

Dow Jones Newspaper Fund

P.O. Box 300
Princeton, NJ 08543-0300
Phone: (609) 452-2820
Fax: (609) 520-5804

Position: Editing Intern

Department: N/A

No. of Positions Offered Annually: 96

Description: All interns selected for this program will spend the summer working as copy editors at daily newspapers, online newspapers and real-time financial news services. Before beginning work, all interns attend pre-internship training lasting from one to two weeks at one of the eight training sites. All expenses for the training are paid. Internships are located across the country; a list of newspapers and news services that hired the pevious year's interns is on the application form. Applicants may not select where they will work but can indicate preferences for newspaper, online newspaper or real-time financial news service.

Qualifications: Applicants must be full-time college juniors, seniors or graduate students at the time they apply. Sincere interest in a newspaper career, work on a campus newspaper or other publication, or previous reporting internship helpful. Journalism major not required. Computer skills helpful for applicants interested in working as online or real-time interns.

Salary: Salary varies depending on hiring media.

Position Dates: Summer

Position Location: Nationwide

Average No. of Applicants Annually: 600-700

Potential for Job Placement: Yes

Application Process: Application to be completed.

Deadline: November 1

Contact: Jan Maressa (E-mail: newsfund@wsj.dowjones.com)

Faber and Faber, Inc.

53 Shore Road
Winchester, MA 01890
Phone: (617) 721-1427
Fax: (617) 729-2783

Position: Editorial Intern

Department: N/A

No. of Positions Offered Annually: 3-4

Description: Editorial intern will spend much of his/her time reading manuscripts currently under consideration by editors. In addition, intern may do market research, proofreading and copy editing. Internship provides an opportunity to see the relationship of the Editorial Department with publishing as a whole.

Qualifications: Proven interest is a plus, but enthusiasm and eagerness to learn are equally important. College students and recent graduates encouraged to apply.

Salary: Unpaid

Position Dates: Fall, Spring and Summer

Position Location: Winchester, MA

Average No. of Applicants Annually: 60

Potential for Job Placement: Yes

Application Process: Send résumé and cover letter stating dates of availability.

Deadline: Rolling

Contact: Adrian Wood

Faber and Faber, Inc.

53 Shore Road
Winchester, MA 01890
Phone: (617) 721-1427
Fax: (617) 729-2783

Position: Marketing Intern

Department: N/A

No. of Positions Offered Annually: 3-4

Description: Intern will work with the Sales and Publicity Departments to research publications and new markets, send out press materials, assist with ongoing projects such as course adoption and special sales and learn about how marketing is an integral part of book publishing today.

Qualifications: Proven interest is a plus, but enthusiasm and eagerness to learn are equally important. College students and graduates are encouraged to apply.

Salary: Unpaid

Position Dates: Fall, Spring and Summer

Position Location: Winchester, MA

Average No. of Applicants Annually: 60

Potential for Job Placement: Yes

Application Process: Send résumé and cover letter stating dates of availability.

Deadline: Rolling

Contact: Adrian Wood

Florida Times-Union

P.O. Box 1949
Jacksonville, FL 32231
Phone: (904) 359-4573

Position: Intern

Department: N/A

No. of Positions Offered Annually: 4

Description: Reporting, copy-editing and photography internships available. Interns will work as regular staffers and weekly meetings will be held with various editors to discuss problems and progress.

Qualifications: Preference given to individuals who have completed their sophomore or junior years in college, individuals who have held summer internships with daily newspapers in the past and individuals interested in print journalism. Applicants who live or attend college in Florida or Georgia are encouraged to apply.

Salary: Salary depends on level of education.

Position Dates: Summer

Position Location: Jacksonville, FL

Average No. of Applicants Annually: 150-200

Potential for Job Placement: Possible

Application Process: Send résumé, cover letter including GPA, at least two references and clips of past work if available.

Deadline: December 1

Contact: Judy Kestler

Harper's Magazine

666 Broadway
New York, NY 10012
Phone: (212) 614-6500

Position: Editorial Intern

Department: N/A

No. of Positions Offered Annually: 12

Description: Each intern is assigned to assist a particular editor, thereby allowing interns a chance to gain a thorough understanding of one specific section of Harper's. All interns work on the Harper's Index and share in being the first readers of unsolicited manuscripts as well as performing general office tasks.

Qualifications: Most interns are graduate and undergraduate students.

Salary: Unpaid

Position Dates: Fall, Spring and Summer

Position Location: New York, NY

Average No. of Applicants Annually: 200

Potential for Job Placement: N/A

Application Process: Application to be completed.

Deadline: June 15 for Fall; October 15 for Spring; February 15 for Summer.

Contact: Susan Burton

Hearst Book Group

1350 Aveunue of the Americas, 4th Floor
New York, NY 10019
Phone: (212) 261-6500
Fax: (212) 261-6518

Position: Intern

Department: Human Resources

No. of Positions Offered Annually: 6

Description: Entry-level positions in which each intern rotates through various departments to gain a full understanding of the book publishing process. Rotations are from three days to two weeks per department. Departments include Editorial, Publicity, Production, Marketing, Sales, Subsidiary Rights, Contracts/Permissions, and Copy Editing. Interns will have heavy clerical responsibilities as well as opportunities to get involved in projects. Interns learn about various departments through hands-on experience, informational luncheons, group intern project networking and other planned activities.

Qualifications: Open to college sophomores and juniors and graduate students. Applicants should have demonstrated desire to work in publishing through related summer positions and internships, office experience and a well-written cover letter.

Salary: $6.00/hour

Position Dates: Summer

Position Location: New York, NY

Average No. of Applicants Annually: 200

Potential for Job Placement: Yes

Application Process: Send résumé and cover letter explaining interest in an internship in book publishing.

Deadline: May 1

Contact: Audrey Schur

Houghton Mifflin

222 Berkeley Street
Boston, MA 02116-3764
Phone: (617) 351-3593

Position: Summer Intern

Department: N/A

No. of Positions Offered Annually: 12

Description: Intern works with experienced personnel and the amount of direct teaching and supervision typically ranges from one to five hours per week. The intern can be expected to gain some knowledge of how college textbooks are developed, produced and marketed and acquire some of the skills related to the process.

Qualifications: Applicants should have advanced computer skills and a strong interest in the publishing industry. Knowledge of a foreign language and marketing and editorial skills helpful.

Salary: $8.00/hour

Position Dates: Summer

Position Location: Boston, MA

Average No. of Applicants Annually: 250-300

Potential for Job Placement: Yes

Application Process: Send résumé and cover letter.

Deadline: April 1

Contact: Nancy Doherty-Schmitt

Intertec Publishing

32 West 18th Street
New York, NY 10011-4612
Phone: (212) 641-5265

Position: Editorial/Marketing Intern

Department: N/A

No. of Positions Offered Annually: 2-4

Description: Interns work with editorial and marketing staff of two leading trade magazines: *Theatre Crafts International* and *Lighting Dimensions*.

Qualifications: Applicant should be computer literate and have some previous work experience and good communication skills.

Salary: $125/week

Position Dates: Fall, Spring and Summer

Position Location: New York, NY

Average No. of Applicants Annually: 12-20

Potential for Job Placement: Minimal

Application Process: Send résumé and cover letter.

Deadline: Rolling

Contact: G. Kavas

Journal Star

One News Plaza
Peoria, IL 61643
Phone: (309) 686-3000

Position: News Intern

Department: N/A

No. of Positions Offered Annually: 6

Description: Full-time internships available with the City Desk and State Desk.

Qualifications: Applicant must have a GPA of at least 3.0 and be a student both the semester before and after the internship. Applicant must have attained at least junior standing.

Salary: $200/week

Position Dates: Fall, Spring and Summer

Position Location: Peoria, IL

Average No. of Applicants Annually: 150

Potential for Job Placement: Possible

Application Process: Send résumé, cover letter explaining interest in the internship, five to ten clips and three to four references.

Deadline: July 15 for Fall; November 15 for Spring; February 1 for Summer.

Contact: Karen Sorensen

Miami Herald

One Herald Plaza
Miami, FL 33132
Phone: (305) 376-3592

Position: Newsroom Intern

Department: N/A

No. of Positions Offered Annually: 12

Description: Reporting, copy editing, photography and art/design/graphics internships available. Duration of internship is 12 weeks.

Qualifications: Applicant should have previous journalism experience.

Salary: $520/week

Position Dates: Summer

Position Location: Miami, FL

Average No. of Applicants Annually: 150

Potential for Job Placement: Possible

Application Process: Send résumé, cover letter and clips.

Deadline: November 1

Contact: Christine Morris

Milwaukee Journal Sentinel

333 West State Street
Milwaukee, WI 53201
Phone: (414) 224-2303
Fax: (414) 224-2347

Position: Intern

Department: N/A

No. of Positions Offered Annually: 8-10

Description: Entry-level journalistic positions available in the following areas: reporting, copy-editing, graphics and photography. Interns will have the opportunity to do real journalism, working closely with editors and mentors.

Qualifications: Applicants should have previous internship experience, published articles or photos and college newspaper experience.

Salary: $400/week

Position Dates: Summer

Position Location: Milwaukee, WI

Average No. of Applicants Annually: 500

Potential for Job Placement: N/A

Application Process: Send résumé, cover letter, clips and references.

Deadline: December 1

Contact: Barbara Dembski

Moline Dispatch Publishing Company

1720 Fifth Avenue
Moline, IL 61265
Phone: (309) 764-4344
Fax: (309) 797-0317

Position: Reporting Intern

Department: N/A

No. of Positions Offered Annually: 5

Description: Interns will cover news and feature stories, functioning as replacements for vacationing beat writers. Internship provides great variety and exposes interns to deadline pressure in a competitive market full of news.

Qualifications: Applicant should be a junior in college majoring in journalism or a related field. Experience on school newspaper a plus. Applicant must be able to provide his/her own car.

Salary: $250/week

Position Dates: Summer

Position Location: Moline, IL

Average No. of Applicants Annually: 80

Potential for Job Placement: Yes

Application Process: Send résumé, cover letter and writing samples.

Deadline: February 1

Contact: Russ Scott

Moline Dispatch Publishing Company

1720 Fifth Avenue
Moline, IL 61265
Phone: (309) 764-4344
Fax: (309) 797-0317

Position: Photography Intern

Department: N/A

No. of Positions Offered Annually: 1

Description: Photography intern shoots news and feature photos for publication in the daily newspaper. Intern functions as a staff photographer with a 40-hour work week.

Qualifications: Applicant should be a junior in college with experience working on school newspaper. Applicant must have own camera equipment and car.

Salary: $200/week

Position Dates: Summer

Position Location: Moline, IL

Average No. of Applicants Annually: 20

Potential for Job Placement: Yes

Application Process: Send résumé, cover letter and samples of work.

Deadline: February 1

Contact: Russ Scott

The Nation

72 Fifth Avenue
New York, NY 10011
Phone: (212) 242-8400
Fax: (212) 463-9712

Position: Intern

Department: N/A

No. of Positions Offered Annually: 24

Description: Interns work in the offices of The Nation magazine. To gain editorial experience, interns check facts, do research, read and evaluate manuscripts and are encouraged to write editorials, articles or reviews for the magazine. On the publishing side, interns assist the advertising, circulation and promotion staff with day-to-day business and in creating and carrying out developmental and research projects for the magazine. Intern duties also include filing, photocopying, running errands and other routine office work. Seven positions are available in New York each semester, and one position is available in Washington each semester. Interns in New York will attend weekly seminars. Internships are full time (10:00 to 6:00), five days a week.

Qualifications: There are no specific requirements but most interns have completed their junior year of college.

Salary: $100/week

Position Dates: Fall, Spring and Summer

Position Location: New York, NY; Washington, D.C.

Average No. of Applicants Annually: 300

Potential for Job Placement: No

Application Process: Send résumé, cover letter, two letters of recommendation and two writing samples (published clips are preferred).

Deadline: July 15 for Fall; November 15 for Spring; April 1 for Summer.

Contact: Peter Meyer/Sandy Wood (E-mail: Institute@TheNation.com)

National Journalism Center

800 Maryland Avenue NE
Washington, DC 20002
Phone: (202) 544-1333
Fax: (202) 544-5368

Position: Intern

Department: N/A

No. of Positions Offered Annually: 60

Description: A reporting apprenticeship.

Qualifications: Applicant must have a college degree, excellent writing ability and prior internship experience.

Salary: $100/week

Position Dates: Fall, Winter, Spring and Summer

Position Location: Washington, DC

Average No. of Applicants Annually: 400

Potential for Job Placement: Job counseling service available.

Application Process: Application to be completed.

Deadline: Half a month prior to start of each session.

Contact: M. Kline

New Republic

1220 19th Street NW, Suite 600
Washington, DC 20036
Phone: (202) 331-7494
Fax: (202) 331-0275

Position: Intern

Department: Intern Program

No. of Positions Offered Annually: 2

Description: One three-month internship from June through August and one nine-month internship from September through May are available. Interns are required to read unsolicited manuscripts, proofread, check facts, run errands and write short articles, book reviews and editorials.

Qualifications: Applicants should have completed their junior or senior year of college. Previous experience in journalism (college newspaper or summer internship) is welcome but not essential. Applicants should be highly motivated individuals with strong administrative, writing and editorial abilities who are willing to work long hours for low pay.

Salary: $200/week

Position Dates: Academic year, Summer

Position Location: Washington, D.C.

Average No. of Applicants Annually: N/A

Potential for Job Placement: N/A

Application Process: Send résumé, cover letter, two recommendations and three to five writing samples.

Deadline: March 1

Contact: N/A

Newsweek

251 West 57th Street
New York, NY 10019
Phone: (212) 445-4409

Position: Summer Editorial Intern

Department: N/A

No. of Positions Offered Annually: 10

Description: *Newsweek*'s summer
internship program is designed for college
juniors entering their senior year,
graduating seniors, graduate students and
professionals with a few years' experience.
Interns do research, fact-checking, reporting
and other editorial tasks in the New York
headquarters. The internship is 13 weeks in
duration.

Qualifications: Applicants should have a
liberal arts background and experience
reporting and writing for high school or
college newspapers or magazines, or for
other publications or at other internships.

Salary: $500/week

Position Dates: Summer

Position Location: New York, NY

Average No. of Applicants Annually:
300-400

Potential for Job Placement: Minimal

Application Process: Send résumé, cover
letter and five samples of published work.

Deadline: January 1

Contact: Abigail Kuflik

Newsweek

251 West 57th Street
New York, NY 10019
Phone: (212) 445-4342
Fax: (212) 445-4929

Position: Public Relations Intern

Department: N/A

No. of Positions Offered Annually: 1

Description: Intern assists on company
newsletter, development of the online
version and in publicizing editorial
exclusives to other news organizations.

Qualifications: Applicant should have
previous journalism experience.

Salary: Salary depends on qualifications.

Position Dates: Summer

Position Location: New York, NY

Average No. of Applicants Annually:
N/A

Potential for Job Placement: Minimal

Application Process: Send résumé, cover
letter and three writing samples.

Deadline: May 1

Contact: Diana Pearson

Penguin Books

375 Hudson Street
New York, NY 10014
Phone: (212) 366-2000

Position: Intern

Department: Various

No. of Positions Offered Annually: 8

Description: Intern will spend time in a variety of departments including Editorial, Marketing and Sales.

Qualifications: N/A

Salary: Unpaid

Position Dates: Summer

Position Location: New York, NY

Average No. of Applicants Annually: 400

Potential for Job Placement: Yes

Application Process: Send résumé and cover letter.

Deadline: Rolling

Contact: Internship Coordinator

Philadelphia Magazine

1818 Market Street
Philadelphia, PA 19103
Phone: (215) 564-7700

Position: Editorial Intern

Department: N/A

No. of Positions Offered Annually: 21

Description: Duties include fact checking, assisting writers with research, and writing short pieces.

Qualifications: Applicant should have previous journalism experience.

Salary: Unpaid

Position Dates: Fall, Spring and Summer

Position Location: Philadelphia, PA

Average No. of Applicants Annually: N/A

Potential for Job Placement: Minimal

Application Process: Send résumé, cover letter and writing samples.

Deadline: August 1 for Fall; November 15 for Spring; April 1 for Summer.

Contact: Benjamin Wallace

Pittsburgh Post-Gazette

34 Boulevard of the Allies
Pittsburgh, PA 15222
Phone: (412) 263-1297

Position: Intern

Department: Internship Program

No. of Positions Offered Annually: 5-8

Description: Thirteen-week internship program that offers a broad exposure to the operation of a diverse, award-winning metropolitan daily newsroom devoted to the events and issues shaping a complex urban region long celebrated for its quality of life.

Qualifications: N/A

Salary: $450-$480/week

Position Dates: Fall, Spring and Summer

Position Location: Pittsburgh, PA

Average No. of Applicants Annually: 200-300

Potential for Job Placement: Possible

Application Process: Send résumé outlining academic, publication and work experience, cover letter, three references and photocopies of five to eight of best published articles. Photography intern candidates should send slides of both black-and-white and color work.

Deadline: December 31

Contact: Matthew Kennedy

The Plain Dealer

1801 Superior Avenue
Cleveland, OH 44114
Phone: (216) 999-5000

Position: Newsroom Intern

Department: N/A

No. of Positions Offered Annually: 13

Description: Internship offers interns opportunity to work for Ohio's largest newspaper. Most of the internships are for reporters, but there is one photography position and one graphic design position as well. All interns work a maximum of 13 weeks and are paid the professional rate.

Qualifications: N/A

Salary: Salary varies depending on qualifications.

Position Dates: Summer

Position Location: Cleveland, OH

Average No. of Applicants Annually: 500

Potential for Job Placement: Possible

Application Process: Send résumé, cover letter, three letters of recommendation and five or more work samples.

Deadline: November 30

Contact: Maxine L. Lynch

Roll Call Newspaper

900 Second Street NE, Suite 107
Washington, DC 20009
Phone: (202) 289-4900
Fax: (202) 289-2205

Position: Editorial Intern

Department: N/A

No. of Positions Offered Annually: 9

Description: Duties include research, proofreading, writing and general office tasks.

Qualifications: Applicant should have a strong desire to pursue a career in journalism.

Salary: Unpaid

Position Dates: Fall, Spring and Summer

Position Location: Washington, DC

Average No. of Applicants Annually: N/A

Potential for Job Placement: Possible

Application Process: Send résumé, cover letter stating dates of availability and at least one writing sample.

Deadline: July 1 for Fall; November 1 for Spring; July 1 for Fall.

Contact: Jane McKee

Science News

1719 N Street NW
Washington, DC 20036
Phone: (202) 785-2255
Fax: (202) 650-0365

Position: Science Writing Intern

Department: Science News

No. of Positions Offered Annually: 3

Description: Interns work as full-time science writers for three months under the guidance of Science News editors and writers. Interns generate many of their own story ideas, reporting and writing one or two published articles a week, including news stories and longer features.

Qualifications: Internship is intended for people planning careers in science writing. Preference given to persons completing advanced degrees in journalism with an emphasis in science writing. Skilled writers working toward an advanced degree in one of the sciences will also be considered.

Salary: $1,200/month

Position Dates: Fall, Spring and Summer

Position Location: Washington, DC

Average No. of Applicants Annually: 50

Potential for Job Placement: Yes

Application Process: Send résumé, cover letter and at least three writing samples.

Deadline: June 15 for Fall; October 15 for Spring; June 15 for Summer.

Contact: Internship Coordinator

Seattle Times

P.O. Box 70
Seattle, WA 98111-0070
Phone: (206) 464-3274

Position: Blethlen Family Newspaper
Minority Intern

Department: The Blethlen Family
Internship

No. of Positions Offered Annually: 12-15

Description: One-year newspaper
internship. Positions available in reporting,
copy editing, photography and graphic art.
Interns spend four months training at the
Walla Walla Union-Bulletin, four months at
the *Yakima Herald-Republic* and the final
four months at the *Seattle Times.*

Qualifications: Open to college graduates
who are African American, Asian American,
Latino, Native American or Pacific Islander.
Interns are required to have a car and should
have a strong desire to pursue their career in
the Pacific Northwest.

Salary: $260-$320/week

Position Dates: One year

Position Location: Seattle, WA

Average No. of Applicants Annually:
N/A

Potential for Job Placement: Yes

Application Process: Send résumé, cover
letter and writing samples.

Deadline: November 15

Contact: Millie Quan

Seattle Times

P.O. Box 70
Seattle, WA 98111
Phone: (206) 464-2200

Position: Newsroom Intern

Department: Various

No. of Positions Offered Annually: 12-15

Description: Most of the positions are for
general-assignment reporters working off
the city desk in suburban bureaus.
Additional openings are for one business
reporter, one copy desk editor, two
photographers, one artist or page designer
and one sports reporter who also has copy-
editing assignments. Those selected are
placed in full-time, paid 12-week positions.

Qualifications: Applicants must be
sophomores, juniors, seniors or graduate
students attending a four-year college or
university who are journalism majors or have
demonstrated a commitment to print
journalism. Previous experience strongly
recommended. Reporting and
photojournalism applicants must have a car.

Salary: $300-$400/week

Position Dates: Summer

Position Location: Seattle, WA

Average No. of Applicants Annually:
100

Potential for Job Placement: Yes

Application Process: Send résumé, cover
letter and writing samples. Reporting and
copy-editing applicants must write a one-
page essay describing why position is
appealing. Photojournalism applicants must
submit 20 samples of work prints.

Deadline: November 15

Contact: Newsroom Intern Coordinator

Society of Professional Journalists

16 South Jackson Street
Greencastle, IN 46135
Phone: (765) 653-8333
Fax: (765) 653-4631

Position: Pulliam/Kilgore Freedom of Information Intern

Department: N/A

No. of Positions Offered Annually: 2

Description: Internship enables students to research and write about freedom of information issues while assiting the Society's Freedom of Information Committee and First Amendment counsel in preparing the annual Freedom of Information Report. Duration of internship is 10 weeks. One position is in Washington, D.C., and one is in Greencastle, Indiana.

Qualifications: Applicant must be a senior or graduate journalism student or law student with journalism background.

Salary: $400/week

Position Dates: Summer

Position Location: Greencastle, IN; Washington, D.C.

Average No. of Applicants Annually: 25

Potential for Job Placement: N/A

Application Process: Application to be completed.

Deadline: February 15

Contact: Internship Coordinator

Vibe Magazine

205 Lexington Avenue
New York, NY 10016
Phone: (212) 522-7092
Fax: (212) 522-4578

Position: Advertising Intern

Department: N/A

No. of Positions Offered Annually: 3

Description: Interns will be expected to take responsibility for certain projects, be relied upon to prospect and make follow-up phone calls to present and potential advertisers and assist account executives and the publisher. In addition, interns will assist in the composing and proofreading of correspondence, maintain and update databases and media kits, execute mailings and provide general office support as needed. Fall and Spring internships are for credit only. Summer internships are paid but salary will vary depending on qualifications.

Qualifications: N/A

Salary: Depends upon qualifications (Summer only)

Position Dates: Fall, Spring and Summer

Position Location: New York, NY

Average No. of Applicants Annually: N/A

Potential for Job Placement: N/A

Application Process: Send résumé and cover letter.

Deadline: August 1 for Fall; December 1 for Spring; March 1 for Summer.

Contact: Kim Ford

Vibe Magazine

205 Lexington Avenue, 6th Floor
New York, NY 10016
Phone: (212) 522-7092
Fax: (212) 522-4578

Position: Advertising/Fashion Intern

Department: N/A

No. of Positions Offered Annually: 4

Description: Intern will perform basic office duties.

Qualifications: Applicant should be proficient in Excel 5.0 and Word.

Salary: Unpaid

Position Dates: Fall, Winter, Spring and Summer

Position Location: New York, NY

Average No. of Applicants Annually: 50

Potential for Job Placement: Possible

Application Process: Send résumé and cover letter.

Deadline: Rolling

Contact: Michelle Castro

Vibe Magazine

205 Lexington Avenue, 6th Floor
New York, NY 10016
Phone: (212) 522-7092
Fax: (212) 522-4578

Position: Advertising/Music Intern

Department: N/A

No. of Positions Offered Annually: 4

Description: Intern will perform basic office duties.

Qualifications: Applicant must have a working knowledge of Macintosh programs.

Salary: Unpaid

Position Dates: Fall, Winter, Spring and Summer

Position Location: New York, NY

Average No. of Applicants Annually: 50

Potential for Job Placement: Possible

Application Process: Send résumé and cover letter.

Deadline: Rolling

Contact: Edwin Philogene

Vibe Magazine

205 Lexington Avenue
New York, NY 10016
Phone: (212) 522-7092
Fax: (212) 522-4578

Position: Art/Photo Intern

Department: N/A

No. of Positions Offered Annually: 2

Description: Intern helps organize photo and assists in layout and scanning of images.

Qualifications: Applicant should have photo/design background and working knowlege of Macintosh programs.

Salary: Unpaid

Position Dates: Fall, Winter, Spring and Summer

Position Location: New York, NY

Average No. of Applicants Annually: 30

Potential for Job Placement: Possible

Application Process: Send résumé and cover letter.

Deadline: Rolling

Contact: Duane Pyous

Vibe Magazine

205 Lexington Avenue, 3rd Floor
New York, NY 10016
Phone: (212) 522-7092
Fax: (212) 522-4578

Position: Circulation/Consumer Marketing Intern

Department: N/A

No. of Positions Offered Annually: 4

Description: Intern assists with direct mail and performs basic clerical tasks.

Qualifications: N/A

Salary: Unpaid

Position Dates: Fall, Spring and Summer

Position Location: New York, NY

Average No. of Applicants Annually: 25

Potential for Job Placement: Possible

Application Process: Send résumé and cover letter.

Deadline: Rolling

Contact: Dana Sacher

Vibe Magazine

205 Lexington Avenue
New York, NY 10016
Phone: (212) 522-7092
Fax: (212) 522-4578

Position: Commuunications Department Intern

Department: Communications Department

No. of Positions Offered Annually: 3

Description: Intern assists Communications Department of *Vibe*. Duties include updating press lists, organizing press clippings and assisting with promotion of any special events. Job involves extensive phone work and some writing.

Qualifications: Applicant must be an enrolled college student and have knowledge of MicrosoftWord and an interest in public relations.

Salary: Unpaid

Position Dates: Fall, Spring and Summer

Position Location: New York, NY

Average No. of Applicants Annually: 25

Potential for Job Placement: No

Application Process: Send résumé and cover letter.

Deadline: Rolling

Contact: Natasha Requena

Vibe Magazine

205 Lexington Avenue, 6th Floor
New York, NY 10016
Phone: (212) 522-7092
Fax: (212) 522-4578

Position: Editorial Intern

Department: Editorial

No. of Positions Offered Annually: 15

Description: Duties are mainly of a clerical nature, providing support to edit staff. No writing is involved in the position.

Qualifications: Applicant should be a college student or recent graduate and should have previous journalism or writing experience as well as knowledge of Macintosh and interest in urban music.

Salary: Unpaid

Position Dates: Fall, Spring and Summer

Position Location: New York, NY

Average No. of Applicants Annually: 100

Potential for Job Placement: Minimal

Application Process: Send résumé, cover letter and clips.

Deadline: Rolling

Contact: Editorial Internship Coordinator

Vibe Magazine

205 Lexington Avenue
New York, NY 10016
Phone: (212) 522-7092
Fax: (212) 522-4578

Position: Marketing Intern

Department: Marketing Department

No. of Positions Offered Annually: 4

Description: Intern assists marketing art manager, marketing associate and marketing director with department projects.

Qualifications: Applicant should be available at least three days a week for three to four hours. Applicant should be proficient in Macintosh computer programs, QuarkXpress, Excel and Word.

Salary: Unpaid

Position Dates: Fall, Winter, Spring and Summer

Position Location: New York, NY

Average No. of Applicants Annually: 50

Potential for Job Placement: Possible

Application Process: Send résumé and cover letter. Qualified candidates will be contacted.

Deadline: Rolling

Contact: Deborah Simon

The Village Voice

36 Cooper Square
New York, NY 10003
Phone: (212) 475-3300
Fax: (212) 475-8944

Position: Editorial Intern

Department: N/A

No. of Positions Offered Annually: 15

Description: Intern will perform research for writers and editors.

Qualifications: Applicant should have excellent writing skills and a strong desire to pursue a career in journalism.

Salary: Unpaid

Position Dates: Fall, Winter, Spring and Summer

Position Location: New York, NY

Average No. of Applicants Annually: 400

Potential for Job Placement: N/A

Application Process: Application to be completed.

Deadline: Rolling

Contact: Frank Ruscitti

Washington Center for Politics and Journalism

P.O. Box 15201
Washington, DC 20003
Phone: (202) 296-8455
Fax: (202) 466-7598

Position: Politics and Journalism Intern

Department: Various

No. of Positions Offered Annually: 26

Description: Interns, selected from nominees submitted by the 46 participating university journalism and communication colleges and direct applicants from other schools, are placed in Washington news bureaus as full-time reporting, writing and broadcasting interns. During their 16 weeks in Washington, they receive twice-weekly seminars about campaign, governance and interest group politics, featuring political practitioners and political journalists. The purpose of the program is to improve the quality of political journalism. Interns at print bureaus always report and write for publication. Interns at broadcast organizations are generally used as news researchers.

Qualifications: Open to college journalists (undergraduates, graduate students and recent graduates). Students should be at least second term juniors when applying. Strong preference will be given to those with reporting and writing experience at school or other newspapers and broadcast outlets.

Salary: $375/month

Position Dates: Fall and Spring

Position Location: Washington, D.C.

Average No. of Applicants Annually: 100

Potential for Job Placement: Minimal

Application Process: Application to be completed.

Deadline: April 1 for Fall; November 1 for Spring.

Contact: Terry Michael
(E-mail: pol-jrnix@netcom.com)

Washington Monthly

1611 Connecticut Avenue NW
Washington, DC 20009
Phone: (202) 462-0128
Fax: (202) 332-8413

Position: Intern

Department: Editorial Department

No. of Positions Offered Annually: 18

Description: Both editorial and business positions available. Editorial interns will gain experience copy editing, fact checking and researching. Business interns will observe all facets of publishing. Internships are Unpaid but can be full or part time.

Qualifications: Previous internship experience and interest in journalism and politics a plus.

Salary: Unpaid

Position Dates: Fall, Spring and Summer

Position Location: Washington, D.C.

Average No. of Applicants Annually: 50-75

Potential for Job Placement: Minimal

Application Process: Send résumé, cover letter and three clips.

Deadline: March 15

Contact: Sherri Eisenberg

Washington Post

1150 15th Street NW
Washington, DC 20071-5508
Phone: (202) 224-7445
Fax: (202) 334-5231

Position: Intern

Department: Newsroom

No. of Positions Offered Annually: 20

Description: Interns work in the newsroom as reporters, copy editors, graphic artists and photographers. The jobs are on the Metro, Business, Style and Sports News desks with an occasional reporter assigned to the Foreign News desk. The program runs for 12 weeks during the summer and the interns work a full-time week.

Qualifications: Applicant must be enrolled as a junior, senior or graduate student at the time of application.

Salary: $784.70/week

Position Dates: Summer

Position Location: Washington, D.C.

Average No. of Applicants Annually: 600

Potential for Job Placement: No

Application Process: Students must call or write for an application.

Deadline: November 1

Contact: William A. Elsen

Washingtonian

1828 L Street NW
Washington, DC 20036-5139
Phone: (202) 296-3600

Position: Editorial Intern

Department: Various

No. of Positions Offered Annually: 6

Description: Duties include fact-checking, research and some writing for the magazine. Editors, writers and heads of Advertising, Promotion, Production, Circulation, Art and Photography Departments meet with interns once or twice a week to discuss their own roles at the magazine and their careers in journalism.

Qualifications: Applicants must be at least juniors in college and have previous journalism experience.

Salary: $5.75/hour

Position Dates: Fall, Spring and Summer

Position Location: Washington, DC

Average No. of Applicants Annually: 300-400

Potential for Job Placement: Possible

Application Process: Send résumé, cover letter and three clips.

Deadline: July 1 for Fall; November 1 for Spring; February 1 for Summer.

Contact: Courtney Rubin

Broadcast Journalism 4

by Julie Hirshfeld

Broadcasting internships are fast paced, time intensive, and the only effective way to get acquainted with the television or radio news business. For many would-be interns, working in broadcasting is about having a good time. But success in broadcasting means taking journalism seriously and taking initiative in order to have real input into the news-gathering and production processes. These are not internships for the weak willed or the lazy. During the application process and the course of your broadcasting internship, you might be called upon to do everything from running pages between the TelePrompTer and the control room, to logging tedious hours of tape, to going out in the field with a camera crew and a correspondent. If you go into it with a sense of adventure and a sense of direction, you'll come out with an education and a network of contacts that will serve you well if you decide to continue in the field.

Think of the process of getting yourself a good broadcasting internship and turning it into a viable employment opportunity as the most important story you'll ever pull together. Go through the who, what, where, when, and why of your internship application process as carefully as you would a news story, complete with research, fact checking, packaging, and pitching the story. Be as scrupulous about the particulars of your internship as you would be about a story, and you will be well on your way to a great experience in the broadcasting industry.

Start Digging

Before you begin sending out inquiries, survey the internship terrain as thoroughly as you can. Remember that you are marketing yourself to internship coordinators and personnel people as an aspiring reporter or production person. By researching internships and targeting those for which you are best suited, you demonstrate your efficiency and conscientiousness.

First, check out the broadcasting internships posted in the career services office at your college or university. If you don't find anything that suits you there, then start digging. Check out the reference section of the library, including the big radio and television industry directories (ask the reference librarian for advice here), to get contact information for the companies that interest you. You can also take to the Internet. Check out the sites of the companies that interest you (sometimes they even post their internships on the sites).

If you have your eye on a particular organization, it can never hurt to express your enthusiasm and lay the groundwork for a future internship by applying there even if you don't meet all the criteria. Just don't put too much energy into these internships that are over your head. Your aim should be to come away from your research with a list of several internships for which you are qualified, and that you have at least some chance of obtaining. Yes, they are out there; you just have to take the time to find them.

Don't hesitate to ask friends, relatives, and people at your college TV/radio stations (or even your college newspaper) about possible internship opportunities. Connections mean a lot in the broadcasting business, and sometimes smaller stations that don't have official internship programs need just as much help as—if not more than—larger operations with entrenched internship programs. If your cousin's sister-in-law is the assistant to a news correspondent, and she happens to be taking the summer off, you might be able to spend your internship replacing her. That's an opportunity you won't find posted, but it could be a great experience.

Use Those Alumni Contacts

Alumni connections can be so useful. My favorite sportscaster in Chicago graduated from Yale, so I decided to write him and call him to see if he could use me as a summer intern. Not only did I get to work with him, but I didn't even have to go through an interview process. The guy turned out to be one of the nicest, most professional, and fun people I've ever come into contact with and I had an incredible summer. Because of his generosity, I was able to experience professional sports like I never thought possible—right on the scene and down on the field. I met many interesting people and gained tremendous insight on the field of broadcasting. To top off the whole experience, the guy took me to a great blues club on my final night on the job, which was, needless to say, a terrific experience. Even the most famous people can be great human beings and take the time to teach you—it's definitely worth a shot.

—Yale sophomore

The final step in your internship research process should be fact checking. The internship listings you will find during your research, and the memories of your contacts in the field may be completely outdated. Consider the story of Jessica, a college junior who wanted more than anything to intern at a local television station not far from her home. She went to her college's career office, pored over the broadcast listings for an entire day, made herself what looked like an impressive list of internship targets, and went home with a smile on her face and an asterisk next to the name of the contact at her preferred station. She sent a letter to the contact, feeling as if she had a pretty good chance of at least getting an interview, but when she hadn't heard back after several months, she called the station to find out what had gone wrong.

It turned out that the contact to whom Jessica had written had left the station six months before, and the new internship coordinator had lost interest in Jessica's application because she hadn't even checked to find out whether she was writing to the correct person. "I'll never forget it," Jessica says. "She said, 'The first thing to know about working here is that little mistakes can translate into big trouble.' " It turned out that the internship was given to somebody more experienced than Jessica anyway, but we can all take a lesson from her experience. Make those fact-checking calls to make sure you have the right name, spelling, and title for the internship coordinator. You wouldn't present a news story without checking the names of those involved; why do it when an internship is at stake?

Get the Details

Read as much as you can about the organization to which you're applying in order to be a knowledgeable candidate and to make sure the internships are the right ones for you. A production secretary at ABC's *Turning Point* who had two consecutive internships at ABC News in New York says that was a key to her getting her foot in the door. "Watch TV [or listen to the radio], read some trade magazines, look at the schedules, figure out the shows you like, and become an expert on them," she says. "Internship coordinators just want to make sure that you're going to be up for whatever is happening, because with broadcast, anything can happen. So know your terms, know some stuff about broadcasting. When it comes down to applying, you have to show enough interest so that they see you're full of ideas, and you'll be a knowledgeable person and an asset to the program." This part of your research will pay off later in the game, in the application and interview stages of the game.

Once you have targeted the places or programs you want to go after, find out what you're getting yourself into. Find out what the internship entails, and make sure it's a good match. If even you don't think it's a good match, it will be difficult to convince an internship coordinator that you're right for it.

An essential note about compensation and broadcast internships: Most of these positions compensate you with college credit rather than a paycheck, so if your school doesn't give college credit for internships, you have some convincing to do. Businesses are required by law to compensate employees—intern or otherwise—for the work they do. So no amount of sweet-talking will convince internship coordinators to break the law and take you on as slave labor. Countless internship candidates have tried it before, and it doesn't fly. With so many candidates to choose from, internship coordinators say they will pass over a well-qualified student for a less impressive one if the better candidate can't get college credit. While many state schools, community colleges, and preprofessional institutions routinely award credit for internships, those of you who attend schools that don't give credit may have to be creative.

A production secretary at ABC's _Prime Time Live_ and a former intern there attended a university that didn't award college credit for internships. So in order to take ABC's offer, she had to find a legal way to produce a document stating that she was getting credit. She went to her local community college and enrolled in a journalism class for which the only requirement was an internship. For the cost of the journalism course, she had a piece of paper to give the internship coordinator at ABC stating that she was indeed receiving credit for the internship. The only catch was a daily journal she had to present at the end of the course to prove she had learned from her internship and should receive the credit. The moral of the story is: The credit you receive doesn't necessarily have to go toward your degree.

For those of you who don't want to pay through the nose to get an internship, there are other options. If you can get a professor or administrator to write a letter arguing that the internship is necessary for a course for which you _will_ receive credit, you may be able to get around the problem. When I was offered an internship at a network in New York during my sophomore year, I went to an administrator at my university who knew me well and was familiar with my interest and experience in journalism. I explained to him that my senior thesis would deal with the effects of media reports on presidential elections, and pointed out that interning for a network would give me the chance to do primary research on the topic. He agreed to write a letter vouching for the fact that the research aspect of my internship would ultimately receive credit as a part of my thesis, and I was accepted for the internship.

This is obviously a very sensitive element of your internship search, and you should be careful not to misrepresent yourself for the sake of getting your dream job. But if you're clever about the compensation/credit issue, you can figure out how the internship does ultimately result in college credit and then get it in writing.

Give Them the Facts

After journalists gather the necessary information for a news story, they think about how to make it relevant to the audience. Why will the audience care about this? Likewise, when marketing yourself you want to consider what intern coordinators care about.

The goal in crafting your résumé should be not only to show past interest, experience, and qualifications in broadcasting, but also to illustrate experience in a broad range of professional situations. One director of human resources says she looks for evidence of a well-rounded and energetic person when she looks at applicants' résumés. "I'm looking for past internships, extracurricular activities, and classes in the field. I'm basically looking for someone who has demonstrated the ability to juggle, because in this particular business, a lot of people do have to juggle on a daily basis. People here have to wear a lot of different hats, so I look for someone who has shown interest in the world that we live in."

Think hard about the qualities that are central to working in broadcasting—among them, inquisitiveness, research skills, assertiveness, accuracy, energy—and include those activities or studies that demonstrate those characteristics. Play up any experience you may have had in journalism or broadcasting, but if you have had none or very little, all is not lost. Show that you can be professional and take a job seriously for an extended period of time, and you will be well on your way to impressing internship coordinators.

While the one-page rule certainly applies as much to broadcasting résumés as any other kind, try not to exclude that volunteer work you did or the tutoring program you were a part of. These activities show that you're adventurous and, as one director of human resources says, have an interest in the world around you that can be so crucial to success in the news business. Just because working consistently at your local library over the past five years doesn't sound glamorous and has nothing to do with broadcasting, don't automatically exclude it from your résumé. It shows both research skills and the ability to take a job and stay with it for a long period of time.

A note on your major: internship coordinators usually gravitate toward candidates who list journalism or mass communications as their majors. If you attend a college or university that doesn't offer such a program, make sure you highlight any classes or extracurricular activities that focus on journalism or broadcasting. My major was an interdisciplinary program called Ethics, Politics, and Economics, so I emphasized the few journalism classes I took, a journalism program I participated in during high school, and the work I did on my college newspaper. One veteran ABC News intern suggests, "There's always something on campus that you an do to show your interest—work on the school paper, work on something that you can point to and show that you did your best to prepare yourself for the responsibilities of a broadcast intern." If you don't major in journalism or mass communications, make sure you include at least a sentence in your cover letter explaining why you didn't, and why your major is beneficial to someone pursuing a career in broadcast journalism.

Finally, presentation is important. The content of your résumé should be more impressive than its design. Don't go too far in trying to stand out visually; if anything, err on the side of simplicity. A manager of professional development and internships at a news network says she looks for a simple résumé that speaks for itself instead of relying on cutesy elements. "I get people all the time who try to impress me or draw attention to their application with fluorescent paper or flowered borders, or résumés that come in elaborate folders that make them look like some consulting firm trying to recruit college students," she says. "You know what's going to make you stand out? Your presentation, your experience. Your cover letter can grab my attention. Your writing sample. There are a lot of ways that you can get my attention; giving me extra things to handle or a résumé that looks like wallpaper is not going to grab me."

Sell Yourself

Once you've pitched a story idea, you have to defend it. Why should people be interested in your piece over another one, why will your facts and figures improve the newscast more than somebody else's might? Likewise, the cover letter should tell a potential employer why you are the best candidate for a position. It's also the place where you can defend your major, explain how your experience is relevant to broadcasting work (if its relevance isn't immediately apparent by looking at the résumé), and perhaps most important, show off your writing skills. According to many internship coordinators, an eloquent letter can be just as valuable as years of experience when it comes to proving yourself as an intern. "Give me an idea of why I should talk to you. What makes you different from the hundreds of résumés that I get? This is where you should explain if you seem less experienced than you should be: 'I don't have a lot of experience, but this is what I bring to the table.' Point out the obvious. This is when you get my attention," says the internship manager of a news network.

If you're having trouble coming up with ideas for your cover letter, try thinking of it as a news item. Start with an interesting lead that will pique the reader's curiosity, lay out the facts, and discuss their significance. While "I am writing to apply for . . ." is a perfectly fine beginning, it never hurts to open with a more aggressive statement like, "My considerable experience and education in broadcasting make me a competitive candidate for the XYZ internship." Introduce yourself in a compelling way, and spend the body of your cover letter briefly explaining the more significant elements of your résumé. You want the internship coordinator to be able to glance from your résumé to your cover letter and see a complete picture of a unique candidate. Point out the obvious and highlight anything that sets you apart from other students in your field, be it a wealth of experience, or little hands-on work but a lot of education that you're eager to use in a broadcast setting. End with a good kicker, preferably one that will make an internship coordinator want to talk to you in person and find out more.

The cover letter is also an appropriate place to mention any contacts or connections you have with the organization to which you're applying. If you met an internship coordinator at a job fair—or anywhere else for that matter—don't hesitate to remind the coordinator where and when you became acquainted. If you were referred by somebody else in the business, use it to your advantage by pointing out that you took the trouble to follow up on the contact.

According to internship coordinators nationwide, the most important point to get across in your cover letter is that you are serious about broadcast journalism, and that you see the internship as a way of laying a foundation for a career in the field. Even if you're not certain this is the business for you, make yourself sound focused and goal oriented; internship coordinators want to feel as if the candidates they pick are good investments that can pay off in the form of successful employees sometime in the future. An internship manager at a news network says that this is what she looks for in a letter. "This business is so unique that in order to succeed, in order to really, really do this, you have to want to do this. It has to be a passion," she says. "You're going to have to work on things you don't want to work on, things you don't agree with, go places you would never even think about going to cover stories that turn your stomach, that make you sad, that just make you angry. And you have to rise above all that, and what makes you rise above all that is the fact that you believe in what you're doing, and that you enjoy what you're doing no matter how bad it is."

Above all, most internship coordinators say they are turned off by students who have too rosy and glamorous a vision of broadcast journalism. So if your only knowledge of the field comes from watching the movie *Broadcast News*, take pains to make your interest sound more substantive than that. An internship manager at a news network says the key is to show strong aspirations based on knowledge, rather than dreams based on the glitz and celebrity of news anchors. "You have people who look at the news and say, 'I think I want to do that,' based on what they see on television. It's not like that. It's not like you read about this guy in a magazine who makes millions of dollars, and you've seen him on TV and say to yourself, 'I could do that.' [It's] more than what you see on television, and some people don't know that. You have to be hungry for this."

Finally, don't leave questions from your résumé—why such a low GPA? why the dearth of experience? why an unrelated major?—unanswered. Deal with them honestly and put the most positive light possible. If your GPA was low because you put in so much time working at your school's radio/TV station or newspaper, point that out. Leave the reader of your cover letter eager to meet you. End your letter with a sentence along the lines of: "I hope you will have the time to meet with me in person in the coming weeks, as I am anxious to introduce myself and share some of my ideas about the XYZ program." A sentence like this can often mean the difference between having your letter placed in the circular file and having your letter placed in a pile of "people to meet with."

Meeting Deadlines and Acing the Interview

Being prompt is a must in the broadcasting business. Journalists work on tight schedules with strict deadlines, and as an internship candidate, you'll have to do the same. No matter how impressive your résumé or how well crafted your cover letter, getting them to the proper person on time is a must if you want a shot at the internship of your choice. So mail out your applications promptly as the first indication of how efficient you are.

Follow up with a phone call two to three weeks after your application will have arrived. Not only will you find out whether your application has reached its destination, you'll also show internship coordinators that you are taking an active role in seeking out the position. This is a second chance to plug yourself for an interview. Just don't be too pushy; be polite and keep the number of calls to a reasonable amount.

Start out by explaining that you're calling to make sure your application arrived safely, ask if the internship coordinator has had a chance to look it over, and then inquire about the possibility of coming in for an interview in the next few weeks. Be flexible about the time and place, and if your contact sounds too harried to meet with you in the near future, assure him or her that you would be happy to call back at another time. Keep track of who you've called and when you said you would call back. Even if the internship coordinator forgets that you promised to call back on a specific date, chances are he or she will remember you when you call back, and be impressed that you're following up yet again.

One former intern says that face-to-face meetings at ABC News were instrumental in landing her first internship. "I still remember going around to each different unit and each producer who might need an intern, and I talked to each one for about five minutes. It took forever, but it was worth it. They knew my face, they knew what I was like, I think they could pretty much tell if I'd be a good person to work with, and I could tell the same about them." Internship coordinators across the board said it helps to be able to put a face with a name and an application. The broadcasting business, after all, is as much about personalities and working well together as any other, so showing your face around the office early on in the process is crucial.

Once you've set up an appointment for an interview, you have your work cut out for you. Learn as much as you can about the particular program or station, and write down some relevant questions and comments that come to mind. Write down a few story ideas and notes on why you think they would be good stories. If you can memorize this, do so. But if you're afraid of forgetting something, jot it down on a reporter's notebook and take it to the interview. Then use that same notebook to jot down details learned during the interview. Taking notes will show interviewers that you are as concerned as they are about finding a good fit. Investigate who is in charge of what, so you can ask to meet people as you go along. Internship coordinators want to hear questions as well as answers in an interview, so prepare yourself not to sit passively, scrutinizing the internship coordinator's paperweight while waiting to field the next question. Broadcast journalists ask questions for a living; prepare yourself to talk nearly the whole time if necessary—or to shut up and listen if that's what's required.

Internship coordinators share many of the same ideas about what constitutes a good broadcast internship interview—all simple things, but all important if you want to make a good impression:

Relax

Says one intern manager, "Sometimes people get so stressed out and so tense that the whole interview is blown out of the water. You can lose out on a job or an internship that you could have had if you allow yourself to become so tense that you can't speak."

Ask Questions

Be an active participant in the conversation. This is a chance to show inquisitiveness (even if you already know the answers) and to flaunt any special knowledge you have of the broadcast business or the particular news operation in question. Again, it can't hurt to ask to meet some of the key players, if they have the time. This doesn't mean asking, "Could you take me by Dan Rather's office so I could get an autograph for my Grandma?" But it's okay to ask to meet a producer or news director, the people you might be working with if you got the internship. Don't be obnoxious, but assert yourself as a self-possessed person who is comfortable with adults and at ease in a professional setting.

Don't Limit Your Answers to One Word

Says one human resources director, "Give me sentences, let me know how you speak, because part of an interview is to find out how you conduct yourself, how you express yourself, in addition to if you can do the job. Can you speak English, can you speak clearly?"

Be on Time and Know Where You're Going

This is basic but very important. You should call if you're going to be late or if you're having trouble finding your way to the office. "If you can't find your way here, how are you going to survive a day in this business?" says one intern manager for a news network.

Make Eye Contact and Have a Firm Handshake

In the interview setting, you are no longer a college student. Be as professional as you can be, and your interviewer will take you seriously. Eye contact is important for on-camera broadcasters, and while there's little chance you will get on the air during your internship, it can't hurt to show you have a future communicating with people in a sincere way. Squash any annoying little habits, such as hair flipping.

Don't Take Yourself Too Seriously

Believe it or not, internship coordinators get bored, too. Don't be afraid to show a sense of humor and tell stories when they seem appropriate. As much as possible, you want your interviewers to be able to identify with you so they see you as someone who could fit in well.

Be Prepared For . . .

Be prepared to talk about the broadcasting business generally and your goals within it. Be ready to take on a hypothetical broadcasting crisis question, such as, "It's one minute to the broadcast, and your correspondent is nowhere to be found. Where do you go, what do you do?" Also anticipate the typical "Where do you see yourself in ten years?" question. If your answer is, "Lying on a beach in Cancun sipping umbrella drinks," think of a more appropriate answer, if only to get you through the interview.

Be Well Groomed

Dress the way someone in the broadcast business would. For women, that can mean a skirt or pants and a blouse, a suit (skirt or pants), or a dress. For men, that means either a full suit or at least a tie and jacket. Don't overdo it; you're not auditioning to be an anchorperson, so keep it simple. But don't show up in jeans or sneakers. Tone down your make-up and jewelry, and—a tip from many internship coordinators—take the rings out of your nose, eyebrows, etcetera, if you have them. They're distracting.

The Internship Itself

Once you land an internship (and congratulations on that), you should live up to and surpass expectations so that you will be remembered when it comes time to look for a job after graduation. If you've come this far in the process, you can be pretty sure you're cut out for the internship. Being a good broadcasting intern is not difficult, but it takes dedication, a time commitment, a good attitude, and a lot of creativity.

If you intern at a large broadcasting operation, being a good intern is about aggressively seeking substantive tasks. You will have to do your share of answering telephones, sending letters and faxes, and filing tapes. You will learn more than you ever wanted to know about how to log tape—how to take a 5,000-page binder of material and write time-codes next to every fifth line as you watch hours upon hours of often not-so-interesting footage. You will place countless labels on yards and yards of tape, filing shots by subject, by date, by person involved.

One former intern was lucky enough to work at ABC during the O.J. Simpson trial. She sat in front of a television, watching every minute of the trial and writing down every shot change and time code. She watched hours of Michael Jackson news segments, logging shots and subjects in preparation for an hour-long show about him. These are not the most glorious moments of an internship, but if you can perform these tasks cheerfully, quickly, efficiently, and thoroughly, you will get noticed by your superiors.

But getting noticed is not your only goal. In order to avoid becoming known simply as "the intern who logs tape like nobody's business," you have to seek out more significant opportunities. Remember that you're there to help out in any way possible, and that it will take some time to gain the trust of the producers and reporters with whom you will ultimately want to work. But whenever you have a free moment, express interest in contributing more to the broadcasting process. Hang around particularly busy producers, and ask if they need help putting together a piece. Become an avid surfer on the Internet and LEXIS-NEXIS (an online legal and business news service), so you can do research and pitch story ideas in your free time. Position yourself as an omnipresent helper during "crashes" (situations in which a story breaks late and the staff has to scramble to pull it together), willing to run tapes, messages, or scripts to wherever they're needed. Make it known that you are reliable in both stressful and everyday situations, so that you will leap to the minds of the overworked producers and reporters when they need something.

Latching onto a staff member who needs a lot of help is often the best route to getting involved in a serious way. If you can make yourself indispensable to somebody who has a lot of input, you will automatically get to do more than those interns who do random tasks for different people during the entire course of the internship. This was the tack one former intern took in her first internship at ABC's *Good Morning America*. She was assigned to help a producer with whom she had mutual interests, and made herself a constant presence in that producer's office. "It was really unbelievable," she recalls. "She let me do everything, because it was like I was her intern. At the very beginning, it was like, 'Look up this, look up that,' but then it really happened quickly where she'd hand me a news article, and just say, 'Flesh this out and see if we can develop a story from it.' I got to do great things, and the more I did, the more she gave me to do. By the end of the summer, she had me pre-interviewing, going on shoots, sitting in the edit room, going out by myself with a camera crew—everything. It was an amazing experience."

The same was true of my own internship at ABC's *Prime Time Live*. Although I wasn't assigned to a particular staff member, I spent all my free time during the first week or so of my internship scoping out a producer who might need an assistant for the summer. I was around late one afternoon the day before the broadcast when a story broke, and I helped a producer and a correspondent put together a segment on very short notice. The next time I heard a page from that producer, I rushed to be the first one to answer it, and she soon involved me in the preparation of a news segment she was producing. While I tried to make myself available for general tasks around the office whenever possible, I quickly became this producer's personal assistant, and she drew me into the production process in many different ways. Because I consistently reported to her, we developed a mutual trust wherein I felt confident making suggestions and giving my input into the stories she was working on, and she felt comfortable putting me in charge of tasks of every kind. I learned how to shoot visual material at the animation stand, put together a clip reel of background footage with an editor, and even how to incorporate words with camera shots in the scripts of news stories. These were indispensable lessons I would never have had the chance to learn if I had spent my entire internship writing time codes on the sides of interview transcripts, and the producer was happy to have the extra help.

If you have an internship at a local station, you may not have to be as active about seeking out a mentor or a consistent source of substantive work. A former intern for such programs as *Extra!*, *Inside Edition*, *American Journal*, *Fox Local News*, and *Dateline NBC*, says a smaller setting makes for more significant roles for interns. "In some ways, you will get more out of an internship at cable or a local news station than from national news. You do learn production stuff at a large operation, but in terms of news gathering, doing shoots, and getting to follow through with stories, it's easier at a smaller place," she says. "Besides, in a smaller setting, it's easier to get to know everyone, so people ask for things more frequently."

Whether you're in a huge, national network office or a small local affiliate, making contacts should be a high priority for you as a broadcasting intern. If you attach yourself to a producer or reporter, you're well on your way to meeting the people who may eventually be able to help you in your quest for a full-time job. But whether you work for one person in particular or everybody in the office, be aware of the fact that these people are in positions to help you later on if you do a good job for them as an intern. Take the opportunities you have as an intern to acquaint yourself with people from all over the organization. Think about how many people would give anything to be in your position, walking around the offices of producers, associate producers, and reporters, just a knock away from chatting with them or running a story idea by them.

Be tactful about these interactions; you can't just barge into the office of a busy executive producer and expect him or her to be willing to chew the fat for 15 minutes. But don't let timidity prevent you from facilitating these meetings whenever possible. Some internship programs are designed in such a way that interns meet with a different member of the broadcasting team—correspondents, legal consultants, editors, etcetera—each week. Attend these meetings, and if they're not offered, don't hesitate to go to your internship coordinator and say, "You know, it would really help me if I could talk to XYZ for a few minutes, and find out what it is she really does all day." Again, being pushy is not to your advantage in these situations. Veteran broadcasting interns share countless story about their annoying peers, who spent their entire internships running around trying to establish a network of job contacts. Don't fall into that trap! It is possible to meet people around the organization and make a good impression they will remember in years to come without kissing up.

Postgraduation Jobs: The Follow-up Story

When your internship is over, your contact with the broadcasting operation shouldn't be. You wouldn't produce a lead story and then cut contact with your sources if you wanted to do a follow-up in the future, so don't do that with your internship, either. If you're going into your senior year right after your internship ends, spend your last few days there talking to whomever you've become close to about the possibility of a job after graduation. If you've had a significant role in producing or putting together a story or group of stories, try to get a tape made of all of your work so you have something to show potential employers. One former intern, whose two summer internships at ABC News led to a job there after graduation, says, "You've got to keep all your contacts; that was really the way that I did it. When it really comes down to the end of the year and you're looking for a job, you need a little mole, a little spy inside to say, 'This is what's available, and this is who to call if you want it.' " Leave your school address and telephone number with those at the station who will be likely to hear about job openings. If you've done a good job during your internship, they probably will be happy to spy for you.

Internship coordinators say they are happy to hear from interns after they've left, so establish a correspondence—mail, E-mail, or telephone—with your closest co-workers at the station. It never hurts to visit the office when you're in the neighborhood; this is a good way to keep in touch and to find out about any positions that are open or likely to open in the near future. When it comes time to apply for a job, send an updated copy of your résumé and your work to your internship coordinator, and ask if she or he would be willing to put them into the right hands for you.

Conclusion: Exploiting Your Luck

If you follow the advice above in pursuing your internships and first job, you are well on your way to beginning a career in broadcasting. But even the most skilled reporters and producers sometimes have to rely on dumb luck for the big breaks that make their stories great, and so will you. Doing a good story is as much about being at the right place at the right time as it is about getting your facts straight and your sources talking. I was extremely lucky during the internship application process; one of the programs to which I had applied happened to pick up one of the stories I broke for my college newspaper. When the producer called to get information about my article, I mentioned that I was a candidate for an internship at the program. Who knows how much these coincidences affect your chances of snagging an internship? They may make all the difference, or none at all. Keep an open mind as you enter the broadcasting industry in search of an internship or a job. Anything and everything can happen, and often does.

CBS News

524 West 57th Street
New York, NY 10019
Phone: (212) 975-5567
Fax: (212) 975-8798

Position: News Production Intern

Department: Production

No. of Positions Offered Annually: 110-130

Description: Duties include but are not limited to research, logging tapes, archive research, time coding scripts, putting scripts together and some clerical work. Internships are for college credit only.

Qualifications: Applicant must be a junior or senior in college, must have a GPA of at least 3.0. Must be majoring in journalism, mass communications, or English. Computer and language skills a plus.

Salary: Unpaid

Position Dates: Fall, Spring and Summer

Position Location: New York, NY

Average No. of Applicants Annually: 300

Potential for Job Placement: Yes

Application Process: Send résumé, cover letter, two letters of recommendation, transcript, writing sample, and letter of credit.

Deadline: Rolling

Contact: Eldra Rodriguez-Gillman (E-mail: erg@CBSNEWS.com)

Children's Television Workshop

1 Lincoln Plaza
New York, NY 10023
Phone: (212) 595-3456
Fax: (212) 875-6088

Position: Intern

Department: N/A

No. of Positions Offered Annually: 60

Description: There are a variety of things that interns may do: research, production, publishing, community education, and new show projects.

Qualifications: Related course work and prior experience in the area in which the intern would like to work.

Salary: Depends on department.

Position Dates: Fall, Spring and Summer

Position Location: New York, NY

Average No. of Applicants Annually: 2,000+

Potential for Job Placement: Yes

Application Process: Send in cover letter and résumé.

Deadline: July 15 for Fall; November 15 for Spring; March 15 for Summer

Contact: Human Resources Department

CNN

One CNN Center
P.O. Box 105366
Atlanta, GA 30348
Phone: (404) 827-1700

Position: Intern

Department: Various

No. of Positions Offered Annually: 200

Description: Intership positions available in the following areas: Booking, Business News, CNNI, CNNfn, CNN Interactive, CNN Newsroom Show, CNN Online, CNN Presents, CNN Sports, Creative Services, Environment Unit, Food and Health Unit, Graphics, Headline News, International Assignment Desk, Medical, News Features, Political, Post Production, Public Relations, Radio, Sales Operations, Science News, Showbiz Today, Spanish, Sports Public Relations, TalkBack, TESI, Travel, Weekend Morning Magazine and World Report.

Qualifications: N/A

Salary: Unpaid

Position Dates: Fall, Winter, Spring and Summer

Position Location: Atlanta, GA

Average No. of Applicants Annually: 400

Potential for Job Placement: Possible

Application Process: Application to be completed.

Deadline: July 1 for Fall; October 1 for Winter; January 1 for Spring; March 1 for Summer.

Contact: Lisa Forniss

Greater Media Cable

95 Higgins Street
Worcester, MA 01616
Phone: (508) 853-1515
Fax: (508) 854-5065

Position: News Intern

Department: N/A

No. of Positions Offered Annually: 18

Description: Interns shoot, edit and help with scripts for the shows. Interns learn how to put a newscast together with two live daily newscasts at 6:30 and 10.

Qualifications: Applicant must be an enrolled college student.

Salary: Unpaid

Position Dates: Fall, Winter, Spring and Summer

Position Location: Worcester, MA

Average No. of Applicants Annually: 100

Potential for Job Placement: Minimal

Application Process: Application to be completed.

Deadline: Rolling

Contact: Martin Morenz

KGO-TV/Channel 7: San Francisco, San Jose, Oakland

900 Front Street
San Francisco, CA 94111
Phone: (415) 954-7958
Fax: (415) 954-7514

Position: Accounting/Finance Intern

Department: Accounting/Finance

No. of Positions Offered Annually: 3-5

Description: Interns will provide general assistance to the controller, manager of accounting, and other members of the business office of a major market television station in areas such as A/P, A/R, fixed assets, and budgeting. Will learn the basic functions of a television finance/accounting department. Duties include spreadsheet work and general clerical duties, but can cover a wide range of activities.

Qualifications: Must be a junior, senior, or graduate student. Must be available for a personal interview and must live in the San Francisco Bay Area during the internship. The internship must be applicable to course credit. Must possess good written and organizational skills. Prefer students with business/finance background. Knowledge of Microsoft Suite helpful.

Salary: $5.00/hour

Position Dates: Fall, Spring and Summer

Position Location: San Francisco, CA

Average No. of Applicants Annually: 300

Potential for Job Placement: N/A

Application Process: Must complete an application form, submit two letters of recommendation, write a one-page rationale, submit a college transcript, a course credit verification, and a résumé.

Deadline: August 1 for Fall; December 1 for Spring; May 1 for Summer

Contact: Kathryn Cox or Sarah Matsuno

KGO-TV/Channel 7: San Francisco, San Jose, Oakland

900 Front Street
San Francisco, CA 94111
Phone: (415) 954-7958
Fax: (415) 954-7514

Position: Graphics Interns

Department: Graphics

No. of Positions Offered Annually: 3-5

Description: An internship in the Graphics Department gives an individual the opportunity to gain hands-on experience with graphic technology. Duties will involve general clerical assistance in addition to researching visual material needed by the department.

Qualifications: Must be a junior, senior, or graduate student. Must be available for a personal interview and must live in the San Francisco Bay Area during the internship. The internship must be applicable to course credit. Intern should have creative and artistic talent. Should be able to handle several tasks simultaneously. Good writing and phone skills. Knowledge of WordPerfect helpful.

Salary: $5/hour

Position Dates: Fall, Spring and Summer

Position Location: San Francisco, CA

Average No. of Applicants Annually: 300

Potential for Job Placement: N/A

Application Process: Must complete an application form, submit two letters of recommendation, write a one-page rationale, submit a college transcript, a course credit verification, and a résumé.

Deadline: August 1 for Fall; December 1 for Spring; May 1 for Summer

Contact: Kathryn Cox or Sarah Matsuno

KGO-TV/Channel 7: San Francisco, San Jose, Oakland

900 Front Street
San Francisco, CA 94111
Phone: (415) 954-7958
Fax: (415) 954-7514

Position: Human Resources Intern

Department: Human Resources

No. of Positions Offered Annually: 3-5

Description: Assists with general responsibilities in a human resources department.

Qualifications: Must be a junior, senior, or graduate student. Must be available for a personal interview and must live in the San Francisco Bay Area during the internship. The internship must be applicable to course credit.

Salary: $5.00/hour

Position Dates: Fall, Spring and Summer

Position Location: San Francisco, CA

Average No. of Applicants Annually: 300

Potential for Job Placement: N/A

Application Process: Must complete an application form, submit two letters of recommendation, write a one-page rationale, submit a college transcript, a course credit verification, and a résumé.

Deadline: August 1 for Fall; December 1 for Spring; May 1 for Summer

Contact: Kathryn Cox or Sarah Matsuno

KGO-TV/Channel 7: San Francisco, San Jose, Oakland

900 Front Street
San Francisco, CA 94111
Phone: (415) 954-7958
Fax: (415) 954-7514

Position: Information Systems Intern

Department: Information Systems

No. of Positions Offered Annually: 3-5

Description: Interns will assist computer systems manager in providing internal support to departments in the areas of desktop application (i.e., MS Office, Lotus, Netscape), operating systems (i.e., Windows and UNIX), and network troubleshooting.

Qualifications: Must be a junior, senior, or graduate student. Must be available for a personal interview and must live in the San Francisco Bay Area during the internship. The internship must be applicable to course credit. Must be proficient with PCs, operating systems, and general business applications, as well as with Novell Netware. Good interpersonal skills and the ability to work independently are needed.

Salary: $5.00/hour

Position Dates: Fall, Spring and Summer

Position Location: San Francisco, CA

Average No. of Applicants Annually: 300

Potential for Job Placement: N/A

Application Process: Must complete an application form, submit two letters of recommendation, write a one-page rationale, submit a college transcript, a course credit verification, and a résumé.

Deadline: August 1 for Fall; December 1 for Spring; May 1 for Summer

Contact: Kathryn Cox or Sarah Matsuno

KGO-TV/Channel 7:
San Francisco, San Jose,
Oakland

900 Front Street
San Francisco, CA 94111
Phone: (415) 954-7958
Fax: (415) 954-7514

Position: Marketing Research Intern

Department: Marketing Research

No. of Positions Offered Annually: 3-5

Description: Intern will assist research director and research associate in all areas of rating research. Major responsibilities include working with Nielsen overnight reports, keeping track of ratings for news, sports, prime time, etc., creating new graphs, updating programming schedules, typing and filing.

Qualifications: Must be a junior, senior, or graduate student. Must be available for a personal interview and must live in the San Francisco Bay Area during the internship. The internship must be applicable to course credit. Knowledge of Microsoft applications desired. Must be detail oriented. Prefer marketing/research majors.

Salary: $5.00/hour

Position Dates: Fall, Spring and Summer

Position Location: San Francisco, CA

Average No. of Applicants Annually: 300

Potential for Job Placement: N/A

Application Process: Must complete an application form, submit two letters of recommendation, write a one-page rationale, submit a college transcript, a course credit verification, and a résumé.

Deadline: August 1 for Fall; December 1 for Spring; May 1 for Summer

Contact: Kathryn Cox or Sarah Matsuno

KGO-TV/Channel 7:
San Francisco, San Jose,
Oakland

900 Front Street
San Francisco, CA 94111
Phone: (415) 954-7958
Fax: (415) 954-7514

Position: News Intern

Department: News

No. of Positions Offered Annually: 3-5

Description: Interns will assist assignment editors in various aspects of the news-gathering process. Responsibilities include monitoring new sources, answering, screening, and following up on phone calls, updating source lists, and other duties as assigned. Interns may accompany reporters on stories. Interns will also work on the news feature "Seven on Your Side," assisting reporters and producers with research for stories, collecting information from various online services, maintaining a news database, following up on viewer letters, and assisting with other duties as assigned.

Qualifications: Must be a junior, senior, or graduate student. Must be available for a personal interview, must reside in the San Francisco Bay Area during the internship, and the internship must be applicable to course credit. Interns should be able to work independently, once they have been given proper instructions and training. Good written and verbal skills desired.

Salary: $5.00/ hour

Position Dates: Fall, Spring and Summer

Position Location: San Francisco, CA

Average No. of Applicants Annually: 300

Potential for Job Placement: N/A

Application Process: Must complete an application form, submit two letters of recommendation, write a one-page rationale, submit a college transcript, a course credit verification, and a résumé.

Deadline: August 1 for Fall; December 1 for Spring; May 1 for Summer

Contact: Kathryn Cox or Sarah Matsuno

KGO-TV/Channel 7: San Francisco, San Jose, Oakland

900 Front Street
San Francisco, CA 94111
Phone: (415) 954-7958
Fax: (415) 954-7514

Position: Programming Intern

Department: Programming

No. of Positions Offered Annually: 3-5

Description: Interns will assist on the weekly home improvement show, _House Doctor._ They will assist in scheduling potential segments, scouting locations, researching segment topics and pre-interviewing guests. Interns may also assist on _Log-on TV,_ a weekly informative and entertaining show for computer users of all levels, or may assist on _Marketplace,_ a weekly business show. Interns will be exposed to all aspects of production on all shows.

Qualifications: Must be a junior, senior or graduate student. Must be available for a personal interview and must reside in San Francisco Bay Area during the internship. The internship must be applicable to course credit. Good writing skills. Knowledge of word processing. Must be able to work independently and handle a variety of tasks simultaneously.

Salary: $5.00/ hour

Position Dates: Fall, Spring and Summer

Position Location: San Francisco, CA

Average No. of Applicants Annually: 300

Potential for Job Placement: N/A

Application Process: Must complete an application form, submit two letters of recommendation, write a one-page rationale, submit a college transcript, a course credit verification, and a résumé.

Deadline: August 1 for Fall; December 1 for Spring; May 1 for Summer

Contact: Kathryn Cox or Sarah Matsuno

KGO-TV/Channel 7: San Francisco, San Jose, Oakland

900 Front Street
San Francisco, CA 94111
Phone: (415) 954-7958
Fax: (415) 954-7514

Position: Promotions Intern

Department: Promotions

No. of Positions Offered Annually: 3-5

Description: Interns will assist the publicity and event director in all areas of publicity, public relations, and event planning. Duties include: writing press releases, working with local TV critics, answering promotion department phones, monitoring local papers, as well as national and press coverage of Channel 7 and its competition, maintaining photo and program files, and assisting at station-sponsored events. Interns will also assist the Promotions Director and Promotions producers with preproduction duties (logging tapes, searching for news footage, and setting up promo shoots).

Qualifications: Must be a junior, senior, or graduate student. Must be available for a personal interview and must reside in San Francisco Bay Area during the internship. The internship must be applicable to course credit. Students with marketing and advertising experience encouraged to apply. Interns should be able to work independently and under time pressure.

Salary: $5.00/hour

Position Dates: Fall, Spring and Summer

Position Location: San Francisco, CA

Average No. of Applicants Annually: 300

Potential for Job Placement: N/A

Application Process: Must complete an application form, submit two letters of recommendation, write a one-page rationale, submit a college transcript, a course credit verification, and a résumé.

Deadline: August 1 for Fall; December 1 for Spring; May 1 for Summer

KGO-TV/Channel 7: San Francisco, San Jose, Oakland

900 Broad Street
San Francisco, CA 94111
Phone: (415) 954-7958
Fax: (415) 954-7514

Position: Public Affairs Intern

Department: Public Affairs/Editorial

No. of Positions Offered Annually: 3-5

Description: Interns will assist the public affairs coordinator and community relations manager in all aspects of the Public Affairs/Editorial Department. Basic responsibilities include answering phones, opening mail, selecting and writing ten-second Community Calendar announcements, overseeing the production of Community Calendars, as well as other duties as assigned.

Qualifications: Must be a junior, senior, or graduate student. Must be available for a personal interview and must live in the San Francisco Bay Area during the internship. The internship must be applicable to course credit. Broadcast production experience or course work helpful, as well as good communication and writing skills, a pleasant phone manner and the ability to work independently.

Salary: $5.00/hour

Position Dates: Fall, Spring and Summer

Position Location: San Francisco, CA

Average No. of Applicants Annually: 300

Potential for Job Placement: N/A

Application Process: Must complete an application form, submit two letters of recommendation, write a one-page rationale, submit a college transcript, a course credit verification, and a résumé.

Deadline: August 1 for Fall; December 1 for Spring; May 1 for Summer

Contact: Kathryn Cox or Sarah Matsuno

KGO-TV/Channel 7: San Francisco, San Jose, Oakland

900 Front Street
San Francisco, CA 94111
Phone: (415) 954-7958
Fax: (415) 954-7514

Position: Sales Intern

Department: Sales

No. of Positions Offered Annually: 3-5

Description: Interns will provide general assistance to sales managers, sales account executives, sales service/traffic and sales assistants in daily office activities. Duties are primarily clerical, but can cover a wide range of activities.

Qualifications: Must be a junior, senior, or graduate student. Must be available for a personal interview and must live in the San Francisco Bay Area during the internship. The internship must be applicable to course credit. Execellent communication skills a must. Should be detail oriented. Knowledge of Windows applications desired. Prefer marketing/communications majors.

Salary: $5.00/hour

Position Dates: Fall, Spring and Summer

Position Location: San Francisco, CA

Average No. of Applicants Annually: 300

Potential for Job Placement: N/A

Application Process: Must complete an application form, submit two letters of recommendation, write a one-page rationale, submit a college transcript, a course credit verification, and a résumé.

Deadline: August 1 for Fall; December 1 for Spring; May 1 for Summer

Contact: Kathryn Cox or Sarah Matsuno

KGO-TV/Channel 7: San Francisco, San Jose, Oakland

900 Front Street
San Francisco, CA 94111
Phone: (415) 954-7958
Fax: (415) 954-7514

Position: Sports Intern

Department: Sports

No. of Positions Offered Annually: 3-5

Description: Interns will assist the sports producer and sports anchors/reporters with the daily activities involved in a major market television Sports Department. Duties range from answering phones and filing to watching and logging televised games and reviewing sports footage.

Qualifications: Must be a junior, senior, or graduate student. Must be available for a personal interview and must live in the San Francisco Bay Area during the internship. The internship must be applicable to course credit. Knowledge of sports is a must. Must possess good organizational skills and the ability to work well with others.

Salary: $5.00/hour

Position Dates: Fall, Spring and Summer

Position Location: San Francisco, CA

Average No. of Applicants Annually: 300

Potential for Job Placement: N/A

Application Process: Must complete an application form, submit two letters of recommendation, write a one-page rationale, submit a college transcript, a course credit verification, and a résumé.

Deadline: August 1 for Fall; December 1 for Spring; May 1 for Summer

Contact: Kathryn Cox or Sarah Matsuno

KGO-TV/Channel 7: San Francisco, San Jose, Oakland

900 Front Street
San Francisco, CA 94111
Phone: (415) 954-7958
Fax: (415) 954-7514

Position: Weather Intern

Department: Weather

No. of Positions Offered Annually: 3-5

Description: Interns will assist weather talent and weather researcher with the preparation of on-air graphics and information for weather forecasts.

Qualifications: Must be a junior, senior, or graduate student. Must be available for a personal interview and must live in the San Francisco Bay Area during the internship. The internship must be applicable to course credit. Ideals candidates should be working towards a degree in meteorology or atmospheric sciences. Familiarity with DIFAX products, domestic data bulletins, and Netscape Web browser a plus.

Salary: $5.00/hour

Position Dates: Fall, Spring and Summer

Position Location: San Francisco, CA

Average No. of Applicants Annually: 300

Potential for Job Placement: N/A

Application Process: Must complete an application form, submit two letters of recommendation, write a one-page rationale, submit a college transcript, a course credit verification, and a résumé.

Deadline: August 1 for Fall; December 1 for Spring; May 1 for Summer

Contact: Kathryn Cox or Sarah Matsuno

KQED-FM

2601 Mariposa Street
San Francisco, CA 94110
Phone: (415) 553-2289
Fax: (415) 553-2241

Position: The California Report Intern

Department: The California Report

No. of Positions Offered Annually: 12-16

Description: Interns will work two to three days a week for at least three months with the staff of The California Report, a statewide news service produced by KQED providing two weekly programs to California public radio stations. Participants will help the program producers, host and reporters, assisting in research, reporting, sound gathering and writing.

Qualifications: Program open to upper division students, graduate students and recent graduates majoring in journalism, communications or broadcasting. Broadcast production experience is desired. People of color, women and persons with disabilities are encouraged to apply. Fluency in languages other than English is helpful.

Salary: Unpaid

Position Dates: Fall and Spring

Position Location: San Francisco, CA

Average No. of Applicants Annually: 200

Potential for Job Placement: N/A

Application Process: Send résumé, cover letter and work samples.

Deadline: Rolling

Contact: Sally Eisele

KQED-FM

2601 Mariposa Street
San Francisco, CA 94110
Phone: (415) 553-2155

Position: News Intern

Department: N/A

No. of Positions Offered Annually: 25

Description: Hands-on program will offer interns the opportunity to gain experience in all aspects of radio news. Interns will work with staff reporters, assist in research, reporting, sound gathering and writing. Interns will also receive training in radio reporting and news writing, effective use of sound, researching stories, field recording and studio editing and story production. As the program is Unpaid, interns will be expected to work two days a week for at least three months.

Qualifications: Program is open to upper division students, graduate students and recent graduates majoring in journalism, communications or broadcasting. Exceptions will be made for applicants with strong experience in related fields. People of color, women and persons with disabilities are encouraged to apply. Fluency in languages other than English is considered a plus.

Salary: Unpaid

Position Dates: Fall, Spring and Summer

Position Location: San Francisco, CA

Average No. of Applicants Annually: 200

Potential for Job Placement: N/A

Application Process: Send résumé, cover letter and work samples.

Deadline: August 15 for Fall; February 15 for Spring; May 15 for Summer.

Contact: Cyrus M. Musiker

Millennium Multi-Media

Box 9704
Laguna Beach, CA 92677

Position: Administrative Assistant

Department: N/A

No. of Positions Offered Annually: 2

Description: General duties of an administrative assistant in a multimedia environment.

Qualifications: A degree and work experience.

Salary: Unpaid

Position Dates: Flexible

Position Location: Laguna Beach, CA

Average No. of Applicants Annually: 100+

Potential for Job Placement: Yes

Application Process: Send cover letter and résumé and references.

Deadline: Rolling

Contact: Human Resources Director

National Public Radio

635 Massachusetts Avenue
Washington, DC 20001-3753
Phone: (202) 414-2000
Fax: (202) 414-2909

Position: Intern

Department: N/A

No. of Positions Offered Annually: 20

Description: Internship positions available in the following areas: Communications, New Media, Human Resources, News, Legal, Marketing, Development, Member Services, Finance, Audience Research, Engineering and Information Technology and Cultural Programming.

Qualifications: Applicant must be a college junior or higher, but no more than six months out of school.

Salary: $5.00/hour

Position Dates: Fall, Spring and Summer

Position Location: Washington, D.C.

Average No. of Applicants Annually: 200

Potential for Job Placement: Minimal

Application Process: Application to be completed.

Deadline: August 15 for Fall; December 15 for Spring; March 30 for Summer.

Contact: Internship Coordinator

NBC

30 Rockefeller Plaza
New York, NY 10112
Phone: (212) 664-2277
Fax: (212) 664-5761

Position: Intern

Department: Various

No. of Positions Offered Annually: 450

Description: Interns work in all departments: Administrative, News, Sports, Finance, Video, etc.

Qualifications: Must receive school credit.

Salary: Commuting expenses only.

Position Dates: Fall, Winter/Spring and Summer

Position Location: New York, NY

Average No. of Applicants Annually: 1,000+

Potential for Job Placement: No

Application Process: Send cover letter and résumé. Include a letter on school letterhead stating that you can receive school credit for the internship.

Deadline: Fall and Winter/Spring: rolling; Summer: April 11

Contact: Internship Coordinator

WXRK

40 West 57th Street, 14th Floor
New York, NY 10019
Phone: (212) 314-9287
Fax: (212) 314-9338

Position: Production/Office Intern

Department: Production

No. of Positions Offered Annually: 45

Description: Interns assist staff on either the Howard Stern Show or in the Promotions Department. Must receive school credit.

Qualifications: Broadcast or journalism major. Computer and typing ability.

Salary: Unpaid

Position Dates: Fall, Spring and Summer

Position Location: New York, NY

Average No. of Applicants Annually: 200

Potential for Job Placement: Slim, but great recommendations given.

Application Process: Send résumé and cover letter.

Deadline: Rolling

Contact: Jodi Salidor

Business

by Daniel P. Weiss

Internships in the business world range from boring and mundane clerical positions to glamorous and exciting positions, from small, local companies to large, international companies. As with most jobs, the type of work and the value of the experience will depend on personal initiative. Successfully completing an internship in the business world will help you earn some money, learn skills that will help you in future career endeavors, and develop contacts for full-time employment. "Having a business internship meant having the opportunity to explore a field I had never even considered," notes a former intern and recent hire at Procter & Gamble Corporation.

Does Size Matter?

All chipper undergraduates who head to their career services departments, searching for ideal business internships, will quickly confront a fork in the road. Business internships are generally divided between large businesses and small businesses. Both paths can lead to successful or wasteful experiences and offer distinct advantages and disadvantages.

Large Companies

Internships with major corporations such as Procter & Gamble, Microsoft, Andersen Worldwide, Chase Manhattan Bank, and General Electric are typically part of a company internship program that encourages participants to work for the company in the long term. The advantages of such internships usually include:

- a higher compensation package
- access to company resources, including training facilities
- enhanced prestige and name recognition
- the possibility of a full-time job offer

The flock of undergraduates who apply for these internship programs face a competitive application process. The difficulty in securing these positions increases their prestige; they are often referred to as great "résumé builders." Future internships in the same corporation are available for those who wish to diversify their experiences.

One former intern for General Electric Capital was offered a full-time position there after completing her internship. She says, "An internship at a large corporation is good for someone who wants to explore different options. You can learn new skills by moving into different businesses within the same company. The first summer I worked with GE, I worked in Stamford, Connecticut, near corporate headquarters. The environment was more competitive and fast paced. The next summer I worked in Pennsylvania, which was much slower and more relaxed than Connecticut. This was important in learning how to deal with different types of people, different goals, and different expectations."

Structured networking opportunities are also more frequent in large corporations. "Working for a large corporation is more cushy. My company supplied all of the extras including a lot of wining and dining. This enabled me to meet the movers and shakers in the company," comments a former General Mills intern. Large corporations have huge budgets to spend on recruiting and intern programs, which are increasingly viewed as the most effective method of attracting and securing top candidates. In fact, Procter & Gamble selects about 80 percent of full-time hires from its corporate internship program, according to Tami Hurwitz, an assistant brand manager and recruiter at the company.

Small Companies

Internships at small companies have become increasingly popular in recent years. The advantages of internships with these smaller firms include:

- increased responsibility
- more hands-on training
- personal attention
- the ability to make substantive, influential changes more quickly

"Smaller firms offer more exposure. I was able to meet people from many different departments at many different levels. A larger corporation has departments which are so large that you can easily get lost within them," comments a Cornell University student who completed a marketing internship with PF Collier & Newfield Publications, Inc. Smaller firms offer less formally structured internships. This lack of restriction allows interns to tailor the position to their interests. Since these smaller firms do significantly less recruiting than do large companies, personal initiative and persistence is especially helpful in securing internships.

What Kind of Positions Are Available?

Students should reflect on what they hope to get out of an internship before deciding which sectors to explore extensively. Internships vary widely between sectors as well as among companies, so a careful investigation of each program is important. Speaking with former interns is highly recommended because they can provide insight into the types of projects you can expect as well as the dynamics of the office.

Sales

Generally, sales interns have a wider selection of locations in which they can work. Sales interns could be asked to track new products and study the in-store marketing approaches of various companies. A large company might have interns working with retail chains while a smaller firm may require interns to spend more time on the phone contacting clients.

The Low-Down on Corporate Law Internships

The benefit of a legal internship is just exposure. The jobs are mostly clerical. I worked in two different practice areas when I interned, and I really got to see what everyone does, from the entry-level associate to the senior partner. The internship really allowed me to have an understanding of what motivates someone to go into corporate law and what kind of dedication it takes to stay in that field.

Most of the big firms have offices in various cities. The type of law you are interested in should factor into where you try to get placed. For example, if you want to learn about public policy, you would probably head to the Washington, D.C., branch of a firm. Or if you want exposure to technology law, you should consider the branch offices in San Francisco. For something like mergers and acquisitions law, New York is one of the major places to be.

If you are more interested in corporate law, you should look into where the big firms have their branch offices and consider quality of life and financial concerns. For example, one of the big-name New York companies might have a division in Phoenix. Not only would your cost of living be lower, but this branch might also be the biggest corporate law office in Phoenix.

—Yale graduate who has interned at several corporate law firms in Houston and New York

Marketing

Marketing internships are often considered the most glamorous of business internships. Market research departments are charged with understanding consumer needs and wants. This sector deals with large amounts of data accumulated through surveys and focus groups. Marketing interns acquire a more general exposure to business, including budgeting, industry bench marking, trend analysis, advertising design, and copywriting.

Finance and Accounting

Internships in finance and accounting are generally reserved for students with a background in these areas. Many large accounting firms offer great technical experience to their interns. Finance sectors of large and small companies are slightly less focused than accounting firms and generally delegate more diverse projects. Finance internships may involve evaluating a targeted company in a mergers-and-acquisitions deal, while accounting internships may require auditing a division. (Investment banking internships are discussed in the chapter on consulting and investment banking.) Students considering an internship in these fields should feel comfortable with financial concepts and numerical calculations.

Manufacturing and Product Supply

Internships in manufacturing and product supply target those students with highly technical backgrounds, often in engineering. Locality is often flexible. Interns are often expected to employ their technical background in investigating efficiency and productivity. Internships in information systems, a growing field, deal with computer technology and integration of company systems. Consulting internships, although unusual, occasionally exist within smaller firms. These internships are beneficial because they provide a wider exposure to all business functions.

Entrepreneurial Positions

Students who truly want to run their own business should look into entrepreneurial internships. These positions, considered less orthodox, are sponsored by corporations with programs that train students to establish and run their own business for the summer. For example, Flying Colors Inc., a Connecticut-based company, assists students in establishing a painting company by providing extensive training and the necessary resources. Students are given significant incentives to build the business because they share in the profits. These opportunities are unique in their ability to provide students with real-life experiences associated with owning a business.

Résumés, Interviews, and Getting the Job

Almost universally, businesses in search of interns are looking for students who exhibit leadership abilities. The personal initiative and motivation associated with a student leader are viewed as imperative to completing intern projects that are valuable to a company. This is especially true in companies with less-structured internship programs. These companies are relying on an intern's ability to identify opportunities to make substantive impacts. Therefore, leadership themes should permeate your internship search and application process. Additionally, you should help potential employers understand why you are interested in working for them and how your qualifications meet their criteria for employment.

Your résumé should consistently highlight those projects or activities that exemplify your ability to analyze problems, think innovatively, and develop strategic solutions. Focus on examples of your ability to lead a group toward successfully setting and achieving goals. Using business jargon in your résumé and cover letter shows a potential employer that you are familiar with the industry and adept at learning and digesting necessary concepts. If you are not familiar with industry jargon, visit the library and find industry-related books that include comprehensive glossaries.

Résumés and cover letters can be sent in response to a career fair, advertisement, personal contact, or just out of general interest. They should always be addressed to an individual, even if you don't have a contact yet. Just call and get the name and correct title of the internship coordinator or personnel manager. Your application should be followed up by a phone call to set up an interview. If a company is recruiting on campus, be sure to sign up for interview and information sessions early.

Business interviews require formality. Intern candidates should dress and act accordingly and remain professional throughout the process. Preparation for the interview should include research about the company, practice interviews, and extensive honing of business acumen. Research about the company should include as much discussion with former and current employees and interns as possible, a computer search of LEXIS-NEXIS (news and legal information services) to learn about recent company activity, and a thorough study of all materials provided by the company before the interview. If possible, practice interviews should include a videotaped interview, which will allow you to observe your own idiosyncrasies, inappropriate habits or gestures, and your overall presentation.

Typical Interview Questions

The following are typical interview questions that you should be prepared to answer:

- Tell me about yourself.
- Why do you want to work for our company? Why do you want to enter this field?
- Tell me about your most rewarding experience.
- Give me an example of how you have shown your leadership abilities.
- Give me an example of an obstacle you have overcome and how you approached this obstacle.
- Tell me about an activity in which you have employed the same skills and abilities that will be necessary during this internship.
- Why did you decide to attend XYZ University?
- What plans have you made for after graduation?
- Where do you see yourself five years from now? Ten years? Twenty years?
- What is your greatest weakness and your greatest strength?

Also be prepared to answer questions about your GPA, academic record and course work, and everything listed on your résumé. "Grades are important but they are not everything. They shouldn't discourage somebody from applying," says a former intern.

Potential business interns should remember that in the world of business, the atmosphere is generally conservative. Dark suits with white or natural colored shirts or blouses are necessities. Women should wear skirts that fall on or below the knee. Belts should match shoes, and shoes should always be polished. Hair should be cut and worn conservatively. Pull long hair back and out of your face.

Remember to arrive at interviews early and prepared. Candidates should find out what they are expected to bring prior to the interview. A leather

Working for a More
Diversified Wall Street

In 1970, Princeton alumni Father Frank Carr, inspired by Martin Luther King's "I Have A Dream" speech, committed himself to increasing opportunities for minorities in business and preparing them for leadership roles in community and the corporate world. With this in mind, he established the Inroads organization in Chicago with 17 companies and 25 interns on board. Since then, Inroads has grown to include more than 900 companies, thousands of interns, and more than 6,000 alumni.

Inroads accepts students ranging from high school seniors to college sophomores. From engineering and computer science to traditional business fields, Inroads helps match students with their areas of interest. Because Inroads is looking to change the long-term future of its members, an Inroads student interns at the same company for several summers in order to develop an in-depth understanding of the company. Minority students must have at least a 3.0 GPA and a 900 SAT score to apply. After this, applicants are screened and filtered into a select talent pool. This group undergoes a two-day training session in which they receive corporate literature, practice résumé writing, and go through mock interviews.

Inroads then secures each student at least one interview with a company in a field that interests him or her. The jobs are paid, with salaries ranging from $7.50 to $16 an hour. But according to an Inroads recruiter, it's not just the work experience—which any internship can offer—that distinguish Inroads internships. Equally as important are the development and training workshops that Inroads provides for its interns. Students are required to attend workshops during the summer on topics ranging from time management to diversity in the workplace. In addition, Inroads stresses community service and throughout the year offers academic support, such as paid tutoring, to make sure students keep up their GPA. The rate of job placement—from internship to full-time employment—is about 50 percent. Students who do not get placed in the companies for whom they intern are often placed in other companies in the same field. Inroads circulates résumés locally and nationally, so about 70 percent of interns are placed after their internships.

Inroads is not alone in offering these special opportunities to minority students. In the past several decades, several programs have developed to help place interns in summer jobs with top-notch companies. One such program is Sponsors for Educational Opportunity (SEO), which locates corporate summer internships for undergraduate students of color. Since 1980, SEO has helped students of color find internships in corporate law, management consulting, investment banking, accounting, and asset management. Big-name companies such as Smith Barney, Merrill Lynch, PaineWebber and Bear Stearns are just a few of the firms that participate in SEO and accept interns each year. SEO interns have mentors at their respective companies and participate in corporate training seminars during the summer.

To qualify, students must have at least a 3.0 GPA. SEO also looks for candidates who demonstrate commitment to community service, leadership in extracurricular activities, maturity, and strong interpersonal skills. SEO generally accepts college juniors and seniors, although it will also consider freshmen and sophomores for some positions. In 1996, SEO accepted about 200 students from an applicant pool of 2,500, coming from more than 70 schools nationwide. SEO has also had excellent placement results, securing full-time employment for 75 percent of its interns. SEO is based in New York City but also conducts interviews in Atlanta, Chicago, California, and Michigan.

Inroads can be contacted at 10 South Broadway, Suite 700, St. Louis, MO 63102 (314) 241-7488.

SEO can be contacted at 23 Gramercy Park South, New York, NY 10003 (212) 979-2040.

portfolio will prove a wise investment if you don't already have one. Inside the portfolio you should have a pad, extra copies of your résumé and cover letter, two stylish pens, and writing samples if necessary. Some companies require a copy of your transcript and/or references.

Typical Questions for Prospective Employers

Prepare six to eight questions about the company and the position and write them out on the pad you will take to the interview. Good examples include:

- What types of projects will I encounter during this internship?
- How much ownership of these projects will I have?
- How much say will I have in determining my projects?
- What are my prospects for full-time employment following an internship at this company?
- What types of intern events are held during the program?
- How much interaction will I have with top management?
- Will there be any opportunities to travel during the internship?
- Do you have a mentorship program?
- What type of evaluation system do you use for interns? What criteria are used in this evaluation process?
- Please explain the rest of the recruitment process. When and how will I be notified of the company's decision?

Arrive for the interview 10 to 15 minutes early and check in with the secretary or manager responsible for setting up the logistics of the interview. During the interview, remember to introduce yourself and extend your hand for the introductory handshake. Speak directly to the interviewer, not the floor. Avoid nervous gestures and the ever-annoying "like" and "um" phrases. If you can't prove that you can focus during the interview, you won't get the job. Speak clearly and slowly and try to remain as calm as possible. Keep in mind the leadership theme when answering questions. Highlight activities listed on your résumé that epitomize your capacity to lead a group. Use industry jargon. Be sure to request a business card before extending your hand once again before leaving.

Immediately afterward, send a thank-you letter to all people involved with your interview. The letter should be written in business format and directly address issues and topics covered during the interview. The only thing left to do then is hope for the best. If you haven't heard anything in about two weeks, follow up with a phone call.

Hopefully, assuming things have gone well, you will end up with several internship offers. It is important to decline in a gracious and professional manner those opportunities that you decided to pass up. Call your contact at each of these companies and explain your decision. Follow this up with a formal business letter reiterating your appreciation of their support. Never accept an offer and then renege. Recruiting and human resources people work together frequently, so you are risking all opportunities when you conduct yourself unprofessionally. Also, it is important to maintain a strong, positive rapport with all contacts made during the internship application process. You never know whom you will need help from in the future.

Arriving for Work

The first day of a business internship can be quite overwhelming for anyone. Information is being shot at you from all directions, and you are unfamiliar with the people and the office. However, interns can take certain precautions to make the first day more manageable.

Arrive early. Interns should ask their managers what time they are expected to arrive to work and where they should report. Human resources personnel often request that interns check in with the HR office before heading to the manager's office. Although most offices are open from 9 A.M. to 5 P.M., many open earlier and some adjust their hours during the summer months. Interns should definitely allow enough time to arrive to work 15 minutes early on the first day. Remaining punctual throughout your internship is of utmost importance. Arriving late to a business meeting is certain to antagonize your boss and diminish the way you are perceived.

Unless otherwise instructed, an intern should maintain the formality of the interview on the first day. The first impression will have a major impact on how people perceive your abilities and competence. Thereafter, follow your boss's lead regarding clothing. Don't take your fashion cues from the secretary. Remember to dress for the job you want, not the job you have. If you dress like you should be making photocopies, then you will probably become familiar with the office machines quickly. Women should not assume they can wear pants, short skirts, or bright colors unless they observe their superiors doing the same. Men should not take off their jackets outside of their office. Former interns frequently espouse the importance of the watch in the day-to-day ensemble. Do not wear a sports watch to work (unless you are a professional diver). People will notice. An inexpensive plain watch is better than the fun Swatch your aunt gave you for Christmas—no matter how much you love the green and purple band. In all cases, avoid excessive or flashy jewelry.

What to bring? Don't forget the portfolio you used during the interview process. Pack a pad, an extra copy of your résumé and any other application materials, and the name and numbers of all contacts. Bring at least two pens. You should also bring a professional planner. As most companies require new employees, including interns, to fill out tax and employment information forms the first day, bring two forms of identification, including a copy of your birth certificate, social security card, and/or passport. Also, don't forget some extra cash. You never know when you might need it. If you are working for a large company, you will probably have the option of participating in a direct deposit program. If that interests you, bring a personal check so you can enroll immediately. Be forewarned: interns won't see their first paycheck for two to three weeks after they are entered into the payroll system.

Spend time the first day learning what resources are available. The quirks of the phone system including voice mail and transferring should be worked out during your first few hours on the job. E-mail has become increasingly important as a medium for communicating in the business world, and you should understand your company's particular capacity. Ask the support staff to help you locate necessary office supplies.

Thoroughly discuss your projects with your manager. Make sure that you feel completely comfortable with what is expected from you. Inquire about contacts and resources available to help you complete the projects. Review deadlines and the process that management will employ to evaluate your performance. Also, get information about company mentorship programs and upcoming intern and office social events.

Tips for Internship Success

The following are some tips provided by former interns who have successfully secured full-time employment.

- Put in longer hours. Companies usually acknowledge commitment and hard work.
- Stay in close contact with your manager. Write memos and weekly updates of your progress, stop by his or her office for advice and feedback, and carefully read any responses.
- Find a mentor. Many companies have formal mentorship programs in place. If not, find a mentor on your own. A mentor will look out for your best interests.
- Inform your manager, mentor, and others of your accomplishments. Don't assume that good news travels fast. Help it travel faster.
- Network. An internship is a great opportunity to meet many people within the company. Take advantage of that opportunity.
- Sit in on meetings with senior management. Learn from the pros.
- Attend intern and office social events. These are the perfect opportunities to build the relationships that will last long after your internship is over.
- Learn how to give a formal presentation and write a formal proposal. These skills will prove invaluable to you throughout your career in business.
- Take notes. Don't be afraid to whip out a paper and pen when a manager is assigning a project or giving some advice. This is expected and appears professional.
- Collect references before leaving the internship, and keep in touch with the office after leaving. References will always make the job search process easier, but company officials are usually hesitant to provide references after you have left. Additionally, the contacts made during an internship will be critical to future networking and career development.

Pitfalls

Here are a few no-nos to avoid in business internships. Remember, perception is important, and you do not want to be perceived as someone who participates in any of these activities.

- Don't make personal phone calls. You never know who is listening. Assume that someone is checking the bills. By the same token, don't write personal E-mail at the office. Modern technology has not provided sufficient protection from nosy co-workers.
- Don't order spaghetti at a business lunch. Avoid all messy meals at business meetings. Your presentation will be less effective with sauce dripping off your chin.
- Don't gossip. What goes around comes around. Many negative reputations are made through the grapevine. Spare yours.
- Don't be rude to the support staff. In fact, go out of your way to demonstrate your appreciation. You will get much farther with sugar than spice.
- Don't read the newspaper at work, unless it's necessary to your job. Otherwise, read the newspaper on the way to work.
- Don't lie to get a sick day. If you get caught taking a phony sick day, or just taking too much time off from a relatively short stay with the company, it could have serious repercussions in terms of full-time offers.
- Don't drink alcohol at business functions. If you are an intern, there's a good chance you're not of legal drinking age. And even if you are of legal age, companies don't want interns under the influence. Stick with juice or soda.
- Don't discuss personal problems. Nobody needs to know that you are running out of Prozac and your girlfriend cheated on you. Save these issues for your psychiatrist.
- Don't fall for "business casual" dress. As far as you are concerned, business casual means you can pull down your tie. It is always better to be overdressed than underdressed.
- Don't discuss salaries. Discussion of compensation is not appropriate at the office.

What's *Bondmath*?

Interested in a career in investment banking? Before you pursue it, you might want to get a flavor for its culture and jargon. Check out some of the following books in order to get oriented to the Wall Street world. One investment banking intern says the Fabozzi books were critical reading in preparing for his internship.

Barbarians at the Gate, by Bryan Burrough

Bear Trap, by Paul Gibson

Liar's Poker, by Michael Lewis

Money of the Mind, by James Grant

Rainmaker, by Anthony Bianco

Random Walk Down Wall Street: Popular Delusions and the Madness of Crowds, by Burton Malkiel

The Handbook of Fixed Income Securities, by Frank Fabozzi

The Handbook of Mortgaged Backed Securities, by Frank Fabozzi

The Handbook of the U.S. Treasury and Government Agency Security, by Frank Fabozzi

Aigner Associates

556 Trapelo Road
Belmont, MA 02178
Phone: (617) 484-5151
Fax: (617) 484-7142

Position: Staff Assistant

Department: N/A

No. of Positions Offered Annually: 2

Description: Staff assistant writes press
releases and recaps, develops media lists
and cuts clips.

Qualifications: Communications, business
or marketing majors preferred.

Salary: Unpaid

Position Dates: Rolling

Position Location: Belmont, MA

Average No. of Applicants Annually:
10-20

Potential for Job Placement: Yes

Application Process: Fax or send résumé
and cover letter.

Deadline: Rolling

Contact: Davyn McGuire

American Association of Advertising Agencies

405 Lexington Avenue, 18th Floor
New York, NY 10171-1801
Phone: (800) 676-9333
Fax: (212) 573-8968

Position: Intern

Department: Diversity Programs

No. of Positions Offered Annually: 60-
75

Description: During the 10-week period of
the MultiCultural Advertising Intern
Program, interns work in major advertising
agencies across the country on such
accounts as American Express, General
Foods, McDonald's and Amtrak. Interns
placed in Boston, Chicago, Detroit and New
York are required to attend seminars after
work once a week and must give a brief final
presentation at the graduation ceremony.
Sixty percent of housing and transportation
costs are coverd.

Qualifications: Applicant must be African
American, Hispanic American, Asian
American or Native American citizen or
permanent resident of the United States who
has completed junior or senior year of
college or is attending graduate school.
Applicant must have a GPA of at least 3.0.

Salary: $300/week

Position Dates: Summer

Position Location: Nationwide

Average No. of Applicants Annually:
200

Potential for Job Placement: Yes

Application Process: Send application,
résumé, two essays, two recommendations,
recent transcript and creative samples.

Deadline: January 5

Contact: Rhonda Jackman

American Management Association

1601 Broadway
New York, NY 10019
Phone: (212) 903-8021
Fax: (212) 903-8163

Position: Human Resources Intern

Department: Human Resources

No. of Positions Offered Annually: 3

Description: Intern projects vary. Possible projects include researching new laws, creating behavioral interview questions, temporary employment analysis and absenteeism analysis.

Qualifications: Applicant should possess excellent communication, computer (Microsoft Office) , research, writing, customer service and organization skills.

Salary: $4.75/hour

Position Dates: Fall, Spring and Summer

Position Location: New York, NY

Average No. of Applicants Annually: N/A

Potential for Job Placement: N/A

Application Process: Send résumé, cover letter and one professional and one academic letter of recommendation. Potential candidates will be interviewed.

Deadline: Rolling

Contact: Jennifer Spillane

American Management Association

1601 Broadway
New York, NY 10019
Phone: (212) 903-8021
Fax: (212) 903-8163

Position: Market Research Intern

Department: N/A

No. of Positions Offered Annually: 3

Description: Duties include: data analysis, competitve analysis, research and survey design.

Qualifications: Applicant should possess excellent communication, organization, research, statistics, computer (SAS, SPSS a plus) , writing and customer service skills. Relevant course work is helpful but not necessary.

Salary: $4.75/hour

Position Dates: Fall, Spring and Summer

Position Location: New York, NY

Average No. of Applicants Annually: N/A

Potential for Job Placement: N/A

Application Process: Send résumé, cover letter and one professional and one academic letter of recommendation. Potential candidates will be interviewed.

Deadline: Rolling

Contact: Jennifer Spillane

American Management Association

1601 Broadway
New York, NY 10019
Phone: (212) 903-8021
Fax: (212) 903-8163

Position: Publishing Intern

Department: N/A

No. of Positions Offered Annually: 5-6

Description: Duties include editing, proofreading, layout design, writing and researching.

Qualifications: Applicant should possess excellent writing, communication and computer skills.

Salary: $4.75/hour

Position Dates: Fall, Spring and Summer

Position Location: New York, NY

Average No. of Applicants Annually: N/A

Potential for Job Placement: N/A

Application Process: Send résumé, cover letter, and one professional and one academic letter of recommendation. Potential candidates will be interviewed.

Deadline: Rolling

Contact: Jennifer Spillane

American Management Association

1601 Broadway
New York, NY 10019
Phone: (212) 903-8021
Fax: (212) 903-8163

Position: Seminar Marketing Intern

Department: N/A

No. of Positions Offered Annually: 3-5

Description: Duties include: competitive analysis, pricing analysis, customer evaluations and feedback and researching topics for marketing seminars.

Qualifications: Applicant should possess good research, writing, communication and analytical skills. Relevant course work helpful but not necessary.

Salary: $4.75/hour

Position Dates: Fall, Spring and Summer

Position Location: New York, NY

Average No. of Applicants Annually: N/A

Potential for Job Placement: N/A

Application Process: Send résumé, cover letter and one academic and one professional letter of recommendation. Potential candidates will be interviewed.

Deadline: Rolling

Contact: Jennifer Spillane

American Society of International Law

2223 Massachusetts Avenue NW
Washington, DC 20008-2864
Phone: (202) 939-6000
Fax: (202) 797-7133

Position: Intern

Department: N/A

No. of Positions Offered Annually: 18

Description: Internship positions available in the following areas: ASIL publications (*American Journal of International Law, International Legal Materials, Proceedings of the Annual Meeting* and *Basic Documents of International Law*), accounting, meetings, internship guide and membership and outreach.

Qualifications: Applicant must possess good researching and typing skills and must be familiar with WordPerfect.

Salary: Unpaid

Position Dates: Fall, Spring and Summer

Position Location: Washington, DC

Average No. of Applicants Annually: 100

Potential for Job Placement: Yes

Application Process: Send résumé, cover letter, writing sample and list of references including telephone numbers.

Deadline: Rolling

Contact: Charles Gnaediger

Barney's New York

575 Fifth Avenue, 11th Floor
New York, NY 10017
Phone: (212) 886-1170
Fax: (212) 450-8489

Position: Advertising Intern

Department: N/A

No. of Positions Offered Annually: 3-6

Description: Intern assists merchandise coordinator, handles phone work, assists business manager in administrative support tasks, assists in researching sources for fitters, groomers and models, assists in timely gathering of merchandise information for ads, assists in contacting media services for media kits and rates and organizes materials for broadcast and print media. Internship is Unpaid and for course credit only.

Qualifications: Open to all majors, but preference given to majors in advertising, marketing, communications and advertising design. Applicants must possess outstanding organization, verbal and written communication skills.

Salary: Unpaid

Position Dates: Fall, Spring and Summer

Position Location: New York, NY

Average No. of Applicants Annually: 100

Potential for Job Placement: Yes

Application Process: Two interviews.

Deadline: Rolling

Contact: Internship Coordinator

Barney's New York

575 Fifth Avenue, 11th Floor
New York, NY 10017
Phone: (212) 886-1170
Fax: (212) 450-8489

Position: Buyer's Intern

Department: N/A

No. of Positions Offered Annually: 6

Description: Intern performs administrative support duties, tracks sales and prepares reports, compiles product and vendor information, communicates with the Distribution Center about status of new receipts and their distribution, communicates with vendors on a regular basis, tracks and coordinates all special orders and assists buyer and other buyer staff in planning and coordinating market visits.

Qualifications: Open to all majors, but preference given to the following areas: fashion buying and merchandising, fashion design, accessories design, cosmetics, fragrances, international trade, jewelry design, menswear, merchandise management/product development, production management, retail management, textile development and marketing, textile/surface design and visual merchandising. Applicant must have previous experience with Excel or other spreadsheet programs.

Salary: Unpaid

Position Dates: Fall, Spring and Summer

Position Location: New York, NY

Average No. of Applicants Annually: 200

Potential for Job Placement: Yes

Application Process: Two interviews.

Deadline: Rolling

Contact: Internship Coordinator

Barney's New York

575 Fifth Avenue, 11th Floor
New York, NY 10017
Phone: (212) 886-1170
Fax: (212) 450-8489

Position: Corporate Human Resources Intern

Department: N/A

No. of Positions Offered Annually: 3

Description: Intern benchmarks, analyzes and organizes reports on compensation analyses, assists in preparation and organization of various training projects, assists in publication and distribution of *Barney's New York Newsletter,* benchmarks and researches ideas for a management training program, assists senior vice president on various HR-related projects and performs administrative support tasks. Internship is Unpaid and is for college credit only.

Qualifications: Open to all majors but preference given to human resources majors or majors that support an HR specialization; PC experience with word processing and spreadsheet skill is required. Excellent written and oral communication skills a must.

Salary: Unpaid

Position Dates: Fall, Spring and Summer

Position Location: New York, NY

Average No. of Applicants Annually: 100

Potential for Job Placement: Yes

Application Process: Two interviews.

Deadline: Rolling

Contact: Internship Coordinator

Barney's New York

575 Fifth Avenue, 11th Floor
New York, NY 10017
Phone: (212) 886-1170
Fax: (212) 450-8489

Position: Graphic Design Intern

Department: N/A

No. of Positions Offered Annually: 3

Description: Intern assists in creation, preparation and publication of the small space advertising campaign, becomes involved in design projects as assigned, contacts illustrators, photographers and other artists, researches sources of materials, assists with paste up, inputs selected copy using design software packages, helps maintain archives, assists designer in planning photo shoots and handles phone work and administrative support tasks. Internship is Unpaid and is only for course credit.

Qualifications: Open to all majors, but preference given to majors in advertising, marketing, communications, advertising design and computer graphics. Knowledge of QuarkXpress, Illustrator, and PhotoShop is necessary.

Salary: Unpaid

Position Dates: Fall, Spring and Summer

Position Location: New York, NY

Average No. of Applicants Annually: 50

Potential for Job Placement: Yes

Application Process: Two interviews.

Deadline: Rolling

Contact: Internship Coordinator

Barney's New York

575 Fifth Avenue, 11th Floor
New York, NY 10017
Phone: (212) 886-1170
Fax: (212) 450-8489

Position: Human Resources Intern

Department: Human Resources

No. of Positions Offered Annually: 6

Description: Intern manages and coordinates applicant pool, experiences the interview process from beginning to end, organizes and tracks all new hires and current employees on the HR system, manages the publication, editing and distribution of the *Barney's New York Newsletter,* assists the HR Manager on various training programs, interacts with operations manager of store, prepares reports on various projects and performs administrative support tasks. Internship is Unpaid and is only for college credit.

Qualifications: Open to all majors but preference given to human resources majors or majors that support an HR specialization; PC experience with word processing skill is required and Windows experience is an asset. Excellent written and oral communication skills are a must.

Salary: Unpaid

Position Dates: Fall, Spring and Summer

Position Location: New York, NY

Average No. of Applicants Annually: 100

Potential for Job Placement: Yes

Application Process: Two interviews.

Deadline: Rolling

Contact: Internship Coordinator

Barney's New York

575 Fifth Avenue, 11th Floor
New York, NY 10017
Phone: (212) 886-1170
Fax: (212) 450-8489

Position: Public Relations Intern

Department: N/A

No. of Positions Offered Annually: 3-6

Description: Intern is involved in fact
checking credit information, assisting in in-
store photography, assisting with fashion
presentations, and assisting in special
events preparation and set-up. Intern will
also assist in administrative tasks and
handle phone work. Internship is for course
credit only.

Qualifications: Open to all majors, but
must have an interest in public relations and
special events planning. Fluency in Japanese
or French is a plus but not required.
Applicant should have polished verbal and
written communication skills and be
organized and able to work confidently in a
fast-paced, deadline-based environment.

Salary: Unpaid

Position Dates: Fall, Spring and Summer

Position Location: New York, NY

Average No. of Applicants Annually:
150

Potential for Job Placement: Yes

Application Process: Two interviews.

Deadline: Rolling

Contact: Internship Coordinator

Benetton USA

597 Fifth Avenue, 11th Floor
New York, NY 10017
Phone: (212) 593-0290
Fax: (212) 371-1438

Position: Communications Department
Assistant

Department: Various

No. of Positions Offered Annually: 3-6

Description: Communications Department
assistant assists in Advertising, Marketing
and Public Relations departments.
Internship is Unpaid; compensation consists
of two Benetton outfits at the end of the
internship.

Qualifications: Applicant should be
computer literate and have relevant work
experience. Knowledge of Italian helpful but
not necessary.

Salary: Unpaid

Position Dates: Fall, Spring and Summer

Position Location: New York, NY

Average No. of Applicants Annually: N/A

Potential for Job Placement: Varies
upon availability.

Application Process: Send résumé and
cover letter.

Deadline: Rolling

Contact: Internship Coordinator

Bozell Public Relations

75 Rockefeller Plaza
New York, NY 10019
Phone: (212) 445-8100
Fax: (212) 275-3554

Position: Public Relations Intern

Department: N/A

No. of Positions Offered Annually: 4-6

Description: Intern assists account staff with writing press releases, planning special events and marketing partnerships and promotions. Internships are typically three to four months in duration.

Qualifications: English, marketing, public relations or journalism majors preferred.

Salary: $800/month

Position Dates: Fall, Spring and Summer

Position Location: New York, NY

Average No. of Applicants Annually: 200

Potential for Job Placement: Yes

Application Process: Send résumé and cover letter stating dates of availability.

Deadline: Three to four months prior to desired start date.

Contact: Lorra Morrill

Bozell Worldwide Public Relations

302 South 36th Street
Omaha, NE 68152
Phone: (402) 978-4278

Position: Intern

Department: N/A

No. of Positions Offered Annually: 4-6

Description: Twelve-week summer internships available in the following agency departments: Account Services, Media, Research, Direct Response, Creative and Public Relations. Interns will have the opportunity to work in the headquarters of a large, successful, full-service public relations and advertising firm.

Qualifications: Relevant course work or professional experience a must.

Salary: $6.00/hour

Position Dates: Summer

Position Location: Omaha, NE

Average No. of Applicants Annually: 100

Potential for Job Placement: Yes

Application Process: Application to be completed.

Deadline: February 15

Contact: Jan Sammons

C. Paul Luongo Company

441 Stuart Street
Boston, MA 02116
Phone: (617) 266-4210
Fax:

Position: Assistant to the President

Department: N/A

No. of Positions Offered Annually: 3

Description: Duties include: new business research and telephone contact, media research and editing.

Qualifications: Applicant should possess good communication, research and administrative skills.

Salary: Unpaid

Position Dates: Fall, Spring and Summer

Position Location: Boston, MA

Average No. of Applicants Annually: 50

Potential for Job Placement: Yes

Application Process: Send résumé and cover letter. Call a month before the internship is to begin, not before.

Deadline: One month before the internship.

Contact: C. Paul Luongo

Century City Partners

9777 Wilshire Boulevard, Suite 611
Beverly Hills, CA 90212
Fax: (310) 777-0249

Position: Intern

Department: N/A

No. of Positions Offered Annually: 4-6

Description: Responsibilities include managing computer database, conducting research and performing telephone and administrative duties.

Qualifications: General office skills a plus.

Salary: Unpaid

Position Dates: Fall, Spring and Summer

Position Location: Beverly Hills, CA

Average No. of Applicants Annually: 150

Potential for Job Placement: Yes

Application Process: Send or fax résumé and cover letter.

Deadline: Rolling

Contact: Brian Faeh

CIGNA

900 Cottage Grove Road
Wilde Building, A-122
Hartford, CT 06152-1122
Phone: (860) 725-2000

Position: Summer Intern

Department: University Relations

No. of Positions Offered Annually: 300

Description: An opportunity to work with one of the world's leading providers of insurance, health care and financial services. Interns may work in Hartford, CT, Philadelphia, PA or other selected field locations.

Qualifications: Accounting, marketing, actuarial science, computer science, computer engineering, general business management, or human resources majors preferred. Applicant must have a GPA of 3.2 or higher, and an interest in a business leadership career.

Salary: Depends on level of education and experience.

Position Dates: Summer

Position Location: Hartford, CT; Philadelphia, PA; nationwide

Average No. of Applicants Annually: 1,000

Potential for Job Placement: Yes

Application Process: Send résumé and cover letter.

Deadline: Rolling

Contact: Internship Coordinator

College Connections

329 East 82nd Street
New York, NY 10028
Phone: (212) 734-2190
Fax: (212) 517-7284

Position: Public Relations Intern

Department: N/A

No. of Positions Offered Annually: 3-4

Description: Interns will work closely with staff in this small firm. There will be many opportunities to learn about the full range of public relations professions and to gain valuable contacts in the industry. Interns are given the opportunity to write pitch letters and press releases, pitch stories to print and broadcast media, compile and update databases and generate mailings. College credit and/or travel expenses and/or stipend will be provided.

Qualifications: Applicants should be in their junior or senior year of college and possess excellent writing skills. Knowledge of Microsoft Word and electronic communication skills preferred.

Salary: Unpaid

Position Dates: Fall, Spring and Summer

Position Location: New York, NY

Average No. of Applicants Annually: 100

Potential for Job Placement: Possible

Application Process: Send résumé, cover letter and one writing sample.

Deadline: Rolling

Contact: Internship Coordinator (E-mail: halstead@halsteadpr.com)

Crown Capital

540 Pacific Avenue
San Francisco, CA 94133
Phone: (415) 398-6330
Fax: (415) 398-6957

Position: Intern

Department: N/A

No. of Positions Offered Annually: 1-2

Description: Intern assists principals of the company in commercial real estate investment and mortgage banking business activities.

Qualifications: Applicant must be at least a junior in college and have top credentials from a top academic institution.

Salary: $500/month

Position Dates: Fall, Spring and Summer

Position Location: San Francisco, CA

Average No. of Applicants Annually: 50

Potential for Job Placement: Yes

Application Process: Send résumé and cover letter.

Deadline: At least two months prior to desired start date.

Contact: David W. Yancey

Dye Van Mol and Lawrence

209 Seventh Avenue North
Nashville, TN 37219
Phone: (615) 244-1818

Position: Public Relations Intern

Department: N/A

No. of Positions Offered Annually: 2-4

Description: Interns acquire on-the-job experience in public relations and gain exposure to the profession and its responsibilities. Interns complete assignments that include research, news writing, editing, special events, proofreading, media audits and internal meetings.

Qualifications: Applicants must be of junior or senior level in college and must demonstrate a high level of competence in the areas of writing, researching and editing.

Salary: $7/hour

Position Dates: Fall, Spring and Summer

Position Location: Nashville, TN

Average No. of Applicants Annually: 200-400

Potential for Job Placement: Possible

Application Process: Application to be completed. Interns are selected based on application review, interviews, work samples and recommendations.

Deadline: June 15 for Fall; November 1 for Spring; March 15 for Summer.

Contact: Deanna Grubs

Earle Palmer Brown

1650 Market Street, 15th Floor
Philadelphia, PA 19103
Phone: (215) 851-9505

Position: Intern

Department: Various

No. of Positions Offered Annually: 60

Description: Positions available in Account Management, Broadcast Production, Graphic Design, Media, Direct Mail, Traffic, Yellow Pages Account Management, Public Relations, Research, New Business, Human Resources. Interns assist account executives or art directors. Interns are given as much responsibility as they can handle. Internship is Unpaid but interns will be provided with a $10/day transportation stipend.

Qualifications: Computer skills a plus.

Salary: Unpaid

Position Dates: Fall, Spring and Summer

Position Location: Philadelphia, PA

Average No. of Applicants Annually: 250

Potential for Job Placement: Possible

Application Process: Send résumé and cover letter stating position choices.

Deadline: Rolling

Contact: Jim Armstrong

Eisner, Petrou and Associates

925 15th Street NW, Suite 900
Washington, DC 20005
Phone: (202) 682-3100

Position: Public Relations Intern

Department: N/A

No. of Positions Offered Annually: 6-8

Description: Intern for full-service public relations agency will gain experience in media relations, research, special events planning and implementation and other public relations opportunities. Intern will be reimbursed for local transportation costs.

Qualifications: Public relations course work or previous internship experience a plus.

Salary: Unpaid

Position Dates: Fall, Spring and Summer

Position Location: Washington, DC

Average No. of Applicants Annually: N/A

Potential for Job Placement: Possible

Application Process: Send résumé and cover letter. Candidates may be interviewed by phone or in person.

Deadline: Rolling

Contact: Marci Luefschuetz

Elite Model Management, Inc.

345 North Maple Drive, Suite 397
Beverly Hills, CA 90210
Phone: (310) 274-9395
Fax: (310) 278-7520

Position: Intern

Department: N/A

No. of Positions Offered Annually: 1

Description: Internship provides intern with the opportunity to observe the inner workings of the most prestigious modeling agency in the world. Intern assists the New Faces divison in which day to day contact with models and scheduling assignments takes place.

Qualifications: Undergraduates interested in the fashion and entertainment business.

Salary: Unpaid

Position Dates: Summer

Position Location: Beverly Hills, CA

Average No. of Applicants Annually: 250

Potential for Job Placement: Possible

Application Process: Send cover letter and résumé. Candidates will be interviewed by Elite staff.

Deadline: March 31

Contact: Mary Beth Hickey

Elkman Advertising and Public Relations

1510 Monument Road
Bala Cynwyd, PA 19004
Phone: (610) 668-1100
Fax: (610) 668-2586

Position: Advertising Intern

Department: N/A

No. of Positions Offered Annually: 4-5

Description: Duties include: ad copyrighting, research, working with account managers. Interns are included in client meetings and photo shoots.

Qualifications: Applicant must be a junior or senior in college and must have good writing and research skills. Applicant must live or go to school in the tristate area (Pennsylvania, New Jersey or Delaware) .

Salary: Unpaid

Position Dates: Fall, Spring and Summer

Position Location: Bala Cynwyd, PA

Average No. of Applicants Annually: 30

Potential for Job Placement: Yes

Application Process: Send résumé and cover letter.

Deadline: July 1 for Fall; November 1 for Spring; March 1 for Summer.

Contact: Internship Director

Elkman Advertising and Public Relations

1510 Monument Road
Bala Cynwyd, PA 19004
Phone: (610) 668-1100
Fax: (610) 668-2586

Position: Creative Arts/Copyrighting Intern

Department: N/A

No. of Positions Offered Annually: 1-2

Description: Duties include: writing and proofing ad copy and designing brochures, newsletters and ads.

Qualifications: Applicants must be juniors or seniors in college and possess good writing skills. Applicants must live or go to school in the tristate area (Pennsylvania, New Jersey or Delaware).

Salary: Unpaid

Position Dates: Fall, Spring and Summer

Position Location: Bala Cynwyd, PA

Average No. of Applicants Annually: 20-30

Potential for Job Placement: Yes

Application Process: Send résumé and cover letter.

Deadline: July 1 for Fall; November 1 for Spring; and March 1 for Summer.

Contact: Internship Director

Elkman Advertising and Public Relations

1510 Monument Road
Bala Cynwyd, PA 19004
Phone: (610) 668-1100
Fax: (610) 668-2586

Position: Media Buying Intern

Department:

No. of Positions Offered Annually: 4-5

Description: Duties include: competitive analyses, research and media planning.

Qualifications: Applicants must be juniors or seniors in college and possess good writing and research skills. Applicants must live or go to school in the tristate area (Pennsylvania, New Jersey or Delaware).

Salary: Unpaid

Position Dates: Fall, Spring and Summer

Position Location: Bala Cynwyd, PA

Average No. of Applicants Annually: 30-40

Potential for Job Placement: Yes

Application Process: Send résumé and cover letter.

Deadline: July 1 for Fall; November 1 for Spring; March 1 for Summer.

Contact: Internship Director

Elkman Advertising and Public Relations

1510 Monument Road
Bala Cynwyd, PA 19004
Phone: (610) 668-1100
Fax: (610) 668-2586

Position: Public Relations Intern

Department: N/A

No. of Positions Offered Annually: 4-5

Description: Duties include: events coordination, writing of publicity materials and research.

Qualifications: Applicants must be juniors or seniors, articulate, eager to learn and have good writing and research skills. Applicant must live or go to school in the tristate area (Pennsylvania, New Jersey or Delaware).

Salary: Unpaid

Position Dates: Fall, Spring and Summer

Position Location: Bala Cynwyd, PA

Average No. of Applicants Annually: 30

Potential for Job Placement: Yes

Application Process: Send résumé and cover letter.

Deadline: July 1 for Fall; November 1 for Spring; March 1 for Summer.

Contact: Internship Director

Federal Reserve Bank of New York

59 Maiden Lane, 39th Floor
New York, NY 10038-4502
Phone: (212) 720-6922

Position: Summer Intern

Department: Human Resources

No. of Positions Offered Annually: 12-15

Description: The summer internship program combines project-oriented work assignments with training and development activities designed to provide an overview to the Federal Reserve Bank of New York and to enhance critical business skills through presentations, analysis, writing and computer projects.

Qualifications: Undergraduate applicants should have completed their junior year of college; master's level applicants should have completed their first year of graduate program. All applicants must have a strong interest in banking, economics or finance and a strong academic record and must be available for in-bank interviews in early spring.

Salary: Stipend to be decided during interview.

Position Dates: Summer

Position Location: New York, NY

Average No. of Applicants Annually: 1,000

Potential for Job Placement: N/A

Application Process: Send résumé suitable for scanning, cover letter and transcript.

Deadline: January 31

Contact: Summer Internship Coordinator

Fenton Communications

1606 20th Street NW, 2nd Floor
Washington, DC 20036
Phone: (202) 745-0707
Fax: (202) 332-1915

Position: Publicity Intern

Department: N/A

No. of Positions Offered Annually: 9-12

Description: Interns work with one account team and participate in all facets of a media campaign, including: organizing logistics involved in press conferences and media briefings; researching and compiling media lists; tracking press coverage through Lexis-Nexis and CompuServe; writing final reports on media coverage for clients; and performing various administrative tasks.

Qualifications: Applicant should have an interest in public relations focusing on environmental and political issues and the ability to handle several tasks simultaneously. Applicant should be proficient in WordPerfect for Windows.

Salary: $100/week

Position Dates: Fall, Spring and Summer

Position Location: Washington, DC

Average No. of Applicants Annually: 200

Potential for Job Placement: Yes

Application Process: Send résumé and cover letter stating dates of availability.

Deadline: At least two months prior to desired start date.

Contact: Valerie Holford

Fortune Public Relations

2319 California Street
Berkeley, CA 94703
Phone: (510) 548-1097
Fax: (510) 841-7006

Position: Media Relations Intern

Department: N/A

No. of Positions Offered Annually: 6

Description: Full range of media relations responsibilites related to promoting food, restaurant and hospitality clients.

Qualifications: Applicant should have an interest in food and travel and possess excellent writing and computer skills.

Salary: Unpaid

Position Dates: Fall, Spring and Summer

Position Location: Berkeley, CA

Average No. of Applicants Annually: 20

Potential for Job Placement: Minimal

Application Process: Call (510) 548-1097 or E-mail Fortunepr@aol.com for application.

Deadline: Rolling

Contact: Tom Walton

Franklin Advertising Associates, Inc.

51 Winchester Street
Newton, MA 02161
Phone: (617) 244-8368
Fax: (617) 244-5897

Position: Account Services Intern

Department: Various

No. of Positions Offered Annually: 3

Description: Intern assists the Account Service Department, office nanager, president and Art Department. Duties include: research, filing, sales, customer service; and administrative work.

Qualifications: Computer knowledge helpful.

Salary: Unpaid

Position Dates: Fall, Spring and Summer

Position Location: Newton, MA

Average No. of Applicants Annually: 100

Potential for Job Placement: Yes

Application Process: Send résumé and cover letter.

Deadline: Rolling

Contact: Christine Peznola

Franklin Advertising Associates, Inc.

51 Winchester Street
Newton, MA 02161
Phone: (617) 244-8368
Fax: (617) 244-5897

Position: Graphic Design Assistant

Department: Art Services

No. of Positions Offered Annually: 3

Description: Intern assists the Art Services Department in the creation and design of ads.

Qualifications: Applicant must be proficient in QuarkXpress, Adobe Illustrator, and Photoshop.

Salary: Unpaid

Position Dates: Fall, Spring and Summer

Position Location: Newton, MA

Average No. of Applicants Annually: 100

Potential for Job Placement: Possible

Application Process: Send résumé and cover letter.

Deadline: Two months befor desired start dage.

Contact: Christine Peznola

General Mills

P.O. Box 113
Minneapolis, MN 55440
Phone: (612) 540-7504
Fax: (612) 540-2445

Position: Intern

Department: Various

No. of Positions Offered Annually: 100

Description: Various positions available in Finance, Accounting, Information Systems, Marketing, Marketing Research, Promotions, Human Resources, Operations, Distribution, Research and Development, Quality Control and Sales departments.

Qualifications: Applicant must have a GPA of at least 3.0.

Salary: Varies by degree and year in school.

Position Dates: Summer

Position Location: Minneapolis, MN

Average No. of Applicants Annually: 2,000

Potential for Job Placement: Yes

Application Process: Send résumé, cover letter, and copy of current transcript.

Deadline: February 1

Contact: Bill Dittmore

Hill, Holiday

200 Clarendon Street
Boston, MA 02116
Phone: (617) 572-3505
Fax: (617) 859-4279

Position: Intern

Department: Various

No. of Positions Offered Annually: 100

Description: Interns work in just about every department. Depending on the responsibilities of the department, intern duties could include: compiling and analyzing client competition, conducting industry analysis, ad layout and storyboard creation, reporting project status, updating media files and discussing new business prospects. Interns will attend weekly seminars conducted by department heads and work on a project from conception to presentation. Interns must receive college credit.

Qualifications: Applicants must be college sophomores, juniors, seniors or graduate students.

Salary: Unpaid

Position Dates: Fall, Spring and Summer

Position Location: Boston, MA

Average No. of Applicants Annually: 400

Potential for Job Placement: Yes

Application Process: Send résumé, cover letter, completed application and writing sample.

Deadline: Rolling

Contact: Jackie Lyman

Inroads, Inc.

10 South Broadway, Suite 700
St. Louis, MO 63102
Phone: (314) 241-7330

Position: Intern

Department: N/A

No. of Positions Offered Annually:
2,200+

Description: Inroads is a referal service for
minorities interested in business,
engineering, applied sciences, and
computers. Inroads prepares the interns for
corporate and community leadership.
Inroads places interns in 49 cities across the
U.S. and in Mexico City. The program begins
June 1 of each year and the interns are part of
Inroads for a full calendar year.

Qualifications: Must have a minimum of a
3.0 GPA, 900+ SAT, and must have an interest
in business or industry.

Salary: Varies based on position.

Position Dates: Summer and Winter break

Position Location: Nationwide and
Mexico City

Average No. of Applicants Annually:
4,000+

Potential for Job Placement: 50%
receive full-time job offers

Application Process: Write for
application.

Deadline: December 31

Contact: Intern Coordinator

Insurance Services Office

7 World Trade Center
New York, NY 10048
Phone: (212) 898-6084
Fax: (212) 898-6071

Position: Actuarial Intern

Department: Human Resources

No. of Positions Offered Annually: 12

Description: Internship provides math
majors with an exciting opportunity to
explore the actuarial profession. Interns will
be given hands-on projects that can be
completed during their summer experience.

Qualifications: Applicant must have a
minimum of at least 24 credits in math, with
some statistics preferred, a minimum GPA of
3.0 and a minimun SAT score of 1300. Math,
applied math, operations research and
statistics majors preferred.

Salary: $450-$550/week

Position Dates: Summer

Position Location: New York, NY

Average No. of Applicants Annually:
250

Potential for Job Placement: Yes

Application Process: Send résumé and
cover letter.

Deadline: February 15

Contact: Nancie Merritt

International Management Group

1 Erieview Plaza, Suite 1300
Cleveland, OH 44114
Phone: (216) 522-1200
Fax: (216) 522-1145

Position: Intern

Department: Various

No. of Positions Offered Annually: 80

Description: Possible areas of placement include: Motorsports, Accounting, Human Resources, Racquet Sports, Investment Advisors, Tax, Golf or Promotions. Each intern can expect to be exposed to the day-to-day operations of each specific department. The program runs for approximately eight weeks. The majority of the intern positions are located in Cleveland, the world headquarters, and in the three New York offices. All intern positions are nonpaying and the intern must therefore receive college credit.

Qualifications: N/A

Salary: Unpaid

Position Dates: Summer

Position Location: Cleveland, OH; New York, NY

Average No. of Applicants Annually: 600

Potential for Job Placement:

Application Process: Send résumé and cover letter.

Deadline: February 15

Contact: Internship Committee

Ketchum Public Relations

292 Madison Avenue
New York, NY 10017
Phone: (212) 448-4200
Fax: (212) 448-4488

Position: Intern

Department: N/A

No. of Positions Offered Annually: 5

Description: Interns are assigned to accounts where they can apply their existing skills and learn new ones. Professional development will come from on-the-job training, management training and informal evaluations. Additional internship opportunities available in Ketchum offices nationwide: Atlanta, Chicago, Dallas, Los Angeles, Miami, Pittsburgh, San Francisco and Washington, D.C.

Qualifications: Applicant should have a strong interest in public relations, be a junior in college, have a GPA of at least 3.0, be a strong writer and be available to work for eight to ten weeks.

Salary: Varies, but internship is paid.

Position Dates: Summer

Position Location: New York, NY and nationwide

Average No. of Applicants Annually: 500

Potential for Job Placement: N/A

Application Process: Send résumé, cover letter and writing samples.

Deadline: March 31

Contact: Rita Masini

Liggett-Stashower Public Relations

1228 Euclid Avenue
Cleveland, OH 44115
Phone: (216) 348-8520
Fax: (216) 736-8118

Position: Public Relations Intern

Department: N/A

No. of Positions Offered Annually: 2

Description: Intern will assist in writing, media relations, special events and planning for one of the agency's largest accounts. Intern will have the opportunity to work with senior professionals, reinforce their writing and media relations skills and observe the day-to-day functions of a full-service public relations firm.

Qualifications: Public relations students entering their senior year preferred but mature juniors will be considered. Applicant must have knowledge of Macintosh and other computer skills and a portfolio which highlights excellent writing and verbal skills.

Salary: $5.00/hour

Position Dates: Summer

Position Location: Cleveland, OH

Average No. of Applicants Annually: 25

Potential for Job Placement: Possible

Application Process: Send résumé and cover letter which includes E-mail address.

Deadline: February

Contact: Marilyn Casey (E-mail: mcasey@liggett.com)

Lobsenz-Stevens, Inc.

460 Park Avenue South
New York, NY 10016
Phone: (212) 684-6300
Fax: (212) 696-4638

Position: Consumer Division Intern

Department: Consumer Division

No. of Positions Offered Annually: 3

Description: Interns in the Consumer Division practice basic public relations skills with entry-level writing and telephone follow-up emphasized. Internship may include some client contact. Internships are for credit only.

Qualifications: Computer skills a plus.

Salary: Unpaid

Position Dates: Fall, Spring and Summer

Position Location: New York, NY

Average No. of Applicants Annually: N/A

Potential for Job Placement: Possible

Application Process: Send résumé and cover letter.

Deadline: Rolling

Contact: Kate McLaughlin

Lobsenz-Stevens, Inc.

460 Park Avenue South
New York, NY 10016
Phone: (212) 684-6300
Fax: (212) 696-4638

Position: Health Care Division Intern

Department: N/A

No. of Positions Offered Annually: 9

Description: Duties include: research, media list development, entry-level writing, clerical assistance, client event assistance, participation in agencywide brainstorm sessions and some media follow-up. All travel expenses are reimbursed.

Qualifications: Applicant should be a flexible team player who is able to reprioritize tasks and projects up to several times a day if necessary.

Salary: $1.50/hour

Position Dates: Fall, Spring and Summer

Position Location: New York, NY

Average No. of Applicants Annually: 25-50

Potential for Job Placement: Possible

Application Process: Send résumé and cover letter.

Deadline: Rolling

Contact: Betsey Aitkenhead

New York State Bar Association

1 Elk Street
Albany, NY 12207
Phone: (518) 463-3200
Fax: (518) 463-4276

Position: Media Services Intern

Department: Department of Media Services and Public Affairs

No. of Positions Offered Annually: 1

Description: Media Services intern will have the opportunity to work with a multidisciplinary communications team that functions much like a single-client public relations agency. Intern will gain exposure to the different techniques used in writing news releases, news articles, brochures and other print materials.

Qualifications: Applicant should be a second semester or graduating senior. Students majoring in communications, public relations or journalism preferred.

Salary: $7.00/hour

Position Dates: Summer

Position Location: Albany, NY

Average No. of Applicants Annually: 20

Potential for Job Placement: No

Application Process: Send résumé and writing samples. Applicant will then be scheduled to take a two-hour writing test administered only in Albany.

Deadline: April 1

Contact: Bradley G. Carr (E-mail: bcarr@nysba.org)

Nike, Inc.

1 Bowerman Drive
Beaverton, OR 97005
Phone: (800) 890-6453

Position: Intern

Department: Various

No. of Positions Offered Annually: 145

Description: Internships available in the following divisions: Sports Marketing, Information Technology, Finance/Accounting, Apparel, Research, Design & Development, Retail, Customer Service, Sales, Production, Human Resources, Legal, Marketing, Corporate Communication and Equipment. Duration of all positions are ten weeks during the summer. Assistance in locating housing provided. Ninety percent of positions in Beaverton, remainder located across the United States. Applicants can find more information at Nike's World Wide Web address: http://www.nike.com.

Qualifications: Open to college juniors, seniors and graduate students.

Salary: $9.45-$16.80/hr

Position Dates: Summer

Position Location: Beaverton, OR; Nationwide

Average No. of Applicants Annually: 1,000

Potential for Job Placement: Yes

Application Process: Application to be completed.

Deadline: Rolling

Contact: Internship Coordinator

Ocean City Advertising Agency

108 West 75th Street, P.O. Box 1759
Ocean City, MD 21842
Phone: (410) 524-5351
Fax: (410) 524-5351

Position: Intern

Department: Various

No. of Positions Offered Annually: 20

Description: Internship positions available in the following departments: Accounting, Advertising, Advertising Media Services, Communications, Computer Science, Editorial Writing and Reporting, Graphic Design and Production, Illustration, Leisure Studies, Marketing, Marketing Research, Personnel Management, Photography, Promotion Management, Public Relations, Sales Promortion and Sports Marketing.

Qualifications: N/A

Salary: Unpaid

Position Dates: Fall, Spring and Summer

Position Location: Ocean City, MD

Average No. of Applicants Annually: N/A

Potential for Job Placement: Yes

Application Process: Call or write for application.

Deadline: Rolling

Contact: Paul D. Jankovic

Oklahoma City 89ers

P.O. Box 75089
Oklahoma City, OK 73147
Phone: (405) 946-8989
Fax: (405) 942-4198

Position: Sales and Marketing Intern

Department: N/A

No. of Positions Offered Annually: 4

Description: Every aspect of professional sport is explored: corporate sales, season tickets, skybox and advertising sales, marketing and promotion of special events. Interns will earn commissions on their sales and their living arrangements will be provided.

Qualifications: Applicants must have a college degree in public relations, communications, marketing or a related field. Previous experience in sales or sport marketplace recommended but not required. Computer experience recommended.

Salary: $600 (stipend)

Position Dates: January to September

Position Location: Oklahoma City, OK

Average No. of Applicants Annually: 75-150

Potential for Job Placement: Yes

Application Process: Send résumé and cover letter with references.

Deadline: November 15

Contact: Nancy Mullins Hixson

Ore-Ida Foods

P.O. Box 10
Boise, ID 83707
Phone: (208) 383-6330
Fax: (208) 383-6570

Position: Marketing Intern

Department: Employment Department

No. of Positions Offered Annually: 3

Description: Intern assists in the implementation and review of the brand's marketing programs, therein learning the fundamental concept of Ore-Ida's marketing philosophy, assists in preparation of annual business review and marketing plan, coordination of marketing activities with those of other company departments and outside support groups, prepares periodic reports relating to each area of responsibility and coordinates with other Heinz affiliates in the development and execution of joint advertising, promotion and trade programs.

Qualifications: Applicant must be a first-year MBA student.

Salary: $3,000/month

Position Dates: Summer

Position Location: Boise, ID

Average No. of Applicants Annually: 100

Potential for Job Placement: Yes

Application Process: Mail or fax résumé, cover letter and transcripts.

Deadline: December 15

Contact: Karey Bertrand

Performance Research

25 Mill Street
Newport, RI 02840
Phone: (401) 848-0111
Fax: (401) 848-0111

Position: Market Research Position

Department: N/A

No. of Positions Offered Annually: 6-8

Description: Duties include traveling throughout the United States, data collection at sporting events, conducting personal interviews, data entry, report generation and independent projects.

Business travel costs are covered. Internship programs are 12 to 14 weeks in duration.

Qualifications: N/A

Salary: $500 (stipend)

Position Dates: Fall, Spring and Summer

Position Location: Newport, RI

Average No. of Applicants Annually: 500

Potential for Job Placement: Yes

Application Process: Send résumé, cover letter and writing sample.

Deadline: One month prior to start date.

Contact: Douglas E. Snow

Ruder Finn

301 East 56th Street
New York, NY 10022
Phone: (212) 593-6332
Fax: (212) 715-1659

Position: Intern

Department: N/A

No. of Positions Offered Annually: 40-45

Description: Training position for Public Relations. Interns will attend seminars, classes and writing workshops while working full time with account groups.

Qualifications: Applicants must possess good writing skills and a bachelor's degree.

Salary: Prorated based on $15,000/year.

Position Dates: Fall, Spring and Summer

Position Location: New York, NY

Average No. of Applicants Annually: 600-800

Potential for Job Placement: Yes

Application Process: Send completed application, résumé, transcript, writing assignments. Candidates will have a case study to review prior to interview.

Deadline: June 1 for Fall; November 1 for Spring; April 1 for Summer.

Contact: Deidra Degn

SDV/ACCI

21144 Mission Boulevard
Hayward, CA 94541
Phone: (510) 530-4280
Fax: (510) 886-3971

Position: Business Analyst

Department: N/A

No. of Positions Offered Annually: 2

Description: Intern will choose between several continuous research projects in the following areas: competitive benchmarking, market research, finance and organizational structure and culture.

Qualifications: Applicant must have just finished or be currently studying for an MBA at one of the top ten business schools.

Salary: Based on previous experience and qualifications.

Position Dates: Fall, Spring and Summer

Position Location: Hayward, CA

Average No. of Applicants Annually: N/A

Potential for Job Placement: Yes

Application Process: Mail or fax résumé and cover letter.

Deadline: Rolling

Contact: Tonia L. Metz

SDV/ACCI

21144 Mission Boulevard
Hayward, CA 94541
Phone: (510) 538-4280
Fax: (510) 886-3971

Position: Information Analyst

Department: N/A

No. of Positions Offered Annually: 4

Description: Information analyst collects, processes and analyzes all information relevant to the business and reports findings to management, develops new information sources, tracks new developments in SDV/ACCI's product markets and provides management with ideas and suggestions for improving service based on the anlayzed information.

Qualifications: Applicant must be MBA or senior B.A. in business, economics, computer science or engineering. Applicant must be Internet savvy and able to work independently.

Salary: Based on qualifications.

Position Dates: Fall, Spring and Summer

Position Location: Hayward, CA

Average No. of Applicants Annually: N/A

Potential for Job Placement: Yes

Application Process: Fax or mail résumé and cover letter.

Deadline: Rolling

Contact: Tonia L. Metz

SDV/ACCI

21144 Mission Boulevard
Hayward, CA 94541
Phone: (800) HOT-HIRE
Fax: (510) 886-4951

Position: Information Systems Assistant

Department: Information Systems

No. of Positions Offered Annually: 2

Description: Information systems assistant assists in the maintenance and development of company's information systems and Web site.

Qualifications: N/A

Salary: Based on qualifications and experience.

Position Dates: Fall, Spring and Summer

Position Location: Hayward, CA

Average No. of Applicants Annually: N/A

Potential for Job Placement: Yes

Application Process: Fax, mail or E-mail résumé and cover letter.

Deadline: Rolling

Contact: Eric Ghere (E-mail: SDVACCI@aol.com)

SDV/ACCI

21144 Mission Boulevard
Hayward, CA 94541
Phone: (510) 538-4280
Fax: (510) 886-3971

Position: Marketing Assistant

Department: N/A

No. of Positions Offered Annually: 3

Description: Intern supports marketing staff, facilitates communication between representatives and maps sales targets in different market segments and provides sales representatives with detailed information on these targets.

Qualifications: Applicant must be an M.B.A. or a senior B.A. student in business or economics with proven interest in marketing.

Salary: Based on qualifications and experience.

Position Dates: Fall, Spring and Summer

Position Location: Hayward, CA

Average No. of Applicants Annually: 9

Potential for Job Placement: Yes

Application Process: Fax or mail résumé and cover letter.

Deadline: Rolling

Contact: Tonia L. Metz

SDV/ACCI

21144 Mission Boulevard
Hayward, CA 94541
Phone: (510) 538-4280
Fax: (510) 886-4931

Position: Recruiting Assistant

Department: N/A

No. of Positions Offered Annually: 2

Description: Recruiting assistant assists recruiting staff in filling open positions for clients and will be familiarized with all the different aspects of the recruiting process.

Qualifications: N/A

Salary: Based on qualifications and experience.

Position Dates: Fall, Spring and Summer

Position Location: Hayward, CA

Average No. of Applicants Annually: 8

Potential for Job Placement: Yes

Application Process: Fax, mail or E-mail résumé and cover letter.

Deadline: Rolling

Contact: Melanie Babasa (E-mail: SDVACCI@aol.com)

Skadden, Arps, Slate, Meagher and Flom, LLP

919 Third Avenue
New York, NY 10022
Phone: (212) 735-3090
Fax: (212) 735-3315

Position: Intern

Department: Legal Assistant Department

No. of Positions Offered Annually: 9

Description: Intern works in the Legal Assistant Department in both corporate transactions and litigation.

Qualifications: Applicant must be at least a junior in college, and must have a strong GPA.

Salary: $10.00/hr

Position Dates: Fall, Winter and Spring

Position Location: New York, NY

Average No. of Applicants Annually: 300

Potential for Job Placement: Yes

Application Process: Send résumé and cover letter.

Deadline: August 1 for Fall; October 1 for Winter; December 1 for Spring.

Contact: Corporate Legal Assistant Manager

Washington Center

1101 14th Street NW, Suite 500
Washington, DC 20005-5622
Phone: (202) 336-7600
Fax: (202) 289-0533

Position: Intern

Department: N/A

No. of Positions Offered Annually: 750

Description: The Washington Center is a referral service that places students in internships in Washington, D.C. All internships are full-time positions with entry-level work. No more than 20 percent of the time may be spent on clerical work. Internships are in all majors and in public, private, and nonprofit organizations. College credit may be available.

Qualifications: Must have a minimum GPA of 2.5, well-written essays, good recommendations.

Salary: Some internships have stipends.

Position Dates: Fall, Spring and Summer

Position Location: Washington, D.C.

Average No. of Applicants Annually: 1,200+

Potential for Job Placement: Some

Application Process: Application consists of transcripts, goals and issues essay, internship request statement, letters of recommendation, and résumé.

Deadline: June 1 for Fall; November 15 for Spring; March 15 for Summer

Contact: Student Services

Widmeyer-Baker Group, Inc.

1875 Connecticut Avenue NW, Suite 800
Washington, DC 20009
Phone: (202) 667-0901
Fax: (202) 667-0902

Position: Graphic Design Intern

Department: N/A

No. of Positions Offered Annually: 4-6

Description: Responsibilities may include: layout and design of various print materials, World Wide Web design, vendor liaison, brainstorming and minimal clerical work.

Qualifications: Applicant should be familiar with desktop publishing, including experience with Adobe PageMaker, Photoshop, Illustrator as well as other programs. Design initiative and knowledge of computer technology a must. Experience in prepress preparation a plus, but not required.

Salary: Stipend to be decided during interview.

Position Dates: Fall, Spring and Summer

Position Location: Washington, D.C.

Average No. of Applicants Annually: 100

Potential for Job Placement: Possible

Application Process: Send résumé and cover letter. Candidates will be interviewed in person or by phone. Portfolio review weighs heavily.

Deadline: August 1 for Fall; December 1 for Spring; April 15 for Summer.

Contact: Art Department Internship Coordinator

Widmeyer-Baker Group, Inc.

1875 Connecticut Avenue NW, Suite 800
Washington, DC 20009
Phone: (202) 667-0901
Fax: (202) 667-0902

Position: Media Relations Fellow

Department: Media Relations

No. of Positions Offered Annually: 10

Description: Duties include: contacting the media for press conferences; writing press releases and media advisories; and researching issues of importance to clients.

Qualifications: Applicant must be a college graduate and have strong writing skills. Public relations experience helpful but not necessary.

Salary: $260/week

Position Dates: Fall, Spring and Summer

Position Location: Washington, D.C.

Average No. of Applicants Annually: 400

Potential for Job Placement: Possible

Application Process: Send résumé, cover letter and writing samples.

Deadline: July 15 for Fall; November 15 for Spring; April 15 for Summer.

Contact: Fellowship Coordinator

Technology

by Chris Grosso

Getting a paid summer internship in a science or technology field is probably easier than in most other fields. You probably already have specialized skills that certain employers will covet. Getting a good internship that will give you quality experience is somewhat harder. In any case, if you work at it, you will almost definitely find something. The key is to start early and give yourself as many options as possible, so that you won't find yourself stuck installing software on some law firm's computers.

The first thing you really need to think about before starting an internship search is the path you want to take after graduation. If you are committed to one of the sciences or to engineering, there is a good chance you might be headed for graduate or professional school. In that case, your decision might be a little different from the person who just wants to earn a little money.

What's Out There

Summer internships in science and technology usually fall into five categories: government research labs, academic research, private sector technology companies, start-ups, and other private sector jobs. Each of these areas has different strengths and weaknesses; you should apply to more than one type in order to keep your options open.

Many government research labs have large internship programs. These programs, at national laboratories such as the Fermi National Accelerator Lab, will give you access to some of the world's most cutting-edge physics research and researchers. For work in the biological sciences, there's the

National Institutes of Health, for example. If you're a math or computer science major, you might want to consider a national defense organization such as the National Security Agency or the Central Intelligence Agency. Often these government internships are paid, look good on your résumé, and can be incredibly exciting (who wouldn't want to spend a summer smashing atoms?). The downside is that these exciting internships attract a lot of applicants from across the country, so you will be competing with a lot of top students from top schools, such as M.I.T., Cal Tech, and Carnegie Mellon.

If research is your top priority, consider working in academic research. Universities always hire students to help with research over the summer. Again, these sorts of jobs are usually great résumé builders, especially if your goal is to go on to academics or graduate school. Unfortunately, you will find that most schools like to hire their own students before outsiders, and the pay is often low. Moreover, to get a job in someone's lab, you often have to network with faculty members. Lastly, recommendations play a big role in getting these kinds of jobs, so you will need to have already established a good set of relationships with professors on campus to get the recommendations that get that job.

For the student interested in more applied work, a job with a technology company might be more fitting. Technology companies often hire interns to help out with special projects. For instance, Microsoft has a large internship program that wins great reviews from students. The other great advantage to working for a technology firm is that you can put yourself on the inside track to a full-time job. But to get a job at a technology company, you are going to need skills. Competition to get an internship at a prestigious software firm, for example, will always be keen. Finally, be prepared for the hours. You might have to work longer hours in the private sector than in the public or academic sectors.

Finally, there's always technology work in the mainstream of most corporations. For example, if you know how to run a computer, there is a pretty good chance you can land a paying job supporting computer users at a big corporation. However, private-sector jobs can range from the glamorous to the mundane. You might be able to land a job doing computer-aided design of memory chips—or you might be doing data entry. In any case, although these kinds of jobs are not as glamorous as a job at Los Alamos, for example, they will usually pay well. And, you almost always can get a job in a firm if you know your way around a computer.

You might be surprised at some of the firms that offer technology internships. Would you guess that Coca-Cola, Ford, and Proctor & Gamble all hire engineering and science students for summer jobs? Do not limit your search to obvious companies such as Hewlett-Packard, Lockheed-Martin, and I.B.M.

Still, most work in the private sector might not be as exciting as working at a small software firm or top-notch lab, as one computer science major discovered doing information technology support work at a major investment bank. "I had a great time and really enjoyed it. The novelty and excitement of working on Wall Street took me a long way. But sometimes I felt as if what I was doing was second class, since it was not the revenue center of the company, but in support of the revenue center. Now, when I'm looking for a full-time job, I want to make sure what I am doing is making the company money."

Finding the Jobs

The best place to start a search for a summer internship in science or technology is at your school's career development office. Many schools, especially those with good engineering programs, have special relationships with major high-technology firms and thus have feeder programs to summer jobs and internships.

Of course, the school's office might not have as many opportunities listed as you would like (otherwise you would not be reading this book), so the next step is the Internet. While for many organizations having an address on the Net remains a luxury, in the sciences and technology it is a necessity. Believe it or not, the Net was originally developed for scientists to share their papers and research, and still remains the central clearinghouse for a lot of scientific information. Most government agencies, high-tech firms, and universities have sites, and many of them list job and internship programs. There are also several sites that specialize in helping you locate summer jobs and internships. (See the chapter on the "Intern-Net" for more information.)

You also should check with the professional organizations of the field in which you are interested. For instance, if you are interested in a job in electrical engineering, check with the Institute of Electrical and Electronics Engineers (IEEE). Some of these organizations have student chapters. And, the national headquarters of these associations often have listings of internships.

Another way to find a summer internship is by talking to the faculty members of your department. Many high-technology fields are small communities, and everyone knows everyone. Also many schools have a lot of adjunct faculty who are often people working for corporations and government agencies. Such adjunct faculty members are great contacts for jobs.

Remember that even organizations that do not have formal internship programs may still be sources of summer jobs. These "informal" internships are often the best kind; the competition usually isn't as stiff as it is in formal internship programs, and chances are good that you will be doing "real work" as opposed to "internship work."

And finally, look for summer jobs on campus. If you attend a large, research-oriented school, such as Yale or University of Michigan, you will have a much easier time finding an academic research job. You might have a harder time finding such a job at a small, liberal arts school, but you can give it a try anyway. Professors sometimes have extra money and small projects they can give undergraduates over the summer. If you can't get paid for it, you might be able to get course credit instead. Even better, a summer internship can often turn into an independent study class or a senior project in the next year.

"I just spent part of the spring walking into random labs and asking around," one student said. "Usually, departments will have brochures listing faculty members and what types of research they do. You can narrow your search from there to the specific stuff you're interested in. The only problem for a lot of people is that they don't know whether they will have the funding to give you a paid position. Professors are almost always willing to let you work for free. The hard part is getting the money."

Crossing Fields: Using
Technology to Shape Policy

Two summers ago I had an internship in the National Security and
International Affairs Division of the White House Office of Science
and Technology Policy (OSTP). I applied for the internship through
the White House Intern Program, but OSTP has recently set up its
own internship program independent of the White House program
for whatever bureaucratic reason. This is an exceptional internship
for those students interested in international science and
technology policy. Because of the highly specialized work that goes
on in this office, student interns—usually one per two- to three-
month period of time—do a variety of projects with very little in the
way of scut work. I worked on a variety of overseas trips done
through this office to expand U.S. scientific cooperation overseas. In
addition, I wrote reports on various subjects that went to other
officials in government, including the president's science advisor
and the president, and represented this division in
intragovernmental and intergovernmental meetings.

This sounds too good to be true, and there are some downsides. The
office has high expectations of interns, and if those expectations are
not met, less rewarding work may be forthcoming. In addition,
there is an expectation of a certain baseline knowledge of
international affairs, if not science per se. Also, despite the fact that
interns have no access to classified material, they still have to go
through a security check, since the office does deal with classified
material through its work with the National Security Council.

—Yale medical student

Laying the Groundwork

Getting an internship in science or technology will require having a good set of skills. Internship coordinators and employers are looking for two things: concrete skills and commitment to the field. Obviously, your choice of major and coursework will limit your options (a physics major is not usually going to get a job in a biology lab).

Make sure at least some of your classes cover "real world" applications, not just theoretical applications. For example, if you are a computer programmer, go beyond academic languages such as Pascal and Scheme and learn industry-standard, multipurpose languages such as C/C++ and Java. Also, try to learn applications such as Lotus Approach, Microsoft Excel, Mathmatica, or another commonly used software package. Software familiarity will give you an advantage in job hunting, even in the sciences. Engineering students should take classes that offer experience in testing and design. Knowing how to use a computer-aided design software application greatly improves your chance of getting a job.

Many schools offer different tracks—a B.S. or a B.A.—in engineering and the sciences. If you are really committed to working in one of these fields, take the B.S. track. Although you will have to take more, sometimes harder courses, the B.S. will be worth it, as it shows a higher level of commitment. Also, it will help you get the skills necessary for success.

Finally, get a job during the school year in a lab or office doing something similar to what you want to do during the summer. For example, if you want an electrical engineering internship designing circuit boards, try to get a job or independent study working for an electrical engineering professor doing similar work. This accomplishes several of your objectives. First, you'll find out if you like the work. Second, it will give you experience and skills you can sell to an employer. Third, you'll be able to use your boss as a reference/recommendation writer in the future. And finally, it might even lead to a summer research job on campus.

The Co-op Option

Many schools, especially those with good engineering programs, offer cooperative work programs. In co-op programs, students might work at job two days a week and take classes three days a week. Some schools, such as Cornell, allow students to take classes during the summer and do fall internships, which generally are a lot less competitive and longer than summer internships. A student doing a fall internship might get an offer for the following summer, or perhaps even a permanent offer.

Your Résumé and Cover Letter Package

While on most résumés experience is the most important element, on résumés oriented to science and technology, skills are the most important element. Employers usually value a skill base over a list of impressive experience and extracurricular activities. So be sure to include on your résumé a list of your technical skills and relevant classes. You might even want to put your skills list above your experience. And don't forget to add information about nontechnical but relevant skills, such as fluency in a foreign language and good writing ability. If you can show that you are an engineering major who can also write very well, you will be at a great advantage. Furthermore, in your descriptions of your work experience, don't be afraid to include detailed descriptions of exactly what you did.

Don't forget to include your grade point average, even if it is somewhat low. Remember that the GPA of a science or engineering major is generally somewhat lower than the GPA of a humanities major. Technology companies realize that a 3.2 in electrical engineering is harder to get than a 3.2 in political science.

Most important, do not lie on your résumé. If you say you can program in C++, you better be able to program in C++. Interviewers will be able to tell right away whether you are telling the truth. Be prepared for the "What was the last program you wrote in C++?" question.

The Microsoft Experience

I interned for two summers at Microsoft and found it to be an amazing experience. Here are some of the things that made the internship experience work well:

- A real job: Often, in software companies, the intern gets the grunge work to do. At Microsoft, our jobs were much like those of the full-time employees around us. The only difference was that they tried to assign us projects that we could reasonably advance or lead to closure in three months.
- A lot of interns: Microsoft hired over 400 interns those two summers. There were always plenty of people my age to go out and do stuff with.
- Well-organized recruiting: They don't just throw your name into a résumé pool. Rather, they search the schools for skilled people, do introductory interviews, and then based on those, invite them to interview with a couple of specific groups. The internship program at Microsoft is seen as a way of finding prospective employees and bringing them to Microsoft right after college. A lot of effort was put into making the interns feel comfortable. For example, Bill Gates invites the interns (in groups of about 50 to 100) to his house every year. After feeding them a great meal, he answers their questions.
- Wining, dining, and benefits: While recruiting, they're very generous about flying you out and taking you out to eat. While you're working for the company, the provide support in finding and paying for an apartment. They have, in the past, subsidized car rentals and provided health club benefits.

—MIT graduate

Along with your cover letter and résumé, consider including a copy of your transcript. Often, employers in science and technology are interested in what courses you have taken.

As for your cover letter, don't blow it off the way many science and technology students do when applying for internships. The cover letter is the one part of your package that can show a bit of your personality. Use it to show enthusiasm for the job for which you are applying. And don't be afraid to add a little personal info; if you love reading Ray Bradbury, you might want to mention it. And, of course, make sure your cover letter is well written. (See the chapter on résumés and cover letters for more information.)

And make sure that somewhere on your résumé or cover letter is the URL for your Web page. A Web site for a techie, especially for a computer programmer, is a must. Put at least your résumé online, as well as other information about you. Show off that fancy Java tic-tac-toe game you wrote or that three-dimensional television you designed. Add some links to other sites that you find interesting.

The Interview

Like with all jobs, the interview for a technology internship is crucial. Before you go on an interview, do your homework. Find out everything you can about the organization—what type of research the lab is doing, what papers it has published, etcetera. The best way to get such information is to search scientific databases for the names of some of the people who work in the organization to find out what they have published. (Check your school's science or engineering library for these databases.) Or you can check out the organization's Internet site. Then read the abstracts of the papers and perhaps the papers themselves. Your interviewer will be impressed with such efforts.

Prepare a mental list of good questions for the interview; remember, the interviewer shouldn't be doing all the talking. Questions do two things. They show the interviewer that you have a clue about what is going on, and they show that you are able to communicate with others. In technology companies and in labs, being able to work in teams is essential. If a researcher feels that she cannot work with you, you won't get the job, no matter how impressive your other qualifications may be. So speak up. For instance, ask what previous interns have done and what types of things they went on to do. But more importantly, show interest in the research. Ask about the implications of possible discoveries made at the lab.

Also, remember that lies will not get you very far in a technical interview. It cannot be overemphasized that in all fields, but especially science and technology, do not say you can do something that you can't do. If you say you know all about cell biology, be ready to be asked the C-terminus of a dibibliomuctase protein. Interviewers will know whether or not you are telling the truth, so tell the truth. They may ask you specific questions about what you've done, or even specific questions to test your knowledge of subject matter.

Finally, many people think that it doesn't matter what you wear to an interview for an internship in science or technology. That's a mistake. In a few cases you might be able to get away with wearing jeans, but it is better to dress as conservatively as possible. Many a student has found that, contrary to popular belief, scientists (especially in the private sector) are pretty spiffy dressers. Be sure to wear, at least, nice shoes, socks, pants, shirt, tie, and a sport jacket, unless you are specifically told not to. A suit would be even better. Once you get the job, however, you will probably be able to dress pretty informally.

Use Your Connections

Even more so than in many other fields, connections are a big help in getting a job offer. There is powerful synergy between research universities and the technology industry. An E-mail from a professor can do wonders for your chances of getting a job. Moreover, be prepared to spend a lot of time on the phone. Talk to plenty of people at the organizations in which you are most interested. Offer to send them copies of papers you have written and the results of projects you have completed.

Making Choices

So what do you do if you receive more than one job offer? As a science or a technology student, you may have an opportunity to be choosy. Remember, future employers and graduate schools will generally be more interested in *what* you did than where you did it. That does not necessarily mean you should turn down a job at Oracle for a job at some tiny software house. Just don't let a prestigious name alone be the deciding factor.

Think carefully about the financial and experience issues involved. Think, too, about whether you might want to work at this place in the future. In general, if you can get an internship at an organization for which you would like to work after graduation, take it. But also remember that working in a professor's lab at your school is not a bad option, especially for a sophomore.

A few words of caution about working on Internet sites. Commercial sites, in particular, often crash and burn within a few months, making the time you invested seem worthless. If you're going to do Web work, it's safest to do it for a well-established firm. The same goes for start-up companies. Start-up companies often offer great opportunities for exciting summer jobs. But for every Microsoft and every Netscape, there are a lot of software houses that went the way of Betamax.

Make the Best of It

It's not the end of the world if you don't land a super internship in a Nobel laureate's lab. Even if your internship ends up being rather mundane—running a database or creating spreadsheets—it's still better than flipping hamburgers or baby-sitting. You'll make some money and you'll get some experience for your résumé.

A.E. Schwartz and Associates

P.O. Box 79228
Waverley, MA 02179-0228
Phone: (617) 926-9111
Fax: (617) 926-0660

Position: Writer/Editor Intern

Department: N/A

No. of Positions Offered Annually: 5

Description: Responsibilities may include: writing, editing and copy editing new and existing materials, writing articles for top training and management journals, compiling, writing and editing manuscripts and training packages, writing video product scripts, self-study guides and workbook reviews, researching supplemental information and reviewing sales, marketing and public relations letters.

Qualifications: Applicant should have strong editorial skills in order to function in a writing, editing and copy editing capacity. Applicant should have strong communications and organizational skills and a knowledge of computers.

Salary: Based on type of projects and quality of work.

Position Dates: Fall, Spring and Summer

Position Location: Waverley, MA

Average No. of Applicants Annually: N/A

Potential for Job Placement: Yes

Application Process: Send résumé and cover letter.

Deadline: Rolling

Contact: Internship Coordinator (E-mail: aes@aeschwartz.com)

A.E. Schwartz and Associates

P.O. Box 79228
Waverley, MA 02179-0228
Phone: (617) 926-9111
Fax: (617) 926-0660

Position: Publishing Intern

Department: N/A

No. of Positions Offered Annually: 5

Description: Responsibilities may include coordination of all publishing aspects and author/publisher correspondence, editing, development, writing and evaluation of new and existing materials, writing for publisher and researching supplemental information. Upon successful completion this position may expand to either a contract consultant or on-staff associate.

Qualifications: Applicant must have good communication and organizational skills and computer knowledge and experience.

Salary: Based on type of project and quality of work.

Position Dates: Fall, Spring and Summer

Position Location: Waverley, MA

Average No. of Applicants Annually: N/A

Potential for Job Placement: Yes

Application Process: Send résumé and cover letter.

Deadline: Rolling

Contact: Internship Coordinator (E-mail: aes@aeschwartz.com)

A.E. Schwartz and Associates

P.O. Box 79228
Waverley, MA 02179-0228
Phone: (617) 926-9111
Fax: (617) 926-0660

Position: Sales and Marketing Intern

Department: N/A

No. of Positions Offered Annually: 5

Description: Responsibilities may include networking with organizations to arrange sponsorship of programs, writing proposals and assisting in all aspects of professional correspondence, researching and marketing new business avenues, telemarketing to potential clients for on-site training programs, placing advertisements, researching and marketing over the Internet and developing and maintaining computer systems for related sales/marketing efforts.

Qualifications: Applicant should be a creative and persistent individual who conceptualizes and articulates clearly.

Salary: Based on type of projects and quality of work.

Position Dates: Fall, Spring and Summer

Position Location: Waverley, MA

Average No. of Applicants Annually: N/A

Potential for Job Placement: Yes

Application Process: Send résumé and cover letter.

Deadline: Rolling

Contact: Internship Coordinator (E-mail: aes@aeschwartz.com)

A.E. Schwartz and Associates

P.O. Box 79228
Waverley, MA 02179-0228
Phone: (617) 926-9111
Fax: (617) 926-0660

Position: Graphic Design Intern

Department: N/A

No. of Positions Offered Annually: 5

Description: Responsibilities may include creating new design concepts for overall organization/image, designing flyers/book covers/sales materials/catalog and exhibit materials, designing specialty and promotion items, writing, editing and copy editing as appropriate and overseeing printing.

Qualifications: Applicant must have strong communication and organizational skills and have experience with computers.

Salary: Based on type of projects and quality of work.

Position Dates: Fall, Spring and Summer

Position Location: Waverley, MA

Average No. of Applicants Annually: N/A

Potential for Job Placement: Yes

Application Process: Send résumé and cover letter.

Deadline: Rolling

Contact: Internship Coordinator (E-mail: aes@aeschwartz.com)

A.E. Schwartz and Associates

P.O. Box 79228
Waverley, MA 02179-0228
Phone: (617) 926-9111
Fax: (617) 926-0660

Position: Public Relations Intern

Department: N/A

No. of Positions Offered Annually: 5

Description: Responsiblities may include facilitating media coverage, newspaper features and talk shows, networking with organizations to arrange media coverage on special projects, follow-up correpsondence, writing letters, articles and press releases and overseeing the placement of advertising.

Qualifications: Applicant must have good communication and organizational skills and experience with computers.

Salary: Based on type of projects and quality of work.

Position Dates: Fall, Spring and Summer

Position Location: Waverley, MA

Average No. of Applicants Annually: N/A

Potential for Job Placement: Yes

Application Process: Send résumé and cover letter.

Deadline: Rolling

Contact: Internship Coordinator (E-mail: aes@aeschwartz.com)

A.E. Schwartz and Associates

P.O. Box 79228
Waverley, MA 02179-0228
Phone: (617) 926-9111
Fax: (617) 926-0660

Position: Internet/Windows Specialist Intern

Department: N/A

No. of Positions Offered Annually: 5

Description: Responsibilities may include designing and creating HTML pages, becoming an Internet resource by exploring new markets and resources, assisting in the delivery of on-line content, integrating Windows95 software packages with existing 3.1, developing more integrated systems with existing and new software, creating a new database structure for existing databases, assisting in the re-design of all desktop publishing/graphic design materials and assisting in the integration of existing software packages.

Qualifications: Applicant should have strong communication and organizational skills.

Salary: Based on type of projects and quality of work.

Position Dates: Fall, Spring and Summer

Position Location: Waverley, MA

Average No. of Applicants Annually: N/A

Potential for Job Placement: Yes

Application Process: Send résumé and cover letter.

Deadline: Rolling

Contact: Internship Coordinator (E-mail: aes@aeschwartz.com)

DesignTech International, Inc.

7401-I Fullerton Road
Springfield, VA 22153
Phone: (703) 866-2000
Fax: (703) 866-2001

Position: Marketing Intern

Department: Marketing

No. of Positions Offered Annually: 3

Description: Projects include developing promotional and packaging material for new products, public relations campaigns, sales analyses and marketing programs to improve sales and customer satisfaction. Room and board are provided.

Qualifications: Undergraduate major in the social sciences, the desire to work in an entrepreneurial environment, and the ability to work independently are all necessary.

Salary: Stipend plus bonus

Position Dates: Winter and Summer

Position Location: Springfield, VA

Average No. of Applicants Annually: 200

Potential for Job Placement: N/A

Application Process: Send cover letter, résumé, and a one- to two-page description on how you would develop a market for a car alarm.

Deadline: Rolling

Contact: Lisa Cole

DesignTech International, Inc.

7401-I Fullerton Road
Springfield, VA 22153
Phone: (703) 866-2000
Fax: (703) 866-2001

Position: Engineering Intern

Department: Engineering

No. of Positions Offered Annually: 3

Description: Projects include involvement with design of new products, primarily in the telephone accessory and auto security areas. Room and board are provided.

Qualifications: Completion of three years of mechanical or electrical engineering courses.

Salary: Stipend plus bonus

Position Dates: Winter and Summer

Position Location: Springfield, VA

Average No. of Applicants Annually: 200

Potential for Job Placement: N/A

Application Process: Send cover letter and résumé.

Deadline: Rolling

Contact: Lisa Cole

DesignTech International, Inc.

7401-I Fullerton Road
Springfield, VA 22153
Phone: (703) 866-2000
Fax: (703) 866-2001

Position: Operations and Finance Intern

Department: Operations and Finance

No. of Positions Offered Annually: 3

Description: Projects include improving manufacturing processes, inventory controls and financial analysis. Room and board are provided.

Qualifications: Undergraduate majoring in economics or business, the desire to work in an entrepreneurial environment, and the ability to work independently are all necessary.

Salary: Stipend plus bonus

Position Dates: Winter and Summer

Position Location: Springfield, VA

Average No. of Applicants Annually: 200

Potential for Job Placement: N/A

Application Process: Send cover letter and résumé.

Deadline: Rolling

Contact: Lisa Cole

Hewlett Packard

3000 Hanover Street
Palo Alto, CA 94086
Phone: (415) 857-6083
Fax: (415) 852-8138

Position: Engineering Intern

Department: Event # 4843

No. of Positions Offered Annually: 150

Description: Engineering interns work in a variety of departments such as Manufacturing, Research and Development, Order Fulfillment and Sales Support. Assignments might include: circuit desing, manufacturability tests, process documentation, control systems, digital signal processing, semiconductor devices, mechanical design, workflow redesign, failure analysis or customer support.

Qualifications: Applicant should have a BS/MS in electrical, mechanical or industrial engineering, excellent written and verbal communication skills, demonstrated ability to work in teams, related PC/workstation skills. Applicant must be authorized to work in the United States and be able to work for ten weeks, full time.

Salary: $2,400/month

Position Dates: Summer

Position Location: Cupertino, CA; Mountain View, CA; Palo Alto, CA; San Francisco, CA; San Jose, CA; Santa Clara, CA; Sunnyvale, CA

Average No. of Applicants Annually: 1,000

Potential for Job Placement: Yes

Application Process: Mail, fax or E-mail (E-mail: résumé@hp.com) résumé and cover letter. Include Event #4843.

Deadline: May 15

Contact: Christine Kavoshi

Hewlett Packard

3000 Hanover Street
Palo Alto, CA 94086
Phone: (415) 857-6083
Fax: (415) 852-8138

Position: Financial Analyst

Department: Event # 4843

No. of Positions Offered Annually: 25

Description: Financial analysis to support business or manufacturing organizations. Duties may include ad hoc analysis, internal audit, budgeting, standard setting, product pricing or investment analysis.

Qualifications: Applicant should have a BS/MBA in Finance, excellent written and verbal communication skills, demonstrated ability to work in teams, related PC/workstation skills and must be able to work ten weeks. Applicant must be authorized to work in the United States.

Salary: $2,400/month

Position Dates: Summer

Position Location: Cupertino, CA; Mountain View, CA; Palo Alto, CA; San Francisco, CA; San Jose, CA; Santa Clara, CA; Sunnyvale, CA

Average No. of Applicants Annually: 1,000

Potential for Job Placement: Yes

Application Process: Mail, fax or E-mail (E-mail: résumé@hp.com) résumé and cover letter. Include Event # 4843.

Deadline: May 15

Contact: Christine Kavoshi

Hewlett Packard

3000 Hanover Street
Palo Alto, CA 94086
Phone: (415) 857-6083
Fax: (415) 852-8138

Position: Software/Information Technology

Department: Event # 4843

No. of Positions Offered Annually: 100

Description: Software Design positions could include: firmware, compilers, GUI development, consumer PCs, graphics or applications software. Information Technology positions could include: development and/or support of applications (accounting, financial systems, marketing analysis), PC/UNIX support and network support.

Qualifications: Applicant should have a BS/MS in computer science or MIS, excellent written and communication skills, demonstrated ability to work in teams and PC/workstation and programming languages skills. Appliant must be authorized to work in the United States and able to work ten weeks, full time.

Salary: $2,400/month

Position Dates: Summer

Position Location: Cupertino, CA; Mountain View, CA; Palo Alto, CA; San Francisco, CA; San Jose, CA; Santa Clara, CA; Sunnyvale, CA

Average No. of Applicants Annually: 1,000

Potential for Job Placement: Yes

Application Process: Mail, fax or E-mail (E-mail: résumé@hp.com) résumé and cover letter. Include Event #4843.

Deadline: May 15

Contact: Christine Kavoshi

Pro-Found Software, Inc.

500 Frank W. Burr Boulevard
Teaneck, NJ 07666
Phone: (201) 928-0400
Fax: (201) 928-1122

Position: Software Development Intern

Department: N/A

No. of Positions Offered Annually: 5

Description: Interns will be offered a unique opportunity to work with senior Pro-Found professionals in all aspects of software development from requirements definition through design and implementation.

Qualifications: Successful candidates must demonstrate high levels of motivation, creativity, and relevant academic achievement and must be proficient in C/C++. UNIX and Windows knowledge is highly desirable.

Salary: Commensurate with experience.

Position Dates: Fall, Spring and Summer

Position Location: Teaneck, NJ

Average No. of Applicants Annually: 250

Potential for Job Placement: Excellent

Application Process: Send cover letter and résumé.

Deadline: Rolling

Contact: Lisa Jayne Nelson, Internship Coordinator

Training Consortium

P.O. Box 79228
Waverley, MA 02179-0228
Phone: (617) 926-9111
Fax: (617) 926-0660

Position: Site Administrator

Department: N/A

No. of Positions Offered Annually: 6

Description: Responsibilities may include: working with the programmer to further develop the site's administration, ensuring the quality and functionality of the web site and helping clients with any questions or problems.

Qualifications: Applicant should be proficient in HTML programming.

Salary: Unpaid

Position Dates: Fall, Spring and Summer

Position Location: Waverley, MA

Average No. of Applicants Annually: 100

Potential for Job Placement: Yes

Application Process: Send résumé and cover letter.

Deadline: Rolling

Contact: Training Consortium.com Internship Coordinator

Training Consortium

P.O. Box 79228
Waverley, MA 02179-0228
Phone: (617) 926-9111
Fax: (617) 926-0660

Position: Graphic Designer

Department: N/A

No. of Positions Offered Annually: 6

Description: Responsibilities may include: creating artwork for the Training Consortium, designing ads for Training Consortium clients and other publications materials for the web site, formatting graphics to be uploaded to the site and providing camera-ready output.

Qualifications: Applicant should have a knowledge of typography and be familiar with graphics packages such as Freehand and CorelDraw.

Salary: Unpaid

Position Dates: Fall, Spring and Summer

Position Location: Waverley, MA

Average No. of Applicants Annually: 100

Potential for Job Placement: Yes

Application Process: Send résumé and cover letter.

Deadline: Rolling

Contact: Training Consortium.com Internship Coordinator

Training Consortium

P.O. Box 79228
Waverley, MA 02179-0228
Phone: (617) 926-9111
Fax: (617) 926-0660

Position: Content Developer

Department: N/A

No. of Positions Offered Annually: 6

Description: Responsibilities may include: researching the Internet and the World Wide Web for appropriate links and content additions and writing and editing new materials for the site.

Qualifications: Applicant should have excellent writing and editing ability.

Salary: Unpaid

Position Dates: Fall, Spring and Summer

Position Location: Waverley, MA

Average No. of Applicants Annually: 100

Potential for Job Placement: Yes

Application Process: Send résumé and cover letter.

Deadline: Rolling

Contact: Training Consortium.com Internship Coordinator

Training Consortium

P.O. Box 79228
Waverley, MA 02179-0228
Phone: (617) 926-9111
Fax: (617) 926-0660

Position: Sales and Marketing Consultant

Department: N/A

No. of Positions Offered Annually: 6

Description: Responsibilities may include: networking with organizations to arrange partnerships within the training and development community, telemarketing to potential clients and marketing the organization's services through E-mails, directories, search engines and announcement sites.

Qualifications: Applicant should have excellent communication skills and knowledge of the workings of search engines and directories.

Salary: Unpaid

Position Dates: Fall, Spring and Summer

Position Location: Waverley, MA

Average No. of Applicants Annually: 100

Potential for Job Placement: Yes

Application Process: Send résumé and cover letter.

Deadline: Rolling

Contact: Training Consortium.com Internship Coordinator

Training Consortium

P.O. Box 79228
Waverley, MA 02179-0228
Phone: (617) 926-9111
Fax: (617) 926-0660

Position: Programmer

Department: N/A

No. of Positions Offered Annually: 6

Description: Possible projects may include: developing various search robots and programming for the Training Consortium site.

Qualifications: Applicant should be proficient in Web programming (HTML, CGI, etc.) and robot development.

Salary: Unpaid

Position Dates: Fall, Spring and Summer

Position Location: Waverley, MA

Average No. of Applicants Annually: 100

Potential for Job Placement: Yes

Application Process: Send résumé and cover letter.

Deadline: Rolling

Contact: Training Consortium.com Internship Coordinator

Science Research 7

by Melissa S. Lee

Interested in finding a science research internship? Don't despair, because there are plenty of them. According to students who have spent their summers at a variety of programs across the country, the key to finding the perfect science research internship is to spend time early on becoming familiar with what is available.

For many, the search begins at their schools' career services offices. If you're lucky, your school has an internship counselor or coordinator who is knowledgeable about the kinds of research internships available. Binders of internship flyers and comments from former interns are also very informative. And big internship sponsors such as the Department of Energy and the National Institutes of Health generally publish their own brochures detailing their various labs and summer research programs.

The Internet is another good source of internship information. A first-year medical student at Northwestern University says the career services office at his undergraduate university was not as helpful as it could have been. Instead, he turned to the Internet. Career services offices at some universities post listings of internships on their sites. The University of Massachusetts, for example, has an informative site on international health internships. The education departments at large government institutions such as the National Aeronautics and Space Administration as well as the National Institutes of Health often post information about their internship programs on their sites. The Space Life Sciences Training Program, a six-week internship run out of the Kennedy Space Center and Florida A&M University, has its own site with photos of and information about the projects that students have worked on in previous years. (To learn more about using the Net to find internships, see the chapter on the "Intern-net" in this book.)

Weighing Your Options: Selecting the Right Science Internship

When you take a look at all the science research internships available, the list might at first seem overwhelming. But if you have a clear sense of what you're interested in, it will be much easier to narrow your search.

Science internships can be classified as either science- or health-related programs. If you are interested in hardcore science research, eliminate those internships geared toward public health or clinical medicine. Should one of the latter categories be of interest, shelve the basic science offerings.

While this should help narrow the choices, keep a few other things in mind as well. Some programs offer stipends but do not provide housing—and the cost of housing might be a serious factor depending on the location of the internship. Rent for an intern attending a National Institutes of Health summer program in Montana would be much less expensive than it would be for an intern living in New York City. If you are able to locate an internship near your home town, you can save yourself some change by living at home and commuting.

Health-Related and Clinical Internships

If you are looking for hands-on application of your science training, or want some clinical experience to prep you for medical school, check out major hospitals and clinics that sponsor summer internships for college students. These allow you direct exposure to the health profession rather than pure science research. Some of these programs provide for more personal interaction than others. But in most cases, you will have the chance to work with patients and, at the very least, observe their treatment and diagnosis.

The first step again is finding a place to work. Your school and nearby medical institutions will probably have information on the bigger programs. If your university is affiliated with a medical center and hospital or has its own medical school, this would be a great place to find out about opportunities on campus. Or you might be able to find out about programs at other institutions.

Again, consider which fields might be of particular interest to you. Would you like exposure to pediatric care, sports medicine, or surgery? Keep in mind that certain fields might allow you more hands-on involvement than others. For example, you might help patients directly at an outpatient physical rehabilitation center, whereas at the cardiovascular department of a hospital, your work would probably have little to do with surgery itself. You should find out about clinics that have special programs targeted at certain groups and that might need interns with special skills. For example, an urban clinic might need bilingual volunteers. If you have special skills that might enhance your experience, be sure to consider these in your search.

If all else fails and you cannot find a major health program to intern with or perhaps have in mind a more focused area to work in, then start forging your own connections. Call your doctor or any doctors you know who are affiliated with a hospital and ask them for advice. They are bound to know other doctors or clinics within their hospital that would be interested in having an intern.

I interned at a child health clinic in Jamaica, New York. I did the basics, taking weights and measurements of patients. But I also found a mentor there, which is always a good idea, and began working on his project. He was evaluating a new asthma program and wanted to find out how it effective it was. I conducted interviews with patients and collected information for his evaluation process.

In general, these types of internships are limited by the law. You do not have any medical training, and so you cannot legally perform many clinical tasks. However, the degree of responsibility you are given does depend on how well you know the people you are interning for. Try to find a mentor. This will allow you to observe in depth the specific procedures performed in the clinic.

The Importance of Lab Shopping

In high school, I worked for a physical chemistry lab at Columbia University and a genetics lab at Cornell University Medical Center. The good part about science research internships is that you get to do "real" work and have a chance to be published; the bad part is that a lot of students don't have the knowledge to understand fully what's going on in the lab. Hence, research is really important if you want to appreciate why you're poking out a mouse's eye to remove the DNA.

At both places I got to work with graduate students, lab technicians, and the professors in charge of the lab. The first two were really helpful in teaching me the basics, and the professors always took the time to explain things to me and discuss my projects. At Columbia, I used to do jigsaw puzzles with the grad student with whom I was working while we waited for the experiments to finish, which was a nice break from the lab.

I'm really big on nice environments, and both labs I worked in were recently built. If environment is important to you, it's important to be aware that a lot of labs are very run down, and you could end up spending your days in a really crappy room.

—Yale student from New York City

Research Positions on Campus

If you have your heart set on a research position, you might find yourself either interning on your own campus or venturing to another campus. There are some major organizations, such as the National Heart Association and Argonne National Labs, that sponsor internships. In addition, the National Institutes of Health and the Department of Energy provide funding for many research positions. These, however, are fairly selective, and the competition can be stiff. Many of these positions require some previous research experience. That means that while you might like to end up at the NIH or at Brookhaven National Laboratories, you'll probably have to start smaller.

Where do you begin? Most universities offer research positions, and many large institutions will have enough to accommodate even those with limited research experience. "There is an advantage to staying at your own school for the summer if you are going to continue to do research during the academic year," advises a senior at Yale. One science major says she started off doing research at the University of Maryland School of Dentistry when she was still in high school. There she acquired her basic research skills and then had the foundation to apply to more selective programs. She says starting in high school gave her a distinct advantage and noted that many places have research opportunities for students who have not yet entered college. She also advises checking out research internships at less competitive universities if you do not yet have extensive research training or have not yet done much science course work.

Each year, the National Science Foundation administers grants that enable institutions across the country to hire students to work on special lab projects and conduct their own research during the summer. The grants vary from year to year and from institution to institution, so it is important to find out what kind of work is being done where. A number of places specialize in optics research, for example. If you are interested in this field, determine which labs are doing the kind of work you find compelling.

Some schools host summer science programs, such as the Howard Hughes Summer Internship at Dartmouth College. If your university does not have such programs available, often professors will have grant money to hire students for the summer. A biology major from Williams College spent a summer at the Woods Hole Oceanographic Institute, but did not work under the established fellowship program for undergraduates. Instead, he was able to find a position working under his thesis advisor, who was able to pay him for his work.

"Professors are a very good resource," comments a senior at Marian College. "They can be very helpful; they just have to know that you are interested." Says another student, "If you are interested in the research of professors at your own school, but are unable to work in their lab, ask them if they know of professors doing similar work at another institution." Being recommended to a lab by your own professor will put you at a distinct advantage over other applicants. And your professors might also have a better sense of what places are good work environments and match the kinds of interests and skills that you have.

Considering Other Options

A recent graduate of Brown University comments that many students interested in science "go outside of academia and work for biotech companies." The journal *Biotech News* is a good source of business reviews of biotech companies. You could also do searches on the Internet to get info on the biotech industry. PointCast (http://www.pointcast.com) is a particularly good tool for this kind of search. It presents up-to-the-minute information about companies and their products and can be personalized according to your interests. You could even check out the yellow pages of the top three biotech cities: San Francisco, Boston, and San Diego (in descending order).

There are, of course, companies in the fields of publishing, policy making, and consulting that would welcome an intern with a science background. For example, certain science magazines prefer students who are skilled in writing and have some science training. Health care consulting is a field in which having analytic and qualitative skills combined with a science background can be a decided advantage. And, of course, many of the large pharmaceutical companies such as Merck and Baxter are worth checking out. While positions with such companies might not be devoted to research, they are often geared toward those with serious science backgrounds.

Going Through the Application Process

Once you determine where you might want to work, you should prepare your application and start making contacts. When I was applying for internships, I had two different forms: one for clinical programs and one for pure science-research programs. For clinical internships, you probably will be writing more about your experience with people and science as well as your interest in medicine. Your interpersonal skills will play a critical role in your list of qualifications. Clinical programs care less about whether you've taken a genetics lab than whether you've volunteered at a hospital. You might also want to point out any specific course work you've done in anatomy or physiology that would distinguish you from research-oriented science majors.

If you choose to go into the private sector, you might be able to follow the standard procedure of sending a cover letter and résumé. But in many cases, and definitely for research positions, these internships require some proof of your academic abilities and interests. For example, one Yale student worked at Brookhaven National Laboratories while still in high school. Her application included an essay explaining what type of research she wanted to do and why. In part, this was to help place her in a lab where her interests would be compatible with the research being conducted.

You might be applying to work not only at a particular institution but with a particular professor in a particular lab. Personal contacts are important in such situations. For the Summer Undergraduate Research Fellowship at Mayo Clinic, a Yale senior made the effort to visit the campus and speak to the director of the program while at home for winter break. Contacting professors within a particular division will enable you to gain specific knowledge of their research. Speaking with them beforehand benefits both parties. You will get a better sense of what they do, and they will get a better sense of who you are and what your qualifications are. If you do have a specific person in mind with whom you'd like to work, be sure to make note of it on your application.

Most important, get started early. Many program deadlines are in January and February, and science internships require some extra preparations — often transcripts must be ordered and recommendations requested long before then. You may have to do some preliminary work, like deciding whom to select as your references and discussing with them what you are interested in doing for your internship. Give your references plenty of time to write letters of recommendation, and always provide them with self-addressed, stamped envelopes. A friendly phone call or E-mail to remind them about the due dates is always a good idea.

Choosing an Internship and Making the Best of It

Some of the internships offered to you might not appear to be what you wanted. But keep an open mind. "I was hoping to do more clinical/human research during my summer at the Space Life Sciences Training Program, and ended up loving my work with plants," says one former intern. Says another student of his internship at the Health Research Training Program, "My job was not the best experience, and was more administrative than I had hoped, but I still learned a lot. The goal is not necessarily to be dramatically successful in finding an internship, but for it to teach you about a subject in general."

Another student offers this advice: "Ideally, one should have two internships. The first summer, you should give it a whirl and be able to experience science outside the classroom. The second summer, your internship choice should be well informed, based on past experience and the skills you have learned."

American Cancer Society

30 Speen Street
Framingham, MA 01701-1800
Phone: (508) 270-4651
Fax: (508) 270-4699

Position: Betty Lea Stone Research Fellowship

Department: N/A

No. of Positions Offered Annually: 4

Description: Cancer-related research.

Qualifications: Must be enrolled in a Massachusetts medical school.

Salary: $3,000

Position Dates: Summer (ten weeks)

Position Location: Framingham, MA

Average No. of Applicants Annually: 12

Potential for Job Placement: N/A

Application Process: Call for an application. Send in application along with two references and transcripts. Forms are sent to the references.

Deadline: March 1

Contact: Jonathon Lyon

American Cancer Society

30 Speen Street
Framingham, MA 01701-1800
Phone: (508) 270-4651
Fax: (508) 270-4699

Position: Alvin T.-Viola D. Fuller Fellowship

Department: N/A

No. of Positions Offered Annually: 10

Description: Cancer-related research.

Qualifications: Must be a Massachusetts resident and a college student (the college does not have to be located in Massachusetts). Looking for applicants with diverse backgrounds.

Salary: $2,500

Position Dates: Summer (ten weeks)

Position Location: Framingham, MA

Average No. of Applicants Annually: 20-60

Potential for Job Placement: N/A

Application Process: Call for an application. Send in completed application along with two references and transcript. Forms are sent to the references.

Deadline: February 1

Contact: Jonathon Lyon

Bermuda Biological Station for Research, Inc.

17 Biological Station Lane
Ferry Reach, St. George's
Bermuda GE 01
Phone: (441) 297-1880
Fax: (441) 297-8143

Position: Volunteer Scientific Intern

Department: N/A

No. of Positions Offered Annually: 20

Description: Interns work under the supervision of a resident scientist, assisting in the work for a period of four to six months. Room and board is provided, but travel expenses are the responsibility of the intern.

Qualifications: Upper division undergraduate standing, or graduates of a university science program.

Salary: Unpaid

Position Dates: Fall, Spring and Summer

Position Location: Bermuda

Average No. of Applicants Annually: 100-200

Potential for Job Placement: Fair

Application Process: Forms available from BBSR Education Department, or at our Web site (http://www.bbsr.edu)

Deadline: June 1 for Fall; October 1 for Spring; February 1 for Summer

Contact: Education Secretary

Brookfield Zoo

3300 Golf Road
Brookfield, IL 60513
Phone: (708) 485-0263
Fax: (708) 485-3532

Position: Graphic Arts Intern

Department: N/A

No. of Positions Offered Annually: 2

Description: Intern will work on a variety of projects involving production of park signage and printed materials. Intern will gain exposure to the silk screening process and MacIntosh computer programs and will experience the different stages of the design process.

Qualifications: Intern must be at least a sophomore in college and have a GPA of at least 2.5.

Salary: Unpaid

Position Dates: Fall, Spring and Summer

Position Location: Brookfield, IL

Average No. of Applicants Annually: 200

Potential for Job Placement: Minimal

Application Process: Complete application and send cover letter, résumé, transcript, and two letters of recommendation.

Deadline: August 1 for Fall; December 1 for Spring; February 1 for Summer.

Contact: Jan Rizzo

Brookfield Zoo

3300 Golf Road
Brookfield, IL 60513
Phone: (708) 485-0263
Fax: (708) 485-3532

Position: Accessibility Department Intern

Department: Accessibility Department

No. of Positions Offered Annually: 1

Description: Intern will gain exposure to programming and services intended to increase access to the zoo by visitors with various disabilities. Intern will assist with hands-on tours of the Children's Zoo, participate in animal outreach visits to groups too ill or disabled to visit the zoo and assist with extended education programs.

Qualifications: Intern must be at least a sophomore in college and have a GPA of at least 2.5.

Salary: Unpaid

Position Dates: Summer

Position Location: Brookfield, IL

Average No. of Applicants Annually: 200

Potential for Job Placement: Minimal

Application Process: Complete application and send cover letter, résumé, transcript, and two letters of recommendation.

Deadline: February 1

Contact: Jan Rizzo

Brookfield Zoo

3300 Golf Road
Brookfield, IL 60513
Phone: (708) 485-0263
Fax: (708) 485-3532

Position: Public Relations/Marketing/Special Events Intern

Department: Public Relations/Marketing/Special Events

No. of Positions Offered Annually: 3

Description: Interns are involved in all aspects of promoting and publicizing the zoo and its special events. Intern will gain exposure to writing press releases, working at special events both on and off site, media relations and advertising.

Qualifications: Intern must be at least a sophomore in college and have a GPA of at least 2.5.

Salary: Unpaid

Position Dates: Fall, Spring and Summer

Position Location: Brookfield, IL

Average No. of Applicants Annually: 200

Potential for Job Placement: Minimal

Application Process: Complete application and send cover letter, résumé, transcript, and two letters of recommendation.

Deadline: August 1 for Fall; December 1 for Spring; February 1 for Summer.

Contact: Jan Rizzo

Brookfield Zoo

3300 Golf Road
Brookfield, IL 60513
Phone: (708) 485-0263
Fax: (708) 485-3532

Position: Audiovisual Services Intern

Department: Audiovisual Services

No. of Positions Offered Annually: 1

Description: Intern will gain hands-on experience in a diverse, fast-paced work environment that provides all photographic, videographic and audiovisual support to all departments of the zoo.

Qualifications: Intern must be at least a sophomore in college and have a GPA of at least 2.5.

Salary: Unpaid

Position Dates: Fall, Spring and Summer

Position Location: Brookfield, IL

Average No. of Applicants Annually: 200

Potential for Job Placement: Minimal

Application Process: Complete application and send cover letter, résumé, transcript, and two letters of recommendation.

Deadline: August 1 for Fall; December 1 for Spring; February 1 for Summer.

Contact: Jan Rizzo

Brookfield Zoo

3300 Golf Road
Brookfield, IL 60513
Phone: (708) 485-0263
Fax: (708) 485-3532

Position: Exhibits Department Intern

Department: Exhibits Department

No. of Positions Offered Annually: 3

Description: Intern learns practical applications of engineering and creative craftsmanship while working with the zoo's staff of exhibit designers. Intern will gain exposure to the variety of trades and materials required to create and produce natural, high-quality habitats for zoo animals.

Qualifications: Intern must be at least a sophomore in college and have a GPA of at least 2.5.

Salary: Unpaid

Position Dates: Fall, Spring and Summer

Position Location: Brookfield, IL

Average No. of Applicants Annually: 200

Potential for Job Placement: Minimal

Application Process: Complete application and send cover letter, résumé, transcript and two letters of recommendation.

Deadline: August 1 for Fall; December 1 for Spring; February 1 for Summer.

Contact: Jan Rizzo

Brookfield Zoo

3300 Golf Road
Brookfield, IL 60513
Phone: (708) 485-0263
Fax: (708) 485-3532

Position: Department of Nutrition Services Intern

Department: Department of Nutrition Services

No. of Positions Offered Annually: 6

Description: Intern will be involved in formulating and preparing daily diets for more than 2,500 zoo animals, as well as distributing food for all animals in the park. Intern will also learn general Commissary operations and work on a project involving specific nutrition-related research, gathering dietary information, computer diet analysis or other aspects of zoo nutrition.

Qualifications: Intern must be at least a sophomore in college and have a GPA of at least 2.5.

Salary: Unpaid

Position Dates: Fall, Spring and Summer

Position Location: Brookfield, IL

Average No. of Applicants Annually: 200

Potential for Job Placement: Minimal

Application Process: Complete application and send cover letter, résumé, transcript and two letters of recommendation.

Deadline: August 1 for Fall; December 1 for Spring; February 1 for Summer.

Contact: Jan Rizzo

Brookfield Zoo

3300 Golf Road
Brookfield, IL 60513
Phone: (708) 485-0263
Fax: (708) 485-3532

Position: Department of Conservation Biology Intern

Department: Department of Conservation Biology

No. of Positions Offered Annually: 2

Description: Intern works with zoo staff in studying the biology, management and conservation of small populations. Intern may select work in a mouse-breeding lab, work in a molecular genetics lab or assist with data collection and tabulation of behavioral data of hooved animals.

Qualifications: Intern must be at least a sophomore in college, have an overall GPA of at least 2.5.

Salary: Unpaid

Position Dates: Fall, Spring and Summer

Position Location: Brookfield, IL

Average No. of Applicants Annually: 200

Potential for Job Placement: Minimal

Application Process: Complete application and send cover letter, résumé, transcript, and two letters of recommendation.

Deadline: August 1 for Fall; December 1 for Spring; February 1 for Summer.

Contact: Jan Rizzo

Brookfield Zoo

3300 Golf Road
Brookfield, IL 60513
Phone: (708) 485-0263
Fax: (708) 485-3532

Position: Zookeeper Intern

Department: N/A

No. of Positions Offered Annually: 60

Description: Zookeeper interns gain valuable hands-on experience in all aspects of captive animal management at an internationally renowned zoological park. Exposure to exhibit maintenance, diet preparation, behavioral observation and documentation, animal husbandry, animal handling and record keeping in the animal area of the intern's selection. Interns also interact with zoo visitors in both formal and informal presentations.

Qualifications: Intern must be at least a college sophomore, have an overall GPA of at least 2.5.

Salary: Unpaid

Position Dates: Fall, Spring and Summer

Position Location: Brookfield, IL

Average No. of Applicants Annually: 200

Potential for Job Placement: Possible

Application Process: Complete application and send cover letter, résumé, transcript, and two letters of recommendation.

Deadline: August 1 for Fall; December 1 for Spring; February 1 for Summer.

Contact: Jan Rizzo

Brookfield Zoo

3300 Golf Road
Brookfield, IL 60513
Phone: (708) 485-0263
Fax: (708) 485-3532

Position: Education Department Intern

Department: Education Department

No. of Positions Offered Annually: 3

Description: Future science educators gain experience in program development and evaluation using informal teaching techniques and assist in implementation of conservation education programs for the zoo's diverse audience.

Qualifications: Intern must be at least a sophomore in college and have a GPA of at least 2.5.

Salary: Unpaid

Position Dates: Fall, Spring and Summer

Position Location: Brookfield, IL

Average No. of Applicants Annually: 200

Potential for Job Placement: Minimal

Application Process: Complete application and send cover letter, résumé, transcript, and two letters of recommendation.

Deadline: August 1 for Fall; December 1 for Winter; February 1 for Summer.

Contact: Jan Rizzo

Crow Canyon Archaeological Center

23390 Country Road K
Cortez, CO 81321
Phone: (970) 565-8975
Fax: (970) 565-4859

Position: Education Internship

Department: N/A

No. of Positions Offered Annually: 6

Description: Interns work closely with experienced teachers to assist them in preparing for programs, teaching curriculum modules, and assisting in field trips. Education interns assist at excavation sites, and in transporting students. Meals and housing are provided. There is a maximum of $350 for travelling reimbursement.

Qualifications: Advanced students with a combined interest in education and anthropology. Current driver's license, first aid and CPR training is required.

Salary: Modest stipend

Position Dates: Fall, Spring and Summer

Position Location: Cortez, CO

Average No. of Applicants Annually: 30

Potential for Job Placement: Some potential

Application Process: Can download applications from our Web site (http://www.crowcanyon.org), or can write or call for applications.

Deadline: Early in the year.

Contact: Internship Coordinator

Crow Canyon Archaeological Center

23390 Country Road K
Cortez, CO 81321
Phone: (970) 565-8975
Fax: (970) 565-4859

Position: Research Intern

Department: Various

No. of Positions Offered Annually: 12

Description: Research internships are offered in Field, Laboratory, and Environmental Archaeology departments. Interns will work closely with experienced professionals to assist them in excavating and recording archaeological contexts, in laboratory processing and analysis, or in studies of present and past environments. In addition, interns will be responsible for helping supervise small groups of program participants in in field or lab work. Interns may also be asked to give lectures or demonstrations to help participants prepare for field or lab work. Meals and housing are provided. There is a maximum of $350 for travel reimbursement.

Qualifications: Advanced undergraduate or graduate in anthropology, archaeology, or related field; ability to work effectively as a team member; ability to perform technical work, make careful observations, and record data legibly and accurately. Strong interest in improving archaeological field and lab skills, and teaching skills.

Salary: Modest stipend.

Position Dates: Fall, Spring and Summer

Position Location: Cortez, CO

Average No. of Applicants Annually: 120

Potential for Job Placement: Some potential

Application Process: Can download applications from Web site (http://www.crowcanyon.org) , or can call or write for applications.

Deadline: Early March

Contact: Internship Coordinator

Frontier Nursing Service

P.O. Box 31
Wendover, KY 41775
Phone: (606) 672-2317

Position: Health Care/Education Intern

Department: N/A

No. of Positions Offered Annually: 16

Description: Couriers (interns) shadow and assist doctors, nurses, midwives, and other health care practicioners in our 40 bed hospital or rural clinics. There are opportunity to take patient vitals, view surgery, serve as patient advocate. Opportunities are also available in health education, teaching assistants, or adult literacy. Couriers are also to deliver supplies on behalf of FNS.

Qualifications: Must be 18 years old and have a vehicle. Should be independent, a self-initiator, and should have a general interest in rural health care.

Salary: Unpaid

Position Dates: 8-12 weeks

Position Location: Wendover, KY

Average No. of Applicants Annually: 80

Potential for Job Placement: N/A

Application Process: Write for application. Completed application must include three letters of reference and a physical form.

Deadline: Rolling

Contact: Karen Thomisee, Volunteer Coordinator

Lunar and Planetary Institute (LPI)

3600 Bay Area Boulevard
Houston, TX 77058-1113
Phone: (281) 486-2196
Fax: (281) 486-2132

Position: LPI Summer Intern

Department: N/A

No. of Positions Offered Annually: 12

Description: An opportunity to participate actively in lunar and planetary research with scientists at LPI and the NASA Johnson Space Center (JSC). Interns will be assigned a project working with an advisor located at LPI or JSC. Interns will be given a maximum of $1,000 towards travel expenses.

Qualifications: Scientific interest, relevant work or training experience.

Salary: $350 per week

Position Dates: June 9 through August 15

Position Location: Houston, TX

Average No. of Applicants Annually: 140

Potential for Job Placement: N/A

Application Process: Send name, address, phone number at school, permanent address and phone number, school, class, GPA, current semester courses and GPA, date spring semester ends, major field of study, three areas of interest, information regarding relevant work experience

Deadline: February 7

Contact: Cecilia M. Hoelscher

Mote Marine Laboratory

1600 Ken Thompson Parkway
Sarasota, FL 34236
Phone: (941) 388-4441
Fax: (941) 388-4312

Position: Intern

Department: Various

No. of Positions Offered Annually: 70

Description: Internships available in both laboratory research programs and support areas. Research interns may work in the following programs: biomedical, chemical fate and effects, coastal resources, environmental assessment and enhancement, fisheries and aquaculture, marine mammals, sea turtles and shark biology or the Southwest Florida Coastal Research Center. Support interns may work in the education or communications department. Duration of internship 8–16 weeks, with 8 weeks being the minimum duration.

Qualifications: Intern must be currently enrolled or recent graduate of accredited university or college. Computer skills are needed for most programs.

Salary: Unpaid

Position Dates: Fall, Spring and Summer

Position Location: Sarasota, FL

Average No. of Applicants Annually: 150

Potential for Job Placement: Minimal

Application Process: Application to be completed.

Deadline: Rolling

Contact: Andrea Davis

National Aquarium in Baltimore

501 East Pratt Street
Baltimore, MD 21202
Phone: (410) 576-8236

Position: Aquarist Intern

Department: Education Department

No. of Positions Offered Annually: 100

Description: Interns assist in care of aquatic specimens. These duties include tank maintenance and cleaning, diet preparation and feeding, cleaning back-up areas and record keeping. Library research may be required.

Qualifications: Intern must be a junior or senior.

Salary: Unpaid

Position Dates: Fall, January, Spring and Summer

Position Location: Baltimore, MD

Average No. of Applicants Annually: 300

Potential for Job Placement: Varies

Application Process: Application to be completed. Transcript must be sent as well.

Deadline: November 1 for January and Spring; April 1 for Summer and Fall.

Contact: Internship Coordinator (E-mail: intern@aqua.org)

National Aquarium in Baltimore

501 East Pratt Street
Baltimore, MD 21202
Phone: (410) 576-8236

Position: Public Relations Intern

Department: Public Relations

No. of Positions Offered Annually: 100

Description: Interns gain experience in writing, media relations and special events. They will actively participate in writing press releases, escorting television and film crews, assisting in the production of press kits and helping to schedule meetings, news conferences and events. Library research is required.

Qualifications: Must be a junior or senior majoring in a related field.

Salary: Unpaid

Position Dates: Fall, January, Spring, and Summer

Position Location: Baltimore, MD

Average No. of Applicants Annually: 300

Potential for Job Placement: Varies

Application Process: Application to be completed. Transcript must be sent as well.

Deadline: November 1 for January and Spring; April 1 for Summer and Fall

Contact: Internship Coordinator (E-mail: intern@aqua.org)

National Aquarium in Baltimore

501 East Pratt Street
Baltimore, MD 21202
Phone: (410) 576-8236

Position: Horticulture Intern

Department: Horticulture

No. of Positions Offered Annually: 100

Description: Interns assist in the care of plants in the Amazon Rainforest exhibit. Duties include plant maintenance, fertilization and propogation, transplantation, display development and library research.

Qualifications: Undergraduates majoring in a field related to the internship.

Salary: Unpaid

Position Dates: Fall, January, Spring and Summer

Position Location: Baltimore, MD

Average No. of Applicants Annually: 300

Potential for Job Placement: Varies

Application Process: Application to be completed. Transcript must be sent as well.

Deadline: November 1 for January and Spring; April 1 for Summer and Fall

Contact: Internship Coordinator (E-mail: intern@aqua.org)

National Aquarium in Baltimore

501 East Pratt Street
Baltimore, MD 21202
Phone: (410) 576-8236

Position: Herpetology Intern

Department: Herpetology

No. of Positions Offered Annually: 100

Description: Interns assist in caring for reptiles and amphibians in the Amazon Rainforest exhibit. Duties include cleaning exhibit and back-up tanks, distributing diets, observation, record keeping and possible library research.

Qualifications: Undergraduate majoring in field related to the internship.

Salary: Unpaid

Position Dates: Fall, January, Spring and Summer

Position Location: Baltimore, MD

Average No. of Applicants Annually: 300

Potential for Job Placement: Varies

Application Process: Application to be completed. Transcript must be sent as well.

Deadline: November 1 for January and Spring; April 1 for Summer and Fall

Contact: Internship Coordinator (E-mail: intern@aqua.org)

National Aquarium in Baltimore

501 East Pratt Street
Baltimore, MD 21202
Phone: (410) 576-8236

Position: Aviculture Intern

Department: Aviculture

No. of Positions Offered Annually: 100

Description: Interns assist in caring for birds in the Amazon Rainforest exhibit. Duties include cleaning exhibit and back-up areas, diet preparation and distribution, and general maintenance. Record keeping and library research required.

Qualifications: Undergraduate majoring in a related field.

Salary: Unpaid

Position Dates: Fall, January, Spring, and Summer

Position Location: Baltimore, MD

Average No. of Applicants Annually: 300

Potential for Job Placement: Varies

Application Process: Application to be completed. Transcript must be sent as well.

Deadline: November 1 for January and Spring; April 1 for Summer and Fall

Contact: Internship Coordinator (E-mail: intern@aqua.org)

National Aquarium in Baltimore

501 East Pratt Street
Baltimore, MD 21202
Phone: (410) 576-8236

Position: Membership Intern

Department: Membership

No. of Positions Offered Annually: 100

Description: Interns assist with the maintenance and promotion of Aquarium memberships. They will be involved in answering inquiries, processing membership applications, assisting with members' trips and workshops and development of special events.

Qualifications: Undergraduates majoring in related fields.

Salary: Unpaid

Position Dates: Fall, January, Spring, and Summer

Position Location: Baltimore, MD

Average No. of Applicants Annually: 300

Potential for Job Placement: Varies

Application Process: Application to be completed. Transcript must be sent as well.

Deadline: November 1 for January and Spring; April 1 for Summer and Fall

Contact: Internship Coordinator (E-mail: intern@aqua.org)

National Aquarium in Baltimore

501 East Pratt Street
Baltimore, MD 21202
Phone: (410) 576-8236

Position: Publications Intern

Department: Publications

No. of Positions Offered Annually: 100

Description: Interns research and write articles for *Watermarks* (a quarterly publication). They will assist with proofreading and production of brochures, reports, flyers and other printed material.

Qualifications: Must be a junior or senior majoring in a field related to the internship.

Salary: Unpaid

Position Dates: Fall, January, Spring and Summer

Position Location: Baltimore, MD

Average No. of Applicants Annually: 300

Potential for Job Placement: Varies

Application Process: Application to be completed. Transcript must be sent as well.

Deadline: November 1 for January and Spring; April 1 for Summer and Fall

Contact: Internship Coordinator (E-mail: intern@aqua.org)

National Aquarium in Baltimore

501 East Pratt Street
Baltimore, MD 21202
Phone: (410) 576-8236

Position: MIS Internship

Department: MIS

No. of Positions Offered Annually: 100

Description: Interns will work with staff to perform system backup and maintenance functions, install PC hardware and software and update user and technical documentation.

Qualifications: Must be a junior or senior majoring in a related field with some experience.

Salary: Unpaid

Position Dates: Fall, January, Spring and Summer

Position Location: Baltimore, MD

Average No. of Applicants Annually: 300

Potential for Job Placement: Varies

Application Process: Application to be completed. Transcript must be sent as well.

Deadline: November 1 for January and Spring; April 1 for Summer and Fall

Contact: Internship Coordinator (E-mail: intern@aqua.org)

National Aquarium in Baltimore

501 East Pratt Street
Baltimore, MD 21202
Phone: (410) 576-8236

Position: Marketing Intern

Department: Marketing and Group Sales

No. of Positions Offered Annually: 100

Description: Interns will assist with the planning and implementation of Aquarium special events and promotions. Experience will be gained in analyzing information gained through zip coding visitors, market research, coupon redemption and visitor admissions. Research is required.

Qualifications: Undergraduate majoring in a related field.

Salary: Unpaid

Position Dates: Fall, January, Spring and Summer

Position Location: Baltimore, MD

Average No. of Applicants Annually: 300

Potential for Job Placement: Varies

Application Process: Application to be completed. Transcript must be sent as well. Application to be completed. Transcript must be sent as well.

Deadline: November 1 for January and Spring; April 1 for Summer and Fall

Contact: Internship Coordinator (E-mail: intern@aqua.org)

National Aquarium in Baltimore

501 East Pratt Street
Baltimore, MD 21202
Phone: (410) 576-8236

Position: Marine Education Intern

Department: Marine Education

No. of Positions Offered Annually: 100

Description: Interns will assist in the creation, revision, and instruction of school group programs, which include hands-on classroom and auditorium style, along with behind the scenes tours. Summer interns actively participate in members' programs, summer camps and visitor programs. A project may be completed.

Qualifications: Undergraduate majoring in a field related to the internship.

Salary: Unpaid

Position Dates: Fall, January, Spring and Summer

Position Location: Baltimore, MD

Average No. of Applicants Annually: 300

Potential for Job Placement: Varies

Application Process: Application to be completed. Transcript must be sent as well.

Deadline: November 1 for January and Spring; April 1 for Summer and Fall

Contact: Internship Coordinator (E-mail: intern@aqua.org)

National Aquarium in Baltimore

501 East Pratt Street
Baltimore, MD 21202
Phone: (410) 576-8236

Position: Mammalogy Intern

Department: Mammology

No. of Positions Offered Annually: 100

Description: Interns will assist in the daily care and maintenance of the marine mammals. Duties include diet preparation, cleaning and maintainence of exhibit and back-up areas, behavioral observation and record keeping.

Qualifications: Intern must be a junior or senior majoring in a field related to the internship. Large-animal experience is highly desirable.

Salary: Unpaid

Position Dates: Fall, January, Spring and Summer

Position Location: Baltimore, MD

Average No. of Applicants Annually: 300

Potential for Job Placement: Varies

Application Process: Application to be completed. Transcript must be sent as well.

Deadline: November 1 for January and Spring; April 1 for Summer and Fall

Contact: Internship Coordinator (E-mail: intern@aqua.org)

National Aquarium in Baltimore

501 East Pratt Street
Baltimore, MD 21202
Phone: (401) 576-8236

Position: Aquaculture Intern

Department: Education Department

No. of Positions Offered Annually: 100

Description: Intern will assist with husbandry staff in the breeding and maintenance of salt water fishes. These duties include tank maintenance and cleaning, diet preparation and feeding, cleaning back-up areas and record keeping. Library research may be required.

Qualifications: Intern must be a junior or senior majoring in a field related to the internship.

Salary: Unpaid

Position Dates: Fall, January, Spring and Summer

Position Location: Baltimore, MD

Average No. of Applicants Annually: 300

Potential for Job Placement: Varies

Application Process: Application to be completed. Transcript must be sent as well.

Deadline: November 1 for January and Spring; April 1 for Summer and Fall.

Contact: Internship Coordinator (E-mail: intern@aqua.org)

National Aquarium in Baltimore

501 East Pratt Street
Baltimore, MD 21202
Phone: (410) 576-8236

Position: Water Quality and Chemistry Intern

Department: Education Department

No. of Positions Offered Annually: 100

Description: Intern will assist in routine quality testing for all exhibit and backup tanks. Duties will include record keeping, use of standard lab equipment such as the Hach spectrophotometer and assisting husbandry staff in troubleshooting water quality problems. A project is required.

Qualifications: Intern must be a junior or senior majoring in a field related to the internship.

Salary: Unpaid

Position Dates: Fall, January, Spring and Summer

Position Location: Baltimore, MD

Average No. of Applicants Annually: 300

Potential for Job Placement: Varies

Application Process: Application to be completed. Transcript must be sent as well.

Deadline: November 1 for January and Spring; April 1 for Summer and Fall.

Contact: Internship Coordinator (E-mail: intern@aqua.org)

National Aquarium in Baltimore

501 East Pratt Street
Baltimore, MD 21202
Phone: (410) 576-8236

Position: Development Intern

Department: Development

No. of Positions Offered Annually: 100

Description: Interns will gather
biographical and financial information on
individuals, corporations and foundations
who are current or potential donors to the
Aquarium. The intern will compile and
organize this information to produce usable
profiles.

Qualifications: Must be a junior or senior
majoring in a related field.

Salary: Unpaid

Position Dates: Fall, January, Spring and
Summer

Position Location: Baltimore, MD

Average No. of Applicants Annually:
300

Potential for Job Placement: Varies

Application Process: Application to be
completed. Transcript must be sent as well.

Deadline: November 1 for January and
Spring; April 1 for Summer and Fall

Contact: Internship Coordinator (E-mail:
intern@aqua.org)

New York Hospital, Cornell Medical Center, Westchester Division

21 Bloomingdale Road
White Plains, NY 10605
Phone: (914) 997-5780
Fax: (914) 997-5958

Position: Summer Pre-Career Program

Department: N/A

No. of Positions Offered Annually: 50

Description: The program combines
structured, staff supervised clinical and
administrative assignments with
professionally conducted seminars and
lectures giving students an opportunity to
explore the many disciplines of a university-
based psychiatric hospital.

Qualifications: Psychology or related
majors and premed students encouraged to
apply.

Salary: Unpaid

Position Dates: Summer

Position Location: White Plains, NY

Average No. of Applicants Annually:
200

Potential for Job Placement: N/A

Application Process: Call or write for an
application. Interview required.

Deadline: April 1

Contact: Diane A. Clark, Director of
Volunteer Services

North Carolina Botanical Garden

3375 Totten Center
Chapel Hill, NC 27599-3375
Phone: (919) 962-0522
Fax: (919) 962-3531

Position: Intern Gardener

Department: N/A

No. of Positions Offered Annually: 2

Description: Work experience with the maintenance of native southeastern U.S. plants as well as native exotic species in the Plant Families Garden, Hubbard Herb Garden and Coker Arboretum.

Qualifications: Preference given to applicants enrolled in or a recent graduate of a program in horticulture, botany, forestry, environmental management or related field, or possessing substantial work experience in one of these areas.

Salary: $7.14/hour

Position Dates: March 20 – October 31

Position Location: Chapel Hill, NC

Average No. of Applicants Annually: 40

Potential for Job Placement: Minimal

Application Process: Application to be completed.

Deadline: February 21

Contact: James L. Ward

NYU Medical Center

400 East 34th Street, Room RR812
New York, NY 10016

Position: Health Career Opportunity Program (HCOP)

Department: Rusk Instituute of Rehabilitation Medicine

No. of Positions Offered Annually: 125

Description: HCOP offers students the opportunity to observe in clinical settings the variety of rehabilitation careers found in a large rehabilitation hospital.

Qualifications: 17 years old or older. Enrolled in a college or university.

Salary: Unpaid

Position Dates: Four weeks in June, July and August

Position Location: New York, NY

Average No. of Applicants Annually: 2,000+

Potential for Job Placement: N/A

Application Process: Must write for an application and information packet.

Deadline: March 1

Contact: Glenn Goldfinger, Director HCOP

Student Conservation Association

P.O. Box 550
Charlestown, NH 03603
Phone: (603) 543-1700
Fax: (603) 543-1828

Position: Conservation Associate

Department: Resource Assistant Program

No. of Positions Offered Annually: 50

Description: Conservation associates serve in six-, nine- or twelve-month positions and assist with a full range of natural/cultural resource management and conservation-related tasks in both field and office settings. Tasks include: archaeological surveys, biological research, historical and cultural resource studies, environmental education, art and graphic design, landscape architecture, prescribed burning and fuels management, recreation management, trail work and forest management. Conservation associates are provided with travel and housing grants, medical insurance, on-the-job transportation and a $160/week subsistence allowance.

Qualifications: Conservation associates must be at least 18 years old. Most conservation associates have completed their undergraduate education and some of them have graduate degrees.

Salary: $160/week (stipend)

Position Dates: Fall, Spring and Summer

Position Location: Nationwide

Average No. of Applicants Annually: N/A

Potential for Job Placement: Possible

Application Process: Application to be completed.

Deadline: Rolling

Contact: Mel Tuck
(E-mail: mel@sca-inc.org)

Student Conservation Association

P.O. Box 550
Charlestown, NH 03603
Phone: (603) 543-1700
Fax: (603) 543-1828

Position: Resource Assistant

Department: Resource Assistant Program

No. of Positions Offered Annually: 1200

Description: Expense-paid internship which allows participants to live and work side by side with conservation and natural resource professionals. Resource assistants serve as volunteer seasonal staff for public and private natural resource management agencies throughout the United States and Canada. Interns receive funds to cover their travel expenses, free housing, a subsistence allowance to help offset food expenses and a uniform allowance when authorized by the cooperating agency.

Qualifications: Resource assistants must be at least 18 years old. Most are college students exploring careers in conservation, and many earn academeic credit for their work experience.

Salary: $160/week (stipend)

Position Dates: Fall and Summer

Position Location: Canada; nationwide

Average No. of Applicants Annually: N/A

Potential for Job Placement: Possible

Application Process: Application to be completed.

Deadline: March 1 for Fall; June 1 for Summer.

Contact: Mel Tuck
(E-mail: mel@sca-inc.org)

Performing Arts

Kate Merkel-Hess

An internship working in performing arts or arts management will give you an opportunity to comb the phone files of prestigious arts institutions—but don't expect to get paid for it.

Simply put, arts organizations in the United States (and around the world for that matter) are generally underfunded and overworked. As a result, these institutions rely heavily on intern and volunteer work and so are a rich source of internships. And, although the theater or box office or dance company you want to work for may need someone to answer phones for an hour a day, often the organization also needs help building sets or designing an advertising campaign. Interns in the arts can be assigned real jobs with real responsibilities, instead of spending their days sending faxes, filing correspondence, and fetching coffee. Your responsibilities might not put you in the limelight, but your exposure to other facets of the industry could be invaluable.

Employers in the arts say they expect interns to be well rounded and hard working. Prima donnas are rare. If you are interested in performance, you might aim for a small company. Who knows? The costume making or piano accompaniment you do now may be your ticket to a full-time, paying job in the future.

Be Devoted and Be Ready to Work Hard

Because organizations are looking for a mélange of skills in their interns, applying for an internship in the field of fine arts is significantly different from faxing off a résumé to a firm on Wall Street or sending clippings to a newspaper. Instead of expecting a résumé of previous internships and a lot of classwork in a specific area, arts employers want you to have a demonstrated interest in "the arts" in general—be it visual, written, or performance—and they look at potential interns in their entirety: personality, experience, work ethic, grades, ability to work with others, and outside interests, to name a few. They anticipate working closely (and sometimes living) with you for two or three months, often under high-pressure conditions, so all these traits become vital.

The application process for an arts internship varies depending on the field in which you're interested. A performance internship is generally applied for first with a résumé and cover letter, and then by audition. Internships in arts management have the most mainstream application process; most require a résumé, cover letter, letters of recommendation and, in the final stages, an interview. Students who have been through the process recommend that you visit the places to which you are applying, if at all possible. Not only does it help to meet the people you would be working for, but if you visit before you send in your application, you may have a better idea what kind of person the organization is seeking.

In general, internship coordinators say they expect interested students to have done some background research. Students should not only know what they want to gain from an internship, but they should know enough about the organization to which they are applying to tell an interviewer why this *specific* organization can provide that experience. "People in the arts work very hard for very little money and it behooves people who want something from them—like an internship—to know something about their art or their work," one national intern coordinator says.

Employers also expect you to bring a certain amount of experience to the table. Jimmy Vaughn, executive director of the South West Theatre Conference, emphasizes that, in addition to basic preparation like good grades and clear objectives, students should read widely and volunteer in a variety of arts organizations in high school and college—even if it's only for a few hours a week.

"Lots of times, the theaters prefer that students don't have experience so they don't have to untrain bad training," Vaughn says. "But it's very important that students get involved in art and theater. No matter what specific field you do, you have to appreciate all the arts."

Both internship coordinators and students say larger organizations have the most prestigious and beneficial internship opportunities in arts management, and of these institutions, not-for-profit theaters and companies offer the most extensive possibilities. These entities have a greater need for staff support than commercial ones do and, experienced students say, are more in tune with the educational model of traditional internships. Since these organizations are likely to be understaffed, student interns have a good chance of getting involved in the nitty-gritty of day-to-day work.

Don't Forget the Perks and the Contacts

Perks in performing arts work range from free concert tickets to equity points (which are necessary for actors to qualify for a performing union) to room and/or board. A student who worked in the public relations department for a government arts office was given tickets to the ballet; a performer in a small theater troupe was invited to attend an important arts gala. Not only will an arts internship give you an opportunity to break into the business, former interns say it will also open your eyes to the diversity and vitality of the national and regional arts scenes.

Students who say their internships were successful—and who were further convinced by their internships to pursue a career in the arts—say the biggest perk may be simply the exposure to the arts. A student who interned at the Royal Opera House in London says that, although she wants to move into voice performance, to her surprise she found that "public relations would not be a bad second choice if performance doesn't work out."

Employers in the arts are generally accommodating and eager to help. In the face of decreasing federal funding and less support from the private sector, arts organizations can be especially grateful to interns for the affordable and unjaded assistance they bring. As one intern says, "I didn't feel like I was furthering my own career. That wasn't my purpose. . . . I was contributing to the field."

The Arts Need You

Although it may not carry much prestige, I would strongly encourage looking into unpaid work with nonprofit, grassroots organizations, specifically those groups that sincerely need manpower because of the severe budgetary restraints under which they operate. More specifically, to those with interests in the arts, I'd like to advocate working for local arts organizations, many of which are reeling from recent federal funding cuts. I've worked for a few such organizations and have found the experiences to be enlightening, sobering, and inspiring. Many of these small offices and smaller staffs manage impressive undertakings in arts advocacy, providing services to artists, facilitating the display of art, aiding in the protest and passing of legislation, etcetera. It's a look behind the scenes of the American art world without any of the glamour, but with all sincerity and ingenuity.

—Stanford student who worked for the Chicago Artists' Coalition (CAC) and the San Francisco Cinematheque

And, as students readily admit, if you are proactive during your internship, you will accumulate a long list of contacts. Boston University sophomore Jennifer Mintzer did just that during her performance internship for Maine State Theatre. The small size of the company meant that Mintzer not only rehearsed every day, but also helped take down sets and do changeovers. By the end of the summer, Mintzer said, many fellow interns were tired and frustrated with the work. Mintzer, on the other hand, sat in on other rehearsals over her long lunches and made attempts to meet as many of the New York theater people who were around. "I picked everyone's brains and scheduled exit interviews," she says. "I talked to basically everyone I could." Her connections and her persistence were helpful in her search for her next internship.

University of Michigan graduate and former National Endowment for the Arts intern Nell Andrew also made an effort to maximize her opportunities in the arts. "You definitely need to keep good ties with the people you work for," she says. "Send notes to keep updated—you will need their recommendations later."

Former interns recommend boldness when it comes to making connections. Keep in contact with employers, ask for the use of their phone files, and schedule exit interviews. It all boils down to one thing: garner the advice and contacts of people already steeped in the industry. Nell Andrew, who has spent several years working for various national arts organizations, notes, "Often arts interns are the first to be hired when jobs open up."

Find Another Way to Support Yourself

But even with the perks and contacts arts internships offer, interns should not expect to make much money, if any. Across the board in the arts (but especially in the nonprofits) organizations have few funds with which to pay interns. Some students work at their internships part time—10 to 20 hours a week—and supplement their income waiting tables or doing part-time secretarial work. Others are able to scrape by with the room-and-board employers sometimes offer. People working in the arts really want to be there and are willing to accept $30 a week (or less) stipends to gain experience and contacts.

"These companies are operating on a shoestring and are willing to engage in what is, in fact, an educational internship," Corey Boniface, manager of operations at the New England Theatre Conference says. "I think everyone understands what the bargain is—you are getting experience while providing entry-level labor."

How to Find Internships in the Performing Arts

There are no hard-and-fast rules when it comes to searching for an internship. The largest, most prestigious organizations may have a cap on the number of interns they accept and the kinds of jobs these interns will perform. Mid-sized and smaller companies are often just as strapped for help but simply don't have the support staff to organize, publicize, and conduct formal internships. A self-directed, focused student might be able to design his or her own program of work in one of these organizations, and the small size of the organization might enable him or her to finish the work and see its immediate impact. Although such self-designed work might not be your idea of a dream job, the initiative you show might help you land a more prestigious or influential internship later.

For vocal and dramatic performers, as well as techies, there is an abundance of regional organizations that can help make the process of searching for an internship much easier. Although not united under any national organization, this loose network of regional auditions is planned by entities such as the New England Theatre Conference and the South Western Theatre Conference. These organizations create a talent-hiring marketplace, usually a weekend-long stream of auditions attended by upwards of 50 different producers. Similar conferences, arranged more like job fairs, are organized for set designers, lighting crews, and costume designers. Deadlines vary, but it is best to begin looking as soon as October or November, since many of the conferences require submission of a résumé by December or January. After their five-minute shot at a monologue or voice piece (students who have attended say you should prepare for this part of the audition as you would any other), students wait for callbacks from the producers.

But attendance at one of these conferences doesn't guarantee an internship. Internships in the arts, especially in performances areas, are very competitive. One Boston University student, a major in vocal performance, discovered this truth the hard way. "I made the mistake of not being very ambitious and thinking things would come to me . . . and they didn't," she says. "You can't send in enough applications. . . . You're going to make mistakes the first couple of times you do it. After you send in five or six applications or talk to five or six theaters, you'll get a better idea of what they want."

Unlike the theater industry, which has hundreds of regional houses scattered around the country, all eager to take on unpaid help in the chorus or backstage, the few dance companies in the United States rarely offer internships and almost never allow interns the chance to dance. Each dancer is expected to be professional, polished, and noticeable on stage. There are prestigious internships at publications such as *Dance* magazine and the *Village Voice* for students interested in writing about dance, and some companies do offer arts management internships, but these also are rare. Most opportunities available in dance are summer workshops with companies and schools. Generally these programs charge tuition, though some offer scholarships to students who need them.

Is the Theater Calling You?

The following directories published by American Theatre Works are good resources for finding theater internships.

• *Summer Theatre Directory:* Issued every December; lists summer internships and apprenticeships; about 385 listings.

• *Regional Theatre Directory:* Issued every May; lists semester and year-long internships for undergraduates taking a semester off or for recent graduates; about 430 listings.

Each book is $16.95 and both are sold in performing arts bookstores. They can also be ordered by calling (802) 867-2223, faxing (802) 867-0144, or by E-mailing theatre@sover.net. For more information, check out the American Theatre Works Web site at http://www.genghis.com//theatre.htm.

Actors Theatre of Louisville

316 West Main Street
Louisville, KY 40202
Phone: (502) 584-1265

Position: Front of House Intern

Department: Apprentice/Intern Office

No. of Positions Offered Annually: 1

Description: Intern will work closely with audience services coordinator. Intern will learn house management skills as well as what goes on in the audience services coordinator position. Intern will be assigned various independent projects relating to house management, audience relations and volunteer coordinating.

Qualifications: Applicant should have strong communication, organizational and people management sklls. Experience in customer service is expected.

Salary: Unpaid

Position Dates: Fall, Spring, Summer and Full Year

Position Location: Louisville, KY

Average No. of Applicants Annually: N/A

Potential for Job Placement: N/A

Application Process: Application to be completed.

Deadline: April 15

Contact: Carol Baker

Actors Theatre of Louisville

316 West Main Street
Louisville, KY 40202
Phone: (502) 584-1265

Position: Stage Management Intern

Department: Apprentice/Intern Office

No. of Positions Offered Annually: 4

Description: Interns work side by side with Equity stage managers, directors and actors, and are involved in the entire rehearsal and performance process for ATL's mainstage productions. In addition, interns will have opportunities to work with visiting companies and directors. The interns will also be involved with all of the apprentice/intern performances and each will be the production stage manager for at least one show. Duties include keeping track of props, pre- and post-show duties, running mainstage productions and assisting at rehearsals.

Qualifications: Applicant should have prior management experience and willingness to work long hours under pressure. An outgoing, assertive personality is a plus.

Salary: Unpaid

Position Dates: Fall, Spring, Summer and Full Year

Position Location: Louisville, KY

Average No. of Applicants Annually: N/A

Potential for Job Placement: N/A

Application Process: Application to be completed.

Deadline: April 15

Contact: Deb Acquavella

Actors Theatre of Louisville

316 West Main Street
Louisville, KY 4202
Phone: (502) 584-1265

Position: Ticket Sales Intern

Department: Apprentice/Intern Office

No. of Positions Offered Annually: 1

Description: Intern works closely with Ticket Sales Director in a 20-station computerized Ticket Sales Department. Intern will learn about ticket sales, event and performance setup, subscription managment, sales reports and analysis, personnel management and group sales. Intern will be assigned various independent projects relating to Ticket Sales and some general clerical duties.

Qualifications: Applicant should have strong organizational, communication and customer service skills and must be able to work approximately 25 hours per week.

Salary: Unpaid

Position Dates: Fall, Spring, Summer and Full Year

Position Location: Louisville, KY

Average No. of Applicants Annually: N/A

Potential for Job Placement: N/A

Application Process: Application to be completed.

Deadline: April 15

Contact: Brian Smith

Actors Theatre of Louisville

316 West Main Street
Louisville, KY 40202
Phone: (502) 584-1265

Position: Sound Intern

Department: Apprentice/Intern Office

No. of Positions Offered Annually: 2

Description: Interns receive experience and training by working with Sound Department staff in the support and creation of designs for all ATL productions. Responsibilities include running performances as Sound Board Operators, assisting the Sound Engineer, Assistant Designers and Designing Apprentices. While all interns will perform some duties in each of these areas, assignments are made based upon each intern's specific interests and goals. There are regular lectures and discussions to explore certain aspects of the design process, to provide interns with a solid technical knowledge of the modern tools of sound design and to review and critique ongoing production work.

Qualifications: Applicant should be interested in sound design or engineering and should have the ability to work on several materials simultaneously.

Salary: Unpaid

Position Dates: Fall, Spring, Summer and Full Year

Position Location: Louisville, KY

Average No. of Applicants Annually: N/A

Potential for Job Placement: N/A

Application Process: Application to be completed.

Deadline: April 15

Contact: Martin Desjardin

Actors Theatre of Louisville

316 Main Street
Louisville, KY 40202
Phone: (502) 584-1265

Position: Literary Intern

Department: Apprentice/Intern Office

No. of Positions Offered Annually: 2

Description: Program is designed to train interns in the fields of literary managment and dramaturgy. Interns work closely with the literary staff in the New Play Program, Classics in Context, Flying Solo Festival, and regular season productions. The New Play Program includes the National Ten-Minute Play Contest and the annual Humana Festival of New American Plays. Interns help screen plays, assist with production dramaturgy and participate in the administration of the contest and playwriting shops. For the Classics in Context Festivals, interns assist with research on classical scripts as well as lectures, films and exhibits. Interns work on the Flying Solo Festival by soliciting submissions, previewing performers and assisting in performer residencies. For regular productions and showcase productions of original ten-minute plays, interns work as dramaturgs, providing research and critical assistance. Work is varied and includes: attending rehearsals, assisting with playwright residencies, library research, reading new plays, writing articles for ATL publications and providing administrative support for various literary projects.

Qualifications: Applicant should be a theater administration, theater or English major. Playwrights welcome to apply.

Salary: Unpaid

Position Dates: Fall, Spring, Summer, Full Year

Position Location: Louisville, KY

Average No. of Applicants Annually: N/A

Potential for Job Placement: N/A

Application Process: Send résumé, cover letter, two letters of recommendation and a five- to ten-page critical writing sample.

Deadline: April 15

Contact: Liz Engelman

Actors Theatre of Louisville

316 West Main Street
Louisville, KY 40202
Phone: (502) 584-1265

Position: Lighting Intern

Department: Apprentice/Intern Office

No. of Positions Offered Annually: 2

Description: Interns are actively involved with the mounting and running of approximately 30 productions in three spaces. In addition to the production work, interns are encouraged to develop drafting, paper work and computer skills directly associated with the regularly scheduled productions. While working directly with the Resident Lighting Designer, it is the intention of the Lighting Department to provide the intern with skills, knowledge and projects to foster artistic growth.

Qualifications: N/A

Salary: Unpaid

Position Dates: Fall, Spring, Summer and Full Year

Position Location: Louisville, KY

Average No. of Applicants Annually:

Potential for Job Placement: N/A

Application Process: Application to be completed.

Deadline: April 15

Contact: Brian Scott

Actors Theatre of Louisville

316 West Main Street
Louisville, KY 40202
Phone: (502) 584-1265
Fax:

Position: Scenic Design Intern

Department: Apprentice/Intern Office

No. of Positions Offered Annually: 1

Description: Internship provides intern with the knowledge and experience required to continue professional growth as a theater artisan. Scenic design intern will be primarily involved in design research, model building and scene painting.

Qualifications: Applicant should have a strong interst and some experience in design, painting and model building. The ability to move more than one project along at a time is necessary.

Salary: Unpaid

Position Dates: Fall, Spring, Summer and Full Year

Position Location: Louisville, KY

Average No. of Applicants Annually: N/A

Potential for Job Placement: N/A

Application Process: Application to be completed.

Deadline: April 15

Contact: Paul Owen/Frazier Marsh

Actors Theatre of Louisville

316 West Main Street
Louisville, KY 40202
Phone: (502) 584-1265

Position: Apprentice/Intern Office Intern

Department: Apprentice/Intern Office

No. of Positions Offered Annually: 1

Description: Intern will assist Apprentice/Intern Directors in the day-to-day operations of the company. Responsibilities will include scheduling, correspondence, travel arrangements, class work, archival correspondence and alumni tracking. Intern will have the opportunity to observe classes, rehearsals, and performances, participate in seminars offered throughout the year and work in other areas of the theater on an as-needed basis.

Qualifications: Intern should be organized, self-motivated and able to work independently and complete tasks on time. Computer skills helpful.

Salary: Unpaid

Position Dates: Fall, Spring, Summer and Full Year

Position Location: Louisville, KY

Average No. of Applicants Annually: N/A

Potential for Job Placement: N/A

Application Process: Application to be completed.

Deadline: April 15

Contact: Jennifer Hubbard/Shannon Mayers

Actors Theatre of Louisville

316 Main Street
Louisville, KY 40202
Phone: (502) 584-1265

Position: Development Intern

Department: Apprentice/Intern Office

No. of Positions Offered Annually: 1

Description: Intern will gain experience in the research, solicitation and acknowledgement of a diverse community of donors, from individual mail contributions to major corporate sponsorships.

Qualifications: Successful applicants will exhibit a strong sense of initiative and self-motivation and have excellent writing and communication skills, a basic familiarity with computers and previous experience.

Salary: Unpaid

Position Dates: Academic Year

Position Location: Louisville, KY

Average No. of Applicants Annually: N/A

Potential for Job Placement: N/A

Application Process: Application to be completed.

Deadline: April 15

Contact: Emily Gnadinger

Actors Theatre of Louisville

316 West Main Street
Louisville, KY 40202
Phone: (502) 584-1265

Position: Public Relations/Marketing Intern

Department: Apprentice/Intern Office

No. of Positions Offered Annually: 2

Description: Internship offers extensive hands-on experience and provides applicant with excellent opportunity to gain solid experience in working with regional, national and international media. Interns gain valuable experience in creating special promotions, handling public information, designing display ads and information/sales material through computer desktop publishing, writing press releases, promotional pieces and program copy, coordinating photo calls and assisting with the theatre's annual subscription campaign.

Qualifications: Applicant should possess excellent communication and organizational skills and the ability to handle multiple priorities and meet deadlines.

Salary: Unpaid

Position Dates: One year

Position Location: Louisville, KY

Average No. of Applicants Annually: N/A

Potential for Job Placement: N/A

Application Process: Application to be completed.

Deadline: April 15

Contact: James Seacat

Actors Theatre of Louisville

316 West Main Street
Louisville, KY 40202
Phone: (502) 584-1265

Position: Casting and Production Managment Intern

Department: Apprentice/Intern Office

No. of Positions Offered Annually: 1

Description: Intern will schedule and organize auditions ATL for pre-professionals from across the country, local auditions for adults, teens and children, as well as arrange specific local casting calls and coordinate the Apprentice Company auditions for mainstage productions. Day-to-day clerical duties include responding to phone and mail inquiries, maintaining files, responding to résumés, checking references and researching information.

Qualifications: Applicants should have strong interpersonal communication skills, a demonstrated ability to work well with a variety of people in a fast-paced situation, excellent writing skills, a working knowledge of computers, good organizational skills and an excellent sense of humor.

Salary: Unpaid

Position Dates: Full year

Position Location: Louisville, KY

Average No. of Applicants Annually: N/A

Potential for Job Placement: N/A

Application Process: Application to be completed.

Deadline: April 15

Contact: Zan Sawyer-Daily

Actors Theatre of Louisville

316 West Main Street
Louisville, KY 40202
Phone: (502) 584-1265

Position: Costumes Intern

Department: Apprentice/Intern Office

No. of Positions Offered Annually: 2

Description: Internships offered in four areas: Assistant to the Designer, Technical Costume, Wardrobe, and Wigs. Each intern is treated as a member of the staff and works closely with seasoned professionals.

Qualifications: Applicant should have good interpersonal and organizational skills and experience within his/her area of focus.

Salary: Unpaid

Position Dates: Fall, Spring, Summer and Full Year

Position Location: Louisville, KY

Average No. of Applicants Annually: N/A

Potential for Job Placement: N/A

Application Process: Application to be completed.

Deadline: April 15

Contact: Delmar Rineheart

Actors Theatre of Louisville

316 West Main Street
Louisville, KY 40202
Phone: (502) 584-1265

Position: Festival Managment Intern

Department: Apprentice/Intern Office

No. of Positions Offered Annually: 1

Description: Intern will provide assistance in the following areas for the Humana Festival of New American Plays and the Classics in Context Festival: events and project coordination, travel and lodging for national and international guests, volunteer coordination, production of numerous publications and flyers and overall coordination of events required for each specific festival.

Qualifications: Applicant should have excellent organizational skills and an ability to deal with many personalities. A courteous attitude when dealing with people is critical. Ability to work with computers is also essential.

Salary: Unpaid

Position Dates: One year

Position Location: Louisville, KY

Average No. of Applicants Annually: N/A

Potential for Job Placement: N/A

Application Process: Application to be completed.

Deadline: April 15

Contact: Joel A. Smith

Actors Theatre of Louisville

316 West Main Street
Louisville, KY 40202
Phone: (502) 584-1265

Position: Arts Administration Intern

Department: Apprentice/Intern Office

No. of Positions Offered Annually: 1

Description: Intern will work with ATL's associate director as well as on projects with other department heads to gain an overview of operations. Areas of experience will include: mentorship in general arts administration, time management skills and scheduling, staff supervisory mentorship, basic public relations and marketing exposure, introduction to international tour management, working with volunteers, arts advocacy introduction, and intensive work with Festival Management.

Qualifications: Applicant should have a good sense of humor, passion for theater, and some basic computer skills.

Salary: Unpaid

Position Dates: One year

Position Location: Louisville, KY

Average No. of Applicants Annually: N/A

Potential for Job Placement: N/A

Application Process: Application to be completed.

Deadline: April 15

Contact: Marilee Herbert-Slater

Actors Theatre of Louisville

316 West Main Street
Louisville, KY 40202
Phone: (502) 584-1265

Position: Company and Volunteer Management

Department: Apprentice/Intern Office

No. of Positions Offered Annually: 1

Description: In addition to working with the year-round ATL staff, the intern will regularly interact with two dyamic volunteer organizations and all of the guest actors and other artists joining ATL for residencies through the season. Internship allows for hands-on facilitation of all residency during contracted employment as well as assistance with day-to-day company management clerical and administrative duties. Intern will also provide constant communication and personal contact with both volunteer support groups, managing multiple projects and deadlines.

Qualifications: Applicant should have strong interpersonal communication skills, desire to work with a variety of personalities, excellent organizational skills, and a well-developed sense of humor.

Salary: Unpaid

Position Dates: One year

Position Location: Louisville, KY

Average No. of Applicants Annually: N/A

Potential for Job Placement: N/A

Application Process: Application to be completed.

Deadline: April 15

Contact: Deb Farmer

Actors Theatre of Louisville

316 West Main Street
Louisville, KY 40202
Phone: (502) 584-1265

Position: Directing Intern

Department: Apprentice/Intern Office

No. of Positions Offered Annually: 2

Description: Directing interns will attend and participate in apprentice acting classes, observe and assist the assistant to the producing director with local casting calls, attend and observe rehearsals for professional company productions, act as assistant to the director on three professional company productions during the season, attend all readings of new plays and subsequent discussions as the Humana Festival of New American Plays is selected, attend specific meetings with the Literary Office staff in order to be prepared to act as an assistant dramaturg on assigned productions in the Humana Festival of New American Plays, attend all production meetings scheduled with directors and their design/technical staff, meet weekly to discuss directing or other issues central to the internship and work on specifically assigned projects.

Qualifications: N/A

Salary: Unpaid

Position Dates: Fall, Spring, Summer and Full Year

Position Location: Louisville, KY

Average No. of Applicants Annually: N/A

Potential for Job Placement: N/A

Application Process: Send résumé, cover letter and two letters of recommendation. An interview will be required.

Deadline: April 15

Contact: Zan Sawyer

American Conservatory Theater

30 Grant Avenue, 6th Floor
San Francisco, CA 94108
Phone: (415) 834-3200

Position: Properties Intern

Department: N/A

No. of Positions Offered Annually: 1

Description: Properties intern works closely with A.C.T. properties staff in the construction and fabrication of properties for the stage. Participation includes meetings with the properties master, directors, stage managers and designers as the working plots for new productions are developed. Interns learn not only the methods and skills necessary to produce properties from time periods, but also learn the overview necessary for the operations and maintenace of properties for the performance.

Qualifications: Art, sculpting, crafts and theater experience highly recommended.

Salary: $165/week

Position Dates: One year

Position Location: San Francisco, CA

Average No. of Applicants Annually: N/A

Potential for Job Placement: Possible

Application Process: Application to be completed.

Deadline: April 15

Contact: Susan West

American Conservatory Theater

30 Grant Avenue, 6th Floor
San Francisco, CA 94108
Phone: (415) 834-3200

Position: Technical Design Intern

Department: N/A

No. of Positions Offered Annually: 1

Description: Interns work under the direction of the design associate and technical supervisor to learn design techniques and construction methods developed by the A.C.T. staff. Drafting and model building are the main areas of concentration in this program. Maintenance of research files provides further exposure to the design process. Interns will have the opportunity to observe A.C.T.'s designers, scenic artists and technicians at work.

Qualifications: N/A

Salary: $165/week

Position Dates: Academic year (September through May)

Position Location: San Francisco, CA

Average No. of Applicants Annually: N/A

Potential for Job Placement: Possible

Application Process: Application to be completed.

Deadline: April 15

Contact: Susan West

American Conservatory Theater

30 Grant Avenue, 6th Floor
San Francisco, CA 94108
Phone: (415) 834-3200

Position: Stage Management Intern

Department: N/A

No. of Positions Offered Annually: 3

Description: Program provides a training
ground for highly motivated persons seeking
exposure and hands-on management
experience in a professional theater. Interns
become integral members of the stage
management team by working alonside
A.C.T. stage management staff. Interns are
involved in development and production of
the shows to which they are assigned.
Internship is a full-time commitment and
stipends will be available.

Qualifications: Applicant must
demonstrate high energy and initiative and
maintain a sensitivity to the demands and
complexities of the rehearsal process.
Previous stage management is required and
a background in acting and technical
theater is helpful.

Salary: $165/week

Position Dates: Academic year (August
through June)

Position Location: San Francisco, CA

Average No. of Applicants Annually: N/A

Potential for Job Placement: Possible

Application Process: Application to be
completed.

Deadline: April 15

Contact: Susan West

American Conservatory Theater

30 Grant Avenue, 6th Floor
San Francisco, CA 94108
Phone: (415) 834-3200

Position: Production Intern

Department: N/A

No. of Positions Offered Annually: 1

Description: Production internships
available on a one-show-only basis. Dates
of commitment vary depending on the
production.

Qualifications: Technical or stage
management experience is helpful.

Salary: $165/week

Position Dates: Seasonal

Position Location: San Francisco, CA

Average No. of Applicants Annually: N/A

Potential for Job Placement: Possible

Application Process: Application to be
completed.

Deadline: April 15

Contact: Susan West

American Conservatory Theater

30 Grant Avenue, 6th Floor
San Francisco, CA 94108
Phone: (415) 834-3200

Position: Assistant Director/Observer Intern

Department: N/A

No. of Positions Offered Annually: 4

Description: Interns will assist in or observe the directing process of an A.C.T. mainstage production. Assistants and observers will have the opportunity to work closely with nationally known directors and A.C.T.'s acting company, thereby gaining an in-depth understanding of the directing process from preproduction design development through rehearsals and previews to the opening night performance. Assistant directorships may also include duties ranging from dramaturgical research and writing to leading panel discussions.

Qualifications: Qualified assistant directors must have at least a master's degree in drama/theater/fine arts with an emphasis on directing and/or equivalent related experience. Directing observer candidates who do not already have such a degree should be enrolled in a program.

Salary: Unpaid

Position Dates: Five-week program, offered year-round.

Position Location: San Francisco, CA

Average No. of Applicants Annually: N/A

Potential for Job Placement: N/A

Application Process: Application to be completed. Finalists will be interviewed before a selection is made.

Deadline: April 15

Contact: Susan West

American Conservatory Theater

30 Grant Avenue, 6th Floor
San Francisco, CA 94108
Phone: (415) 834-3200

Position: Sound Design Intern

Department: N/A

No. of Positions Offered Annually: 1

Description: Intern works with the resident sound designer in mounting each production. Intern will work closely with the designer in determining the artistic and technical needs for all shows, attending all technical and dress rehearsals and working in the sound studio to create each show's requirements.

Qualifications: Experience with studio techniques is required and a familiarity with theater is highly recommended.

Salary: $165/week

Position Dates: Academic year (September through May)

Position Location: San Francisco, CA

Average No. of Applicants Annually: N/A

Potential for Job Placement: Possible

Application Process: Application to be completed.

Deadline: April 15

Contact: Susan West

American Conservatory Theater

30 Grant Avenue, 6th Floor
San Francisco, CA 94108
Phone: (415) 834-3200

Position: Graphic Design Intern

Department: N/A

No. of Positions Offered Annually: 2

Description: Interns will assist the graphic artist in all phases of the design of marketing materials and will observe creative sessions and carry out design duties as assigned by the graphic artist.

Qualifications: Design education or experience and a working knowledge of Photoshop, Illustrator, QuarkXpress, and PageMaker is required.

Salary: Unpaid

Position Dates: Year-round, Fall, Spring and Summer

Position Location: San Francisco, CA

Average No. of Applicants Annually: N/A

Potential for Job Placement: N/A

Application Process: Application to be completed.

Deadline: April 15

Contact: Susan West

American Conservatory Theater

30 Grant Avenue, 6th Floor
San Francisco, CA 94108
Phone: (415) 834-3200

Position: Marketing/Public Relations Intern

Department: N/A

No. of Positions Offered Annually: 4

Description: Interns will assist the staff in all phases of producing and trafficking sales materials, developing and executing promotions, budget analysis and expense tracking and database administration. Intern will observe deparmental strategy and creative sessions as assigned by the director of marketing and public relations. Interns will also learn the basics of public and press relations by assisting the public relations manager in day-to-day operations and observing long-range planning sessions. Duties may include: writing, editing and proofing media releases, assisting in press list maintenance, photo production and distribution, archive maintenance, accompanying artists to and from press engagements and handling information requests from the public and the press.

Qualifications: N/A

Salary: Unpaid

Position Dates: Fall, Spring and Summer

Position Location: San Francisco, CA

Average No. of Applicants Annually: N/A

Potential for Job Placement: N/A

Application Process: Application to be completed.

Deadline: April 15

Contact: Susan West

American Conservatory Theater

30 Grant Avenue, 6th Floor
San Francisco, CA 94108
Phone: (415) 834-3200

Position: General Artistic Staff Intern

Department: N/A

No. of Positions Offered Annually: 6

Description: Interns assist A.C.T.'s artistic director and artistic staff with various aspects of administration. Interns may be assigned to a specific member of the staff in a specific department (Casting or Literary) or may assist on general clerical and administrative matters, depending on how the individual's interest and background meet departmental needs.

Qualifications: Applicant must demonstrate education and experience related to the field of assignment.

Salary: Unpaid

Position Dates: Fall, Spring and Summer

Position Location: San Francisco, CA

Average No. of Applicants Annually: N/A

Potential for Job Placement: N/A

Application Process: Application to be completed.

Deadline: April 15

Contact: Susan West

American Conservatory Theater

30 Gary Avenue, 6th Floor
San Francisco, CA 94108
Phone: (415) 834-3200

Position: Wig Conservation and Makeup Intern

Department: N/A

No. of Positions Offered Annually: 1

Description: Intern will work under the supervision of the wig master, learning to construct hand-tied wigs and facial hair and some special effects items. Intern will also work backstage and maintain wigs during performances and learn makeup techniques.

Qualifications: Applicant should be a focused individual who has an interest in hairdressing and haircutting.

Salary: $165/week

Position Dates: Academic year (September through May)

Position Location: San Francisco, CA

Average No. of Applicants Annually: N/A

Potential for Job Placement: Possible

Application Process: Application to be completed.

Deadline: April 15

Contact: Susan West

American Conservatory Theater

30 Grant Avenue, 6th Floor
San Francisco, CA 94108
Phone: (415) 834-3200

Position: Costume Rentals Intern

Department: N/A

No. of Positions Offered Annually: 1

Description: Costume rental staff is responsible for maintaining A.C.T.'s large stock of period costumes as well as renting constumes to the public for business, personal and theatrical use. Intern will gain experience furnishing rehearsal costumes to mainstage A.C.T. productions and in creating new garments to complete large scale rentals as well as manufacturing of accessories and hair.

Qualifications: Design ability is required. Applicant must have the ability to work well with people.

Salary: $165/week

Position Dates: Academic Year (September through May)

Position Location: San Francisco, CA

Average No. of Applicants Annually:

Potential for Job Placement: Possible

Application Process: Application to be completed.

Deadline: April 15

Contact: Susan West

American Conservatory Theater

30 Grant Avenue, 6th Floor
San Francisco, CA 94108
Phone: (415) 834-3200

Position: Lighting Design Intern

Department: N/A

No. of Positions Offered Annually: 1

Description: Intern will work as the assistant to the resident lighting designer in mounting each production. Intern's full-time responsibilities include attending all production meetings, maintaining records necessary for the upkeep of the light plot inventory, drafting designs for special effects, assisting the designers in hanging and focusing lighting instruments and in supervising technical rehearsals. Intern must also attend all technical and dress rehearsals for each of the mainstage productions of the season.

Qualifications: Applicant must have a strong background and experience in theatrical lighting.

Salary: $165/week

Position Dates: Academic year (September through April)

Position Location: San Francisco, CA

Average No. of Applicants Annually: N/A

Potential for Job Placement: Possible

Application Process: Application to be completed.

Deadline: April 15

Contact: Susan West

American Conservatory Theater

30 Grant Avenue, 6th Floor
San Francisco, CA 94108
Phone: (415) 834-3200

Position: Publications Intern

Department: N/A

No. of Positions Offered Annually: 2

Description: Interns assist publications
staff with producing A.C.T.'s programs,
subscriber newsletters and study guides.
Duties include soliciting and editing artistic
bios, word processing, proofreading, copy
editing, research and possible writing
assignments. Position requires a minimum
time commitment of two months.

Qualifications: Applicant must
demonstrate education and experience
related to field of assignment.

Salary: Unpaid

Position Dates: Fall, Spring and Summer

Position Location: San Francisco, CA

Average No. of Applicants Annually: N/A

Potential for Job Placement: N/A

Application Process: Application to be
completed.

Deadline: April 15

Contact: Susan West

American Repertory Theatre

64 Brattle Street
Cambridge, MA 02138
Phone: (617) 496-2000
Fax: (617) 495-1705

Position: Intern

Department: Various

No. of Positions Offered Annually: 20

Description: Internship positions available
in the following areas: Artistic Management,
Box Office, Financial Management, Fund-
raising, House Management, Literary
Management, Marketing/Public Relations,
Production Management, Voice and
Movement Coaching, Stage Management,
Running Crew, Scene Shop, Paint
Department, Costume and Prop Shops and
Lighting. Internships are full-time
commitments. Internships can be be three,
six, nine, or twelve months.

Qualifications: N/A

Salary: Unpaid

Position Dates: Fall, Spring, Summer, and
one year

Position Location: Cambridge, MA

Average No. of Applicants Annually:
100

Potential for Job Placement: Minimal

Application Process: Application to be
completed.

Deadline: Varies depending on internship
position.

Contact: Internship Director

Berkeley Repertory Theatre

2025 Addison Street
Berkeley, CA 94704
Phone: (510) 204-8901
Fax: (510) 841-7711

Position: Intern

Department: Various

No. of Positions Offered Annually: 12

Description: Internship positions available in the following ares: Development, Marketing, Administration, Properties, Costumes, Sound, Lighting, Scenic Construction, Scenic Painting, Stage Management, Literary and Education. Housing is provided for a limited number of interns.

Qualifications: N/A

Salary: $300/month (stipend)

Position Dates: Academic year

Position Location: Berkeley, CA

Average No. of Applicants Annually: 200

Potential for Job Placement: Possible

Application Process: Send résumé, three letters of recommendation, and three references.

Deadline: March 15 for Stage Management; April 15 for all others.

Contact: Internship Coordinator

College Light Opera Company

162 South Cedar Street
Oberlin, OH 44074
Phone: (216) 774-8485

Position: Orchestra Musician

Department: N/A

No. of Positions Offered Annually: 18

Description: Orchestra musicians play in the pit orchestra for the nine summer productions. Room and board provided.

Qualifications: Appliant should have previous educational or professional experience.

Salary: $500 (stipend)

Position Dates: Summer

Position Location: Falmouth, MA

Average No. of Applicants Annually: 350-400

Potential for Job Placement: Yes

Application Process: Application to be completed.

Deadline: Rolling

Contact: Robert A. Haslun

College Light Opera Company

162 South Cedar Street
Oberlin, OH 44074
Phone: (440) 774-8485

Position: Business Staff Intern

Department: N/A

No. of Positions Offered Annually: 4

Description: Two box office treasurers, one publicity director and one assistant business manager taken on each summer. Room and board are provided.

Qualifications: Previous experience a plus.

Salary: $1,000 (stipend)

Position Dates: Summer

Position Location: Falmouth, MA

Average No. of Applicants Annually: 350-400

Potential for Job Placement: Yes

Application Process: Application to be completed.

Deadline: Rolling

Contact: Robert A. Haslun

College Light Opera Company

162 South Cedar Street
Oberlin, OH 44074
Phone: (216) 774-8485

Position: Singer/Actor

Department: N/A

No. of Positions Offered Annually: 32

Description: Singing actors will perform in the nine summer productions. Room and board provided.

Qualifications: Previous experience a must.

Salary: Unpaid

Position Dates: Summer

Position Location: Falmouth, MA

Average No. of Applicants Annually: 350-400

Potential for Job Placement: Yes

Application Process: Application to be completed.

Deadline: Rolling

Contact: Robert A. Haslun

College Light Opera Company

162 South Cedar Street
Oberlin, OH 44074
Phone: (212) 774-8485

Position: Stage and Costume Crew

Department: N/A

No. of Positions Offered Annually: 12

Description: Crew members build sets and costumes for nine productions during the summer season. Room and board provided.

Qualifications: Previous experience a plus.

Salary: $1,000 (stipend)

Position Dates: Summer

Position Location: Falmouth, MA

Average No. of Applicants Annually: 350-400

Potential for Job Placement: Yes

Application Process: Application to be completed.

Deadline: Rolling

Contact: Robert A. Haslun

Creede Repertory Theater

Box 269
Creede, CO 81130

Position: Intern

Department: Various

No. of Positions Offered Annually: 10

Description: Interns will work in the following departments: Set Construction, Costume Construction, Lights/Sound, Business/Box Office, Stage Managements. Interns can gain practical experience in theater construction, running crews, and maintenance.

Qualifications: N/A

Salary: $115/week

Position Dates: Summer

Position Location: Creede, CO

Average No. of Applicants Annually: 1,000

Potential for Job Placement: Yes

Application Process: Send for application. Must have three letters of recommendation.

Deadline: March 1

Contact: Richard Baxter

Jacob's Pillow Dance Festival

P.O. Box 287F
Lee, MA 01238
Phone: (413) 637-1322
Fax: (413) 243-4744

Position: Business Office Intern

Department: Business Office

No. of Positions Offered Annually: 1

Description: The internship offers a wide exposure to the daily financial aspects of the Pillow. Duties include reconciliation of box office, food service and retail operations records, the development and monitoring of institutional and project budgets, and data entry into our computerized accounting records. Weekly shifts in the box office and store are required. Room and board are provided. College credit is available.

Qualifications: This position demands a personal sense of diplomacy and confidentiality combined with an ample sense of humor. This position also requires a basic knowledge of accounting principles and spreadsheet software experience.

Salary: $100/month

Position Dates: Summer

Position Location: Lee, MA

Average No. of Applicants Annually: 200

Potential for Job Placement: Limited

Application Process: Send résumé, cover letter with primary interest and goals and expectations of internship, two letters of recommendation, and two work-related references.

Deadline: March 3

Contact: Lesley Farlow

Jacob's Pillow Dance Festival

P.O. Box 287F
Lee, MA 01238
Phone: (413) 637-1322
Fax: (413) 243-4744

Position: Marketing and Press Intern

Department: Marketing and Press

No. of Positions Offered Annually: 3

Description: Interns participate in the promotion of the festival through the use of house publications, paid advertisements, and the press. Working with professional staff, responsibilities include hosting groups, guiding tours of the festival grounds, on-site displays, advertisement preparation, staffing the information booth, various grass-roots marketing efforts, writing press releases, hosting press visits, arranging interviews, maintenance of press records, and working with visiting artists to prepare weekly program materials, as well as weekly shifts in the box office. Interns will use word processing and desktop publishing systems. Room and board are provided. College credit is available.

Qualifications: Computer experience is a plus.

Salary: $100/month

Position Dates: Summer

Position Location: Lee, MA

Average No. of Applicants Annually: 200

Potential for Job Placement: Limited

Application Process: Send résumé, cover letter with primary interest and goals and expectations of internship, two letters of recommendation, two work-related references, and two writing samples.

Deadline: March 3

Contact: Lesley Farlow

Jacob's Pillow Dance Festival

P.O. Box 287F
Lee, MA 01238
Phone: (413) 637-1322
Fax: (413) 243-4744

Position: Programming/Special Projects

Department: Programming

No. of Positions Offered Annually: 1

Description: The programming/special projects intern works closely with the executive director and the assistant producer to gain professional experience in all phases of festival programming. Duties include general assistance in technical and production work for special projects. Opportunity to serve as liasion for guest artists performing on the outdoor stage and for artists-in-residence. Room and board are provided. College credit is available.

Qualifications: Knowledge of Fundmaster, WordPerfect, PageMaker, MS Windows and DOS helpful. Good written and oral communication skills, interest in dance development and education are essential.

Salary: $100/month

Position Dates: Summer

Position Location: Lee, MA

Average No. of Applicants Annually: 200

Potential for Job Placement: Limited

Application Process: Send résumé, cover letter with primary interest and goals and expectations of internship, two letters of recommendation, and two work-related references.

Deadline: March 3

Contact: Lesley Farlow

Jacob's Pillow Dance Festival

P.O. Box 287F
Lee, MA 01238
Phone: (413) 637-1322
Fax: (413) 243-4744

Position: Archives/Preservation Intern

Department: Archives/Preservation

No. of Positions Offered Annually: 1

Description: Working alongside the director of preservation, the archives/preservation assistant will help create links between the Pillow's extensive archives and the resident artists/students as well as the general public. Room and board are provided. College credit available.

Qualifications: Professional experience required.

Salary: $100/month

Position Dates: Summer

Position Location: Lee, MA

Average No. of Applicants Annually: 200

Potential for Job Placement: Limited

Application Process: Send résumé, cover letter with primary interest and goals and expectations of internship, two letters of recommendation, and two work-related references.

Deadline: March 3

Contact: Lesley Farlow, Education Program Director

Jacob's Pillow Dance Festival

P.O. Box 287F
Lee, MA 02138
Phone: (413) 637-1322
Fax: (413) 637-4744

Position: Operations Intern

Department: N/A

No. of Positions Offered Annually: 1

Description: The intern assists the director of operations in the day-to-day activities of managing a busy multitheater dance festival. The operations intern will assist in materials and equipment procurement, studio and space scheduling, budget tracking, phone system and computer network maintenance, along with administrative duties. Room and board are provided. College credit available.

Qualifications: N/A

Salary: $100/month

Position Dates: Summer

Position Location: Lee, MA

Average No. of Applicants Annually: 200

Potential for Job Placement: Limited

Application Process: Send résumé, cover letter with primary interest and goals and expectations of internship, two letters of recommendation, and two work-related references.

Deadline: March 3

Contact: Lesley Farlow

Jacob's Pillow Dance Festival

P.O. Box 287F
Lee, MA 01238
Phone: (413) 637-1322
Fax: (413) 243-4744

Position: Video Internship

Department: Video

No. of Positions Offered Annually: 1

Description: The video intern will work with staff videographer to document various activities of the season. Responsibilities include taping performances, classes, and rehearsals. Other responsibilities include the maintenance of the video equipment. Room and board are provided. College credit is available.

Qualifications: Familiarity with basic video and editing equipment, as well as experience taping dance is required. Still photography skills desirable.

Salary: $100/month

Position Dates: Summer

Position Location: Lee, MA

Average No. of Applicants Annually: 200

Potential for Job Placement: Limited

Application Process: Send résumé, cover letter with primary interest and goals and expectations of internship, two letters of recommendation, and two work-related references.

Deadline: March 3

Contact: Lesley Farlow

Jacob's Pillow Dance Festival

P.O. Box 287F
Lee, MA 02138
Phone: (413) 637-1322
Fax: (413) 243-4744

Position: Education/Resources Intern

Department: Education/Resources

No. of Positions Offered Annually: 1

Description: The intern will participate in the daily operation of the School and its programs, supervising scholarship duties, scheduling, maintaining records, assisting in special events, coordinating artists' housing, hospitality and travel needs, and facilitating various conferences and community workshops. Room and board are provided. College credit available.

Qualifications: N/A

Salary: $100/month

Position Dates: Summer

Position Location: Lee, MA

Average No. of Applicants Annually: 200

Potential for Job Placement: Limited

Application Process: Send résumé, cover letter with primary interest and goals and expectations of internship, two letters of recommendation, and two work-related references.

Deadline: March 3

Contact: Lesley Farlow

Jacob's Pillow Dance Festival

P.O. Box 287F
Lee, MA 01238
Phone: (413) 637-1322
Fax: (413) 243-4744

Position: Technical Theater/Production Intern

Department: Technical Theater/Production

No. of Positions Offered Annually: 11

Description: Interns gain professional experience working as running crew for over 20 productions in the Pillow's two theater spaces and on the informal outdoor stage. Participants work closely with both the resident professional staff and visiting designers, stage managers and artists. Interns rotate through all "crew" positions and will be exposed to most aspects of production. Room and board are provided. College credit available.

Qualifications: N/A

Salary: $100/month

Position Dates: Summer

Position Location: Lee, MA

Average No. of Applicants Annually: 200

Potential for Job Placement: Limited

Application Process: Send résumé, cover letter with primary interest and goals and expectations of internship, two letters of recommendation, and two work-related references.

Deadline: March 3

Contact: Lesley Farlow, Education Program Director

John F. Kennedy Center for the Performing Arts

Washington, DC 20566
Phone: (202) 416-8807
Fax: (202) 416-8802

Position: Advertising Intern

Department: Education Department

No. of Positions Offered Annually: 6

Description: Kennedy Center Advertising is the in-house ad agency that creates, produces and places campaigns to generate ticket sales for the Center's performances. Assignments for interns include traffic and production management, media planning and buying, broadcast production assistance, promotional event planning and management, ad placements, copy editing, scheduling, obtaining approvals, filing, invoicing, vendor negotiation, cost estimating and copywriting assignments. More information is available on the Web site: http://www.kennedy-center.org.

Qualifications: N/A

Salary: $650/month

Position Dates: Fall, Spring and Summer

Position Location: Washington, D.C.

Average No. of Applicants Annually: 30

Potential for Job Placement: Possible

Application Process: Send résumé, cover letter stating career goals and computer skills, two current letters of recommendation, official transcript and writing sample of no more than three pages in length.

Deadline: June 1 for Fall; November 1 for Spring; March 1 for Summer.

Contact: Darrell M. Ayers

John F. Kennedy Center for the Performing Arts

Washington, DC 20566
Phone: (202) 416-8807
Fax: (202) 416-8802

Position: National Symphony Orchestra Education Intern

Department: Education Department

No. of Positions Offered Annually: 3

Description: Intern learns about and assists with organization and implementation of special concerts for young people and families, administration of training programs and competitions for high school musicians, responding to phone inquiries, researching programming issues, working with volunteers and compiling reports, study materials and program notes for NSO education programs. More information available on the Web at http://www.kennedy-center.org.

Qualifications: N/A

Salary: $650/week

Position Dates: Fall, Spring and Summer

Position Location: Washington, D.C.

Average No. of Applicants Annually: 30

Potential for Job Placement: Possible

Application Process: Send résumé, cover letter stating career goals and computer skills, two current letters of reccommendation, official transcript and a writing sample of no more than three pages in length.

Deadline: June 1 for Fall; November 1 for Spring; March 1 for Summer.

Contact: Darrell M. Ayers

John F. Kennedy Center for the Performing Arts

Washington, DC 20566
Phone: (202) 416-8807
Fax: (202) 416-8802

Position: Volunteer Management Intern

Department: Education Department

No. of Positions Offered Annually: 3

Description: Intern assists with volunteer management, publication of the Friends of the Kennedy Center newsletter and community relations. Intern works directly with volunteers in all facets of the program. More information can be found on the Web at http://www.kennedy-org.com.

Qualifications: N/A

Salary: $650/month

Position Dates: Fall, Spring and Summer

Position Location: Washington, D.C.

Average No. of Applicants Annually: 30

Potential for Job Placement: Possible

Application Process: Send résumé, cover letter stating career goals and computer skills, two current letters of recommendation, official transcript and a writing sample of no more than three words in length.

Deadline: June 1 for Fall; November 1 for Spring; March 1 for Summer.

Contact: Darrell M. Ayers

John F. Kennedy Center for the Performing Arts

Washington, DC 20566
Phone: (202) 416-8807
Fax: (202) 416-8802

Position: Alliance for Arts Education Network Intern

Department: Education Department

No. of Positions Offered Annually: 3

Description: The alliance is a network of state organizations that brings together educators, community leaders, arts organizations and concerned citizens to plan and implement programs and activities in support of arts education. Intern learns about and assists with services for state alliances and the general public, the dissemination and gathering of information on arts education-related issues, the publication of an arts education newsletter, planning and implementation of Governance Committee meetings, national meetings and other conferences, the administration of grants and recognition programs and the administration of new initiatives and special projects. More information can be found on the Web at http://www.kennedy-center.org.

Qualifications: N/A

Salary: $650/month

Position Dates: Fall, Spring and Summer

Position Location: Washington, D.C.

Average No. of Applicants Annually: 30

Potential for Job Placement: Possible

Application Process: Send résumé, cover letter stating career goals and computer skills, two recent letters of recommendation, official transcript and a writing sample of no more than three pages in length.

Deadline: June 1 for Fall; November 1 for Spring; March 1 for Summer.

Contact: Darrell M. Ayers

John F. Kennedy Center for the Performing Arts

Washington, DC 20566
Phone: (202) 416-8807
Fax: (202) 416-8802

Position: Fellowships of the Americas Intern

Department: Education Department

No. of Positions Offered Annually: 3

Description: Program assists young to mid-career performing artist in establishing careers beyond the borders of their native countries. The program provides extensive support and guidance in defining advanced training opportunities for the fellowship recipients. Intern learns how to develop professional relationships with international artists, the art of diplomatic communication skills, how to collaborate with leading organizations as well as grant application and panel management. More information available on the Web at http://www.kennedy-center.org.

Qualifications: Applicant must have proficient language skills in Spanish, Portuguese or French.

Salary: $650/month

Position Dates: Fall and Spring

Position Location: Washington, D.C.

Average No. of Applicants Annually: 30

Potential for Job Placement: Possible

Application Process: Send résumé, cover letter stating career goals and computer skills, two recent letters of recommendation, offical transcript and a writing sample of no more than three pages in length.

Deadline: June 1 for Fall; November 1 for Spring.

Contact: Darrell M. Ayers

John F. Kennedy Center for the Performing Arts

Washington, DC 20566
Phone: (202) 416-8807
Fax: (202) 416-8802

Position: Youth and Family Programs Intern

Department: Education Department

No. of Positions Offered Annually: 3

Description: Each year the program typically produces three or four new shows, tours nationally and presents 15 to 20 national and international companies in a total of nearly 250 performances for young people and their families. Intern learns about and assists with all aspects of presenting and producing including work on scheduling, marketing, press, contracting and overall administration and production-related needs including assisting with the mounting of the Kennedy Center-produced shows, both in-house and touring. More information available on the Web at http://www.kennedy-center.org.

Qualifications:

Salary: $650/month

Position Dates: Fall, Spring and Summer

Position Location: Washington, DC

Average No. of Applicants Annually: 30

Potential for Job Placement: Possible

Application Process: Send résumé, cover letter stating career goals and computer skills, two recent letters of recommendation, official transcript and a writing sample of no more than three pages in length.

Deadline: June 1 for Fall; November 1 for Spring; March 1 for Summer.

Contact: Darrell M. Ayers

John F. Kennedy Center for the Performing Arts

Washington, DC 20566
Phone: (202) 416-8807
Fax: (202) 416-8802

Position: Professional Development Opportunities Intern

Department: Education Department

No. of Positions Offered Annually: 3

Description: Intern learns about and assists with the administration and implementation of arts education events for teachers. Duties include attending and evaluating educational events and performances, coordinating technical and logistical details and assisting with the preparation of teacher resource materials. More information available on the Web at http://www.kennedy-center.org.

Qualifications: N/A

Salary: $650/month

Position Dates: Fall, Spring and Summer

Position Location: Washington, DC

Average No. of Applicants Annually: 30

Potential for Job Placement: Possible

Application Process: Send résumé, cover letter stating career goals and computer skills, two current letters of recommendation, official transcript and a writing sample of no more than three pages in length.

Deadline: June 1 for Fall; November 1 for Spring; March 1 for Summer.

Contact: Darrell M. Ayers

John F. Kennedy Center for the Performing Arts

Washington, DC 20566
Phone: (202) 416-8807
Fax: (202) 416-8802

Position: Performing Arts Centers and Schools Intern

Department: Education Department

No. of Positions Offered Annually: 1

Description: Program is designed to create and encourage partnerships throughout the nation between arts-presenting organizations and their local school systems with a special emphasis on the professional development of teachers. Intern learns about and assists with the coordination and implementation of a national conference and a training institute for new teams. Internship provides opportunity to communicate with arts administrators and educators from across the country and to learn about the many issues surrounding education reform and the professional development of teachers.

Qualifications: N/A

Salary: $650/month

Position Dates: Spring

Position Location: Washington, DC

Average No. of Applicants Annually: 10

Potential for Job Placement: Possible

Application Process: Send résumé, cover letter stating career goals and computer skills, two current letters of recommendation, official transcript and a writing sample of no more than three pages in length.

Deadline: November 1

Contact: Darrell M. Ayers

John F. Kennedy Center for the Performing Arts

Washington, DC 20566
Phone: (202) 416-8807
Fax: (202) 416-8802

Position: Performance Plus Education Intern

Department: Education Department

No. of Positions Offered Annually: 3

Description: Program produces adult arts education events in ballet, dance, music, theater and jazz using the artists performing at the Kennedy Center. Intern assists with implementation of all events and attends and evaluates those events. Specific duties include preparing attendance and evaluative reports, drafting correspondence for mass mailing, assisting with technical and logistical details, working with volunteers and assisting with the marketing needs of the program. More information available on the Web at http://www.kennedy-center.org.

Qualifications: N/A

Salary: $650/hour

Position Dates: Fall and Spring

Position Location: Washington, D.C.

Average No. of Applicants Annually: 30

Potential for Job Placement: Possible

Application Process: Send résumé, cover letter stating career goals and computer skills, two current letters of recommendation, official transcript and a writing sample of no more than three pages in length.

Deadline: June 1 for Fall; November 1 for Spring.

Contact: Darrell M. Ayers

John F. Kennedy Center for the Performing Arts

Washington, DC 20566
Phone: (202) 416-8807
Fax: (202) 416-8802

Position: Membership Intern

Department: Education Department

No. of Positions Offered Annually: 3

Description: This is a development/fund-raising internship. Intern learns about and assists with the membership fund-raising campaigns for the Kennedy Center Stars and the National Symphony Orchestra Association. Intern also learns about and assists with day-to-day planning and management of fund-raising campaigns using direct mail and telemarketing techniques. Other specific areas include, but are not limited to, administrative support, proofreading and liaison work with outside computer and printing vendors and telemarketing firms. More information can be found on the Web at http://www.kennedy-center.org.

Qualifications: N/A

Salary: $650/month

Position Dates: Fall, Spring and Summer

Position Location: Washington, D.C.

Average No. of Applicants Annually: 30

Potential for Job Placement: Possible

Application Process: Send résumé, cover letter stating career goals and computer skills, two current letters of recommendation, official transcript and a writing sample of no more than three pages in length.

Deadline: June 1 for Fall; November 1 for Spring; March 1 for Summer.

Contact: Darrell M. Ayers

John F. Kennedy Center for the Performing Arts

Washington, DC 20566
Phone: (202) 416-8807
Fax: (202) 416-8802

Position: Membership Services and Circles Fund Intern

Department: Education Department

No. of Positions Offered Annually: 3

Description: This is a development/fund-raising internship. The Membership Services and Circles Fund Office is responsible for the acquisition, retention and servicing of members for the National Symphony Orchestra Association and Kennedy Center Stars as well as the cultivation and solicitation of $1,000+ contributing members of the Kennedy Center Circles Fund. Intern learns about and assists with the fulfillment of member benefits and events, database management, financial processing and reporting of individual memberships and donations, planning and implementation of Circles Fund solicitation mailings, cultivation events and support functions for the Circles Fund Committee.

Qualifications: N/A

Salary: $650/month

Position Dates: Fall, Spring and Summer

Position Location: Washington, D.C.

Average No. of Applicants Annually: 30

Potential for Job Placement: Possible

Application Process: Send résumé, cover letter stating career goals and computer skills, two current letters of recommendation, official transcript and a writing sample of no more than three pages in length.

Deadline: June 1 for Fall; November 1 for Spring; March 1 for Summer.

Contact: Darrell M. Ayers

John F. Kennedy Center for the Performing Arts

Washington, DC 20566
Phone: (202) 416-8807
Fax: (202) 416-8802

Position: Grant Programs Intern

Department: Education Department

No. of Positions Offered Annually: 3

Description: This is a development/fund-raising internship. The Grant Programs Office is responsible for foundation and corporate grant activity for the Kennedy Center and National Symphony Orchestra. Intern assists in drafting proposals, applications and final reports for the National Endowment for the Arts and other governmental sources, foundations and corporate sponsorships. Intern may interact with Center and NSO programming staff, finance, education and press staff to obtain necessary information. Intern also has limited office duties and assists occasionally with special events such as galas and benefits. More information can be found on the Web at http://www.kennedy-center.org.

Qualifications: N/A

Salary: $650/month

Position Dates: Fall, Spring and Summer

Position Location: Washington, D.C.

Average No. of Applicants Annually: 30

Potential for Job Placement: Possible

Application Process: Send résumé, cover letter stating career goals and computer skills, two recent letters of recommendation, official transcript and a writing sample of no more than three pages in length.

Deadline: June 1 for Fall; November 1 for Spring; March 1 for Summer.

Contact: Darrell M. Ayers

John F. Kennedy Center for the Performing Arts

Washington, DC 20566
Phone: (202) 416-8807
Fax: (202) 416-8802

Position: Corporate Fund Intern

Department: Education Department

No. of Positions Offered Annually: 3

Description: Development/fund-raising position. The Corporate Fund generates nearly $3 million each year in contributions for the Kennedy Center, primarily through solicitations of the Corporate Fund Board, which is comprised of approximately 30 CEOs from prominent corporations around the country. Intern will gain a thorough understanding of how the Center manages this national corporate fund-raising campaign. In addition, intern will learn how this campaign markets the Center's education programs in order to demonstrate the Center's national impact to corporations across the country. More information can be found on the Web at http://www.kennedy-center.org.

Qualifications: N/A

Salary: $650/month

Position Dates: Fall, Spring and Summer

Position Location: Washington, D.C.

Average No. of Applicants Annually: 30

Potential for Job Placement: Possible

Application Process: Send résumé, cover letter stating career goals and computer skills, two current letters of recommendation, official transcript and a writing sample of no more than three pages in length.

Deadline: June 1 for Fall; November 1 for Spring; March 1 for Summer.

Contact: Darrell M. Ayers

John F. Kennedy Center for the Performing Arts

Washington, DC 20566
Phone: (202) 416-8807
Fax: (202) 416-8802

Position: Constituency Relations Intern

Department: Education Department

No. of Positions Offered Annually: 3

Description: Development/fund-raising internship. Constituency Relations Office is responsible for three donor membership groups: the President's Advisory Committee on the Arts, National Committee for Performing Arts and the National Symphony Orchestra Trustees. From member relations to event planning, the intern learns every aspect of donor servicing. Duties include financial, special events and press release management as well as day-to-day administrative duties. There is a high level of interaction with committee members as well as Kennedy Center employees. More information can be found on the Web at http://www.kennedy-org.com.

Qualifications: N/A

Salary: $650/month

Position Dates: Fall, Spring and Summer

Position Location: Washington, D.C.

Average No. of Applicants Annually: 30

Potential for Job Placement: Possible

Application Process: Send résumé, cover letter stating career goals and computer skills, two current letters of recommendation, official transcript and a writing sample of no more than three pages in length.

Deadline: June 1 for Fall; November 1 for Spring; March 1 for Summer.

Contact: Darrell M. Ayers

John F. Kennedy Center for the Performing Arts

Washington, DC 20566
Phone: (202) 416-8807
Fax: (202) 416-8802

Position: Management Information Services Intern

Department: Education Department

No. of Positions Offered Annually: 3

Description: This department provides the common framework by which other administrative/financial, educational and production work is undertaken using existing computer programs and by the development of new computer programs. The intern experiences all aspects of this Center-wide service department including software and hardware installation, training, maintenance and help-line support as well as participating in the development and implementation of a computer programming need. More information can be found on the Web at http://www.kennedy-center.org.

Qualifications: N/A

Salary: $650/month

Position Dates: Fall, Spring and Summer

Position Location: Washington, D.C.

Average No. of Applicants Annually: 30

Potential for Job Placement: Possible

Application Process: Send résumé, cover letter stating career goals and computer skills, two current letters of recommendation, official transcript and a writing sample of no more than three pages in length.

Deadline: June 1 for Fall; November 1 for Spring; March 1 for Summer.

Contact: Darrell M. Ayers

John F. Kennedy Center for the Performing Arts

Washington, DC 20566
Phone: (202) 416-8807
Fax: (202) 416-8802

Position: Speical Event Planning Intern

Department: Education Department

No. of Positions Offered Annually: 3

Description: Intern assists coordinators in a variety of tasks, including preparation of invitation mailings, maintenance of guest lists and production of event-related materials. Intern is aditionally responsible for many daily functions within the office and will have the opportunity to attend several of the events planned. More information available on the Web at http://www.kennedy-center.org.

Qualifications: N/A

Salary: $650/month

Position Dates: Fall, Spring and Summer

Position Location: Washington, D.C.

Average No. of Applicants Annually: 30

Potential for Job Placement: Possible

Application Process: Send résumé, cover letter stating career goals and computer skills, two current letters of recommendation and a writing sample of no more than three pages in length.

Deadline: June 1 for Fall; November 1 for Spring; March 1 for Summer.

Contact: Darrell M. Ayers

John F. Kennedy Center for the Performing Arts

Washington, DC 20566
Phone: (202) 416-8807
Fax: (202) 416-8802

Position: Public Relations Intern

Department: Education Department

No. of Positions Offered Annually: 6

Description: Interns learn about and assist press representatives with media coverage for Kennedy Center and National Symphony Orchestra performances and institutional events. Duties include assisting with phone contacts, ticket requests, opening nights, press releases, media lists, press kits and Stagebills. More information can be found on the Web at http://www.kennedy-center.org.

Qualifications: N/A

Salary: $650/month

Position Dates: Fall, Spring and Summer

Position Location: Washington, DC

Average No. of Applicants Annually: 30

Potential for Job Placement: Possible

Application Process: Send résumé, cover letter stating career goals and computer skills, two current letters of recommendation, official transcript and a writing sample of no more than three pages in length.

Deadline: June 1 for Fall; November 1 for Spring; March 1 for Summer.

Contact: Darrell M. Ayers

John F. Kennedy Center for the Performing Arts

Washington, DC 20566
Phone: (202) 416-8807
Fax: (202) 416-8802

Position: Programming Intern

Department: Education Department

No. of Positions Offered Annually: 3

Description: Intern is involved in many areas of programming through administrative and hands-on execution, including database management and calendar coordination, preparation for touring companies, management of supernumeraries files, auditions and casting, assistance with festival operations, event planning and implementation and logistics. Intern also maintains public information and fields phone inquiries, works with volunteers and comiles reports for the department. More information can be found on the Web at http://www.kennedy-org.com.

Qualifications: N/A

Salary: $650/month

Position Dates: Fall, Spring and Summer

Position Location: Washington, D.C.

Average No. of Applicants Annually: 30

Potential for Job Placement: Possible

Application Process: Send résumé, cover letter stating career goals and computer skills, two current letters of recommendation, official transcript and a writing sample of no more than three pages in length.

Deadline: June 1 for Fall; November 1 for Spring; March 1 for Summer.

Contact: Darrell M. Ayers

John F. Kennedy Center for the Performing Arts

Washington, DC 20566
Phone: (202) 416-8807
Fax: (202) 416-8802

Position: Orchestra Promotion/Administration Intern

Department: Education Department

No. of Positions Offered Annually: 3

Description: Intern learns about and supports orchestra production and administration during the National Symphony Orchestra's summer season. Areas may include concert production and operations, artistic administration, education and orchestra personnel. Intern works with the NSO production staff in preparation for and in production of NSO rehearsals and at various summer venues such as the Wolf Trap, the U.S. Capital, the Kennedy Center and Carter Barron Amphitheater as well as assists with the NSO's annual Mozart Festival. More information can be found on the Web at http://www.kennedy-center.org.

Qualifications: N/A

Salary: $650/month

Position Dates: Summer

Position Location: Washington, DC

Average No. of Applicants Annually: 30

Potential for Job Placement: Possible

Application Process: Send résumé, cover letter stating career goals and computer skills, two current letters of recommendation, official transcript and a writing sample of no more than three pages in length.

Deadline: March 1

Contact: Darrell M. Ayers

John F. Kennedy Center for the Performing Arts

Washington, DC 20566
Phone: (202) 416-8807
Fax: (202) 416-8802

Position: Festival Management Intern

Department: Education Department

No. of Positions Offered Annually: 1

Description: Intern learns about and assists with the technical and administrative coordination of the Kennedy Center American College Theater Festival, a national educational theater program designed to indentify and promote quality in college-level theater. Duties include but are not limited to travel arrangements for national festival cast and crew, coordination of student design and acting awards, press and promotion of festival, meeting and escorting arriving national festival companies and distributing tickets. More information can be found on the Web at http://www.kennedy-center.org.

Qualifications: N/A

Salary: $650/month

Position Dates: Spring

Position Location: Washington, DC

Average No. of Applicants Annually: 10

Potential for Job Placement: Possible

Application Process: Send résumé, cover letter stating career goals and computer skills, two current letters of recommendationa and a writing sample of no more than three pages in length.

Deadline: November 1

Contact: Darrell M. Ayers

John F. Kennedy Center for the Performing Arts

Washington, DC 20566
Phone: (202) 416-8807
Fax: (202) 416-8802

Position: ArtsEdge Intern

Department: Education Department

No. of Positions Offered Annually: 3

Description: ArtsEdge is the evolving national arts and education information network that provides online information services and access to databases nationally. Intern assists with and learns how to research, collect and organize information to be disseminated through the ArtsEdge network. Additional responsibilities include responding to inquiries about ArtsEdge and requests for specific information or resources. More information can be found on the Web at http://www.kennedy-center.org.

Qualifications: Applicant must possess strong writing and organizational skills, as well as computer-based knowledge and skills.

Salary: $650/month

Position Dates: Fall, Spring and Summer

Position Location: Washington, D.C.

Average No. of Applicants Annually: 30

Potential for Job Placement: Possible

Application Process: Send résumé, cover letter stating career goals and computer skills, two current letters of recommendation, official transcript and one writing sample.

Deadline: June 1 for Fall; November 1 for Spring; March 1 for Summer.

Contact: Darrell M. Ayers

John F. Kennedy Center for the Performing Arts

Washington, DC 20566
Phone: (202) 416-8807
Fax: (202) 416-8802

Position: Major Gifts Intern

Department: Education Department

No. of Positions Offered Annually: 3

Description: The overarching goal of the Major Gifts Office is to secure unrestricted, outright and deferred six- and seven-figure contributions from individuals nationally and internationally who wish to support the Kennedy Center and National Symphony Orchestra. As a member of the Major Gifts team, intern observes and participates in processes associated with prospect identification, cultivation, solicitation and donor stewardship, all of which are critical components of building the level of financial support from the Kennedy Center Board of Trustees and other current and prospective contributors to the Annual Fund and the Endowment Fund. More information can be found on the Web at http://www.kennedy-center.org.

Qualifications: N/A

Salary: $650/month

Position Dates: Fall, Spring and Summer

Position Location: Washington, D.C.

Average No. of Applicants Annually: 30

Potential for Job Placement: Possible

Application Process: Send résumé, cover letter stating career goals and computer skills, two current letters of recommendation, official transcript and a writing sample of no more than three pages in length.

Deadline: June 1 for Fall; November 1 for Spring; March 1 for Summer.

Contact: Darrell M. Ayers

Maine State Music Theatre

14 Maine Street
Brunswick, ME 04011
Phone: (207) 725-8769
Fax: (207) 725-1199

Position: Intern

Department: Various

No. of Positions Offered Annually: 30

Description: Internship positions available in the following areas: performance, carpentry, paints, props, sound, electrics, stage management, box office, house management, marketing, administration, costumes and music direction. Stipend, room and board provided.

Qualifications: N/A

Salary: $50/Production; $30/Peformance.

Position Dates: Summer

Position Location: Brunswick, ME

Average No. of Applicants Annually: 300

Potential for Job Placement: Minimal

Application Process: Application to be completed.

Deadline: March 31

Contact: Julie Ray

Manhattan Theatre Club

453 West 16th Street
New York, NY 10011
Phone:
Fax: (212) 691-9106

Position: Intern

Department: Various

No. of Positions Offered Annually: 15

Description: Internships available in the following areas: development, literary, Business, musical theater, production assistant, general management, education, running crew, writers in performance, offices of artistic and managing directors, casting, marketing/public relations and management information systems. A full-time internship providing interns with intensive training in one department, attendance at departmental and full-staff meetings, individual projects under the guidance of experienced supervisors, weekly artistic and management seminars and invitations to special events.

Qualifications: N/A

Salary: $110/week

Position Dates: Fall, Spring, Summer and full theatre season.

Position Location: New York, NY

Average No. of Applicants Annually: N/A

Potential for Job Placement: N/A

Application Process: Send résumé, cover letter stating first three departmental preferences and two letters of recommendation. Interview may be scheduled.

Deadline: Rolling

Contact: Intern Coordinator

New Dramatists

424 West 44th Street
New York, NY 10036
Phone: (212) 757-6960
Fax: (212) 265-4738

Position: Intern

Department: Various

No. of Positions Offered Annually: 25

Description: Internships available in the following areas: stage management/casting, literary management and development/publicity. Interns work as general office support and have many chances to specialize in their chosen field. Travel stipend provided for full-time interns.

Qualifications: Applicants should have a good knowledge of theater and a passion for new plays.

Salary: Unpaid

Position Dates: Fall, Spring and Summer

Position Location: New York, NY

Average No. of Applicants Annually: 125

Potential for Job Placement: Minimal

Application Process: Send résumé and cover letter. Interview will be scheduled.

Deadline: Rolling

Contact: Stephen Haff

Playhouse on the Square

51 South Cooper
Memphis, TN 38104
Phone: (901) 725-0776

Position: Intern

Department: N/A

No. of Positions Offered Annually: 11

Description: One internship available in each of the following areas: administrative, stage manager, props, tech, lighting and costumes. Internships are for the full or half season, contractually agreed upon in advance. Housing is provided.

Qualifications: Applicants should have an undergraduate degree in theater.

Salary: $100/week

Position Dates: Fall, Spring and Summer

Position Location: Memphis, TN

Average No. of Applicants Annually: N/A

Potential for Job Placement: Yes

Application Process: Application to be completed.

Deadline: Rolling

Contact: Carrie Fairchild

Qually and Company

2238 Central Street
Evanston, IL 60201-1457
Phone: (847) 864-6316
Fax: (847) 864-1796

Position: Intern

Department: Various

No. of Positions Offered Annually: 7

Description: Internships available in the following areas: graphic design, art direction, computer production, accounts and new business development.

Qualifications: N/A

Salary: Unpaid

Position Dates: Year round

Position Location: Evanston, IL

Average No. of Applicants Annually: 200

Potential for Job Placement: Possible

Application Process: Send résumé, cover letter and portfolio samples. Follow up with a phone call in a few weeks.

Deadline: Six to eight months prior to desired start date.

Contact: Mike Iva

Williamstown Theatre Festival

100 East 17th Street, 3rd Floor
New York, NY 10003
Phone: (212) 228-2286
Fax: (212) 228-9091

Position: Technical/Administrative Intern

Department: N/A

No. of Positions Offered Annually: 60

Description: Internship positions available in the following areas: design, tech, production, general management, directing, company management, stage management, production management, cabaret management, box office, house management, publicity, photography, literary management and graphic design. Housing fee of $450 for the summer.

Qualifications: Applicant should have educational and/or professional experience in chosen area of interest.

Salary: Unpaid

Position Dates: Summer

Position Location: Williamstown, MA

Average No. of Applicants Annually: 500

Potential for Job Placement: Yes

Application Process: Application to be completed.

Deadline: Rolling

Contact: Anne Lowrie

Williamstown Theatre Festival

100 East 17th Street, Third Floor
New York, NY 10003
Phone: (212) 228-2286
Fax: (212) 228-9091

Position: Acting Apprentice

Department: Apprentice Admissions

No. of Positions Offered Annually: 75

Description: Apprentices take classes with
professional theater artists, work in all
technical and administrative departments
and serve as running crew on festival
productions. Apprentices have the
opportunity to audition for festival
productions. Fee of $2,400 for room, board
and tuition for the ten-week program.

Qualifications: No previous experience
necessary.

Salary: Unpaid

Position Dates: Summer

Position Location: Williamstown, MA

Average No. of Applicants Annually:
200

Potential for Job Placement: Yes

Application Process: Application to be
completed.

Deadline: Rolling

Contact: Anne Lowrie

Museums and Galleries

by Bettina R. Lerner

Museum internships are among the most useful and instructive for a college student or recent grad considering a career in the arts. For this reason, they are the most sought-after internships and more than often the most selective as well. This is especially true for summer internships. For example, The Metropolitan Museum of Art in New York City, which has one of the top internship programs in this field in the nation, regularly accepts about 20 undergraduate and ten graduate interns from an applicant pool of more than 600 undergraduate and 150 graduate students.

Of the many internship opportunities available in the arts, museums seem to offer the most structured and established programs. Interns report having coordinated schedules that allow them to work only on certain days of the week, and participate in field trips to other museums or hear weekly lectures from administrators and artists on other days. Furthermore, some museums will rotate their interns through the various departments and allow them to become acquainted with the different areas of museum work. Although the interns are definitely exposed to their share of grunt work, this is in large part made up for by the truly educational aspects of the program. "I really looked forward to the times we spent listening to the talks given by the curators of the different departments. It felt almost like being in school again, but in a school where all the lectures were directly relevant to my life—and there was no homework," says one intern of her experience as an intern at the Museum of Modern Art in New York City.

Museum Departments

Interns at museums generally work for one or two specific departments within the institution. It is to your advantage to know in advance what departments offer internships at a particular museum and indicate your preference and reasons for choosing that particular area. The names of the departments may vary from institution to institution, but the following is a list of the departments most commonly found in large and small museums alike.

Archives

Interns in archive departments usually work with documents pertaining to the specific museum's history. Articles that appear in periodicals, magazines, and catalogs that refer to particular pieces in the permanent collections, or to temporary exhibits, flow in and out of this office. Interns generally spend most of their time sorting through old and new materials, and updating the database.

"The bulk of the work that I enjoyed doing at the Isamu Noguchi Garden Museum was in the archives of the foundation, looking for articles to include in the new Web site for the museum and gathering information for the updated and complete bibliography," recalls one former intern. "Sifting through dusty articles in old file cabinets may not sound glamorous at first, but I learned more than I could have hoped for about the artist. Also, archival work is among the most independent work one can do at a museum. The work I did was all unsupervised, so I could spend as much time as I wanted just reading original documents from the early 1920s and reorganizing the files. I felt like I was actually doing constructive and helpful work for the museum."

Administration

Interns in this department usually assist in the financial aspects of museum administration and in issues concerning the personnel at the museum. Interns cited this kind of work as valuable in terms of the high degree of exposure they had to all the areas and levels of museum operation, and the large amounts of time they spent working on a one-to-one basis with museum employees. Internship coordinators suggest a general interest in administration and management is helpful when applying for such a position, as well as some basic background in accounting and finance.

Conservation

Conservation departments are responsible for the maintenance of the works kept in the museum. It is always preferable to have taken a course in conservation prior to applying to this kind of department. At the very least, interns are generally expected to have some knowledge of chemistry and basic artistic techniques in order to qualify for this kind of internship.

"Conservation can be at times challenging and at other times menial. I spent most of my summer cleaning out fountains and wiping down stone sculptures with different detergents, but it was an excellent opportunity to spend a lot of time in contact with valuable works of art. I learned a lot about an individual artist's approach to sculpture by seeing details in an up-close and personal way—some days, I could almost feel the artist's hand working with the stone," recalls a former intern.

Curatorial

Interns working in this department spend at least some time doing research for upcoming exhibitions. This can include researching and acquiring works as well as assisting with the actual organization and installation of works for a particular show. Most larger museums will have separate curatorial departments for the different media represented, such as sculpture, painting, and photography. Coordinators often emphasize the importance of foreign language skills for interns in this department.

Design

Working in this department requires extensive knowledge of page layout and design software. Interns help with the layout of the brochures and catalogs accompanying exhibits. An intern at the Museum of Modern Art in New York City was responsible for the design of the internship program's 1996 application form.

Education

This department offers the opportunity to develop programs designed for teaching and interacting with the community. Interns may be responsible for designing the structure of activities for student visitors of various ages. In some cases interns actually work with the students themselves. Knowledge of both art and art history as well as education theory is helpful for this kind of internship.

Says one former museum intern, "I spent three summers working with the Raiders of the Fine Arts program at the Brooklyn Museum as an assistant art teacher. The program was designed for youth 4 to 18 years old, but has been expanded to include adult classes as well. We drew heavily on the museum's collection and had the kids sketch and draw for different works and then use these sketches for a larger project that they completed at the end of the program. Because I had participated as a student beginning in sixth grade, I was especially attached to the program and got a lot out of the contact with the kids and the different perspectives that they had on the works that had inspired them."

Interning in a museum's education departments may also include giving talks and tours through the museum's collection or working in the visitor services department. Preparing an individualized tour is a large part of an intern's work in the education department of The Metropolitan Museum of Art, for example.

Public Affairs

The main focus of this department is the distribution of information about the museum to the media as well as the public. Projects vary a lot from one museum to another, but generally include organizing the various forms of advertising and press releases to domestic and international media. Intern coordinators cite writing and foreign language skills as the most useful qualities for interns working in this area.

Publications

Most museums produce several printed publications a year. Interns working in this department will be exposed to many aspects of publishing, including research, writing, and marketing of a museum's catalogs and magazines. Applicants to this department should highlight any notable editorial and writing skills that they possess.

In addition to those mentioned above, some museums also have more specialized departments for legal matters, registrar, grant-making, library and resource collections, and retail operations.

The Application Process

Try to choose one or two areas that you are already familiar with, or in which you would like to gain experience. In your application, describe your specific interest in that field(s). However, since museums often rotate their interns through different departments, or assign interns to departments simply on the basis of availability, be sure to sound like you're flexible.

Because these internships are so well planned and coordinated, particularly in the summer, they are very selective. The selection process begins with the application itself, which can be very detailed in some cases. Museums that provide applications for the internship will generally ask you to list work experience and relevant course work in art history or art, and may require a personal statement of about 500 words describing your interest in museum work and your career goals.

It is important to take some time to fill out the application carefully. Because there are a large number of applicants, a messy application will indicate to whomever is reading it that you do not have a genuine interest in the internship. As several intern coordinators have noted, the greatest strength that a candidate can possess is a true interest in art and a real commitment to the program to which they are applying.

As important as enthusiasm may be, it is equally important for a coordinator to see evidence of a strong background in art and art history. For this reason, applications will often ask you to provide a separate list of the art or art history courses you have taken, in addition to a copy of your transcript. Even if the application asks you to submit only a résumé, transcript, and cover letter, always submit a list of relevant classes that you have taken as well. When listing these courses, keep in mind the kind of museum to which you are applying. For a list submitted to the Museum of Modern Art, list classes in modern art first. For museums that focus on the art of a specific culture, it would be a good idea to emphasize any courses you've taken on the history and art of that culture.

While some museums may require at least eight to ten courses in art history, it is important to keep in mind that museum internships are not exclusively reserved for art and art history majors. In the past, many museums, including The Metropolitan Museum of Art, have accepted undergraduate English and history majors into their summer internship programs. Besides listing specific classes that you have taken, it may also be helpful to list any traveling you might have done, and the museums you have visited in the United States and abroad. This will show that you have a culturally rich background and an overall interest in art.

Institutions that do not have application forms generally request a cover letter, personal statement, or both. The personal statement allows you to express yourself in a less formal way than an application would, and you should be sure to use this to your advantage. Often, a personal statement will ask you to describe yourself, your career goals, your interest in art and museum work, and your interest in the specific internship for which you are applying. Be as specific as possible. In describing your career goals, highlight the elements in your background that have helped you come to your decision. Finally, the personal statement gives you the opportunity to present yourself as a well-rounded individual. In addition to your travel experience, mention any foreign languages you speak. These details will help the intern coordinators form a picture of you as an individual.

Finally, your résumé should reflect the office and communication skills that you possess. Most museum interns do spend a great deal of time working in offices. Since some museum work involves dealing with the public by giving tours or information to visitors, it is important for the coordinators to see evidence of communication and leadership skills, which will be helpful both in the offices and in dealing with the public.

Galleries

Most interns who have worked in both galleries and museums agree that the two experiences diverge, and are in many ways incomparable. To begin with, many galleries do not have access to the same kinds of funding as museums, and are less willing to offer stipends to interns. Some might cover only minimum expenses for their interns, notably transportation and lunch costs. Others will not offer any compensation at all. While museums tend to inform colleges and universities about their internship opportunities, far fewer galleries post such opportunities at schools or in general internship listings. So finding a gallery to work in may be more challenging and require more legwork. Finally, galleries will not offer the same kinds of structured internships as museums. Consequently, interns at galleries tend to have greater amounts of filing and other grunt work required of them than do interns at museums.

However, galleries offer an entirely different perspective on the art market, and one that many interns claim brings you closer to art and artists than museum internships do. "Galleries have always been the ones to take chances on artists' work and the public's understanding of the work. Artists are generally well known to galleries before any work is purchased by a museum," says a former intern. Interns working at galleries in New York report having direct contact with the fast-paced world of artistic communities. The day-to-day work is balanced with invitations to openings and contact with artists and buyers, giving interns a clear feel for the artistic community and the lifestyle that accompanies it.

Finding an internship at a gallery may also be an open opportunity for an intern to create his or own experience. This may well begin with the very search for the right gallery. A local newspaper, art guide, or art magazines such as *Artforum* and *Art in America* offer listings of those galleries representing the most prominent artists. It is a good idea to choose those whose upcoming shows interest you because of either the artist represented or the media in which it most commonly deals. It is a good idea to choose seven to ten galleries.

Regardless of the differences between museums and galleries, both internship opportunities tend to require many of the same skills from their applicants. A background in general art and art history are expected, as well as more detailed knowledge of the kind of media and time period that the specific gallery commonly deals in. Remember to include a list of classes that you have taken in these fields. Stating any previous administrative work you may have done may also prove beneficial.

The Auction House Alternative

Interns who have worked at auction houses (such as Sotheby's or Christie's) rather than museums or galleries claim that working for these houses is a unique and rewarding experience. One intern who worked at Christie's in New York describes her experience. "My day-to-day work may have been tedious at times and included general office and a lot cataloging, but it was also exciting because of the great amount of time that I spent handling art work. Also, the kinds of internships that auction houses run provide interns the opportunity to deal with people on many different levels. That summer, I was able to interact with clients and discuss with them different works they were interested in—a task that proved challenging and educational."

The large auction houses sometimes require interns to show relative expertise in certain areas of art history, such as Eastern Asian arts, in order to qualify for certain programs. Their internship programs often include a lecture series and field trips to museums.

Buffalo Bill Historical Center

720 Sheridan Avenue
Cody, WY 82414
Phone: (307) 578-4005
Fax: (307) 587-5714

Position: Intern

Department: Various

No. of Positions Offered Annually: 12

Description: Interns are placed in one of the Center's four museums (Buffalo Bill Museum, Cody Firearms Museum, Plains Indian Museum, or Whitney Gallery of Western Art) and the McCracken Research Library as well as the Education, Public Relations, Collections or Development departments.

Qualifications: Preference given to upper-level undergraduate students and graduate students.

Salary: $1,000/month (when funding is available)

Position Dates: Fall, Spring and Summer

Position Location: Cody, WY

Average No. of Applicants Annually: 25

Potential for Job Placement: Minimal

Application Process: Application to be completed.

Deadline: Rolling

Contact: Sharon Schroeder

Buffalo Bill Historical Center

720 Sheridan Avenue
Cody, WY 82414
Phone: (307) 578-4005
Fax: (307) 587-5714

Position: Native American Intern

Department: N/A

No. of Positions Offered Annually: 4

Description: Interns have the opportunity to work with one of the world's finest Plains Indian collections and to develop the skills needed to enter the museum profession.

Qualifications: Applicants must have completed at least two years of college and be tribally enrolled members of an American Indian nation.

Salary: $1,000/month

Position Dates: Fall, Spring and Summer

Position Location: Cody, WY

Average No. of Applicants Annually: 12-15

Potential for Job Placement: Minimal

Application Process: Application to be completed.

Deadline: Rolling

Contact: Sharon Schroeder

The Cloisters

Fort Tryon Park
New York, NY 10040
Phone: (212) 650-2280
Fax: (212) 795-3640

Position: Intern

Department: N/A

No. of Positions Offered Annually: 8

Description: Interns are responsible for conducting gallery workshops with groups of New York City day campers and for developing a public gallery talk, which they will deliver in the last week. Integral aspects of the program are intensive training sessions in The Cloisters collection and in museum teaching techniques as well as field trips to New York City institutions and meetings with curators and conservators.

Qualifications: Applicants are expected to be mature individuals who are able to work independently and in a group. All undergraduate college students may apply, with special consideration given to first- and second-year students.

Salary: $2,250 (stipend)

Position Dates: Summer

Position Location: New York, NY

Average No. of Applicants Annually: 250

Potential for Job Placement: Possible

Application Process: Application to be completed.

Deadline: February 1

Contact: Dr. Michael Norris

Denver Art Museum

100 West 14th Avenue Parkway
Denver, CO 80204
Phone: (303) 640-4433
Fax: (303) 640-5627

Position: Education Intern

Department: Education Department

No. of Positions Offered Annually: 12

Description: Internship positions available in the following areas: outreach to culturally diverse audiences, school programs, family programs, adult programs and visitor evaluation. For internship of over one month duration, interns must commit to spend a minimum of 20 hours per week of service at the museum; for internships of only one month in duration, interns must commit to spend 40 hours per week at the museum.

Qualifications: Preference given to interns who will be receiving academic credit from their sponsoring institution.

Salary: Unpaid

Position Dates: Fall, Spring and Summer

Position Location: Denver, CO

Average No. of Applicants Annually: N/A

Potential for Job Placement: N/A

Application Process: Application to be completed.

Deadline: Rolling

Contact: Rogene Cuerden

Hermitage Association

4580 Rachel's Lane
Hermitage, TN 37076-1331
Phone: (615) 889-2941

Position: Intern

Department: N/A

No. of Positions Offered Annually: 15

Description: Interns will participate in all phases of field excavation and laboratory processing of finds, thereby learning the basics of historical archaeology. Five and two-week sessions available. Five-week sessions are intended for advanced undergraduates and early-phase graduate students who have had some field training in archaeology and who are looking for more experience in a research-oriented setting. Two-week sessions are primarily intended for advanced undergraduates and graduate students in such fields as history, African American studies, American studies, folklore and geography. Participants receive room and board in addition to the stipend.

Qualifications: N/A

Salary: $200/week

Position Dates: Summer

Position Location: Hermitage, TN

Average No. of Applicants Annually: 200

Potential for Job Placement: N/A

Application Process: Send letter stating interest in program to receive application.

Deadline: April 10

Contact: Dr. Larry McKee

J. Paul Getty Trust

P.O. Box 2112
Santa Monica, CA 90407-2112
Phone: (310) 230-7156
Fax: (310) 454-8156

Position: Graduate Intern

Department: Education Department

No. of Positions Offered Annually: 20

Description: Interns will work in the Getty Museum and other programs of the Getty Trust. Interns will receive full health care coverage in addition to their salary.

Qualifications: Applicant must be currently enrolled in a university program leading to a graduate degree in art history or another field related to the internship or have completed a relevant graduate degree no more than six months prior to application date.

Salary: $13,837 (9 months); $20,00 (12 months)

Position Dates: 9- and 12-month programs available.

Position Location: Santa Monica, CA

Average No. of Applicants Annually: 225

Potential for Job Placement: Minimal

Application Process: Application to be completed.

Deadline: January 1

Contact: Dr. Andrew J. Clark (E-mail: interns@getty.edu)

J. Paul Getty Trust

P.O. Box 2112
Santa Monica, CA 90407-2112
Phone: (310) 451-4565
Fax: (310) 230-7076

Position: Summer Undergraduate Intern

Department: Education Department

No. of Positions Offered Annually: 15

Description: Each intern will be assigned
to one Getty Program and will work with a
mentor on specific projects. As a group,
interns meet every other week to discuss
aspects of their work, participate in seminars
or take field trips.

Qualifications: Applicants should have an
interest in exploring careers in the arts and
humanities and issues of diversity.
Applicants must be currently enrolled in an
accredited college or university and must
have completed at least two semesters or
three quarters of college at the time of
application. Students from all backgrounds
and disciplines are encouraged to apply.

Salary: $3,300 (stipend)

Position Dates: Summer

Position Location: Santa Monica, CA

Average No. of Applicants Annually:
400-550

Potential for Job Placement: Minimal

Application Process: Application to be
completed.

Deadline: March 1

Contact: Jennifer Hickman (E-mail:
summerinterns@getty.edu)

Los Angeles Municipal Art Gallery

4800 Hollywood Boulevard
Los Angeles, CA 90027
Phone: (213) 485-4581
Fax: (213) 485-8396

Position: Intern

Department: Education Department

No. of Positions Offered Annually: 15

Description: Interns will work in the
Education Department. Tasks may include:
writing curricula for art education programs,
leading tours and providing administrative
support. Internship provides excellent
training in art museum education.

Qualifications: Applicants should have a
background in art, studio art, art history or
education and a desire to work with
children.

Salary: Unpaid

Position Dates: Fall, Spring and Summer

Position Location: Los Angeles, CA

Average No. of Applicants Annually:
25

Potential for Job Placement: Possible

Application Process: Application to be
completed.

Deadline: One month prior to desired start
date.

Contact: Education Coordinator

Museum of Contemporary Art

220 East Chicago Avenue
Chicago, IL 60611-2604
Phone: (312) 280-2660
Fax: (312) 397-4095

Position: Intern

Department: Various

No. of Positions Offered Annually: 75

Description: Internship positions available in the following departments: Audience Development, Marketing, Media, Accounting, Administration, Collections and Exhibitions, Curatorial, Development (annual fund or corporate, foundation and government relations) , Editorial, Education, Graphic Design, Information Systems and Library, Membership, Photo Archives, Public Relations, Performance Programs, Registrar, Retail and Wholesale and Spedial Events and Hospitality.

Qualifications: N/A

Salary: Unpaid

Position Dates: Fall, Spring and Summer

Position Location: Chicago, IL

Average No. of Applicants Annually: 250-300

Potential for Job Placement: N/A

Application Process: Application to be completed.

Deadline: August 15 for Fall; November 15 for Spring; March 15 for Summer.

Contact: Human Resources Manager

Museum of Modern Art

11 West 53rd Street
New York, NY 10019-5498
Phone: (212) 708-9795
Fax: (212) 708-9889

Position: Curatorial Intern

Department: Curatorial Department

No. of Positions Offered Annually: 1

Description: Intern works in the Curatorial Department.

Qualifications: Open to recent graduates interested in pursuing a curatorial career. Minority graduates of art history, museum studies, studio art and related studies encouraged to apply.

Salary: Amount of stipend depends on available funding.

Position Dates: 12 months

Position Location: New York, NY

Average No. of Applicants Annually: N/A

Potential for Job Placement: Possible

Application Process: Application to be completed.

Deadline: June 1

Contact: Internship Coordinator

Museums and Galleries

261

Museum of Modern Art

11 West 53rd Street
New York, NY 10019-5498
Phone: (212) 708-9795
Fax: (212) 708-9889

Position: Noble 12-Month Intern

Department: Management and Development

No. of Positions Offered Annually: 2

Description: Stipends awarded to two interns who will work specifically in Management and Development departments.

Qualifications: Applicants must be college graduates whose academic and/or professional experience combines art history with the following areas: art administration, musuem studies, arts management and development.

Salary: Amount of stipend depends on available funding.

Position Dates: 12 months

Position Location: New York, NY

Average No. of Applicants Annually: N/A

Potential for Job Placement: N/A

Application Process: Application to be completed.

Deadline: June 1

Contact: Internship Coordinator

Museum of Modern Art

11 West 53rd Street
New York, NY 10019-5498
Phone: (212) 708-9795
Fax: (212) 708-9889

Position: Intern

Department: Various

No. of Positions Offered Annually: 100

Description: Internship postions available in the following departments: Curatorial, Curatorial Support, Administrative and Public Service. Stipends are awarded to summer interns based on available funding. No stipends are available for academic-year terms.

Qualifications: Summer program open to college juniors and seniors and graduate students. Fall and Spring programs open to high school, college, graduate students and currently employed museum/art institution professionals.

Salary: Unpaid

Position Dates: Fall, Spring and Summer

Position Location: New York, NY

Average No. of Applicants Annually: 1,000

Potential for Job Placement: N/A

Application Process: Application to be completed.

Deadline: Rolling

Contact: Internship Coordinator

Smithsonian Institution

900 Jefferson Drive SW, MRC 427
Washington, DC 20560
Phone: (202) 357-3102
Fax: (202) 357-3346

Position: Intern

Department: Center for Museum Studies

No. of Positions Offered Annually: 700

Description: Internship opportunities include, but are not limited to historical research, scientific research, collections care and management, public programming and special events, exhibit design, public affairs, development and education. Most of the internships are located in the Washington D.C. area although some are located in New York, Boston and Panama. Additional information on the various specific internship positions available may be found in the free booklet "Internships and Fellowships" or on the Internet at http://www.si.edu./organiza/offices/musstud/intern.htm.

Qualifications: Varies depending on the program.

Salary: Unpaid

Position Dates: Fall, Winter, Spring and Summer

Position Location: Boston, MA; New York, NY; Panama; Washington, DC

Average No. of Applicants Annually: N/A

Potential for Job Placement: N/A

Application Process: Application to be completed.

Deadline: Varies depending on the program.

Contact: Elena Piquer Mayberry (E-mail: siintern@sivm.si.edu)

Solomon R. Guggenheim Museum

1071 Fifth Avenue
New York, NY 10128
Phone: (212) 423-3557

Position: Intern

Department: Internship Programs

No. of Positions Offered Annually: 75

Description: Internships available in the following departments: Archives/Library, Art Service and Production, Conservation, Curatorial, Design, Development, Director's Office, Education, Finance, Information Technology, Legal, Membership, Personnel, Photography, Public Affairs, Publications, Registrar, Special Events and Volunteer Services.

Qualifications: Open to undergraduate and graduate students who wish to supplement their course work with practical museum training. Spring and Fall interns must commit a minimum of two days per week for three months. Summer interns must work full time for nine weeks.

Salary: Unpaid

Position Dates: Fall, Spring and Summer

Position Location: New York, NY

Average No. of Applicants Annually: 225

Potential for Job Placement: N/A

Application Process: Application to be completed.

Deadline: August 1 for Fall; December 1 for Spring; February 1 for Summer.

Contact: Internship Coordinator

Entertainment

by Yen-Wen Cheong

Entertainment internships can be exceptionally rewarding and fun, but can involve grueling hours, low pay (if any), and petty tasks. Interest in the industry and a good attitude can get you noticed and will keep you going when you're wondering why, as a college student, you're sweeping the floor — for the third time that day.

There are two types of entry-level workers in entertainment: interns and production assistants, or "PAs," as novices are known in the industry. The difference is that interns are generally unpaid college students, while PAs are usually low-paid college students or graduates. In addition, interns are usually able to work 9:00 to 5:00 while PAs are often required to work much longer hours. Most PAs work about 50 hours a week. Both interns and PAs work in departments such as art, business, hair and makeup, talent, wardrobe, and writing.

Be Flexible and Keep Things Flowing Smoothly

In an industry epitomized by the saying, "It's not what you know, it's who you know," your best asset may actually be a sincere interest in entertainment. Interns should be "hard working and . . . have a good attitude. The people who have those qualities are the people who get hired," one production manager says.

Although ambition and interest are prerequisites for internships in any field, union laws make them particularly important in the entertainment industry. "Because of union rules, it's really hard to get the hands-on experience. [But interns] can absorb everything even though it's not hands-on, like touching the equipment—they can gain the experience in another way," says the office manager of a popular children's television show.

Many internship coordinators say they do not expect résumés loaded with production experience. Instead they look for students with the potential to contribute and learn. They need students who are willing to schmooze with top stars and escort VIPs on set, and who are also quick to step in when a crisis situation develops—like when a costume needed for a shoot is 40 minutes away at the costume designer's studio, or when the stage manager discovers he needs speaker wire from the local electronics store at the last minute.

Although a background in communications is helpful, it is not a requirement. In other words, don't despair if your course work is heavy on English and history rather than media and marketing. "Communications [courses are] a plus, always, just because [those students] have a better feel for what is going on around them. [But] it's not mandatory as long as [students are] generally interested in entering this field," one office manager says.

Even if your school doesn't offer communications courses, you may be able to clock some time with the local television or radio station. "If your school doesn't offer [communications courses], you have to go into the community," says a University of Michigan graduate, now the office manager of a popular television show.

For most of the year studios are in the preproduction phase. Writers are crafting scripts, talent coordinators are seeking actors, production managers are securing funding. When filming or taping commences, days can get hectic. The best studio managers and taping schedules try to prevent obstacles on the set. Because union laws decree that actors and camera crews be paid by the hour, it is essential that time-consuming obstacles be kept to a minimum. Glitches translate into lost time and, more importantly, wasted money. This means that someone behind the scenes—the intern or PA—has to keep things rolling smoothly, despite the inevitable snags. Someone might send you off to buy a needed item, and then send you trekking off to the same store for the very same item half an hour later.

Because entertainment internships can involve menial tasks, it's extremely important that interns be interested in the field. Even a prestigious internship can get tedious when all it has to offer is a name with clout. "An intern has to be interested in what they want to do or they can be discouraged. You try to do your best every day, but you don't want to commit [to something in which you're not interested] for three months," says a former *Prime Time Live* intern who found she was more interested in children's shows than news.

Intern coordinators say the best interns are the ones who are willing to perform any job, no matter how big or how small. We're "looking for someone who's passionate about [entertainment]—someone who's willing to do the legwork and the small jobs [and who is] enthusiastic about learning the industry," says one office manager and intern coordinator.

Producers, directors, and other industry bigwigs notice effort and interest and may make job offers to particularly competent interns. Because studios and theaters hire most personnel for time periods varying from a few months to a few years, permanent jobs in the entertainment industry are virtually nonexistent. So sticking your foot in a VIP's door is crucial to advancement.

Working in the Television Industry

TV series follow cyclical schedules. Some do their preproduction in the fall, winter, and spring, and then tape in the summer. Others tape on a weekly basis throughout the fall, winter, and spring and then take a break for the summer. So first find a show with a schedule that coincides with yours. Depending on how much flexibility your schedule allows, you might want to time your internship to coincide with the peak period of the department in which you are interested. For example, the hair and makeup department doesn't do much in the preproduction phase. Conversely, creative staff, including script writers, will cover the most ground in the preproduction phase, although changes are always made during taping.

But don't pigeonhole yourself into any one department; if you set your heart on the script department and the script department doesn't need help, you could end up without a job. On the other hand, if you're willing to take a stab at animation, you might find yourself having a lot of fun and making important contacts. Many people working in entertainment started out in areas outside their primary interest, then made the most of their experience by using it as a springboard to future jobs.

One way to find a television internship is to brainstorm a list of shows for which you'd like to work. Some shows—such as *Late Night with David Letterman* and *Sesame Street*—have established internship programs. Others may require extra initiative on your part. If the show on which you've set your heart absolutely does not offer internships, you might want to approach the network that broadcasts the show.

Interning with Carmen Sandiego

Students nationwide owe a lot of their geography knowledge to Carmen. College students grew up with the *Carmen Sandiego* computer game; high school students can hum the catchy tune of the first Carmen Sandiego television series, *Where in the World Is Carmen Sandiego?* The original Carmen show has been replaced by *Where in Time Is Carmen Sandiego?*

Interns for this show are hired in the art, office/studio, and hair and makeup departments and work two eight-hour days a week. The environment is friendly and casual—many employees are themselves recent college graduates. They are generally obliging and willing to share their knowledge of their departments.

Interns get an educational look at the inner workings of a television show, both behind the scenes and on the set. Office/studio interns get the broadest exposure to the production process, performing duties from answering phones, aiding talent coordinators, accompanying visitors to the set, and helping out when tasks arise during taping.

Working in the Film Industry

One of the most effective ways of finding out about available film work is to check published listings and certain Internet sites for the latest shooting schedules. For example, the Mayor's Office of Film, Theatre, and Broadcasting in New York City publishes a list of films shooting in New York. The list is updated weekly and also appears on the Web at http://www.ci.nyc.ny.us/html/filmcom/html/tech.html. Students who snag choice movie assignments are the ones on the ball. Production listings change frequently, so keep checking them. Often, productions need help over the course of several weeks, although the job can last anywhere from a few days to a few months.

In this sense, film internships can offer flexibility unknown in most in other fields. If you're busy for most of the summer but want to get a feel for the industry for a couple of weeks before you start school, chances are you might be able to land a brief job working on a film or TV movie. The downside is that plum jobs often demand immediate availability. Thus, New York and Los Angeles residents have the advantage over students located elsewhere.

Surf These

The following Internet sites might be helpful in tracking down a film or television internship:

- **American Film Market:** http://www.afma.com
- **The Film Zone:** http://filmzone.com
- **Global Film and Media Access:** http://www.global-film.com
- **The Independent Feature Film Project:** http://www.ifp.org
- **The Independent Film Channel Market:** http://www.ifctv.com
- **The Internet Movie Database:** http://us.imdb.com
- **JVIII NYC Film Production Resource Locator:**
  http://www.panix.com/jviii/filmictr/jv3filmi.html
- **Production Weekly:** http://users.aol.com/prodweek
- **The Sundance Channel:** http://www.sundancefilm.com
- **The Writer's Guild of America:** http://www.wga.org

Working in the Music Industry

Most internships in the music industry are in the recording industry. Major companies, such as the Elektra Entertainment Group, PolyGram, and Sony Music Entertainment, have offices not only in New York and Los Angeles but also in many other cities. Thus music internships offer opportunities for students who can't afford (or refuse to pay) the sky-high rents of New York and Los Angeles.

Celebrity Kids Who've Had Entertainment Internships

- Bill Boesky (son of Wall Street's infamous Ivan): *Late Night with David Letterman*
- Karis Jagger (daughter of rocker Mick): *Young Indiana Jones* (TV series)
- Gwynneth Paltrow (daughter of actress Blythe Danner): Williamstown Theatre Festival
- Melissa Rivers (daughter of biting talk show host Joan): CBS News and *Rescue 911*

Archive Films, Inc.

530 West 25th Street
New York, NY 10001
Phone: (212) 675-0115
Fax: (212) 645-2137

Position: Intern

Department: Various

No. of Positions Offered Annually: 10

Description: Internship positions available
in the following departments: Film and
Photo Research, Film Sales, Marketing and
Acquisitions/Duplications. Duties include
preparing tape transfers to NTSC, PAL and
VHS formats, repairing and splicing 35mm
and 16mm original film and searching
archive's computer database to answer
client questions. Internship is unpaid but
interns will receive a small transportation
and meal stipend.

Qualifications: Applicant should have a
strong interest in twentieth century cultural
and film history and experience handling
16mm or 35mm film and making video
duplications.

Salary: unpaid

Position Dates: Fall, Spring and Summer

Position Location: New York, NY

Average No. of Applicants Annually:
100

Potential for Job Placement: Yes

Application Process: Call or write for
application and information.

Deadline: Rolling

Contact: Justin Barke

Assistant Directors Training Program

15503 Ventura Boulevard
Encino, CA 91436
Phone: (818) 386-2545

Position: Assistant Director Trainee

Department: N/A

No. of Positions Offered Annually: 20

Description: Year-long internship in which
interns are required to complete 400 days of
on-the-job training. During training,
interns will be assigned to work on episodic
television, television movies, pilots, mini-
series and feature films with various studios
and production companies. The program is
designed to give interns a basic knowledge
of the organization and logistics of motion
picture and television production.

Qualifications: Applicants must be a
mininum of 21 years of age and have the
legal right to work in the United States.

Salary: $439-$539/week

Position Dates: Applicants accepted on an
annual basis.

Position Location: Encino, CA

Average No. of Applicants Annually:
1,200

Potential for Job Placement: N/A

Application Process: Application to be
completed.

Deadline: November 15

Contact: Elizabeth Stanley

Charlie Rose

499 Park Avenue
New York, NY 10022
Phone: (212) 940-1600

Position: Intern

Department: Internship Program

No. of Positions Offered Annually: 12

Description: Duties include assisting in research and production of a daily talk show.

Qualifications: Applicants hould have an interest in politics, news, film and television.

Salary: unpaid

Position Dates: Fall, Spring and Summer

Position Location: New York, NY

Average No. of Applicants Annually: 60-100

Potential for Job Placement: Yes

Application Process: Send résumé and cover letter stating dates of availability.

Deadline: Rolling

Contact: Cara Famelet

Comedy Central

1775 Broadway, 10th Floor
New York, NY 10019
Fax: (212) 767-4257

Position: Sales Research Intern

Department: N/A

No. of Positions Offered Annually: 3

Description: Intern provides general office support and works on Neilson database. Students must receive college credit to participate in the program.

Qualifications: Applicant must be proficient in Microsoft Word and Microsoft Excel.

Salary: $500 (stipend)

Position Dates: Fall, Spring and Summer

Position Location: New York, NY

Average No. of Applicants Annually: 3

Potential for Job Placement: Yes

Application Process: Send résumé and cover letter.

Deadline: July 31 for Fall; October 21 for Spring; February 28 for Summer.

Contact: Mandy Preville

Comedy Central

1775 Broadway, 10th Floor
New York, NY 10019
Fax: (212) 767-4257

Position: Programming Intern

Department: N/A

No. of Positions Offered Annually: 6

Description: Interns provide general office support and assist staff with research, development, production, on-air promotions, marketing and sales. Students must receive college credit to participate.

Qualifications: Applicant should be detail-oriented and proficent in Excel.

Salary: $500 (stipend)

Position Dates: Fall, Spring and Summer

Position Location: New York, NY

Average No. of Applicants Annually: 20

Potential for Job Placement: Yes

Application Process: Send résumé and cover letter.

Deadline: July 31 for Fall; October 31 for Spring; February 28 for Summer.

Contact: Mandy Preville

Comedy Central

1775 Broadway, 10th Floor
New York, NY 10019
Fax: (212) 767-4257

Position: Production Intern

Department: N/A

No. of Positions Offered Annually: 15

Description: Interns will act as Production Assistants on various programs. Student must receive college credit to participate in the program.

Qualifications: Applicant must possess excellent interpersonal skills and have a strong interest in a career in entertainment. Administrative and computer skills a plus.

Salary: $500 (stipend)

Position Dates: Fall, Spring and Summer

Position Location: New York, NY

Average No. of Applicants Annually: 30

Potential for Job Placement: Yes

Application Process: Send résumé and cover letter.

Deadline: July 31 for Fall; October 31 for Spring; February 28 for Summer.

Contact: Mandy Preville

Comedy Central

1775 Broadway, 10th Floor
New York, NY 100219
Fax: (212) 767-4257

Position: Programming Development Intern

Department: Programming/Development

No. of Positions Offered Annually: 6

Description: Intern will review scripts and submissions and provide general office support. Students must receive college credit to participate in the program.

Qualifications: Excellent interpersonal skills, prior entertainment industry experience a plus, flexibility, administrative and computer skills.

Salary: $500 (stipend)

Position Dates: Fall, Spring and Summer

Position Location: New York, NY

Average No. of Applicants Annually: 10

Potential for Job Placement: Yes

Application Process: Send résumé and cover letter.

Deadline: July 31 for Fall; October 31 for Spring; February 28 for Summer.

Contact: Mandy Preville

Comedy Central

1775 Broadway, 10th Floor
New York, NY 10017
Fax: (212) 767-4257

Position: Media Relations Intern

Department: Media Relations

No. of Positions Offered Annually: 6

Description: Assist with day-to-day public relations efforts. Maintain network press digest. Update press releases and executive bios, maintain press tape library, coordinate press kits and provide general office support. Students must receive college credit to participate in the program.

Qualifications: Good computer skills are required. Organizational skills, interpersonal skills, flexibility.

Salary: $500 (stipend)

Position Dates: Fall, Spring and Summer

Position Location: New York, NY

Average No. of Applicants Annually: 20

Potential for Job Placement: Yes

Application Process: Send résumé and cover letter.

Deadline: July 31 for Fall; October 31 for Spring; February 28 for Summer.

Contact: Mandy Preville

Comedy Central

1775 Broadway, 10th Floor
New York, NY 10019
Fax: (212) 767-4257

Position: Ads Sales Planning and Operations Intern

Department: Ad Sales Planning and Operations

No. of Positions Offered Annually: 3

Description: Develop and maintain filing system. Review projection reports on a weekly basis to make sure all AADV and ADV sheets are accounted for. Re-do AADV and ADV sheets as actual ratings. Track usage of inventory and check new contract reports. Students must receive college credit to participate in the program.

Qualifications: Excel and Word. Detail oriented and flexible. Excellent organizational and interpersonal skills are necessary.

Salary: $500 (stipend)

Position Dates: Fall, Spring and Summer

Position Location: New York, NY

Average No. of Applicants Annually: 10

Potential for Job Placement: Yes

Application Process: Send résumé and cover letter.

Deadline: July 31 for Fall; October 31 for Spring; February 28 for Summer.

Contact: Mandy Preville

Comedy Central

1775 Broadway, 10th Floor
New York, NY 10019
Fax: (212) 767-4257

Position: Affiliate Relations Intern

Department: Affiliate Relations

No. of Positions Offered Annually: 3

Description: Update and maintain local ad sales database, produce local ad sales kits, produce monthly local ad sales mailing, provide general office support. Students must receive credit to participate in the program.

Qualifications: Applicant should be proficient in Microsoft Excel and Microsoft Word and have excellent organizational and interpersonal skills.

Salary: $500 (stipend)

Position Dates: Fall, Spring and Summer

Position Location: New York, NY

Average No. of Applicants Annually: 5

Potential for Job Placement: Yes

Application Process: Send résumé and cover letter.

Deadline: July 31 for Fall; October 31 for Spring; February 28 for Summer.

Contact: Mandy Preville

Comedy Central

1775 Broadway, 10th Floor
New York, NY 10019
Fax: (212) 767-4257

Position: On-Air Promotions Intern

Department: N/A

No. of Positions Offered Annually: 6

Description: Intern provides general office support, assists on external shoots and screenings and assists production assistants. Students must receive college credit to participate.

Qualifications: Previous production, programming or entertainment industry experience a plus.

Salary: $500 (stipend)

Position Dates: Fall, Spring and Summer

Position Location: New York, NY

Average No. of Applicants Annually: 15

Potential for Job Placement: Yes

Application Process: Send résumé and cover letter.

Deadline: July 31 for Fall; October 31 for Spring; February 28 for Summer.

Contact: Mandy Preville

Comedy Central

1775 Broadway, 10th Floor
New York, NY 10019
Fax: (212) 767-4257

Position: Human Resources Intern

Department: Human Resources

No. of Positions Offered Annually: 3

Description: Intern will provide general office support and assist with various human resources initiatives and projects as needed. Students must receive academic credit to participate in the program.

Qualifications: Applicant must be proficient in Microsoft Excel.

Salary: $500 (stipend)

Position Dates: Fall, Spring and Summer

Position Location: New York, NY

Average No. of Applicants Annually: 5

Potential for Job Placement: Yes

Application Process: Send résumé and cover letter.

Deadline: July 31 for Fall; October 31 for Spring; February 28 for Summer.

Contact: Mandy Preville

Comedy Central

1775 Broadway, 10th Floor
New York, NY 10019
Fax: (212) 767-4257

Position: Programming/Market Research
Intern

Department: Various

No. of Positions Offered Annually: 3

Description: Intern provides support to
programming, marketing and new business
departments, coordinates focus group
materials and provides general office
support. Students must receive college
credit to participate in the program.

Qualifications: Applicant should be
proficient in Microsoft Excel and Lotus.

Salary: $500 (stipend)

Position Dates: Fall, Spring and Summer

Position Location: New York, NY

Average No. of Applicants Annually:
10

Potential for Job Placement: Yes

Application Process: Send résumé and
cover letter.

Deadline: July 31 for Fall; October 31 for
Spring; February 28 for Summer.

Contact: Mandy Preville

Comedy Central

1775 Broadway, 10th Floor
New York, NY 10019
Fax: (212) 767-4257

Position: Online Intern

Department: N/A

No. of Positions Offered Annually: 3

Description: Intern will provide online
administrative assistance, respond to online
correspondence via E-mail and organize the
online archive. Students must receive
college credit to participate in the program.

Qualifications: Prior Web experience a
plus. Web knowledge required.

Salary: $500 (stipend)

Position Dates: Fall, Spring and Summer

Position Location: New York, NY

Average No. of Applicants Annually:
10

Potential for Job Placement: Yes

Application Process: Send résumé and
cover letter.

Deadline: July 31 for Fall; October 31 for
Spring; February 28 for Summer.

Contact: Mandy Preville

Late Show with David Letterman

1697 Broadway
New York, NY 10019
Phone: (212) 975-5806

Position: Intern

Department: Various

No. of Positions Offered Annually: 54

Description: *Late Show*'s interns are assigned to work in one of the following departments: Writing, Research, Production, Talent, Mailroom, Music, Tickets, Graphics, Executive Producer's Office and America On-line Office. All interns perform general office tasks as well as tasks specific to their departments. Internships must be for course credit.

Qualifications: All majors welcome to apply. Prior office and internship experience and communications courses helpful but not required.

Salary: Unpaid

Position Dates: Fall, Spring and Summer

Position Location: New York, NY

Average No. of Applicants Annually: 500

Potential for Job Placement: Yes

Application Process: Send résumé and cover letter. Résumés are reviewed and those selected will meet with *Late Show* staff members during each semester's interview process.

Deadline: June 1 for Fall; October 1 for Spring; March 1 for Summer.

Contact: Janice Penino

Lucasfilm Ltd.

P.O. Box 2009
San Rafael, CA 94912-2009
Phone: (415) 471-3400

Position: Intern

Department: Human Resources

No. of Positions Offered Annually: 90

Description: Program exposes students to the entertainment industry and provides practical on-the-job experience. Assignments may be available in such departments as THX, Licensing, Marketing, Publicity, Finance/Accounting, Human Resources, Information Systems, Merchandising, Research, Graphic Design, Guest Services, Food Services and Corporate Fitness. Fall and Spring internships are unpaid and students must therefore receive college credit.

Qualifications: Prospective interns must be junior, senior or graduate-level students with a GPA of at least 3.3. Applicants for Fall and Spring positions must be enrolled at an accredited college located within commuting distance of the internship location.

Salary: $4.25/hour

Position Dates: Fall, Spring and Summer

Position Location: San Rafael, CA

Average No. of Applicants Annually: 500

Potential for Job Placement: N/A

Application Process: Application to be completed.

Deadline: July 31 for Fall; October 31 for Spring; March 30 for Summer.

Contact: Internship Coordinator

Metro-Goldwyn-Mayer/United Artists

1350 Sixth Avenue, 24th Floor
New York, NY 10019
Phone: (212) 708-0407
Fax: (212) 582-2846

Position: Publicity/Promotions Intern

Department: Publicity/Promotions

No. of Positions Offered Annually: 20

Description: Intern duties include: answering phones, mailings, work screenings, set-up of promotions, researching promotional partners and helping with press junkets and premieres. Interns must receive college credit.

Qualifications: Applicants should be familiar with WordPerfect and Excel and feel comfortable making cold calls.

Salary: unpaid

Position Dates: Fall, Spring and Summer

Position Location: New York, NY

Average No. of Applicants Annually: 100

Potential for Job Placement: Minimal

Application Process: Mail or fax résumé and cover letter.

Deadline: Rolling

Contact: Elizabeth Bondy

Mitch Schneider Organization

14724 Ventura Boulevard, Suite 410
Sherman Oaks, CA 91403
Phone: (818) 380-0400
Fax: (818) 380-0430

Position: Intern

Department: N/A

No. of Positions Offered Annually: 10

Description: Responsibilities include assisting in writing news items, organizing mailings, making follow-up phone calls, updating computer datatbase information and researching media and various business contacts. Interns will gain experience working in a music public relations film.

Qualifications: Candidates should have a desire to gain experience in the music public relations industry. Communication and writing skills and computer experience preferred. Open to college students, college graduates, graduate students, career changers and individuals interested in the music industry and public relations work.

Salary: unpaid

Position Dates: Fall, Spring and Summer

Position Location: Sherman Oaks, CA

Average No. of Applicants Annually: 40-60

Potential for Job Placement: Yes

Application Process: Mail or fax résumé and cover letter. In-person interview recommended.

Deadline: Rolling

Contact: Thanh-Thanh Dang

New Breed Entertainment

134 West 26th Street, Suite 770
New York, NY 10001
Phone: (212) 255-0672
Fax: (212) 627-0208

Position: Intern

Department: Various

No. of Positions Offered Annually: 4

Description: Intern will perform all types
of duties, having hands-on experience in
various departments such as Retail,
Marketing and Promotions.

Qualifications: N/A

Salary: unpaid

Position Dates: Fall, Spring and Summer

Position Location: New York, NY

Average No. of Applicants Annually:
150

Potential for Job Placement: Yes

Application Process: Send résumé and
cover letter.

Deadline: Rolling

Contact: Internship Coordinator

PolyGram

825 Eighth Avenue
New York, NY 10019
Phone: (212) 333-8320

Position: Intern

Department: Various

No. of Positions Offered Annually: 150

Description: Opportunities available in
Marketing, Promotions, Publicity, Sales and
Distribution. Interns will learn aspects of the
music business, provide administrative
support and handle projects relating to
artists. Interns must receive college credit to
participate in the program.

Qualifications: N/A

Salary: unpaid

Position Dates: Fall, Spring and Summer

Position Location: New York, NY

Average No. of Applicants Annually:
400

Potential for Job Placement: Yes

Application Process: Send résumé and
cover letter.

Deadline: Rolling

Contact: Jennifer Monahan

Wall Street Music

1189 East 14 Mile Road
Birmingham, MI 48009-2025
Phone: (810) 646-2054
Fax: (810) 646-1957

Position: Intern

Department: Various

No. of Positions Offered Annually: 9

Description: Internship positions available in the following departments: Media/Promotion, Radio and Club Promotion and Engineering/Production.

Qualifications: N/A

Salary: Unpaid

Position Dates: Fall, Spring and Summer

Position Location: Birmingham, MI

Average No. of Applicants Annually: 120

Potential for Job Placement: N/A

Application Process: Application to be completed.

Deadline: Rolling

Contact: Tim Rochon (E-mail: wallstmus@aol.com)

Politics and Government

by Daniel P. Weiss

Internships in the political arena are some of the most competitive and highly sought-after internships out there. Students who are interested in possible careers in law or government vie annually for those coveted spaces on senators' staffs or in the White House. At the outset, you might be intimidated, and it may seem impossible that you will be chosen from the overwhelming number of applicants. But with a bit of advanced planning and dedication, you can bring into reach the internship to which you aspire. Before long, you may find yourself hobnobbing with gubernatorial bigwigs and carving your path to political infamy.

First, you should take a moment to weigh the pros and cons of a political internship. Applying is time consuming, so an informed choice is well in order before you take the first step. Whether they are in Washington, D.C., or elsewhere in the country, political internships can be stressful and, in some instances, might seem like more trouble than they are worth. Here are a few considerations, some big and some small, to keep in mind before you begin.

The Payoffs and the Drawbacks

If you are looking to make a lot of money, a political internship is probably not for you. There are a few internships that pay, so don't rule it out entirely based on financial constraints. But your run-of-the-mill stint with a congressperson probably won't pay off those college loans.

On top of that, you having political internship can get costly. Most of these positions require a certain standard of dress. That usually means business attire—no casual clothes unless otherwise stated. For men, this means ties and dress shirts along with jackets (that can usually be shed in the office). For women, plan on blouses and dress pants, skirts, or suits. So push the jeans, sneakers, and t-shirts to the side of your closet and check out what remains. You would probably need two or three different outfits.

Other expenses include rent, transportation (including travel), and food. Can you afford to rent or sublet an apartment for the summer? Will you have access to public transportation, or will you have to find some other means of getting to and from work? These factors could affect your decision about whom to work for. For example, if you were to accept an unpaid internship with a congressperson, you might want to choose the office closest to your home (even if it's smaller) to cut down on transportation and living expenses.

So why would you want an internship in politics? Because it's a great way to learn about the inner workings of government. A job in a politician's office is a mind-opening opportunity and a chance to see firsthand whether a career in government or law is right for you. But don't delude yourself with visions of accompanying your senator to dinner or sitting behind her at a committee meeting. Be prepared to do anything from helping prepare policy to opening letters, answering phones, and filing. You have to be realistic and know that there is menial work to be done in any office, and someone has to do it. The days can be long and sometimes unrewarding, but overall there are very few people who regret spending their summer in a politician's office.

So what can you hope to get out of a foray into the world of politics? As always, it varies from one internship to another, but most students will find that they are able to play a substantive role in the policy and direction of the office. Research and policy statements are sometimes delegated to interns. There is also the possibility of making real contacts in the political world and building a base of experience for later years. If, for example, you were to work for one of your senators the summer after your freshman year, with a good recommendation and a phone call from the senator's office, you might find yourself in an internship with much more responsibility and prestige the following summer. By the time you enter the job hunt, you might be able to show a progression of internships that showcase your talents and trustworthiness.

You can also gain valuable experience in office management and interpersonal skills in a political internship. As any good politician knows, smooth interpersonal skills are a must for survival in the political arena.

If a political internship still sounds like your cup of tea, it's time to consider specifically what kind of internship you want. There are many categories of political internships, and your personal interests and availability will dictate which type is best for you.

Considering Your Options: From the Capitol to Your Town

Congressional Internships

An internship with a senator or congressional representative is prestigious and difficult to obtain. These positions are almost exclusively for people of college age and older, and most of the internships are based in Washington, D.C. However, certain congresspeople will take on interns in their home state office. Such positions are a good alternative for students who can't afford or don't want to work in D.C. Some students have received these internships after completing their freshman year, although it is usually the older students with more college experience who are delegated more responsibility. However, these positions can still be great career moves for younger students. When they do eventually end up in D.C., they will be given more substantive duties and will be better accustomed to a political office environment.

If this type of internship sounds appealing, here are a few facts to bear in mind. Members of Congress generally take on five to ten interns per summer. For senators, this figure leans toward the higher end because they have bigger staffs and more projects to delegate. There is usually a hierarchy among the interns, based on experience and age. These internships may not last the entire summer; some of them start in June and run to the first or second week in August (Congress goes on vacation in August). While some of these internships are paid, many are not, and none of them is paid very well. The pay from one internship to another varies according to the congressperson's budget, the specific position, and the length of time of the position. For example, if you were to apply for an internship late in the game, the office might write back and offer you an unpaid position on staff in place of nothing at all.

If you are hoping to work for a congressperson, the phrase that should echo again and again in your mind is *earlier is better*. Call or write as early as possible. For a summer position, you should definitely start thinking about applying before your school's winter break. Even if the people in the office laugh and say they won't be accepting applications for a few months, at least they won't be laughing and saying the deadline has long since passed.

Another important pointer, specifically with respect to congressional internships, is to keep your options open by applying to more than one office. Contact as many offices (both near you and in other places you would consider living/working) as you can think of, and solicit information from each about internships. Think of it like the college application process. You probably wouldn't apply to one college only (unless it was a sure bet). You also wouldn't tell a college that you weren't really interested in attending and were far more interested in another college. So even though you might be scoping out several places, always indicate that you would be overjoyed to join the staff of each particular office.

Start with congresspeople in your home state. Each state has two senators and a number of representatives. These politicians might be more receptive to hiring a "local." In addition, you might be more familiar with the issues your own congresspeople are addressing than you would be working for someone in another state. Or consider the congresspeople of the state in which you attend school. In fact, your school might have special connections to a particular congressperson in that state and could help with the search for an internship. Your school might even be the alma mater of one of these politicians, which could work to your advantage.

After you've covered the home base, then check out congresspeople from other states. Do research about them and the issues and legislation that affect their regions. You might have to offer a really compelling reason to be considered over the local internship candidates. So if you have a strong case, be sure to state it. ("I am very interested in Senator X's efforts in environmental legislation. I am a biology major intending to pursue policy in

Making Your Campaign Internship a Winner

The best way to succeed is by taking care of business—whatever someone needs at any given time. You need to be really flexible because you will be working for a number of people. Undertake any task willingly, no matter who gives it.

You will have to do some menial duties but the payoffs are there. Word gets around the office about which interns are excelling at their work. If you can earn a good reputation among your supervisors, they will give you more interesting projects because they'll know you are capable.

Projects include mass mailings and a ton of phone work, calling constituents and reminding them to vote. More interesting projects include fund-raising work or anything that lasts more than just a single day, such as convention planning. You should try to find and approach somebody who is working on a long-term project and needs consistent help, rather than waiting for work to come your way. Volunteering for small projects is the best way to build your reputation, but once you've done that, aim for something bigger that will keep you occupied on a regular basis.

—An intern for the 1996 Clinton-Gore campaign

this field and believe I would learn a lot from exposure to the senator's lobbying and research initiatives in environmental protection.")

State Government Internships

State government positions include jobs with state representatives and state senators, jobs in the governor's office, and general legislative aid jobs (working for the state government generally instead of for a specific legislator). If you live close enough to the state capital, you can live at home and commute to the internship.

State legislators generally hire far fewer interns than their national counterparts. This varies from state to state but most take only one or two. This, however, is not necessarily a bad thing. The competition for these positions is usually less intense than for the national positions, and sometimes the pay is actually better. I had an internship with my state representative that paid $2,400 for eight weeks of work, which was pretty decent for a political internship. Keep in mind that the legislator has no say in how much you are paid. The money depends on whether the legislature approves an internship program for that summer while they are in session.

Money aside, an internship with a state legislator is different from a congressional position in many respects. Because the staff is smaller and there are fewer responsibilities in the office, you will most likely work with only one or two people on a daily basis. In general, state legislative sessions close in July, so you probably won't be on staff for most of August, unless there is a different setup in your particular state. There is also a distinct possibility that you will be working directly, and on a regular basis, with the state congressperson. At a senator's office, you may meet your employer a few times, watch him or her rush in and out during the day. If you're lucky, at the end of the summer he or she might even know your name. Not so at a state legislator's office. Most of these politicians are around often, and in such small offices they cannot help but take notice of the intern extraordinaire (that's you).

Responsibilities in these state internships vary greatly. Most include substantive roles for the first-time intern, including attending sessions, researching, preparing policy, and directing inquiries. It makes a lot of sense to start your political internship career with one of these positions because it builds a solid frame of reference for future jobs and gives you the best chance to have an impact on the office you work in and the agency you work for.

The application process for these positions is generally fairly informal. It would not be out of the ordinary for you to write a letter of interest to your state representative or senator close to or during winter break and express your interest in a summer position. If you don't receive word back by the end of January, make a quick phone call to confirm that the office has received your letter and registered your interest. See if you can get a timetable for the decision-making process and set a further date for communication.

Connections can play a very important part in your application for an internship in the state legislature. Also if you've ever met the legislator or if your parents know him or her, be sure to mention that in the letter.

Don't ignore the possibility of working for state legislators outside of your own district. Try first for your own legislator, but if you really want to work at the state level, send applications to three or four offices to ensure that you have a good chance of being accepted for at least one post.

County/City/Town Government Internships

County, city, and town governments might also have internship positions available, and even if they don't, they might be willing to create one without much trouble. Working for your local government is a viable option, especially for those of you who live in sections of the country with strong county governments. There are plenty of roles to play in such administrations.

These local internships are ideal for students who are looking for a restful summer, away from the hustle and bustle of a capital city. You could end up working with people you already know, making the transition to an office environment much more comfortable. While the work may not be very rigorous or varied, the pressure isn't overwhelming, either.

Sometimes, however, local internships can be very challenging. Most local governments don't have interns and are often short-staffed, so you could end up doing something more substantive than photocopying. When talking to local officials about interning, you should definitely try to pinpoint what their needs are and what you can offer them. If there is a project that requires attention, sell yourself as the person to do the job. Let them know that you are choosing a local position precisely because you want more hands-on experience. You can stuff envelopes anywhere. But because you know everything about and everyone in Your Town, USA, you already have the necessary background to take on serious tasks.

If you're worried that such local positions might be too relaxing, consider working with the government of a nearby big city. Big-city government offices are intense and fast paced. Still, you're less likely to get noticed there than in a small, local government office. Just keep in mind that working locally entails living at home, seeing a lot of the same people you grew up

Biting the Big Apple

Live in New York City and want to intern in local politics and goverment? The New York City Department of Personnel publishes its own summer internship guide, which describes city administrative and political internships. For more information, write to the NYC Department of Citywide Administrative Services, Division of Citywide Personnel Services, 2 Washington Street, New York, NY 10004.

with, and working in somewhat familiar settings. These could be deciding factors either for or against this sort of internship.

Branching Out: Other Political Internships

Classic political internships are traditionally found in the legislative branch. However, there are also valuable internship opportunities in the executive and judicial branches of government. These internships are among the most competitive in the country. Generally, students who apply for these already have some background in political internships or in student politics. These internships programs are particularly rewarding because they often include seminars and special opportunities designed especially for interns. Internships in the judicial branch are few and far between and are mostly reserved for law school students, but it never hurts to call and ask if there is anything available for undergrads.

During a campaign year, there are numerous positions for enterprising college and high school students. These are almost always unpaid internships, but the work is plentiful and the help is greatly appreciated. If you have interned for the candidate before or have extensive office experience, then the chances of doing something important and substantive increase greatly. You might find yourself responsible for recruiting voters in your age group, for example.

Extragovernmental jobs are increasingly considered to be political positions, even though they aren't directly connected to the government. Lobbying agencies and special interest groups usually accept interns, and you can gain political experience just as easily working for them as you can working for a government. It's important to see how the government works from the outside and how outside forces work on the government. Groups such as Greenpeace, the National Rifle Association, the Christian Coalition, and the American Civil Liberties Union either have internship programs or might create a position for you. (See the chapter on advocacy internships for more information.)

Getting on the Political Bandwagon

Once you've decided what kind of political internship you want, it's time to get serious and devote your energy to pursuing this goal. First and foremost, there is no real substitute for your own ingenuity and improvisation. Be willing to go all out.

During the fall semester, compile a list of offices and organizations for whom you would like to work the following summer. Contact them, asking for application forms and any literature they might have (your school's career services office might also have some information). By winter break, you should have narrowed down your list.

Over the break, fill out your applications and send them out. Enclose a résumé even if the application doesn't ask for one. Try to tailor your résumé to an organization by emphasizing any strengths you have that would interest that particular group. For example, if you are applying to Greenpeace, highlight any community service or volunteering that you've done, even if it was in high school. If you are applying for a traditional government internship, place emphasis on your organizational skills and your ability to get the job done. Show yourself as task oriented and efficient, capable of meeting deadlines and of completing quality work.

Your cover letter is important. It's usually the first thing that gets read, and it's the most effective way for you to show your enthusiasm for the job and to reveal who you are as a person. Always customize each letter to show your interest in that specific group. Do a little research in order to make your application stand out above the rest. If you are applying for a job with a senator or a congressperson, find out which bills he or she is sponsoring and mention the legislation in your letter. ("Congresswoman Doe, I have been tracking your antitobacco efforts closely as it is an issue I feel strongly about. Here on campus, I have been a member of a student coalition to ensure smoke-free buildings for all community members.") Show how informed you are. Read any recent publication the group might have published, and comment on it in your letter.

Cover letters and résumés are also critical places to point out what makes you a "political type." You might have served in a political organization on your school's campus. For example, during the last election, you might have done some campaigning for local or national candidates. You might be a member of your school's Democrat or Republican student group. You may have participated in political debates.

Involvement in the student government suggests a general interest in organizing and helping to rally a community. Highlight any special goals you accomplished in office. For example, as a representative in your student senate, you managed to improve facilities in your dorm. What does this have to do with your congressperson's political agenda? Not much. But it shows you have a knack for representing people and negotiating their demands. Point out any leadership positions you have held with any group; again, these illustrate your ability to balance a host of interests and still achieve some group goal. Any management role you have had, whether it be director of a play or editor of a student newspaper, can be used to exemplify your leadership, interpersonal, and organizational skills. Finally, draw some links between your experiences and the ways in which these would be further enhanced by an internship.

Recommendations from people who can attest to your organizational skills and energy are an important bonus. If you can't think of anyone, don't fret. Lack of references won't totally sink your application. But consider all possibilities—a teacher who knows you pretty well, a leader of an extracurricular activity (including sports), an employer. Make sure that the recommendations are more than just generally glowing endorsements of you. Have your references highlight specific accomplishments or traits that showcase why you would make an excellent addition to someone's staff. Limit the number of recommendations to three.

From the Front Lines of Justice

In my summer internship with the Department of Justice, Special Litigation section, I was sent to a state incarceration facility to assist in the deposition of inmates for a trial against the prison. The D.O.J. was suing the prison for the mistreatment of prisoners and violations of constitutional rights. One of the big areas of investigation was how prisoners were treated in the maximum security area, and that was where I was supposed to depose a witness.

No one ever tells you specifically how to treat murderers—when you are in the same room with them there is a feeling that is unexplainable to someone else, precluding the effectiveness of advice. The guy I was talking to had killed two people ("Ya know, I was working then as a carny, and, carny, it's a hard life, and some guy had some Jim Beam, and, ya know I wouldn't have even been at that if as a kid my dad wasn't a bastard, and some guys were shovin', and ya know, he used to put out cigarettes on my arms, and then I made a stupid mistake, and now I'm here") and while in prison needed protection, which he did not receive. He was in complete restraints—leg shackles, handcuffs, chest restraint, bright orange jumpsuit, and a gag attached if it proved necessary.

Throughout the deposition I waited to understand how this man was different from me. I waited, listening to how he answered questions and what he said when challenged and how he responded when the guard came to take him away, for the thing that made us different. I waited to discover the thing that proved he was a murderer and I wasn't, and that it was fair that he was in jail and I was free, and why he would be gagged and I wore a tie, and why he had scars from where he had attempted suicide "just so I could get out" and I was a summer intern at the Department of Justice, pretending I understood the world well enough to ask a man about his life, when I couldn't even understand who the man was. All I really learned was how we are the same.

—Yale history major

The FBI Wants You

Internships in the executive branch of the national government allow you to work for some of the most exciting agencies in the country. For example:

Central Intelligence Agency
Defense Information Systems Agency
Defense Nuclear Facilities Safety Board
Department of Agriculture
Department of Commerce
Department of Labor
Department of State
Department of Treasury
Executive Office of the President
Federal Bureau of Investigation
National Security Agency
U.S. Information Agency
White House Intern Program

Waiting It Out

If you haven't heard anything by the middle to end of February, write a quick note or call to check on the status of your application and to make sure that the internship coordinators have received it. Find out if they have a timetable for the decision-making process, and what other stages are involved, such as interviews or second applications. Interviews are common for positions that are highly competitive and are usually conducted over the phone.

Be ready to answer questions based on prior experiences and on your expectations of the internship. Be sure to sound enthusiastic and natural. Don't be nervous, and try not to hesitate too much when you are asked questions. Your interviewers will be analyzing you not only by what you say but also by how you say it. In addition to the tough questions, they may ask you about mundane things, like which days you can work, travel arrangements, and what other internships you are applying for. Have this information handy, because it will expedite the decision-making process. Most important, be yourself and try to enjoy it.

When you finally receive word about their decision, it's up to you to move quickly. If the news is good, start looking for a place to live, and make travel arrangements (if necessary). Make a dry run a few days before the start of your internship so that you don't get lost on the first day of work. Visit the office ahead of time and introduce yourself. That way, you won't feel like a complete stranger when you show up for work.

If the news is bad, then the fight for a decent summer internship is far from over. Hopefully, you applied for more than one job. But if you end up with no offers at all, then it's time for Plan B. This will take a little frantic legwork, but it might just pay off. Call around to different organizations, particularly lobbying groups or local/municipal agencies, to see if they have any positions open for the summer. So it's a little late in the game—you might luck out. Just be aware that you might have to be very flexible—for example, agreeing to work for free. Even a senator's office might accept a volunteer. In fact, there are very few groups that will turn down a volunteer, especially an enthusiastic one. Bear in mind that present sacrifices could reap future rewards; interning in a small, municipal office for free could get you in the door of your state senator the following summer.

If you are determined to find a political internship, you have many options open to you. Not all are easy, and few will be handed to you on a platter. But by planning ahead and pursuing intensely, you should be able to find the right match. Once you have the internship, you can use the time to make connections in the political world. Your internship experience will provide invaluable insight into the political arena—and let you know whether or not you belong there.

Brookings Institution

1775 Massachusetts Avenue NW
Washington, DC 20036-2188
Phone: (202) 797-6000
Fax: (202) 797-6004

Position: Governmental Studies Intern

Department: Governmental Studies Program

No. of Positions Offered Annually: 25

Description: Full- and part-time positions available. Main responsibility of the intern is to provide research assistance for the program's current projects. Interns will have the chance to participate in substantive and independent research in areas of American government such as the appropriations process, omnibus legislation, campaigns and elections, executive branch restructuring, welfare reform and criminal justice policy.

Qualifications: Applicant must be college junior, senior or graduate student with background in American government and political science.

Salary: Unpaid

Position Dates: Fall, Spring and Summer

Position Location: Washington, D.C.

Average No. of Applicants Annually: 140

Potential for Job Placement: N/A

Application Process: Send résumé, cover letter, transcript, two letters of recommendation and a short (three- to five-page) writing sample.

Deadline: Rolling

Contact: Assistant to the Program Director

Brookings Institution

1775 Massachusetts Avenue NW
Washington, DC 20036-2188
Phone: (202) 797-6000
Fax: (202) 797-6004

Position: Information Technology Intern

Department: Information Technology Services

No. of Positions Offered Annually: 2

Description: Full- and part-time internships available throughout the year. Duties of intern are to assist information technology staff in providing user support, computer service and Web page development to Brookings.

Qualifications: Experience with computers is required.

Salary: Unpaid

Position Dates: Fall, Spring and Summer

Position Location: Washington, D.C.

Average No. of Applicants Annually: 2

Potential for Job Placement: N/A

Application Process: Send résumé and cover letter.

Deadline: Rolling

Contact: Manager of Information Services

Brookings Institution

1775 Massachusetts Avenue NW
Washington, DC 20036-2188
Phone: (202) 797-6000
Fax: (202) 797-6004

Position: Public Affairs Intern

Department: Public Affairs

No. of Positions Offered Annually: 3

Description: This internship offers the challenge of assisting in the day-to-day activities of a busy public affairs office. Duties include responding to telephone inquiries from the general public, media, government, academic and other organizations in the U.S. and abroad, assisting in the production of the *Media Guide,* updating press lists and completing other office duties as assigned.

Qualifications: Applicant must be an undergraduate majoring in mass communications, public relations, journalism, or a related subject.

Salary: Unpaid

Position Dates: Fall, Spring and Summer

Position Location: Washington, DC

Average No. of Applicants Annually: 35-40

Potential for Job Placement: N/A

Application Process: Send résumé and cover letter.

Deadline: Rolling

Contact: Internship Coordinator

Brookings Institution

1775 Massachusetts Avenue NW
Washington, DC 20036-2188
Phone: (202) 797-6004
Fax: (202) 797-6004

Position: Economic Studies Intern

Department: Economic Studies Program

No. of Positions Offered Annually: 4

Description: Responsibilties include: verification of statistical data, verifying of manuscript materials, econometric modeling, literature searching and working with statistical, spreadsheet and word processing software.

Qualifications: Applicant should be an undergraduate senior majoring in math or economics or a graduate student of economics.

Salary: Unpaid

Position Dates: Summer

Position Location: Washington, D.C.

Average No. of Applicants Annually: 10

Potential for Job Placement: N/A

Application Process: Send résumé and cover letter.

Deadline: Rolling

Contact: Intern Coordinator

Carter Center

453 Freedom Parkway
Atlanta, GA 30307
Phone: (404) 420-5151
Fax: (404) 420-5196

Position: Intern

Department: N/A

No. of Positions Offered Annually: 120

Description: The internship program has special appeal for those who wish to combine academic study with practical application and experience. Interns participate in Carter Center projects related to contemporary international and domestic issues. Interns must commit a minimum of 15 hours per week for at least one semester. Interns are given long-term and short-term research projects. Duties may also include administrative duties. Academic credit available

Qualifications: Open to undergraduates, graduate students, and professional students who have demonstrated superior academic ability and who have course work, professional or personal experience, and career interests related to the Carter Center.

Salary: Unpaid

Position Dates: Fall, Spring and Summer

Position Location: Atlanta, GA

Average No. of Applicants Annually: 400

Potential for Job Placement: N/A

Application Process: Application to be completed. Sealed transcripts and confidential letters of recommendation must also be sent.

Deadline: June 15 for Fall; October 15 for Spring; March 15 for Spring

Contact: Internship Coordinator

Center for California Studies, California State University

The Center for California Studies
California State University
Sacramento, CA 95819-6081

Position: Jessie Marvin Unruh Assembly Fellow

Department: N/A

No. of Positions Offered Annually: 18

Description: The fellowship offers college graduates full-time legislative staff experience coupled with a graduate seminar conducted by California State University, Sacramento. Health care is provided.

Qualifications: Applicants must have completed a bachelor's degree by the October start of the fellowship. Individuals with advanced degrees or those in mid career are also encouraged to apply.

Salary: $1,538/month (stipend)

Position Dates: One year (October to September)

Position Location: Sacramento, CA

Average No. of Applicants Annually: 300

Potential for Job Placement: Possible

Application Process: The application includes academic, employment and activities information, transcripts from colleges attended, personal and policy statements, and three letters of reference.

Deadline: February 19

Contact: Mimi Morris, Director

Connecticut Judicial Volunteer Program

2275 Silas Deane Highway, P.O. Box 390
Rocky Hill, CT 06067
Phone: (860) 563-5797
Fax: (860) 563-5797

Position: Judicial Volunteer Intern

Department: Various

No. of Positions Offered Annually: 800

Description: Interns are placed in adult probation, juvenile matters, family division, or state attorney and public defender's offices statewide. Interns will aquire inside knowledge of the criminal court process and legal system.

Qualifications: College juniors, seniors, law students, graduates, and paralegal students with good communication skills, mature attitude, and interest in the Criminal Justice System are eligible.

Salary: N/A

Position Dates: Fall, Spring and Summer

Position Location: Rocky Hill, CT

Average No. of Applicants Annually: 1,000

Potential for Job Placement: Good

Application Process: Call program supervisor for an application.

Deadline: Rolling

Contact: Volunteer/Intern Services, Office of Adult Probation

Illinois Legislative Staff Intern Program

UIS, PAC 472
Springfield, IL 62794-9243
Phone: (217) 786-6602
Fax: (217) 786-6542

Position: Legislative Research Intern

Department: Legislative Research

No. of Positions Offered Annually: 4

Description: Interns work in the Legislative Research Unit performing various types of research.

Qualifications: Must have a B.A.

Salary: $1,600/month

Position Dates: September 16 to July 31

Position Location: Springfield, IL

Average No. of Applicants Annually: 100

Potential for Job Placement: Yes

Application Process: Application to be completed. Must also send in official transcript, and three letters of recommendation, and have an interview.

Deadline: March 1

Contact: Program Coordinator

Illinois Legislative Staff Intern Program

UIS, PAC 472
Springfield, IL 62794-9243
Phone: (217) 786-6602
Fax: (217) 786-6542

Position: Partisan Staff Intern

Department: Partisan Staff

No. of Positions Offered Annually: 16

Description: Full-time position. Sixteen interns will work with the partisan staff in analyzing bills and drafting legislation.

Qualifications: Must have a B.A.

Salary: $1,600/month

Position Dates: October 1 to August 15

Position Location: Springfield, IL

Average No. of Applicants Annually: 100

Potential for Job Placement: Yes

Application Process: Application to be completed. Must send in official transcript and three letters of recommendation, and must have an interview.

Deadline: March 1

Contact: Program Coordinator

Institute for Policy Studies

1601 Connecticut Avenue NW, #500
Washington, DC 20009
Phone: (202) 234-9382
Fax: (202) 387-7915

Position: Intern

Department: Various

No. of Positions Offered Annually: 20

Description: Interns will work on a specific project. Interns should indicate on their application which projects best suit them: Africa Project, Corportate Accountability/National Tax Policy/Feminist Agenda Project, Cuba Project, Global Communities Project, Global Economic Integration Project, The Good Society Project, Human Rights Award Event, Membership Development/Publication Promotions, Pathways to the 21st Century, Press/Public Relations, Social Action Leadership School for Activists (SALSA), State of the District Project, Sustainable Communities Project, Sustainable Energy and Environmental Network, Databook Research and Writing, and Public Trust and Action Campaign (PTRAC). An administrative assistant is also needed.

Qualifications: Desire to work in an intellectually challenging environment.

Salary: Unpaid

Position Dates: Fall, Spring and Summer

Position Location: Washington, D.C.

Average No. of Applicants Annually: N/A

Potential for Job Placement: N/A

Application Process: Application form, cover letter, résumé, a brief writing sample (no more than five pages), and a transcript.

Deadline: Rolling

Contact: Intern Coordinator, IPS

New York City Fellowship Programs

2 Washington Street, 15th Floor
New York, NY 10004
Phone: (212) 487-5698
Fax: (212) 487-5715

Position: Government Scholar

Department: N/A

No. of Positions Offered Annually: 25

Description: Interns are given full-time positions in city government.

Qualifications: College sophomores, juniors, or senior who are interested in pursuing a career in municipal government. All majors and levels of experience welcome.

Salary: $3,000 (stipend)

Position Dates: Summer

Position Location: New York, NY

Average No. of Applicants Annually: 350

Potential for Job Placement: N/A

Application Process: Call office in October for an application.

Deadline: January 13

Contact: Natalie Thompson

New York City Fellowship Programs

2 Washington Street, 15th Floor
New York, NY 10004
Phone: (212) 487-5698
Fax: (212) 487-5715

Position: Urban Fellow

Department: N/A

No. of Positions Offered Annually: 25

Description: Interns are given full-time positions in city government.

Qualifications: Recent college graduate, no more than two fall semesters out of college.

Salary: $18,000/year and health insurance

Position Dates: Academic year

Position Location: New York, NY

Average No. of Applicants Annually: 350

Potential for Job Placement: Positive

Application Process: Call office in October for application.

Deadline: January 20

Contact: Natalie Thompson, Assistant Director

Public Defender Service for D.C.

451 Indiana Avenue NW
Washington, DC 20001
Fax: (202) 626-8437

Position: Intern Investigator and Case-Assistant

Department: Trial Division

No. of Positions Offered Annually: 100

Description: Interns work one-on-one with one or two attorneys in the trial division. A thorough, pretrial investigation of the facts of each case is a prerequisite to providing our clients with the highest quality representation.

Qualifications: All majors encouraged. Fluency in a second language is a plus. Strong oral and written communication skills necessary.

Salary: Unpaid

Position Dates: Fall, Winter Break, Spring and Summer

Position Location: Washington, D.C.

Average No. of Applicants Annually: 300-500

Potential for Job Placement: N/A

Application Process: Application to be completed. Send résumé.

Deadline: Rolling

Contact: Kesha Taylor, Intern Coordinator

Securities and Exchange Commission (SEC)

450 Fifth Avenue NW
Washington, DC 20549
Phone: (202) 942-4150

Position: Summer Law Student Intern

Department: N/A

No. of Positions Offered Annually: 25

Description: Provides legal assistance and research for staff attorneys.

Qualifications: First- or second-year law students. Top 20% of class. Law review or moot court. Securities industry course work.

Salary: $13-$14/hour

Position Dates: Summer

Position Location: Washington, D.C.

Average No. of Applicants Annually: 300

Potential for Job Placement: Some

Application Process: Send cover letter, résumé, law school transcript, writing sample, and three references.

Deadline: Second Friday in February

Contact: Liz Persell, Attorney Recruitment Coordinator

Securities and Exchange Commission (SEC)

450 Fifth Street NW
Washington, DC 20540
Phone: (202) 942-4150

Position: Clerk

Department: N/A

No. of Positions Offered Annually: 30

Description: To provide office assistance to attorneys, accountants, and securities compliance examiners.

Qualifications: Computer literate. Typing skills.

Salary: $8-$9/hour

Position Dates: Summer

Position Location: Washington, D.C.

Average No. of Applicants Annually: 500

Potential for Job Placement: None

Application Process: Submit government application (OF-612) and transcript.

Deadline: March 15

Contact: Arlene Green, Summer Recruitment Coordinator

Securities and Exchange Commission (SEC)

450 Fifth Street NW
Washington, DC 20549
Phone: (202) 942-4150

Position: Law Intern

Department: N/A

No. of Positions Offered Annually: 20

Description: Interns work with attorneys to learn more about federal securities laws.

Qualifications: B average, law review or moot court, interest in security field

Salary: Unpaid

Position Dates: Summer

Position Location: Washington, D.C.

Average No. of Applicants Annually: 200

Potential for Job Placement: Good

Application Process: Send cover letter, résumé, law school transcript, short writing sample, and three references.

Deadline: First week in March

Contact: Candyce Pare, Division of Enforcement

Supreme Court of the United States

Supreme Court of the United States, Room 5
Washington, DC 20543
Phone: (202) 479-3415

Position: Judicial Intern

Department: N/A

No. of Positions Offered Annually: 2

Description: Interns work full time and perform some routine office tasks that include clipping and copying news articles and preparing memoranda and correspondence. They also conduct background research for speeches and review legislation on the federal judicial system. Interns will also be given a long-term research project to complete.

Qualifications: 1) High intellectual development, including an ability to think clearly, speak articulately, and write cogently; substantial research experience; some course work on constitutional law or on the Supreme Court; a demonstrated capacity to absorb extensive information and to analyze, summarize, and derive conclusions from it. 2) Ability and willingness to work closely with others in a complex and sensitive organization. 3) Capacity to undertake a variety of tasks as assigned and to function with a low profile. 4) Unusual trustworthiness and discretion. 5) Self-sustaining motivation and initiative.

Salary: Unpaid

Position Dates: Fall, Spring and Summer

Position Location: Washington, D.C.

Average No. of Applicants Annually: 80

Potential for Job Placement: N/A

Application Process: Send in a cover letter, résumé, an official transcript, a writing sample (i.e., a short term paper), three letters of recommendation, and an essay on the importance of the U.S. constitutional system.

Deadline: June 1 for Fall; October 10 for Spring; March 10 for Summer

Contact: Office of the Administrative Assistant to the Chief Justice

United States Chamber of Commerce

1615 H Street NW
Washington, DC 20062-2000
Fax: (202) 463-5328

Position: Intern

Department: Various

No. of Positions Offered Annually: 100

Description: The Chamber offers internships in the following departments: Accounting, Art, Broadcast, Congressional Affairs/International, Domestic Policy, GAIN/Grassroots Action, Human Resources, Magazine Marketing, Media Relations, Membership, Planning and Marketing, Publishing, and Regional Offices. All internships will require some writing and research. Interns may receive credit, but it is not guaranteed.

Qualifications: Applicants must be in their junior or senior year of college or currently enrolled in graduate programs.

Salary: Local transportation allowance

Position Dates: Year round

Position Location: Washington, D.C.

Average No. of Applicants Annually: 300 to 400

Potential for Job Placement: Yes

Application Process: Application to be completed. Must also send in cover letter, résumé, a writing sample, and an academic letter of recommendation.

Deadline: Rolling

Contact: Internship Coordinator, Human Resources Department

University of Illinois for Illinois General Assembly

UIS, PAC 466
Springfield, IL 62794-9243
Phone: (217) 786-6574
Fax: (217) 786-6542

Position: Science Writing Intern

Department: Legislative Research

No. of Positions Offered Annually: 2

Description: The positions are for the Legislative Research Unit, the general bipartisan research agency of the General Assembly. The LRU answers a wide variety of inquiries from legislators, and often publishes articles on scientific topics in its legislative newsletter, *First Reading*.

Qualifications: Applicants must have a B.A. by the start of the internship and have at least a 3.0 GPA. Applicants must write clearly and have critical thinking skills.

Salary: $1,600 per month

Position Dates: September 16 to July 31

Position Location: Springfield, IL

Average No. of Applicants Annually: 10 to 20

Potential for Job Placement: Good

Application Process: Call or E-mail (aldrich@uis.edu) for application.

Deadline: March 1

Contact: Ann Aldrich, Program Assistant

University of Illinois for Illinois General Assembly

UIS, PAC 466
Springfield, IL 62794-9243
Phone: (217) 786-6574
Fax: (217) 786-6542

Position: Partisan Staff Intern

Department: N/A

No. of Positions Offered Annually: 16

Description: Major duties are researching issues, drafting bills, and analyzing bills and agency budget requests to prepare for committee and floor action. General office support will also be expected.

Qualifications: Must have a B.A. at the start of the internship.

Salary: $1,600 per month

Position Dates: October 1 to August 15

Position Location: Springfield, IL

Average No. of Applicants Annually: 100 to 150

Potential for Job Placement: Good

Application Process: Call or E-mail (aldrich@uis.edu) for application.

Deadline: March 1

Contact: Ann Aldrich, Program Assistant

University of Illinois for Illinois General Assembly

UIS, PAC 466
Springfield, IL 62794-9243
Phone: (217) 786-6574
Fax: (217) 786-6542

Position: Research Intern

Department: Legislative Research Unit

No. of Positions Offered Annually: 2

Description: The Legislative Research Unit researches a wide variety of questions on public issues for legislators. Legislators use this research to develop programs, support or oppose bills, and aid other legislative activities.

Qualifications: Applicants must have a B.A. by the start of the internship.

Salary: $1,600 per month

Position Dates: September to July

Position Location: Springfield, IL

Average No. of Applicants Annually: 100

Potential for Job Placement: Good

Application Process: Call or E-mail (aldrich@uis.edu) for application.

Deadline: March 1

Contact: Ann Aldrich, Program Assistant

Woodrow Wilson International Center for Scholars

1000 Jefferson Drive SW
Washington, DC 20560
Phone: (202) 357-2429
Fax: (202) 357-4439

Position: Intern

Department: N/A

No. of Positions Offered Annually: 60

Description: Interns search for source materials at area institutions, and are responsible for analyzing and summarizing the materials. Interns will compile bibliographies and proofread and edit written work. The interns benefit from participation in the international and intellectual ambiance of an institution dedicated to the highest scholarly pursuits.

Qualifications: Juniors, seniors, and graduate students are eligible.

Salary: Unpaid

Position Dates: Fall, Spring and Summer

Position Location: Washington, D.C.

Average No. of Applicants Annually: 500

Potential for Job Placement: None

Application Process: Send résumé, transcript, and two letters of references.

Deadline: Fall: August 1; Spring: November 1; Summer: March 20

Contact: Bahman Amini, Internship Coordinator

Advocacy

by Duncan P. Levin

Take a look at the sidebar that starts on the next page. It contains the Bill of Rights, the first ten amendments to the Constitution of the United States of America. It's sacred land. The first eight amendments outline the fundamental rights and freedoms of every American citizen. The last two amendments explicitly forbid Congress from creating any new laws that might violate the first eight. If there's a mission statement for any public-interest advocacy group, it is to be a watchdog for the people and protect these fundamental rights.

Keeping in mind the Bill of Rights, think about some of the significant things that took place in 1996. Colorado's antihomosexual Amendment 2 initiative—which would have resulted in homosexual Colorado citizens' being treated differently under the law than heterosexual citizens—was struck down by the U.S. Supreme Court. A federal three-judge panel ruled against a new law that would criminalize "indecent" speech—whatever that is—on the Internet. The Virginia Military Institute was required to admit women, a great victory for equal rights. Referenda passed in California and Arizona that push for legalization of marijuana for medicinal use.

But remember, too, that in 1996 the death penalty was resurrected in Oregon and New York. The first triple execution in the United States took place (in Alabama) in 1996, as well as the first firing-squad execution since 1977. In 1996, FBI wire-tapping reached record levels. (According to the American Civil Liberties Union, the FBI is planning to *more than double* the number of private calls it listens in on within the next eight years.) The president signed into legislation "welfare reform" bills that wind up hurting America's

United States Bill of Rights

Amendment I

Congress shall make no law respecting an establishment of religion, or prohibiting the free exercise thereof; or abridging the freedom of speech, or of the press; or the right of the people peaceably to assemble, and to petition the Government for a redress of grievances.

Amendment II

A well regulated Militia, being necessary to the security of a free State, the right of the people to keep and bear Arms, shall not be infringed.

Amendment III

No Soldier shall, in time of peace be quartered in any house, without the consent of the Owner, nor in time of war, but in a manner to be prescribed by law.

Amendment IV

The right of the people to be secure in their persons, houses, papers, and effects, against unreasonable searches and seizures, shall not be violated, and no Warrants shall issue, but upon probable cause, supported by Oath or affirmation, and particularly describing the place to be searched, and the persons or things to be seized.

Amendment V

No person shall be held to answer for a capital, or otherwise infamous crime, unless on a presentment or indictment of a Grand Jury, except in cases arising in the land or naval forces, or in the Militia, when in actual service in time of War or public danger; nor shall any person be subject for the same offense to be twice put in jeopardy of life or limb; nor shall be compelled in any criminal case to be a witness against himself, nor be deprived of life, liberty, or property, without due process of law; nor shall private property be taken for public use, without just compensation.

Amendment VI

In all criminal prosecutions, the accused shall enjoy the right to a speedy and public trial, by an impartial jury of the State and district wherein the crime shall have been committed, which district shall have been previously ascertained by law, and to be informed of the nature and cause of the accusation; to be confronted with the witnesses against him; to have compulsory process for obtaining witnesses in his favor, and to have the Assistance of Counsel for his defense.

Amendment VII

In suits at common law, where the value in controversy shall exceed twenty dollars, the right of trial by jury shall be preserved, and no fact tried by a jury, shall be otherwise reexamined in any Court of the United States, than according to the rules of the common law.

Amendment VIII

Excessive bail shall not be required, nor excessive fines imposed, nor cruel and unusual punishments inflicted.

Amendment IX

The enumeration in the Constitution, of certain rights, shall not be construed to deny or disparage others retained by the people.

Amendment X

The powers not delegated to the United States by the Constitution, nor prohibited by it to the States, are reserved to the States respectively, or to the people.

---

underprivileged citizens. In the United States, police can get away with horrific beatings, and freedom of expression and speech sometimes isn't all that free.

These are just a few of the flagrant violations of the Bill of Rights that occur in our nation. If reading about them sends a shiver down your spine, then an internship in public advocacy might be a good match for you. Also, if you think you may want to go on to law school but aren't too psyched to spend your days in a suit working on corporate litigation, public advocacy groups are a great place to work. On the other hand, if making money is what gets you up in the morning, find a different field. Nearly all public advocacy internships are very competitive and involve long hours for no pay.

High school students will probably have the most difficult time getting internships with these groups. The competition is fierce (for example, the American Civil Liberties Union hires three summer interns from a pool of 150 applicants), and most groups also hire college and law school students. But if you're and high school student wondering how you can compete with college and law school students, don't worry. Most organizations actually like to hire high school students—and have set quotas for them—because they offer cheap labor. High school students spend most of their time doing "clerical work." In other words, they fax, copy, send, run, walk, file, answer, lick, stamp, and mail. But they also get a great chance to see exciting legal cases in progress from behind the scenes. And, think of it this way: if you are in high school and you're going to wind up faxing, copying, and mailing during your summer anyway, why not do it in an exciting place that serves a good cause?

For college students, the jobs are a bit more varied. While clerical work is still included in the job description, they get the chance to conduct some research for legal cases and work a bit more closely with lawyers. Law school students, naturally, can do more substantial work on legal cases.

Finding a Cause That's Right for You

Advocacy groups fight for their causes by mustering political clout, working with media, and putting together education campaigns to make the public aware of their causes. As you're probably starting to realize, these groups cover a lot of territory, from human rights to animal rights to environmental protection.

Despite much of the civil rights progress that has been made in the past few decades, there are still hundreds of cases of discrimination each year. Ensuring equal treatment of all people covers a lot of ground: ensuring that women are earning the same wages as men for doing the same work; ensuring that people of certain ethnic groups are not denied housing by discriminatory landlords; ensuring that public schools offer equal opportunity to all students regardless of sex, race, and socioeconomic backgrounds.

In addition to safeguarding people's rights, advocates might also seek to promote minority groups and help secure them new opportunities in society.

For example, there are various advocacy groups concerned with increasing voter turnout among women and minorities. Thus, advocacy groups take both reactive and proactive measures. The NAACP and the Women's Legal Defense Fund are just two examples of such groups.

Keep in mind that there are advocacy groups that work against each other. For example, there are groups that fight for the elimination of guns (especially assault rifles) from the streets; however, there are also advocacy groups that fight for the right of the people to bear arms (guaranteed by the Second Amendment). Abortion is a similar issue. Pro-choice groups are as easy to find as pro-life groups.

The key here is to take a stand—no matter how controversial. If you believe that women should have the right to wear fur coats, head to the Fur Manufacturer's Association of America, where you'll spend your summer lobbying Congress, talking to the press, writing packets of information, and talking to supporters and critics alike. On the other hand, if you would rather protect the rights of the fur-bearing animals, try a group like People for the Ethical Treatment of Animals (PETA), where you'll spend the summer lobbying Congress, talking to the press, writing packets of information, and talking to supporters and critics alike. These groups do remarkably similar things with their time, except for the fact that they're fighting the same battle from different sides. One of the best ways to find a cause you care about and a group that advocates it is by keeping up with current events.

After you've picked an area or two of interest, it's time to get the names of groups working in those areas. (Start with the listing at the end of this chapter.) If you already know the name of a group in your field of interest, call them. Even if they aren't a perfect fit for you, they'll probably be able to point you in the right direction.

So, let's say, for example, that you are upset by the lack of term limits in Congress. If you're aware that Public Citizen, Ralph Nader's outfit in Washington, D.C., has a division called "Public Citizen's Congress Watch," you're in business. Give them a call, ask for the internship coordinator, and ask that they send you information and an annual report. It's also okay to ask the internship coordinator for the names of other organizations that deal with similar issues. That's a quick way to get the lowdown on other groups for whom you might want to work.

But suppose you didn't know about Nader's group. There are a number of ways to find organizations that fit your interests. You could search the bookstore or library (with the help of a reference librarian) for directories of public-interest advocacy groups, particularly in your field of interest. Another method would be to use NEXIS, an online business news service full of articles about people and organizations. NEXIS can be extraordinarily helpful. If you have access to this database (most schools do), just do a search for your topic of interest (in this case, "term limits and public-interest group"), and you'll come up with pertinent articles. And, yes, it's true that not all of these groups will have internship programs, but many will. Also, the ones that don't might be interested in starting a program—you could be their first intern ever!

If you know your way around a browser, you can also use the Internet to search for public-advocacy organizations. Using your favorite search engine (such as Infoseek or Excite), enter a word or phrase that represents what you're looking for, as described above in the section on NEXIS. Even if it's a bit too broad, it will get you started. You can narrow down the searches as you go along (for example, after you get thousands of hits from "Congressional term limits," search those hits for "public advocacy"). With any luck, you'll find direct links to the sites of these organizations, many of which will have information about internship programs. Even if you don't get direct links, at least you'll have the names of these groups, and then you can do a search to find out if these groups have sites on the Internet. And, even if a group doesn't have its own site on the Net, you'll probably be able to find information about the group in another site—at the very least, an address and phone number. (See the chapter on using the "Intern-Net" for more information.)

Once you've got a list of the groups you want to apply to, get going on the phone.

Profile:
Center for National Security Studies

The Center for National Security Studies (CNSS) in Washington, D.C., is a civil liberties advocacy group, founded in 1974, to work for control of the Federal Bureau of Investigation and Central Intelligence Agency and the intelligence community in the United States. The folks who work there spend countless hours trying to get the government to declassify mountains of classified documents that the intelligence community is withholding from the public scrutiny. The group's mission statement reads in part: "The existing mechanisms of accountability and control are not self-enforcing; they must be exercised by citizens. When the Executive Branch acts improperly, neither Congress nor the courts can be relied upon to respond to their own initiative. Defense of human rights and constitutional procedures in the face of claims of national security is a never-ending task that requires constant vigilance and public awareness. The Center for National Security Studies plays that role."

CNSS has seriously influenced a great amount of domestic legislation including: the Intelligence Oversight Act of 1980, which mandates that the Executive Branch tell Congress about covert operations, and its post-Iran-Contra revision in 1991; the Classified Procedures Act, which formed rules regarding the use of classified documents in criminal trials; and reforms to immigration laws. They have also been instrumental in the formulation of the President Kennedy Assassination Records Act of 1992, which set strict standards for the declassification of secret government documents. Recently, CNSS teamed up with the Helsinki Foundation for Human Rights in Warsaw, Poland, to begin a legal-reform project in Eastern and Central Europe to push for better oversight and accountability of the secret services in 14 countries.

CNSS has recently begun sponsoring summer internship positions for college students in its D.C. office. For more information call them at (202) 994-7060.

The Cover Letter

There really isn't a tried-and-true formula for getting their attention. But a key element in getting an internship in public advocacy is to care (or, if you don't, to at least look like you care). This means, but doesn't mandate, a lot of community service on your record: a demonstrated interest in public advocacy work during your summers or school vacations that transcends a school's average community service requirement. And, yes, working with disabled birds off the coast of Madagascar can help get you get a job fighting Internet censorship bills, as unrelated as the two may seem at first glance.

So what should you play up to get that competitive edge? First, don't worry too much about your GPA. Unless your record is peppered with Cs and Ds, you'll be fine. If you are a straight C student, you might want to explain why. Are you having troubles at home? Do you need better glasses? It may just be that you care more about your extracurrics (which just so happen to include saving the inhabitants of a small village in Northern Kenya) than you do about impressing your teachers. Whatever the case may be, the cover letter is the perfect place to explain yourself.

Use this letter to highlight your service endeavors. Use it to say why you should be hired over all of the other high school or college students who will also be applying. Are you hard working? Motivated? A self-starter? Yes? Then tell them—and give examples.

Some of the larger public advocacy groups have offices around the country. (For example, the ACLU has offices in every state except, for some reason, South Dakota.) If you're willing (or happy) to work somewhere other than New York City or Washington, D.C., mention that. Your chances of getting the internship you want will improve.

The Résumé

Okay, the key here is to tell the truth, the whole truth, and nothing but the truth. But, while you're at it, make it look like you care about things. Law experience and a social conscience are two things that most internship coordinators in public advocacy say they want to see more than anything else. Most students don't have the first one, so don't sweat it too much. But social conscience is a good thing to develop (even if you're not applying for advocacy internships). So, if you spend your afternoons working as a waiter but every other week tutor inner-city children in mathematics, then consider breaking the chronological format and put the tutoring highest on your résumé.

If you speak a foreign language, don't forget to include that. Many public-interest groups are involved in international work, so being able to converse in Albanian or Japanese could be a big plus. Also, if you're experienced with the Internet, especially in Web site construction, make sure you note it. Many public-interest groups are looking to publicize themselves with a Web site, and you could be the one to help them out.

(See the chapter on résumés and cover letters for more information.)

A Final Few Words

Research, research, research! Any internship coordinator will tell you to do your homework. "In these days of the Internet, we're really impressed when someone's done research on us," explains the president of a Washington, D.C.–based advocacy organization. "We love to see someone who's made an effort in their cover letter to tell us about the work we do and how they would be a perfect match."

Here's another reason to do your homework: people with gender-bending names—such as Pat and Terry—often get letters misaddressing them as Mr. or Ms. Those letters and résumés go straight into the round file. If in doubt, do yourself a favor—call the organization and ask. Also, be sure to get the job description right.

20/20 Vision

1828 Jefferson Place NW
Washington, DC 20036
Phone: (202) 833-2020
Fax: (202) 833-5307

Position: Intern

Department: N/A

No. of Positions Offered Annually: 9

Description: Interns are assigned to specific projects and/or staff members depending on the intern's interests and 20/20 Vision's priorities at the time. The departments include: Legislation, Media and Promotion, Field, Development and Membership. There are three interns in each session. College credit is available

Qualifications: Interns should have some knowledge of the congressional process and of environmental and/or peace issues; excellent communication skills; computer experience (Macintosh preferred) ; an eye for details; the ability to work independently while still being part of a small office team and a sense of humor. Interns are expected to work full time for a period equivalent to an academic semester, or the traditional summer vacations months.

Salary: Stipend available

Position Dates: Fall, Spring and Summer

Position Location: Washington, D.C.

Average No. of Applicants Annually: 140+

Potential for Job Placement: N/A

Application Process: Mail, fax, or E-mail (vision@igc.apc.org) a cover letter, résumé, and three references.

Deadline: Rolling

Contact: Internship Coordinator

Accuracy in Media

4455 Connecticut Avenue NW, Suite 330
Washington, DC 20008
Phone: (202) 364-4401
Fax: (202) 364-4098

Position: Research Interns

Department: N/A

No. of Positions Offered Annually: 10

Description: Intern will do research, writing, and office work.

Qualifications: Writing experience and interest in journalism.

Salary: $125/week

Position Dates: Fall, Spring and Summer

Position Location: Washington, D.C.

Average No. of Applicants Annually: 60

Potential for Job Placement: Yes

Application Process: Send résumé, cover letter, and writing samples

Deadline: Rolling for the year; mid-May for Summer

Contact: Internship Coordinator

American-Arab Anti-Discrimination Committee

4201 Connecticut Avenue NW, Suite 500
Washington, DC 20008
Phone: (202) 244-2990
Fax: (202) 244-3196

Position: Organizing and Special Events Intern

Department: Organizing and Special Events

No. of Positions Offered Annually: 4

Description: Responsibilities include: assisting director with work involving the national network of local chapters, monitoring and mobilizing activists to work on projects, issues, action alerts and campaigns, assisting with planning national convention in D.C. and assisting in chapter mailings.

Qualifications: Intern should possess excellent organizing skills, good writing and oral communications skills, proficiency in WordPerfect 5.1 DOS and Windows. Community or campus organizing experience is useful but not required.

Salary: $500 stipend

Position Dates: Summer

Position Location: Washington, D.C.

Average No. of Applicants Annually: 10

Potential for Job Placement: N/A

Application Process: Application to be completed.

Deadline: March 30

Contact: Intern Coordinator

American-Arab Anti-Discrimination Committee

4201 Connecticut Avenue NW, Suite 500
Washington, DC 20008
Phone: (202) 244-2990
Fax: (202) 244-3196

Position: Education Intern

Department: Education

No. of Positions Offered Annually: 4

Description: Intern works closely with the director of education in mobilizing a grassroots network of chapters and activists in outreach to educators to dispel stereotypes of Arabs and to encourage creative teaching, curriculum and instructional programs about the Arab world in elementary and high schools. Part- or full-time positions available.

Qualifications: Intern must possess excellent writing skills, and knowlege of the Middle East, Arab world or the Arab-American community. Education majors especially welcome. Preference given to graduate students, juniors and seniors.

Salary: $500 stipend

Position Dates: Summer

Position Location: Washington, D.C.

Average No. of Applicants Annually: 10

Potential for Job Placement: N/A

Application Process: Application to be completed.

Deadline: March 30

Contact: Internship Coordinator

American-Arab Anti-Discrimination Committee

4201 Connecticut Avenue NW, Suite 500
Washington, DC 20008
Phone: (202) 244-2990
Fax: (202) 244-3196

Position: Media and Publications Intern

Department: Media and Publications

No. of Positions Offered Annually: 4

Description: Internship provides experience in journalism, public relations and publishing. Responsibilities include: writing articles for *ADC Times*, helping write, edit and design *Annual Activity Report*, assisting in maintenance of video, book library and departmental filing system, monitoring the media and responding to public and media information requests.

Qualifications: Intern must possess excellent writing skills, good organizational abilities, interest in Middle Eastern, Arab or Arab-American issues, experience in writing for publication, proficiency in WordPerfect 5.1. Journalism or communication/public relations majors preferred; knowledge of desktop publishing programs a plus. Preference given to graduate students, seniors and juniors.

Salary: Unpaid

Position Dates: Summer

Position Location: Washington, D.C.

Average No. of Applicants Annually: 10

Potential for Job Placement: N/A

Application Process: Application to be completed.

Deadline: March 30

Contact: Internship Coordinator

American-Arab Anti-Discrimination Committee

4201 Connecticut Avenue NW, Suite 300
Washington, DC 20008
Phone: (202) 244-2990
Fax: (202) 244-3196

Position: Legal Intern

Department: N/A

No. of Positions Offered Annually: 12

Description: Intern works closely with attorneys on cases and legal matters involving immigration law, civil rights and human rights law, international law and treaties, drafts client letters and press releases on legal matters, conducts research, assists in the organization of the human rights information bank in Arab nations and in the organization of the Pro Bono Legal Services Program. Full- or part-time available. Possibility of arranging accreditation with law schools.

Qualifications: Intern must have completed at least one year of law school and possess excellent writing and legal research skills.

Salary: $700 (stipend)

Position Dates: Fall, Spring and Summer

Position Location: Washington, D.C.

Average No. of Applicants Annually: 50

Potential for Job Placement: N/A

Application Process: Application to be completed.

Deadline: Rolling for Fall and Spring; March 30 for Summer

Contact: Intern Coordinator

American Israel Public Affairs Committee (AIPAC)

440 First Street NW, Suite 600
Washington, DC 20001
Phone: (202) 639-5267
Fax: (202) 347-4918

Position: Intern

Department: Various

No. of Positions Offered Annually: 44

Description: Internship positions are available in various departments: Legislative, Foreign Policy Issues, Political Affairs, Development, and Political Leadership Development. Interns help AIPAC provide information to decision makers and work to sensitize members of Congress to the importance of the U.S.-Israel relationship. Eight to 12 interships are offered in both the Fall and the Spring terms. Twenty internships are offered in the Summer term. There are also a variety of locations: Washington D.C., Los Angeles, San Francisco, Chicago, Seattle, and Jerusalem.

Qualifications: N/A

Salary: Stipend for Summer Interns only

Position Dates: Fall, Spring and Summer

Position Location: Chicago, IL; Jerusalem; Los Angeles, CA; San Francisco, CA; Seattle, WA; Washington, DC

Average No. of Applicants Annually: 350

Potential for Job Placement: Yes

Application Process: To apply send in a cover letter stating your interest in interning at AIPAC, a résumé, two letters of recommendation, a one-page essay about pro-Israel involvement, and a passport size photo.

Deadline: September 15 for Fall; January 15 for Spring; March 15 for Summer

Contact: Brian Shankman

American Rivers

1025 Vermont Avenue NW, Suite 720
Washington, DC 20005
Phone: (202) 547-6900
Fax: (202) 347-9240

Position: Development Intern

Department: Development

No. of Positions Offered Annually: 4

Description: Intern will work with development staff on research, membership drives, special events, cause-related marketing, foundation grant proposals, responses to inquiries and general office duties.

Qualifications: Open to college students or graduates from a variety of backgrounds. Interest in marketing as well as desire to work for a nonprofit helpful.

Salary: $1,000 (stipend)

Position Dates: Fall, Winter, Spring and Summer

Position Location: Washington, D.C.

Average No. of Applicants Annually: 50-75

Potential for Job Placement:

Application Process: Send résumé, cover letter stating dates of availability, a brief writing sample and list of three references.

Deadline: Rolling

Contact: Judith Rath

American Rivers

1025 Vermont Avenue NW, Suite 720
Washington, DC 20005
Phone: (202) 547-6900
Fax: (202) 347-9240

Position: Communications Intern

Department: Communications

No. of Positions Offered Annually: 4

Description: Intern will work with the director of strategic communications on research, communications projects, press releases, press conferences and other major media events. Intern will also assist with general office duties.

Qualifications: Open to college students and graduates from a variety of backgrounds, particularly those with interest in journalism and the media.

Salary: $1,000 (stipend)

Position Dates: Fall, Winter, Spring and Summer

Position Location: Washington, D.C.

Average No. of Applicants Annually: 50-75

Potential for Job Placement:

Application Process: Send résumé, cover letter stating dates of availability, a brief writing sample and a list of three references.

Deadline: Rolling

Contact: Judith Rath

American Rivers

1025 Vermont Avenue NW, Suite 720
Washington, DC 20005
Phone: (202) 547-6900
Fax: (202) 347-92940

Position: Conservation Intern

Department: Various

No. of Positions Offered Annually: 8

Description: Interns will work in one or more of the following program areas: Hydropower, Floodplain, Urban Rivers and Wild and Scenic Rivers. Intern will also assist the director of legislative programs and the outreach coordinator on a number of conservation functions and special projects.

Qualifications: Open to college students or graduates from a variety of backgrounds. Knowledge or interest in environmental science, particularly river conservation is helpful.

Salary: $1,000 (stipend)

Position Dates: Fall, Winter, Spring and Summer

Position Location: Washington, D.C.

Average No. of Applicants Annually: 100

Potential for Job Placement: N/A

Application Process: Send résumé, cover letter stating dates of availability, a brief writing sample, and a list of three references.

Deadline: Rolling

Contact: Judith Rath

Arms Control Association

1726 M Street NW, Suite 201
Washington, DC 20036
Phone: (202) 463-8270
Fax: (202) 463-8273

Position: Intern

Department: N/A

No. of Positions Offered Annually: 10

Description: Interns are involved in all facets of ACA's work including: researching and writing about national security, defense and arms control; assisting in editing ACA's monthly journal *Arms Control Today*; monitoring Capitol Hill activities and supporting analysts in administrative tasks. Interns' commuting expenses will be reimbursed.

Qualifications: Applicant should have a background in foreign affairs and should have completed relevant course work.

Salary: $25/week (stipend)

Position Dates: Fall, Spring and Summer

Position Location: Washington, D.C.

Average No. of Applicants Annually: 200

Potential for Job Placement: Minimal

Application Process: Send résumé, cover letter and three- to five-page writing sample.

Deadline: August 15 for Fall; December 15 for Spring; and April 30 for Summer.

Contact: Erik Leklem

Center for Campus Organizing (CCO)

Box 748
Cambridge, MA 02142
Phone: (617) 354-9363
Fax: (617) 547-5067

Position: Public Relations Intern

Department: Public Relations

No. of Positions Offered Annually: 10

Description: Help promote CCO by coordinating outreach to the media; organize special fund-raising events; expand CCO's membership base by direct mail, advertisements, networking and other creative means; work with all aspects of promotions and some grant writing; create promotional displays, literature, and paraphernailia.

Qualifications: N/A

Salary: Need-based stipend

Position Dates: Flexible

Position Location: Cambridge, MA

Average No. of Applicants Annually: 100

Potential for Job Placement: N/A

Application Process: Application to be completed. Must also send cover letter and résumé.

Deadline: Rolling

Contact: Internship Coordinator (E-mail: cco@igc.apc.org)

Center for Campus Organizing (CCO)

Box 748
Cambridge, MA 02142
Phone: (617) 354-9363
Fax: (617) 547-5067

Position: Campus Organizer

Department: N/A

No. of Positions Offered Annually: 10

Description: Maintain contact with and coordinate mailings for CCO's campus contact participants; assist student activists nationwide via E-mail and telephone contact; assist with National Days of Action and shared office work.

Qualifications: N/A

Salary: Need-based stipend

Position Dates: Flexible

Position Location: Cambridge, MA

Average No. of Applicants Annually: 100

Potential for Job Placement: N/A

Application Process: Application to be completed. Must also send cover letter and résumé.

Deadline: Rolling

Contact: Internship Coordinator (E-mail: cco@igc.apc.org)

Center for Campus Organizing (CCO)

Box 748
Cambridge, MA 02142
Phone: (617) 354-9363
Fax: (617) 547-5067

Position: Researcher

Department: N/A

No. of Positions Offered Annually: 10

Description: Help develop a guide for student activists researching their campus; help maintain active records and listings of foundations funding right-wing campus activity; research current right-wing legal initiatives affecting affirmative action and funding of political activity on campus; assist with shared office work.

Qualifications: N/A

Salary: Need-based stipend

Position Dates: Flexible

Position Location: Cambridge, MA

Average No. of Applicants Annually: 100

Potential for Job Placement: N/A

Application Process: Application to be completed. Must also send cover letter and résumé.

Deadline: Rolling

Contact: Internship Coordinator (E-mail: cco@igc.apc.org)

Center for Campus Organizing (CCO)

Box 748
Cambridge, MA 02142
Phone: (617) 354-9363
Fax: (617) 547-5067

Position: Assistant Office Manager

Department: N/A

No. of Positions Offered Annually: 10

Description: Compile, maintain, and distribute a national events calendar for campus activities; work as a right-hand to Office Manager to ensure smooth operation of the office; assist with processing requests for information and shared office work.

Qualifications: N/A

Salary: Need-based stipend

Position Dates: Flexible

Position Location: Cambridge, MA

Average No. of Applicants Annually: 100

Potential for Job Placement: N/A

Application Process: Application to be completed. Must also send cover letter and résumé.

Deadline: Rolling

Contact: Internship Coordinator (E-mail: cco@igc.apc.org)

Center for Campus Organizing (CCO)

Box 748
Cambridge, MA 02142
Phone: (617) 354-9363
Fax: (617) 547-5067

Position: Publications and Journalism Intern

Department: N/A

No. of Positions Offered Annually: 10

Description: Assist with the layout and design of "Infusion: Tools for Action and Education;" assist in program development for the Campus Alternative Journalism Project.

Qualifications: N/A

Salary: Need-based stipend

Position Dates: Flexible

Position Location: Cambridge, MA

Average No. of Applicants Annually: 100

Potential for Job Placement: N/A

Application Process: Application to be completed. Must also send cover letter and résumé.

Deadline: Rolling

Contact: Internship Coordinator (E-mail: cco@igc.apc.org)

Center for Campus Organizing (CCO)

Box 748
Cambridge, MA 02142
Phone: (617) 354-9363
Fax: (617) 547-5067

Position: Computer Specialist

Department: N/A

No. of Positions Offered Annually: 10

Description: Maintain CCO's Web site and CANET, our campus activist E-mail network; perform computer-related maintenance tasks as needed; assist with shared office work.

Qualifications: N/A

Salary: Need-based stipend

Position Dates: Flexible

Position Location: Cambridge, MA

Average No. of Applicants Annually: 100

Potential for Job Placement: N/A

Application Process: Application to be completed. Must also send cover letter and résumé.

Deadline: Rolling

Contact: Internship Coordinator (E-mail: cco@igc.apc.org)

Council on Economic Priorities

30 Irving Place, 9th Floor
New York, NY 10003
Phone: (212) 420-1133
Fax: (212) 420-0988

Position: Public Service Intern

Department: N/A

No. of Positions Offered Annually: 10

Description: Internship positions are available in the following departments: Corporate Social Responsibility, Child Labor and International Sourcing, Environment, International Security and Marketing and Communications.

Qualifications: Applicant must possess excellent research and communications skills, ability to interpret and synthesize information, thoroughness and meticulous attention to details and PC experience (WordPerfect and Paradox) . Internet knowledge a plus. CEP encourages applications from minority students.

Salary: Modest stipend provided.

Position Dates: Summer

Position Location: New York, NY

Average No. of Applicants Annually: N/A

Potential for Job Placement:

Application Process: Send résumé, cover letter indicating area of interest, transcript and a three-page writing sample.

Deadline: Rolling

Contact: Internship Coordinator

The Feminist Majority

1600 Wilson Boulevard, Suite 801
Arlington, VA 22209

Position: Intern

Department: N/A

No. of Positions Offered Annually: 23

Description: Each internship provides a wide variety of responsibilities such as monitoring press conferences and congressional hearings, researching, writing, policy analysis, organizing events and demonstrations.

Qualifications: Previous progressive activism on women's issues. Diversity in academic disciplines welcome. Must be currently enrolled in a college or a university. Must be available to work full time. An equal opportunity employer.

Salary: $70/week (stipend for Spring and Fall)

Position Dates: Fall, Spring and Summer

Position Location: Arlington, VA

Average No. of Applicants Annually: 200

Potential for Job Placement: N/A

Application Process: Cover letter, résumé, a short writing sample (three to five pages) , and two letters of reference.

Deadline: Rolling

Contact: Christine Onyango, Intern Coordinator

Heritage Foundation

214 Massachusetts Avenue NE
Washington, DC 20002
Phone: (202) 546-4400
Fax: (202) 608-6136

Position: Intern

Department: N/A

No. of Positions Offered Annually: 130

Description: Intern will perform a variety of research and administrative assignments under direction of department. Departments taking interns during the year include: Academic Programs, The Asian Studies Center, Business Relations, Coalition Relations, Domestic and Economic Policy Studies, The Executive Offices, Foreign and Defense Policy Studies, Government Relations, Information Marketing, Lectures and Educational Programs and Public Relations. Interns will have the opportunity to work in a large conservative think-tank.

Qualifications: Applicants must possess strong research and writing skills and knowledge of conservative, free-market ideas.

Salary: $8/day for Fall, Spring; $250/week for Summer

Position Dates: Fall, Spring and Summer

Position Location: Washington, D.C.

Average No. of Applicants Annually: 300

Potential for Job Placement: N/A

Application Process: Send résumé, cover letter stating reason for interest in the internship, a two- to four-page writing sample and two letters of recommendation.

Deadline: Rolling

Contact: Intern Coordinator

Korean American Coalition

3421 West Eighth Street, 2nd Floor
Los Angeles, CA 90005
Phone: (213) 380-6175
Fax: (213) 380-7990

Position: Intern

Department: N/A

No. of Positions Offered Annually: 20

Description: Program begins with Korean
American Coalition (KAC) Leadership
Conference. At conclusion of conference,
interns spend four days per week with
sponsor, gaining insight into operations of a
corporate, legal, political, or media office
and one day per week at KAC office. Provides
excellent opportunity to learn about issues
affecting Korean American community.

Qualifications: N/A

Salary: $1,000 (stipend)

Position Dates: June 22 to August 22

Position Location: Los Angeles, CA

Average No. of Applicants Annually:
200-300

Potential for Job Placement: N/A

Application Process: Application and
interview.

Deadline: February 15

Contact: Kimberly Yu

National Asian Pacific American Legal Consortium

1629 K Street NW, Suite 1010
Washington, DC 20006
Phone: (202) 296-2300
Fax: (202) 296-2318

Position: Intern

Department: N/A

No. of Positions Offered Annually: 12

Description: Interns will assist staff on
special research projects, press releases and
program development, attend congressional
hearings and press briefings and perform
some administrative tasks.

Qualifications: Open to undergraduates
and law students. Applicants must possess
good writing skills.

Salary: Depends on funding

Position Dates: Fall, Spring and Summer

Position Location: Washington, D.C.

Average No. of Applicants Annually:
100

Potential for Job Placement: N/A

Application Process: Send résumé, cover
letter, transcript and writing sample.

Deadline: July 15 for Fall; December 15 for
Spring; March 15 for Summer.

Contact: Jayne Park (E-mail:
hn5598@handsnet.org)

National Wildlife Federation

1400 16th Street NW
Washington, DC 20036
Phone: (202) 797-6800
Fax:

Position: Legal Intern

Department: N/A

No. of Positions Offered Annually: 10

Description: Position offers students hands-on lawyering experience in federal courts, government agencies and Congress. Interns work on a wide range of natural resource and conservation issues and participate in some of the most significant environmental legal work in the United States. Each intern assists an attorney and takes on at least one extensive research program. Fall and Spring semester interns are not paid.

Qualifications: Applicants should have completed at least three semesters of law school. It is recommended that students complete courses in constitutional, administrative and environmental law before the internship. Although the Federation imposes no strict cutoff, those selected generally rank within the top third of the class.

Salary: $340/week (Summer only)

Position Dates: Fall, Spring and Summer

Position Location: Washington, D.C.

Average No. of Applicants Annually: 400

Potential for Job Placement: N/A

Application Process: Send résumé, cover letter, writing sample, law school transcript and list of references.

Deadline: April 1 for Fall; November 1 for Spring; March 1 for Summer.

Contact: Leevannah Washington

National Wildlife Federation

1400 16th Street NW
Washington, DC 20036
Phone: (202) 797-6800

Position: Conservation Intern

Department: N/A

No. of Positions Offered Annually: 12

Description: Internships are offered in two 24 week sessions (January–June and July–December). Much of an intern's time is spent researching environmental policy issues and covering congressional activity. Responsibilities may include attending congressional hearings, briefings and seminars, drafting testimony to be presented by the Federation to congressional and executive panels, lobby on environmental legislation, and assisting generally in the activities of the program.

Qualifications: Applicants must be college graduates with academic background or work experience in wildlife biology, wetlands ecology, natural resource and land management, environmental science/policy, biology, energy, international environmental/developmental issues, political science, grassroots organizing and journalism. Excellent writing and speaking abilities required. Applicants must be able to conduct independent research on difficult environmental policy issues and must be prepared to advocate the positions of the NWF.

Salary: $275/week

Position Dates: Fall, Spring and Summer

Position Location: Washington, D.C.

Average No. of Applicants Annually: 400

Potential for Job Placement: N/A

Application Process: Send résumé, cover letter indicating area of interest, names and telephone numbers of three to five academic or professional references and a two- to four-page sample of academic or professional writing.

Deadline: Rolling

Contact: Leevannah Washington

The Population Intitute

107 Second Street NE
Washington, DC 20009

Position: Future Leaders of the World (FLW) Program

Department: N/A

No. of Positions Offered Annually: 6

Description: Staff assistants participate in all organizational activities, seeking practical solutions to population-related problems. Work with public policy, assisting on legislative alerts, providing information to legislators and key staff, and following up on community leaders recruited during field trips across the nation. Or work as a media coordinator, the duties of which include the maintenance of of a press list, liaison with media, writing, reporting, proofreading and editing. During the Sping session, work as a field coordinator to plan and implement trips around the nation for speakers of the Institute. During the Fall, manage special programs, such as the Global Media Awards, World Population Awareness Week, The Combines Federal Campaign, and an in-depth research or development project.

Qualifications: Applicants must be able to demonstrate leadership qualities, international experiences and perspectives, a good academic record and strong writing and oral skills. Candidates should also have a sense of purpose and commitment, and must be interested in a career in public or nonprofit service. Applicants must have completed at least two years of college and be over 21 years of age, but under 25.

Salary: $1,000/month

Position Dates: Fall and Spring

Position Location: Washington, D.C.

Average No. of Applicants Annually: N/A

Potential for Job Placement: N/A

Application Process: Send a cover letter, résumé, three recommendations (two from academic sources) and an official transcript.

Deadline: September 1 for Spring; April 1 for Fall

Contact: Devinka Abeysinghe

Women's International League for Peace and Freedom

777 United Nations Plaza
New York, NY 10017
Phone: (212) 682-1265
Fax: (212) 286-8211

Position: Office Assistant

Department: N/A

No. of Positions Offered Annually: 4

Description: Intern will attend United Nations meetings, briefings, conferences and parallel nongovernmental organizations, prepare written and oral reports and perform light administrative tasks (correpsondence, typing, filing and answering telephones calls).

Qualifications: Applicant should possess good writing and reading skills, a sense of order and initiative and knowledge of Macintosh.

Salary: Unpaid

Position Dates: Fall, Spring and Summer

Position Location: New York, NY

Average No. of Applicants Annually: N/A

Potential for Job Placement: N/A

Application Process: Send résumé, cover letter and the name, address and telephone number of one reference.

Deadline: Rolling

Contact: Pamella Saffer

Women's Legal Defense Fund

1875 Connecticut NW, Suite 710
Washington, DC 20009
Phone: (202) 986-2600
Fax: (202) 986-2539

Position: Family Economic Security Intern

Department: Family Economic Security

No. of Positions Offered Annually: 5

Description: Will assist WLDF's advocacy efforts in the areas of welfare, child support, family policy. Activities will include analyzing data on the economic status of women and children in the states, gathering reports of the impact of changes in welfare policy on women and families, and reviewing literature on custody and child support issues.

Qualifications: Candidates majoring in a social science preferred. Candidates should have basic quantitative and library research skills and possess excellent oral and written communications skills. Excellent organizational skills and the ability to meet fast-paced deadlines are essential. Proficiency in WordPerfect 6.1 required. Database and Internet experience a plus.

Salary: Unpaid

Position Dates: Fall, Spring and Summer

Position Location: Washington, D.C.

Average No. of Applicants Annually: 300+

Potential for Job Placement: N/A

Application Process: Specify internship(s) of interest. Submit letter of interest, résumé, writing sample, transcripts, and references.

Deadline: March 1 for Summer; Rolling for Fall and Spring

Contact: Internship Coordinator

Women's Legal Defense Fund

1875 Connecticut Avenue NW, Suite 710
Washington, DC 20009
Phone: (202) 986-2600
Fax: (202) 986-2539

Position: Communications Intern

Department: Communications

No. of Positions Offered Annually: 5

Description: Will assist the Communications Department in educating the public on WLDF's key issues through extensive work with the print and electronic media. Activities include maintaining follow-up contacts with the media and tracking WLDF statements, coordinating speaking engagements, responding to requests for information and producing and distributing daily news clip packages.

Qualifications: Interest in public relations, mass communications or related field preferred. Candidates must be attentive to detail and possess excellent oral and written communication skills. Excellent organizational skills and the ability to meet fast-paced deadlines are essential. Proficiency in WordPerfect 6.1 required, Internet experience a plus.

Salary: Unpaid

Position Dates: Fall, Spring and Summer

Position Location: Washington, D.C.

Average No. of Applicants Annually: 300+

Potential for Job Placement: N/A

Application Process: Specify internship(s) of interest. Submit letter of interest, résumé, writing sample, transcripts, and references.

Deadline: March 1 for Summer; Rolling for Fall and Spring

Contact: Internship Coordinator

Women's Legal Defense Fund

1875 Connecticut Avenue NW, Suite 710
Washington, DC 20009
Phone: (202) 986-2600
Fax: (202) 986-2539

Position: Law Clerk for Women's Health Program

Department: Women's Health

No. of Positions Offered Annually: 6

Description: Will work with the deputy director to improve women's access to affordable, quality health care, including the full range of reproductive health services. Activities include researching and analyzing women's health care, monitoring federal and state legislation, and attending and reporting back from relevant Congressional hearings, briefings, and other meetings.

Qualifications: Candidates with two years of law school and/or background in women's health issues preferred. Must be attentive to detail and possess excellent oral and written communication skills. Excellent organizational skills and the ability to meet fast-paced deadlines are essential. Proficiency in WordPerfect required, Internet experience a plus.

Salary: Unpaid

Position Dates: Fall, Spring and Summer

Position Location: Washington, D.C.

Average No. of Applicants Annually: 300+

Potential for Job Placement: N/A

Application Process: Specify internship(s) of interest. Submit letter of interest, résumé, writing sample, transcripts, and references.

Deadline: March 1 for Summer; Rolling for Fall and Spring

Contact: Internship Coordinator

Women's Legal Defense Fund

1875 Connecticut Avenue NW, Suite 710
Washington, DC 20009
Phone: (202) 986-2600
Fax: (202) 986-2539

Position: Law Clerk for Work and Family Program

Department: Work and Family

No. of Positions Offered Annually: 6

Description: Will assist WLDF's advocacy efforts in the areas of equal employment, family friendly workplace policy, and employment rights for women of color. Activities include working on implementation of existing employment laws, monitoring activities of federal agencies responsible for enforcing anti-discrimination laws, and attending and reporting back from relevant Congressional hearings, briefings, and other meetings.

Qualifications: Candidates must be attentive to detail amd possess excellent oral and written communication skills. Excellent organizational skills and the ability to meet fast-paced deadlines are essential. Proficiency in WordPerfect required, Internet experience is a plus.

Salary: Unpaid

Position Dates: Fall, Spring and Summer

Position Location: Washington, D.C.

Average No. of Applicants Annually: 300+

Potential for Job Placement: N/A

Application Process: Specify internship(s) of interest. Submit letter of interest, résumé, writing sample, transcripts, and references.

Deadline: March 1 for Summer; Rolling for Fall and Spring

Contact: Internship Coordinator

Women's Legal Defense Fund

1875 Connecticut Avenue NW, Suite 710
Washington, DC 20009
Phone: (202) 986-2600
Fax: (202) 986-2539

Position: Law Clerk for Family Economic Security Program

Department: Family Economic Security

No. of Positions Offered Annually: 6

Description: Will assist with WLDF's advocacy efforts in the areas of welfare reform and child support to foster security for women and their families. Activities include researching and analyzing child support and welfare reform issues at the national and state levels, drafting reports, memoranda and other materials and attending and reporting back from relevant Congressional hearings, briefings and other meetings.

Qualifications: Candidates with two years of law school and a background in poverty or family law preferred. Must be attentive to detail and possess excellent oral and written communication skills. Excellent organizational skills and the ability to meet fast-paced deadlines are essential. Proficiency in WordPerfect required, Internet experience a plus.

Salary: Unpaid

Position Dates: Fall, Spring and Summer

Position Location: Washington, D.C.

Average No. of Applicants Annually: 300+

Potential for Job Placement: N/A

Application Process: Specify internship(s) of interest. Submit letter of interest, résumé, writing sample, transcripts, and references.

Deadline: March 1 for Summer; Rolling for Fall and Spring

Contact: Internship Coordinator

Women's Legal Defense Fund

1875 Connecticut Avenue NW, Suite 710
Washington, DC 20009
Phone: (202) 986-2600
Fax: (202) 986-2539

Position: Employment Advocacy Intern

Department: Employment Advocacy

No. of Positions Offered Annually: 5

Description: Will assist with WLDF's advocacy efforts in the areas of equal employment, family-friendly workplace policy, and employment rights for women of color. Activities include working on implementation of existing employment laws, monitoring activities of federal agencies responsible for enforcing anti-discrimination laws, monitoring and developing legislative initiatives on employment issues, and public education.

Qualifications: Candidates must be attentive to detail and possess excellent oral and written communication skills. Excellent organizational skills and the ability to meet fast-paced deadlines are essential. Proficiency in WordPerfect 6.1 required. Database and Internet experience a plus.

Salary: Unpaid

Position Dates: Fall, Spring and Summer

Position Location: Washington, D.C.

Average No. of Applicants Annually: 300+

Potential for Job Placement: N/A

Application Process: Specify internship(s) of interest. Submit letter of interest, résumé, writing sample, transcripts, and references.

Deadline: March 1 for Summer; Rolling for Fall and Spring

Contact: Internship Coordinator

Women's Legal Defense Fund

1875 Connecticut Avenue NW, Suite 710
Washington, DC 20009
Phone: (202) 986-2600
Fax: (202) 986-2539

Position: Development Intern

Department: Development

No. of Positions Offered Annually: 5

Description: Will assist in the day-to-day operations of the fund-raising department. Spring and summer interns' primary responsibility will be to assist development staff in planning and execution of WLDF's annual spring luncheon. Past luncheons have honored dignitaries such as Attorney General Janet Reno, First Lady Hillary Rodham Clinton, Vice President Al Gore, and President Bill Clinton, raised over $500,000, and included more than 1,500 guests. Interns will be responsible for coordination of luncheon appeal mailing, maintenance of donor records, follow-up with donors, assistance with on-site registration and other administrative duties as assigned.

Qualifications: Candidates must be attentive to detail and possess excellent oral and written communication skills. Excellent organizational skills and the ability to meet fast-paced deadlines are essential. Proficiency in WordPerfect 6.1 required. Database and Internet experience a plus.

Salary: Unpaid

Position Dates: Fall, Spring and Summer

Position Location: Washington, D.C.

Average No. of Applicants Annually: 300+

Potential for Job Placement: N/A

Application Process: Specify internship(s) of interest. Submit letter of interest, résumé, writing sample, transcripts, and references.

Deadline: March 1 for Summer; Rolling for Fall and Spring

Contact: Internship Coordinator

Women's Sports Foundation

Eisenhower Park
East Meadow, NY 11554
Phone: (800) 227-3988
Fax: (516) 542-4716

Position: Intern

Department: Various

No. of Positions Offered Annually: 20

Description: Internship positions available in the following departments: Administration, Advocacy, Athlete Services, Community Programs, Development/ Marketing, Education, Awards and Grants, Information Services, Communications and Special Events. Minimun internship duration is three months; maximum duration is one year.

Qualifications: N/A

Salary: $350-$1,000/month

Position Dates: Fall, Spring and Summer

Position Location: East Meadow, NY

Average No. of Applicants Annually: N/A

Potential for Job Placement: N/A

Application Process: Application to be completed.

Deadline: Rolling

Contact: Associate Executive Director

World Federalist Association

418 Seventh Street SE
Washington, DC 20003
Phone: (202) 546-3950
Fax: (202) 546-3749

Position: Intern

Department: N/A

No. of Positions Offered Annually: 15

Description: Duties include: membership outreach programs, organizing assemblies, providing materials to assist local chapters, writing news releases, pitching WFA events to the media, calling media outlets to inform them about WFA activities, researching world order and United Nations reform issues, lobbying activities and tracking legislation. Interns will obtain an understanding of the federalist movement, increase their knowledge of how interest groups interact with the political process and effect change in the political system, gaining first-hand exposure to the intricacies of the legislative process.

Qualifications: Open to college and graduate students interested in addressing problems such as environmental degradation, human rights violations, population growth and global militarism. Applicants should have strong written and oral skills.

Salary: $5/day

Position Dates: Fall, Spring and Summer

Position Location: Washington, D.C.

Average No. of Applicants Annually: N/A

Potential for Job Placement: N/A

Application Process: Send résumé and cover letter describing interest in working with WFA and goals for the internship. Applicants should then call the Internship Coordinator to schedule an interview.

Deadline: At least one month prior to desired start date.

Contact: Internship Coordinator (E-mail: wfa@igc.apc.org)

Public Service

by Sara Schwebel

A summer internship is not just a summer job. An intern doesn't drive whining kids to Little League or twirl a whistle at the swimming pool. No, an intern puts on a suit and drives downtown to work in an important-looking office building where fresh flowers sit in front of the elevator every day. An intern gets treated to a five-star lunch the first day of work and a gala party at the end of the summer. Right?

Well, not in the public service sector. If you want a public service internship, you'll have to get used to pinching pennies. There is a lot of work to be done, and funding is always scarce. After interning with a nonprofit group, you'll never look at a spreadsheet the same way again, and unlike your friends interning on Capitol Hill, you'll feel guilty about calling long distance on the office tab.

So why would you want to intern in the public service sector? Reasons abound. We know the world isn't perfect, and as much as we try to change it from our college campuses, it's hard to make serious progress. We're strapped by financial barriers and administrative policy, by the lack of transportation, the exams, and the problems that crowd our schedule and prevent us from getting out and *doing*. As students, we lack the expertise — the legal, financial, and educational training — that allows professionals to see and understand the bigger picture.

Moreover, as students, we are frustrated that so many people around us "do good" simply to smooth their path into Yale Law or Harvard Med. Nonprofit organizations, whether operating at a community level or out of national offices in New York or Washington, D.C., face similar problems: big goals and tight funding. But with an eye fixed on local and national politics and a hand reaching out to help the homeless down the street, there is a sense of strength and defiance in the office. Nonprofits are plucky.

Ann Yoders, the intern coordinator for Project Vote Smart, describes the nonprofit, nonpartisan organization as "very idealistic, very genuine." Based in Colorado and Boston, Project Vote Smart strives to provide voters with accurate, up-to-date information about candidates and political issues. Project Vote Smart conducts research for campaigners, operates a hotline, and maintains a Web site. As with many nonprofits, it places an emphasis on providing all employees—from interns on up through senior staff members—with the freedom to learn and grow. "We really look for how [applicants] would fit into a grassroots, idealistic environment. It's a unique experience," Ann says.

This embrace of idealism is another way in which public service internships differ from most other internships. Many grassroots nonprofits are filled with recent college graduates who believe passionately in their cause. Idealism is an accepted mindset, not a taboo concept. While employees in a consulting firm may put in extra hours trying to hack their way to the top of the corporate ladder, people in nonprofits log extra hours because they believe in what they're doing. When hiring, intern coordinators are on the lookout for people who understand the difference.

"A girl called me this morning from Columbia University in New York and said she spent the last three summers doing internships in D.C. and it wasn't her cup of tea. Because there was so much back stabbing and trying to impress the boss, it was not a conducive environment in which to grow and learn. She asked me to describe our program to see if it was what she wanted," Ann says.

The public service sector expects and demands genuineness. So if you're looking for an internship simply to pad your résumé, public service is probably not for you. While it is fairly easy to bluff your way through an interview, talking about why you want to fight world hunger or save some rain forest species, it is quite another thing to keep up a front for six to ten weeks if you would rather be at the beach.

Hard Work That's Worth It

Take it from one Yale student who worked at a family domestic violence shelter over a summer: it's hard but definitely worth it. The shelter houses victims of domestic violence while they look for new housing and, in some cases, apply for federal aid. There she worked with the children of the residents, providing care for them and counseling them, for example, on how to handle touchy personal issues.

"It wasn't easy but it was incredibly rewarding," she explains. "You need to be willing to open yourself up to something you haven't been exposed to before, and you'll learn so much from the people you're advocating for. There are literally hundreds of underfunded places that need people to help them out."

Getting a Public Service Internship

There is a wide range of fields and an even greater breadth of internship experiences available in the public service sector. Some internships focus on the legwork behind policy change—researching social issues, preparing brochures, and writing speeches, for example. Others involve hands-on work with people in need—for example, leading a summer program for children of low-income families, or organizing social activities at a local homeless shelter.

There are many organizations in big cities such as Washington, New York, Philadelphia, and Los Angeles that have established internship programs. But even more internships are available at the local, grassroots level. Keep this in mind when you are searching on the Web or flipping through the organizations listed in this book. While they are a good place to start, you should always go one step further. Get out and knock on doors—you'll be surprised by how many nonprofits are willing to start an internship program just for you.

Whether you apply for a competitive internship in a major city or ask a small, local nonprofit to take you on as an intern, remember that public service organizations hold themselves to high standards. While they are always in need of a helping hand, not just any hand will do. Small offices often have only three or four full-time staff members, and they depend on each other to create a positive, energized working environment. The last thing they want is an arrogant or cynical intern getting in the way. Generally, public service internships are not extremely competitive; however, intern coordinators are wary of taking anyone who will not fit into their organizational style or who will detract from their positive image.

Having an impeccable GPA and impressive SAT scores won't get you anywhere if you come across as ignorant of the organization's work and indifferent to its mission. On the other hand, good intentions are of little value if you lack the skills to carry out the organization's work. A nonprofit that is trying to change public opinion or government policy needs interns who are up-to-date on current events and office skills.

One intern coordinator for an immigrant workers center says he looks at applicants' résumés to see if they are familiar with computers and such standard office procedures as preparing a bulk mailing. "We look for people who already have a skill we can use. If someone comes in and doesn't know office skills, we have to teach about both the organization and the office," he says. "That's why interns can be more of a burden than a help sometimes."

One project coordinator for a Chinese Americans organization says he gets about 100 applications for eight to ten internship spots. What distinguishes the applications of those who get the internships? A successful application shows him that the applicant not only has taken the time to learn about the organization, but also has done community service work in a related field. "You'd be surprised at what people send in," he says. "We get a lot of applications from people who aren't knowledgeable about the organization."

The key to getting an internship in the public service sector is three pronged. *Know* about the organization and how it works; *care* about what the organization is trying to accomplish; and *have marketable skills* that will aid the organization in reaching its goals. Your cover letter, résumé, and interview should emphasize your familiarity with the organization's goals and leadership style, your personal commitment to its work, and experience (including volunteer work) that would make you an asset to the organization.

Making the Most of Your Public Service Internship

Interns have the opportunity to shadow professionals on a daily basis, carrying out individual projects as they gain confidence, skills, and experience. For that reason, it is important to select an internship that will provide a supportive environment in which you can make—and learn from—mistakes.

Let's say you land an internship at the fictitious "Center for Crayons." The organization works to develop and distribute ideas for inexpensive art projects to children's homes, orphanages, and shelters throughout the United States. When you receive the letter of acceptance, you are ecstatic. As a double major in art and childhood education, you have many ideas for projects and are eager to prepare program material and pilot it with local children. When you arrive for your first day of work, however, you are handed a stack of envelopes to stuff. You find out that your internship consists of photocopying, stapling, and fetching coffee. Or you discover that the Center for Crayons carries out its productive work in branch offices across the country, and the main headquarters, where you work, is used primarily for fund-raising.

An internship that is not geared toward your interests and abilities will not be a worthwhile experience. Sandra Canfield, a master's candidate in international politics at American University, has interned at four public service organizations. She knows the difference between a good internship experience and a bad one. "At my last internship, I ended up doing something very different than I expected and I was miserable. It's very important to be clear. The best thing to do is to let [the organization] know what you're looking for and to ask exactly what you will be doing," Canfield says. "There are tons of [internship] opportunities; you just have to keep looking for the one you want."

As an example of a positive internship experience, Sandra points to her internship at Visions in Action, an international nonprofit organization that sends volunteers to Africa and Latin America to work in international development. During her third week in the office, she was already writing the organization's newsletter for a major international conference.

Positive internship experiences such as that one give interns the opportunity to design their own internships and immerse themselves in many areas of the organization's work. In a group that has only two or three full-time staff members, there is always plenty of work to go around. One associate director says his small organization in Washington, D.C., is growing but still depends on interns to carry out daily work. He himself started at the organization as an intern. "Interning at a small organization has its pros and cons," he says. "I got to do some really great stuff, and I played a big role in getting things going [as an intern]. The groundwork was laid by the interns, and we continue to rely on them a lot."

But in small organizations, no one is freed from grunt work, least of all interns. Tasks such as filing and retrieving documents, photocopying, and answering the phones are routine in most intern experiences. Usually, full-time staff members have to do these things, too. Whether an intern works in a large or small office, the chance to do more important and challenging tasks often comes only if the intern demonstrates that he or she has the necessary drive, skills, and initiative. Some groups will take only students who prove themselves right from the start.

"We like our interns to think critically," says Kimberly Smith, a policy assistant in the Washington, D.C., office of Family Service America's Office of Public Policy. "When there are policy issues on the Hill, [interns] have to be able to know what is involved and how to react." Family Service America interns are expected to keep up with local and national policies involving issues such as welfare reform, food stamps, health care, and Medicaid. Interns are on the Hill two or three times a day, and the most aggressive interns have business cards and know how to network.

Internships that involve hands-on social service work also vary as a direct result of students' self-initiative. Sarah Baker, a Yale student who interned at the Salvation Army Homeless Shelter in Philadelphia, began her internship in June with a research project that involved interviewing former shelter residents. Although she completed the interviews, she spent most of her internship hours leading arts-and-crafts activities for the shelter's youngest residents. "The thing about public service is there is so much to do. I could have worked at any part of shelter and made a difference," she says.

Good Public Relations

If the idea of big business, a large office, and corporate accounts interests you, do not look for an internship at Fenton Communications. But Fenton may be the best place to gain an introduction to public relations for progressively/socially responsible issues, the environment, grassroots organizing, and nonprofit political action groups. As an intern, I was involved with every aspect of publicity campaigns. At Fenton, I performed research, coordinated press conferences, and pitched story ideas to the media. Fenton gives its interns these opportunities to challenge themselves because when full-time positions do become available, the interns get priority consideration.

You can find out more about Fenton Communications by contacting them in Washington, D.C., at (202) 822-5200 or by checking out their Web site, which lists internships (http://www.fenton.com).

—Matt Bockner

Talking Dollars and Cents

The same holds true for internships. While editorial interns at the *Washington Post* can rake in several hundred dollars a week, interns at the nearby Peace Action Education Fund consider themselves lucky to get a $50 stipend. That doesn't do much to offset the expense of renting a tiny room in the nation's capital. But according to interns and intern coordinators, paid public service internships are the exception rather than the rule.

"If you come down [to D.C.] to get money, forget it. All the interns here are encouraged to come in [to the Visions in Action office] a couple of days a week and to work in a local restaurant or retail store in the evenings and on the other days," Sandra Canfield says.

One intern coordinator says it is standard practice for his interns to balance paying jobs with their internships. Because all internships are unpaid, he says interns are given more flexibility than staff members. "For unpaid interns, we're really, really flexible. We want them to be at work on time, but we realize they are not being compensated."

What a Public Service Internship Can Do for You

While it may not help you fatten your bank account, an internship at a nonprofit organization can give you tremendous insight into what a career in the public service sector would be like—the kind of people you would work with, the kind of projects that would fill your days, the kind of skills needed to succeed.

Professional fields differ in the value they place on academic education and practical experience. While the public service sector values academic training, it places a strong emphasis on the kind of practical experience gained through summer or term-time internships. If you plan to go into the public service sector right out of college, an internship is an absolute necessity. "An internship is critical for anybody considering any type of [nonprofit] career [because] it allows [students] to get a broad understanding of how other people in the field are approaching the issue," says Marcel Bolintiam, an information services director for Community Information Exchange, a national nonprofit organization providing information on affordable housing.

For that reason, many career-minded, socially conscious people continue interning in nonprofit organizations even as they study for advanced degrees. As Sandra Canfield explains, "It's not enough if you want to do it, you need the skills to do it. The best way to do that is to do an internship. It's great for making connections."

One former intern at the Boulder, Colorado–based Association for Experimental Education (AEE), a nonprofit organization committed to furthering experimental learning and teaching, found her internship not only provided her with valuable perspective but also opened doors to employment. Leaders of other nonprofit organizations knew that an intern for AEE would be skilled. "It's very prestigious to have that on a résumé. AEE is very well known in the field," she says.

342

Every Day Is Earth Day

If you're interested in working in environmental protection, check out the National Wildlife Federation's _Conservation Directory,_ which lists and describes most conservation organizations (including government agencies) nationally and internationally. It costs $20 and can be purchased by contacting the NWF at 1412 16th St. NW, Washington, DC 20036.

But after several successful job interviews, the former intern went back to AEE and now serves as the organization's office manager. Her experience is not unique. More than one former intern has found that their public service internships provided more than contacts and letters of recommendation; they led to full-time jobs. Ann Yoders, the intern coordinator for Project Vote Smart (and a 1995 Vote Smart intern), said it is common practice for the organization to hire its interns. "It's just smart for the organization to do that," she says. As an intern, "you've spent ten weeks and you're oriented to the project. Our interns are considered staff while they are here, and they are given a lot of leeway and responsibility."

But even for those less interested in building a career out of public service, interning can be a worthwhile way to spend the summer months. Postgraduate programs in everything from medicine to law to education smile upon internships. And these days, they smile particularly widely on internships that combine practical experience with bettering society. Community service is "in."

Most public service interns will tell you that the right internship—the kind where you _do_ rather than watch—has even greater implications. If you pick an organization run by enthusiastic people who are constantly turning out ideas, you can walk away from the internship with the skills to return to your campus or community and fight for change as well as the moral support and confidence to do so.

Summerbridge: The Ultimate
Internship for Future Teachers

The tables are turned on Summerbridge interns. Instead of staying up nights slaving over homework, they stay up nights coming up with homework to assign.

Summerbridge is an innovative program that readies middle school students for high school college preparatory programs. With 35 sites from San Francisco to Providence, Rhode Island, Summerbridge employs 850 high school and college students every year. Summerbridge students, about 80 percent of whom are people of color, are selected for their academic potential. While they benefit from the program's intelligent and enthusiastic interns/teachers, the interns themselves benefit from the instruction of supervisory master teachers, who are full-time educators.

"It's really become a twin goal," says Beth Porter, the assistant director of development for Summerbridge National. "We prepare elementary and middle school students to succeed in academically rigorous programs in high school, and we try to encourage teachers to go into education. It's one of the few programs where you can try out teaching without teacher credentials." The result, interns say, is a program in which the teachers learn as much, if not more, than the students.

"For anyone considering teaching, it's the best short-term thing you can do to see if it's for you," says Kevin Robbins, who worked at the Denver Summerbridge while a student at Princeton University. "My interest was to get some in-class teaching experience. My rationale was that if I'm interested in teaching in a public school, which will have classes of 20 to 30, it makes sense to find out if I like teaching in a class of seven."

Whether Summerbridge interns are college seniors contemplating a career in education or 18-year-olds fresh out of high school, they become teachers responsible for everything from writing lesson plans to grading papers. Teaching responsibilities differ from site to site, but most programs require interns to lead academic and extracurricular classes five days a week. Much of the work, however, is not spelled out in the job description.

"A lot of it is not expertise in [academic subjects], but just being able to communicate with kids," says Sarah Russell, a Yale student who taught at a Summerbridge program in Concord, Massachusetts. "You're kind of a counselor, too, making sure the girls don't starve themselves."

Many past interns have described the program as demanding the impossible. Teachers must create classrooms dynamic enough to inspire learning through the long, hot days of summer. Even for experienced teachers, that's a tall order, and Summerbridge faculty spend hours discussing the best way to meet the challenge. "You work from 8 A.M. up until 8 P.M. every day. It was really an intense job," says Lorenzo Moreno, who interned at the Denver Summerbridge after graduating from Cate, an independent school in California. "I'd get to the site completely tired and have two cups of black coffee."

Because the Summerbridge program is an internship, interns are not left to fight their battles alone. When they first arrive at their Summerbridge site—usually an independent school in a major metropolitan area—interns begin a one- or two-week training program under the direction of professional educators. Orientation begins with a review of current educational literature and culminates in a practice teaching session. The master teachers then remain available to Summerbridge interns throughout the summer, evaluating work and giving advice as needed. Professional guidance is supplemented by the scores of Summerbridge interns who return to the program repeatedly. "What I really loved about the job was that there was such an emphasis on the teacher side, on personal growth and professional development," Lorenzo says. "I learned so much about myself as a human being."

For many interns, the personal growth extends beyond the classroom. When high school and college students apply for a

Summerbridge internship, they indicate in which cities they would be willing to teach. They are offered a job at only one site, and must fend for themselves in whatever city they are placed.

Five-time Summerbridge teacher Mark Scheel worked for Summerbridge as both a high school student in Rhode Island and a college student at Johns Hopkins University. "I still have yet to find a social environment like Summerbridge," Scheel says. "You are surrounded by amazing, hard-working, socially conscious people—you can't help being driven by this energy. You'll drive to a mountain and climb up it and watch the sunrise. It was great. I conquered San Francisco in eight weeks."

Summerbridge Internships: The Facts
Competitiveness: In 1996, 1,400 people applied for 850 teaching positions. Approximately half selected are high school students and half college students.

Pay: Small stipend that usually covers transportation to site and money for incidentals.

Future Employment: Résumé referral system for interns who want to continue in education. Upon request, Summerbridge will send résumés and letters of recommendation to independent schools across the country.

To request an application, call the Summerbridge National Program Office at (415) 749-2037, or contact your local Summerbridge office. **Note:** Six Summerbridge sites are also Americorps sites and operate year round. Internships at these sites are available for the summer and academic school year.

—Sara Schwebel

American Committee on Africa

17 John Street, 12th Floor
New York, NY 10038
Phone: (212) 962-1210
Fax: (212) 964-8570

Position: Intern

Department: N/A

No. of Positions Offered Annually: 6

Description: Interns will perform general office work, as well as some other specialized tasks.

Qualifications: Must have two or three references.

Salary: Unpaid

Position Dates: Fall, Spring and Summer

Position Location: New York, NY

Average No. of Applicants Annually: N/A

Potential for Job Placement: N/A

Application Process: Application to be completed. Must submit a writing sample.

Deadline: July 1 for Fall; January 1 for Spring; February 28 for Summer

Contact: Internship Coordinator

American Red Cross

8111 Gatehouse Road
Falls Church, VA 22042
Phone:
Fax: (703) 206-8572

Position: Presidential Intern

Department: Varies

No. of Positions Offered Annually: 12

Description: This ten-week summer internship is for minority students at the national headquarters in the Washington D.C. metropolitan area. Because sponsoring a presidential intern is a competitive process, specific departments vary from year to year. Past sponsors include Biomedical Services, Finance, Development, Human Resources, International Social Services, Health and Safety Services, and Information Services. Interns will have entry-level professional assignments working on a discrete project.

Qualifications: Applicants must be minority undergraduate or graduate students and must be U.S. citizens who are currently enrolled in school or who have graduated the semester immediately prior to the internship. Specific requirements vary from position to position.

Salary: $8.40/hour

Position Dates: Summer

Position Location: Washington, D.C.

Average No. of Applicants Annually: 200

Potential for Job Placement: Possible

Application Process: Positions are posted in mid-March at career services offices of local area colleges and universities. Students residing outside the Washington, D.C. area should write for position listing which is available in early March.

Deadline: April 15

Contact: Colleen Matan

American Red Cross

8111 Gatehouse Road
Falls Church, VA 22042
Phone: (703) 206-8566

Position: Volunteer

Department: Office of Volunteers

No. of Positions Offered Annually: 10

Description: Volunteer positions available both at the national headquarters and at local chapters across the country. Contact the National Office of Volunteers for volunteer opportunities at the national headquarters. Contact local chapters for all other opportunities.

Qualifications: N/A

Salary: Unpaid

Position Dates: Fall, Spring and Summer

Position Location: Nationwide

Average No. of Applicants Annually: N/A

Potential for Job Placement: N/A

Application Process: Contact headquarters or local chapter for information.

Deadline: Rolling

Contact: N/A

American Woman's Economic Development Corporation (AWED)

71 Vanderbilt Avenue, #320
New York, NY 10169

Position: Training and Counseling Intern

Department: N/A

No. of Positions Offered Annually: 4

Description: The intern will assist training and counseling department with various duties. Organization trains women how to start and manage their own business.

Qualifications: Undergraduates or graduate students. Interest in entrepreneurship.

Salary: Unpaid

Position Dates: Fall, Spring and Summer

Position Location: New York, NY

Average No. of Applicants Annually: 40

Potential for Job Placement: Possible.

Application Process: Send résumé and writing sample.

Deadline: Rolling

Contact: Persephone Zill, Director of Training

Best Buddies International

100 Southeast Second Street, Suite 1990
Miami, FL 33131
Phone: (305) 374-5305

Position: Intern

Department: N/A

No. of Positions Offered Annually: 3

Description: Intern may work in a variety of departments: Public Relations, Marketing, Development, Special Events, or Finance.

Qualifications: Applications reviewed on an individual basis.

Salary: Unpaid

Position Dates: Summer

Position Location: Miami, FL

Average No. of Applicants Annually: 5

Potential for Job Placement: N/A

Application Process: Send résumé and cover letter.

Deadline: Rolling

Contact: Director of Administration

Bet Tzedek Legal Services

145 South Fairfax Avenue, Suite 200
Los Angeles, CA 90036
Phone: (213) 939-0506
Fax: (213) 939-1040

Position: Law Clerk

Department: N/A

No. of Positions Offered Annually: 50

Description: Law clerks conduct legal research, negotiate, perform factual investigation, provide advocacy and prepare legal documents.

Qualifications: N/A

Salary: Small stipend provided.

Position Dates: Summer

Position Location: Los Angeles, CA

Average No. of Applicants Annually: 200

Potential for Job Placement: Possible

Application Process: Send résumé and cover letter.

Deadline: February 1

Contact: Personnel Director/Volunteer Coordinator

Public Service

$125.00

Bet Tzedek Legal Services

145 South Fairfax Avenue, Suite 200
Los Angeles, CA 90036
Phone: (213) 939-0506
Fax: (213) 939-1040

Position: Intake Assistant

Department: N/A

No. of Positions Offered Annually: 150

Description: Duties include: prescreening
clients for financial and case-type eligibility
by telephone, arrange appointments based
on legal issues and deadlines and provide
information and referrals. Position may
involve promotion to legal assistant
position, which involves observing and
conducting in-person client consultations
and investigations and preparing
correspondence and forms under attorney
supervision.

Qualifications: N/A

Salary: Unpaid

Position Dates: Fall, Spring and Summer

Position Location: Los Angeles, CA

Average No. of Applicants Annually:
300

Potential for Job Placement: No

Application Process: Send résumé and
cover letter.

Deadline: Rolling

Contact: Personnel Director/Volunteer
Coordinator

Boston University Sargent Camp

36 Sargent Camp Road
Hancock, NH 03449
Phone: (603) 525-3311

Position: Teaching Intern

Department: N/A

No. of Positions Offered Annually: 16

Description: A teaching intern is
responsible for instructing and facilitating
groups of 10 to 12 students in all aspects of
the program. Curriculum includes wetland,
wildlife and forest ecology, astronomy, night
exploration, history of early settlers, team
problem solving, group dynamics, and low
and high challenge rope courses. Room and
board are provided.

Qualifications: Minimum of 18 years old,
current first aid and CPR certification,
experience working with children, good
communication skills, comfortable working
long hours outdoors, desire to learn and the
ability to live and work as part of a team.
Bachelor's degree and/or experience in
environmental education and/or adventure
education a plus.

Salary: $85-$135/week (stipend)

Position Dates: Three-, six- or nine-month
positions

Position Location: Hancock, NH

Average No. of Applicants Annually:
20

Potential for Job Placement: N/A

Application Process: Application packet
to be completed.

Deadline: Rolling

Contact: Marijean Legnard Parry

Breckenridge Outdoor Education Center

P.O. Box 697
Breckenridge, CO 80424
Phone: (800) 383-BOEC

Position: Intern

Department: N/A

No. of Positions Offered Annually: 20

Description: The objective of the internship is to provide empowerment through outdoor education and adaptive skiing for individuals and groups of all abilities. Room and board are provided.

Qualifications: People with outdoor experience and a love of working with people.

Salary: $50/month

Position Dates: Winter and Summer

Position Location: Breckenridge, CO

Average No. of Applicants Annually: 80

Potential for Job Placement: Competitive

Application Process: Call for an application.

Deadline: September 15 for Winter; March 20 for Summer

Contact: Earl Richmond

Brethren Volunteer Service

1451 Dundee Avenue
Elgin, IL 60120
Phone: (847) 742-5100
Fax: (847) 742-5100

Position: U.S. Intern

Department: N/A

No. of Positions Offered Annually: 50

Description: Volunteers work at solving deep-rooted problems (i.e. homelessness, racism). BVS projects seek to advocate justice, work for peace, serve basic human needs, and maintain the integrity of creation. There are medical benefits and loan deferrals. Room and board are provided.

Qualifications: Must be willing to commit for one year. In order to serve in the U.S. must be 18 years of age with high school diploma or equivalency exam. Specialized skills can be used on some projects but not required.

Salary: $45/month (stipend)

Position Dates: Fall, Spring and Summer

Position Location: Nationwide

Average No. of Applicants Annually: 100

Potential for Job Placement: Varies.

Application Process: Application to be completed, essays, references, transcripts, medical exams, and $15 fee.

Deadline: Six weeks prior to starting date.

Contact: BVS Recruitment

Brethren Volunteer Service

1451 Dundee Avenue
Elgin, IL 60120
Phone: (847) 742-5100
Fax: (847) 742-6103

Position: Oversees Intern

Department: N/A

No. of Positions Offered Annually: 25

Description: Volunteers work at solving deep-rooted problems (i.e. peace issues, community building) . BVS projects seek to work for peace, advocate justice, serve basic human needs, and maintain the integrity of creation. There are medical benefits and loan deferals. Room and board are provided.

Qualifications: 21 years of age, college degree (bachelor's) , flexibility, $400 travel fee, must commit to two years of service.

Salary: $45/month (stipend)

Position Dates: Fall, Spring and Summer

Position Location: Worldwide

Average No. of Applicants Annually: 30

Potential for Job Placement: Unlikely

Application Process: Application to be completed, essays, references, résumé, medical forms, and $15 fee.

Deadline: Six weeks prior to start of the program.

Contact: BVS Recruitment

Camp Courageous of Iowa

12007 120th Street, Box 418
Monticello, IA 52310-0418
Phone: (319) 465-5916
Fax: (319) 465-5919

Position: Camp Counselor and Activity Specialist

Department: N/A

No. of Positions Offered Annually: 10

Description: Work with children and adults that have disabilities in a camp setting. Room and board are provided.

Qualifications: Experience helpful but not required.

Salary: $80/month (stipend)

Position Dates: Fall, Spring and Summer

Position Location: Monticello, IA

Average No. of Applicants Annually: 30-40

Potential for Job Placement: Yes

Application Process: Application to be completed. References and interview required.

Deadline: Rolling

Contact: Mike Maher

Camp Fire Boys and Girls, Inc.— Georgia Council

100 Edgewood Avenue, Suite 528
Atlanta, GA 30303
Fax: (404) 527-7139

Position: Public Relations Intern

Department: N/A

No. of Positions Offered Annually: 2

Description: The position will be responsible for publicizing council activities and promotions for special events, and assisting in the maintenance of membership records. The interns will be responsible for writing press releases and distributing them to appropriate outlets, creating flyers for programs, attending Community Relations Committee meetings of the board of directors, assisting in alumni relations development, following up on all assignments in a timely manner. Work within the limits of the Camp Fire budget, assist other staff will special projects offering expertise and support in areas of public relations, development and marketing as time permits.

Qualifications: Should have a commitment to excelllence in youth development and should be a self-starter who possesses strong communication and human relations skills. Coursework in public relations or marketing or nonprofit desirable. Software proficiency in Word for Windows. PageMaker and Access skills desirable but not required.

Salary: Unpaid

Position Dates: Fall, Spring and Summer

Position Location: Atlanta, GA

Average No. of Applicants Annually: 4

Potential for Job Placement: Some

Application Process: Send résumé and a list of 3 references.

Deadline: Rolling

Contact: Linda Woodworth, Communications Manager

Catholic Charities, Diocese of Metuchen

288 Rues Lane
East Brunswick, NJ 08816
Phone: (908) 257-6100
Fax: (908) 651-9834

Position: Clinical Intern

Department: N/A

No. of Positions Offered Annually: 40

Description: Intern provides mental health services in traditional mental health and family service offices, in partial hospitalization programs, and in non-traditional settings such as in-home.

Qualifications: Must be enrolled in a BSW, MSW, Ph.D. program.

Salary: Unpaid

Position Dates: Fall, Spring and Summer

Position Location: East Brunswick, NJ

Average No. of Applicants Annually: 60-70

Potential for Job Placement: N/A

Application Process: Contact Educational Coordinator.

Deadline: Rolling

Contact: Patricia A. Moore, Educational Coordinator

Chrysalis, A Center for Women

2650 Nicollet Avenue S
Minneapolis, MN 55408
Phone: (612) 870-2420
Fax: (612) 870-2403

Position: Group Facilitator

Department: N/A

No. of Positions Offered Annually: 10

Description: Meet weekly with a small group of women who support each other. Groups include: Self-Worth and Empowerment, Women of Color, Lesbian Support, Single Moms, and others. Thirty-six hours of training provided.

Qualifications: Prior experience as support group member or facilitator highly recommended.

Salary: Unpaid

Position Dates: Once a week for a year. Flexible starting dates.

Position Location: Minneapolis, MN

Average No. of Applicants Annually: N/A

Potential for Job Placement: Possible, but not frequent.

Application Process: Interview and reference check.

Deadline: Rolling

Contact: Tiffany Muller, Volunteer Coordinator

Chrysalis, A Center for Women

2650 Nicollet Avenue S
Minneapolis, MN 55408
Phone: (612) 870-2420
Fax: (612) 870-2403

Position: Phone Resource Counselor

Department: N/A

No. of Positions Offered Annually: 10

Description: Provide support to women over the phone regarding various issues such as divorce, domestic violence, relationships, self-esteem, crisis intervention, etc. Also provide information to callers about where to seek further information.

Qualifications: Counseling experience and knowledge of community resources helpful.

Salary: Unpaid

Position Dates: Once a week for a year. Flexible starting dates.

Position Location: Minneapolis, MN

Average No. of Applicants Annually: N/A

Potential for Job Placement: Possible, but not frequent.

Application Process: Interview and reference check

Deadline: Rolling

Contact: Tiffany Muller, Volunteer Coordinator

City of Cambridge

57 Inman Street
Cambridge, MA 02139
Phone: (617) 349-4601
Fax: (617) 349-4669

Position: Economic Development Intern

Department: Economic Development

No. of Positions Offered Annually: 2

Description: Interns will work closely with Economic Development personnel in the following capacities: analyze permits and licensing processes which affect Cambridge businesses and development, assist in coordinating new signage proposal for City buildings, coordinate committee doing research on computer technologies used to streamline permits and licensing processes, research and update data on local biotechnology businesses and leading Cambridge employers, finalize a directory of women-owned businesses for publication, maintain development database of current projects within the City of Cambridge, organize departmental photos and drawings used for public relations into a usable system, other duties as directed and needed by Economic Development personnel.

Qualifications: Applicants must be an undergraduate or graduate student. Experience with Windows, MS Word, MS Excel, and MS Access is preferred. Interns must have excellent oral and written communication skills. Interns must be able to work independently and cooperatively in a group setting.

Salary: $10/hour (undergraduate); $13/hour (graduate)

Position Dates: Summer (ten weeks)

Position Location: Cambridge, MA

Average No. of Applicants Annually: N/A

Potential for Job Placement: N/A

Application Process: Fax or send résumé and cover letter.

Deadline: May 21

Contact: Derrick L. Woody, Project Administrator

CityArts, Inc.

525 Broadway, Suite 700
New York, NY 10012
Phone: (212) 966-0377
Fax: (212) 966-0551

Position: Intern

Department: N/A

No. of Positions Offered Annually: 10

Description: Interns will assist artists. Interns will also be responsible for some public relations work, fund-raising, and marketing work.

Qualifications: Artist assistants should be interested in the fine arts. Experience in community service and with children is desirable. General office work experience is a plus, but not necessary. Commitment to the arts.

Salary: Unpaid

Position Dates: Fall, Spring and Summer

Position Location: New York, NY

Average No. of Applicants Annually: 100+

Potential for Job Placement: N/A

Application Process: Send in résumé and cover letter, indicating area of interest.

Deadline: Rolling

Contact: Internship Coordinator

Coro Fellows Program in Public Affairs

St. Louis, MO
Phone: (314) 621-3040

Position: Coro Midwestern Center Public Affairs Intern

Department: N/A

No. of Positions Offered Annually: 12

Description: The nine month program is a full-time graduate level program involving field assignments, seminars, interviews, public service projects. The program is for individuals who have a serious desire to improve the quality of life in their communities. The program provides hands-on experience in the real world of public affairs. Stipends available to help with living expenses.

Qualifications: Applicant should posses a B.A. in any major and/or equivalent work experience. Must demonstrate leadership potential and commitment to public service.

Salary: Unpaid

Position Dates: Academic Year

Position Location: St. Louis, MO

Average No. of Applicants Annually: 300

Potential for Job Placement: N/A

Application Process: Application to be completed, which includes essays, transcripts, four letters of recommendation, and a $50 fee. Finalists will be interviewed in early April.

Deadline: Mid-February

Contact: Andy Thorp

Coro Fellows Program in Public Affairs

San Francisco, CA
Phone: (415) 986-0521

Position: Coro Northern California Public Affairs Intern

Department: N/A

No. of Positions Offered Annually: 12

Description: The nine-month program is a full-time graduate-level program involving field assignments, seminars, interviews, public service projects. The program is for individuals who have a serious desire to improve the quality of life in their communities. The program provides hands-on experience in the real world of public affairs. Stipends available to help with living expenses.

Qualifications: Applicant should posses a B.A. in any major and/or equivalent work experience. Must demonstrate leadership potential and commitment to public service.

Salary: Unpaid

Position Dates: Academic year

Position Location: San Francisco, CA

Average No. of Applicants Annually: 300

Potential for Job Placement: N/A

Application Process: Application to be completed, which includes essays, transcripts, four letters of recommendation, and a $50 fee. Finalists will be interviewed in early April.

Deadline: Mid-February

Contact: Gracie Cornejo

Coro Fellows Program in Public Affairs

New York, NY
Phone: (212) 248-2935

Position: Coro Eastern Center Public Affairs Intern

Department: N/A

No. of Positions Offered Annually: 12

Description: The nine-month program is a full-time graduate-level program involving field assignments, seminars, interviews, public service projects. The program is for individuals who have a serious desire to improve the quality of life in their communities. The program provides hands-on experience in the real world of public affairs. Stipends available to help with living expenses.

Qualifications: Applicant should possess a B.A. in any major and/or equivalent work experience. Must demonstrate leadership potential and commitment to public service.

Salary: Unpaid

Position Dates: Academic year

Position Location: New York, NY

Average No. of Applicants Annually: 300

Potential for Job Placement: N/A

Application Process: Application to be completed which includes essays, transcripts, four letters of recommendation, and a $50 fee. Finalists will be interviewed in early April.

Deadline: Mid-February

Contact: William Malpica

Coro Fellows Program in Public Affairs

Los Angeles, CA
Phone: (213) 623-1234

Position: Coro Southern California Public Affairs Intern

Department: N/A

No. of Positions Offered Annually: 12

Description: The nine-month program is a full-time graduate-level program involving field assignments, seminars, interviews, public service projects. The program is for individuals who have a serious desire to improve the quality of life in their communities. The program provides hands-on experience in the real world of public affairs. Stipends available to help with living expenses.

Qualifications: Applicant should posses a B.A. in any major and/or equivalent work experience. Must demonstrate leadership potential and commitment to public service.

Salary: Unpaid

Position Dates: Academic year

Position Location: Los Angeles, CA

Average No. of Applicants Annually: 300

Potential for Job Placement: N/A

Application Process: Application to be completed which includes essays, transcripts, four letters of recommendation, and a $50 fee. Finalists will be interviewed in early April.

Deadline: Mid-February

Contact: Dorothy Gamoning

Criminal Justice Clinic, Georgetown University Law Center

III F Street NW
Washington, DC 20001
Phone: (202) 662-9575
Fax: (202) 662-9681

Position: Investigative Intern

Department: N/A

No. of Positions Offered Annually: 30

Description: The Juvenile and Criminal Justice Clinics provide representation to indigent clients charged with criminal offenses in DC and Maryland. Interns are trained in investigation and criminal law and are then assigned to attorneys in the Clinics. Responsibilities include locating and interviewing witnesses, taking witness statements, meeting with clients, serving subpoenas and collecting evidence, researching the criminal backgrounds of witnesses, photographing and measuring crime scenes, preparing exhibits for courts, participating in the development of case strategy and theory and generally assisting attorneys in and out of court. Interns attend a lecture series to expose them to other aspects of the criminal justice system. For interns interested in attending law school, they may meet with the Director of Admissions for Georgetown Law, train on Westlaw and Lexis, have free access to the library and a 15% discount on LSAT preparatory courses offered by Kaplan and Princeton Review.

Qualifications: Open to students in college, college graduates or graduate students. Juniors and seniors in college are given preference over freshmen and sophomores. All majors are eligible. Previous exposure to or experience in the fields of law, criminal justice or public service helpful but not required. Applicants must be able to demonstrate strong communication skills and be able to devote a sufficient amount of time to the internship.

Salary: Unpaid

Position Dates: Fall, Spring and Summer

Position Location: Washington, D.C.

Average No. of Applicants Annually: 400-500

Potential for Job Placement: No

Application Process: Application to be completed. Interviews are conducted with most candidates.

Deadline: March 15 for Fall; December 1 for Spring; April 1 for Summer.

Contact: Helen Mould

DC Rape Crisis Center

P.O. Box 34125
Washington, DC 20043
Phone: (202) 232-0789

Position: Intern

Department: Various

No. of Positions Offered Annually: 22

Description: Internships available in the following departments: Counseling and Advocacy, Development/Public Relations, and Community/Education.

Qualifications: Women of color and from diverse backgrounds desired. Women interested in psychology and women's studies desired.

Salary: Unpaid

Position Dates: Fall, Spring and Summer

Position Location: Washington, D.C.

Average No. of Applicants Annually: 200+

Potential for Job Placement: N/A

Application Process: Application to be completed. Must also send résumé. Will be contacted for an interview.

Deadline: Rolling

Contact: Arlette del Toro

Fight Crime: Invest in Kids

1334 G Street NW, Suite B
Washington, DC 20005-3107
Phone: (202) 638-0690
Fax: (202) 638-0673

Position: Intern

Department: Various

No. of Positions Offered Annually: 12

Description: Interns can work in the following departments: Fund-raising, Research, Press and Media, and Organizing. Interns will be doing much research and writing. The internship is a full-time position and lasts the equivalent of a semester. Interns will be reimbursed for living expenses up to $500.

Qualifications: Excellent research and writing skills.

Salary: Unpaid

Position Dates: Fall, Spring and Summer

Position Location: Washington, D.C.

Average No. of Applicants Annually: 100+

Potential for Job Placement: N/A

Application Process: Send résumé, cover letter, and brief writing sample.

Deadline: June 1 for Fall; November 1 for Spring; March 1 for Summer

Contact: Intern Coordinator

Fourth World Movement

7600 Willow Hill Drive
Landover, MD 20785
Phone: (301) 336-9489
Fax: (301) 336-0092

Position: Intern

Department: N/A

No. of Positions Offered Annually: 12

Description: Three-month internship that
provides the intern with an introduction to
the approach and work of grassroots
volunteer work. Work will include data
entry, working on a newsletter, and
discussing videos and documents. Housing
is provided.

Qualifications: Applicants must have a
commitment to seeing an end to poverty.

Salary: Unpaid

Position Dates: Fall, Spring and Summer

Position Location: Landover, MD

Average No. of Applicants Annually:
80

Potential for Job Placement: Some

Application Process: Application to be
completed. Interview is required.

Deadline: Rolling

Contact: Internship Coordinator

Gould Farm

Gould Farm
Monterey, MA 01245
Phone: (413) 528-1804
Fax: (413) 528-5051

Position: Mental Health Intern

Department: N/A

No. of Positions Offered Annually: 12

Description: Hands-on experience at a
unique residential rehabilitation program
for the mentally ill on a working farm. Lead
small work groups, help in treatment
planning and integrating clients back into
the general community. Room and board
are provided.

Qualifications: Ideal for social work or
psychology major. Must be interested in
human service. Level of maturity is more
important than degree. Driver's license is a
must.

Salary: $250/month

Position Dates: Fall, Spring and Summer

Position Location: Monterey, MA

Average No. of Applicants Annually:
100

Potential for Job Placement: Very good

Application Process: Send résumé, cover
letter, and three references. An interview is
required.

Deadline: Rolling

Contact: Paula Snyder, Human Resources
Manager

Human Service Alliance

3983 Old Greensboro Road
Winston-Salem, NC 27101
Phone: (910) 761-8745
Fax: (910) 722-7882

Position: Intern

Department: N/A

No. of Positions Offered Annually: 35

Description: Interns engage in hands-on care of terminally ill patients, giving medications, keeping patient records, preparing meals, and housekeeping. Room and board are provided.

Qualifications: Positive attitude and willingness to work on a team.

Salary: Unpaid

Position Dates: Fall, Spring and Summer

Position Location: Winston-Salem, NC

Average No. of Applicants Annually: 70

Potential for Job Placement: N/A

Application Process: Application to be completed. Three letters of reference and a telephone interview are required.

Deadline: Rolling

Contact: Sanford Danziger

Immigrant Workers' Resource Center

25 West Street
Boston, MA 02111
Phone: (617) 542-334
Fax: (617) 542-334

Position: Intern

Department: N/A

No. of Positions Offered Annually: 5

Description: Aid in organizing immigrant communities, assist in office, fund-raising.

Qualifications: Fluency in Spanish helpful but not required.

Salary: Unpaid

Position Dates: Year round

Position Location: Boston, MA

Average No. of Applicants Annually: 10

Potential for Job Placement: Yes

Application Process: Send résumé and cover letter.

Deadline: Rolling

Contact: Executive Director

Interlocken Center for Experimental Learning

RR2 Box 165
Hillsboro, NH 03244
Phone: (603) 478-3166
Fax: (603) 478-5260

Position: Summer Camp Counselor

Department: N/A

No. of Positions Offered Annually: 50

Description: Responsible for teaching classes in art, theater, wilderness, waterfront, sports, and other areas, as well as being responsible for the health and well-being of campers.

Qualifications: Experience working with youth, skills in teaching areas, love of children, and a minimum age of 19.

Salary: $1,200 plus d.o.e.

Position Dates: Summer

Position Location: Hillsboro, NH

Average No. of Applicants Annually: 500

Potential for Job Placement: No

Application Process: Send résumé and cover letter.

Deadline: Rolling

Contact: Judi Wisch, Staffing Director

Interlocken Center for Experimental Learning

RR2 Box 165
Hillsboro, NH 03244
Phone: (603) 478-3166
Fax: (603) 478-5260

Position: Travel Program Leader

Department: N/A

No. of Positions Offered Annually: 20

Description: Co-lead a small group of teenagers on a travel adventure in the U.S., Canada, Europe, or the Caribbean: biking, wilderness, environment, performing arts, leadership training.

Qualifications: Minimum age of 24. Intensive experience working with teenagers out in the field. Expertise in the program area.

Salary: $1,000-$1,500

Position Dates: Summer

Position Location: Hillsboro, NH

Average No. of Applicants Annually: 750

Potential for Job Placement: No

Application Process: Send résumé and cover letter.

Deadline: Rolling

Contact: Judi Wisch, Staffing Director

International Partnership for Service-Learning

815 Second Avenue, Suite 315
New York, NY 10017
Phone: (212) 986-0989
Fax: (212) 986-5039

Position: Intern

Department: N/A

No. of Positions Offered Annually: 300

Description: A wide variety of service placements are available in each location. Students are often placed according to their request. Service examples include teaching/tutoring, health care (including the physically and mentally handicapped), youth recreation, helping the elderly, community development, cultural and heritage projects, environmental projects and womens' issues.

Qualifications: Some students bring existing skills to their service, for example experience with health issues or child care. These skills are valued but not required. Applicants must possess, at minimum, a college degree.

Salary: Unpaid

Position Dates: One year, Fall, Spring, and Summer

Position Location: Jamaica

Average No. of Applicants Annually: 300+

Potential for Job Placement: Not likely

Application Process: Application to be completed and a $250 deposit is required.

Deadline: July 1 for Fall; November 1 for Spring; May 1 for Summer

Contact: Howard Berry, President

Japanese Exchange Teaching Program (JET Program)

2520 Massachusetts Avenue NW
Washington, DC 20008
Phone: (202) 939-6772

Position: Intern

Department: N/A

No. of Positions Offered Annually: 1,100

Description: Assistant language teachers (1,000) placed in public junior or senior high schools. Over 100 positions available as coordinators for international relations, who are placed in local government offices.

Qualifications: Teaching, tutoring, or coaching experience.

Salary: 3,600,000 Yen/year

Position Dates: One year

Position Location: Japan

Average No. of Applicants Annually: 3,600

Potential for Job Placement: N/A

Application Process: Application to be completed, two-page essay, two letters of recommendation, a transcript, a copy of bachelor's degree or letter saying that you will graduate in June.

Deadline: First week in December

Contact: JET Program Coordinator, Embassy of Japan

Massachusetts Public Interest Research Group (MASSPIRG)

29 Temple Place
Boston, MA 02111
Phone: (617) 292-4800
Fax: (617) 292-8057

Position: Political/Environmental Intern

Department: Various

No. of Positions Offered Annually: 20

Description: Internships are available in all four of the program departments: Toxics, Solid Waste, Energy, Consumer. Intern activities will include researching and writing reports, conducting surveys, organizing citizen and environmental groups around a campaign, investigating unfair consumer activities, assisting with press conferences, and working with legislators.

Qualifications: Commitment to public interest issues, ability to take initiative and work independently. Strong communication skills a must. Political and issue experience a plus.

Salary: Unpaid

Position Dates: Fall, Spring and Summer

Position Location: Boston, MA

Average No. of Applicants Annually: N/A

Potential for Job Placement: Yes

Application Process: Send résumé and cover letter.

Deadline: Rolling

Contact: Internship Coordinator

Middle Earth, Inc.

299 Jacksonville Road
Warmister, PA 18974
Phone: (215) 443-0280

Position: Student Teacher

Department: N/A

No. of Positions Offered Annually: 5

Description: Interns will work in the following fields: psychology, sociology and criminal justice. Interns work with students who have a history of poor school adjustment characterized by academic failure, truancy, and disruptive behavior.

Qualifications: Good interpersonal skills, understanding of applied psychology, and an interest in adolescents.

Salary: Unpaid

Position Dates: Academic year

Position Location: Warmister, PA

Average No. of Applicants Annually: 10

Potential for Job Placement: High

Application Process: Call or write for application.

Deadline: Rolling

Contact: Elizabeth A. Quigley

Organization of Chinese Americans, Inc. (OCA)

1001 Connecticut Avenue NW, Suite 707
Washington, DC 20036
Phone: (202) 223-5500
Fax: (202) 296-0540

Position: OCA Congressional Internship

Department: N/A

No. of Positions Offered Annually: 10

Description: Work in a congressional office and participate in the legislative process. Only open to OCA members or College Affiliate members.

Qualifications: Must be a college or graduate student having demonstrated an interest in public affairs. Must have good oral and written communication skills. Must work for a minimum of ten weeks.

Salary: $1,500 for ten weeks

Position Dates: Fall, Spring and Summer

Position Location: Washington, D.C.

Average No. of Applicants Annually: 75+

Potential for Job Placement: N/A

Application Process: Application to be completed, résumé (including extracurricular activities), transcript, one-page essay about why you want to participate in program, two letters of reference, and an interview.

Deadline: July 15 for Fall; November 15 for Spring; March 15 for Summer

Contact: Executive Director

Organization of Chinese Americans, Inc. (OCA)

1001 Connecticut Avenue NW, Suite 707
Washington, DC 20036
Phone: (202) 223-5500
Fax: (202) 296-0540

Position: OCA National Internship

Department: N/A

No. of Positions Offered Annually: 10

Description: Work in the OCA National Office under the Executive Director and participate in many functions mandated by the OCA mission.

Qualifications: Must be a college or graduate student having demonstrated an interest in public affairs. Must have good oral and written communication skills. Must work for a minimum of 10 weeks.

Salary: $1,500 for ten weeks

Position Dates: Fall, Spring and Summer

Position Location: Washington, D.C.

Average No. of Applicants Annually: 75+

Potential for Job Placement: N/A

Application Process: Application to be completed, résumé (including extracurricular activities), transcript, one-page essay about why you want to participate in program, two letters of reference, and an interview.

Deadline: July 15 for Fall; November 15 for Spring; March 15 for Summer

Contact: Executive Director

Organization of Chinese Americans, Inc. (OCA)

1001 Connecticut Avenue NW, Suite 707
Washington, DC 20036
Phone: (202) 223-5500
Fax: (202) 296-0540

Position: OCA Government Internship

Department: N/A

No. of Positions Offered Annually: 10

Description: Work in a federal agency in Washington D.C. and learn about policy making (please indicate area of interest). Only open to OCA Members or Affiliate College members.

Qualifications: N/A

Salary: $1,500 for ten weeks

Position Dates: Fall, Spring and Summer

Position Location: Washington, D.C.

Average No. of Applicants Annually: 75+

Potential for Job Placement: N/A

Application Process: Application to be completed, résumé (including extracurricular activities), transcript, one-page essay about why you want to participate in program, two letters of reference, and an interview.

Deadline: July 15 for Fall; November 15 for Spring; March 15 for Summer

Contact: Executive Director

Outdoors Wisconsin Leadership School

Box 210
Williams Bay, WI 53191
Phone: (414) 245-5531
Fax: (414) 245-9068

Position: Adventure Education Instructor

Department: N/A

No. of Positions Offered Annually: 4

Description: Following an intensive training period, covering activity leadership, facilitation and technical skills, interns take a leadership role in all program areas including: group facilitation, technical support, program design and evaluation, facility construction and maintenance, and administrative duties. The program is located at George Williams College. Room and health plan provided.

Qualifications: College graduate or senior year status, preferably with some course work in related areas such as psychology, communications, education, recreation or outdoor leadership. Good communication skills, experience leading groups, and a high level of energy and enthusiasm for creating powerful learning experiences for others are a must.

Salary: Hourly pay and overtime available

Position Dates: March to Mid-November

Position Location: Williams Bay, WI

Average No. of Applicants Annually: 30-50

Potential for Job Placement: N/A

Application Process: Send a cover letter, résumé, three academic and/or work references.

Deadline: November or December

Contact: Cathy Coster, Director of Adventure Education

Peace Action Education Fund

1819 H Street NW, Suite 420
Washington, DC 20006
Phone: (202) 862-9740
Fax: (202) 862-9762

Position: Intern

Department: N/A

No. of Positions Offered Annually: 6

Description: Interns work with program staff on the following issues: nuclear disarmament and arms trade campaign.

Qualifications: Interest in peace and justice issues.

Salary: $50/week

Position Dates: Fall, Spring and Summer

Position Location: Washington, D.C.

Average No. of Applicants Annually: 30

Potential for Job Placement: N/A

Application Process: Application to be completed, includes writing samples, letters of reference, and résumé.

Deadline: Rolling

Contact: Craig Lamberton

Peace Corps

6 World Trade Center, Room 611
New York, NY 10048
Fax: (212) 466-2473

Position: Intern

Department: Various

No. of Positions Offered Annually: 30

Description: Interns will work in the New York regional office in various departments: Communications, Public Affairs, Business, Marketing, etc.

Qualifications: Interest in volunteer work and experience in various fields in necessary.

Salary: Unpaid

Position Dates: Winter/Spring and Summer

Position Location: New York, NY

Average No. of Applicants Annually: 60+

Potential for Job Placement: Many interns volunteer in Peace Corps afterwards

Application Process: Send cover letter and résumé. An interview is also required.

Deadline: January 15 for Winter/Spring; April 15 for Summer

Contact: Internship Coordinator

Rock Creek Foundation

1107 Spring Street, Suite C
Silver Spring, MD 20910
Phone: (310) 589-6675
Fax: (310) 588-1567

Position: Intern

Department: Variety

No. of Positions Offered Annually: 40

Description: At least a three-month position, working at least six hours per week. A variety of departments are offered to meet each specific individual's needs. Examples of positions are as follows: tutor, recreation specialist, support counselor, mentor, community integration specialist, career advisor, job coach, technical trainer, service learning specialist, group leader, computer aide, and marketing coordinator. College credit is available.

Qualifications: Interest in working with adults who have special needs.

Salary: Unpaid

Position Dates: Fall, Spring and Summer

Position Location: Silver Spring, MD

Average No. of Applicants Annually: 200

Potential for Job Placement: Yes

Application Process: Send cover letter requesting application and résumé.

Deadline: Rolling

Contact: Beth Albaneze, Director

Schuylkill Center for Environmental Education

8480 Hagy's Mill Road
Philadelphia, PA 19128
Phone: (215) 482-7300
Fax: (215) 482-8158

Position: Intern

Department: N/A

No. of Positions Offered Annually: 4

Description: Interns will teach environmental education lessons outdoors and natural history to members. There is some weekend work. Interns will also be responsible for maintenance of museum and exhibits.

Qualifications: Teaching background is preferred. Majoring in Environmental Education or Biology is also preferred.

Salary: $1,600 (stipend)

Position Dates: Fall and Spring

Position Location: Philadelphia, PA

Average No. of Applicants Annually: 12

Potential for Job Placement: Possible, but unlikely

Application Process: Send a cover letter, résumé, and two references.

Deadline: Rolling

Contact: Gayle White

Southface Energy Institute

241 Pine Street
Atlanta, GA 30308
Phone: (404) 872-3549
Fax: (404) 872-5089

Position: Staff Assistant

Department: N/A

No. of Positions Offered Annually: 12

Description: Approximately half of the work week will be spent in general staff assistance (answering phones, preparing mailings, maintaining membership databases, participating in staff meetings, etc.). The remainder of the time will be spent giving tours of demo house facilities to the public, performing general maintenance tasks, and preparing and participating in educational projects.

Qualifications: Interns must have completed one year of college or equivalent work and education experience.

Salary: Starts at $335/month and housing

Position Dates: Year round

Position Location: Atlanta, GA

Average No. of Applicants Annually: 200

Potential for Job Placement: Good

Application Process: Send for application.

Deadline: Rolling

Contact: Steve Byers

St. Vincent's Hospital

P.O. Box 12407
Birmingham, AL 35202-2407
Phone: (205) 939-7000
Fax: (205) 930-2104

Position: Personnel Internship

Department: Personnel

No. of Positions Offered Annually: 10

Description: Assist the personnel department with employment, staffing, unemployment compensation, reference checking, and benefit administration.

Qualifications: Minimum of sophomore year in college. Previous experience with Windows strongly preferred.

Salary: Unpaid

Position Dates: Year round

Position Location: Birmingham, AL

Average No. of Applicants Annually: 10-15

Potential for Job Placement: N/A

Application Process: Send résumé and cover letter.

Deadline: Rolling

Contact: Amy Anzalone

Starlight Foundation

1560 Broadway, Suite 402
New York, NY 10036
Phone: (212) 354-2878
Fax: (212) 354-2977

Position: Intern

Department: N/A

No. of Positions Offered Annually: 8

Description: Interns are involved in children's services. Interns plan hospital parties, and are also involved in marketing, public relations, and fund-raising. It is a three day per week commitement for three months.

Qualifications: Excellent communication skills.

Salary: Unpaid

Position Dates: Fall and Summer

Position Location: New York, NY

Average No. of Applicants Annually: 30-40

Potential for Job Placement: Not much.

Application Process: Application to be completed.

Deadline: Rolling

Contact: Internship Coordinator

Wediko Children's Services

264 Beacon Street
Boston, MA 02116
Phone: (617) 536-2747
Fax: (617) 536-9489

Position: Intern

Department: N/A

No. of Positions Offered Annually: 100

Description: Interns act as caregivers for children with emotional disorders at the center in Hillsborough, New Hampshire. Room and board are provided.

Qualifications: Two years of college experience. No academic requirements, but most major in psychology, education, or human services.

Salary: $900-$1,500

Position Dates: Summer

Position Location: Hillsboro, NH

Average No. of Applicants Annually: 300

Potential for Job Placement: N/A

Application Process: Application to be completed. Must send résumé.

Deadline: Rolling, but positions are filled by the end of March.

Contact: Summer Program Coordinator

Wildlife Habitat Council

1010 Wayne Avenue, Suite 920
Silver Spring, MD 20910
Fax: (301) 588-4629

Position: Media Relations/Public Relations Intern

Department: Media Relations/Public Relations

No. of Positions Offered Annually: 1

Description: Intern will assist the Communications Director and the Editor. Intern will maintain a media list and will complete some writing assignments. Interns must provide general office support.

Qualifications: Good writing, organizational, and communication skills are a must. Interest in wildlife conservation is desirable.

Salary: Unpaid

Position Dates: Flexible

Position Location: Silver Spring, MD

Average No. of Applicants Annually: N/A

Potential for Job Placement: Some

Application Process: Send cover letter and résumé.

Deadline: Rolling

Contact: Jarid Goldman, Communications Director

Wildlife Habitat Council

1010 Wayne Avenue, Suite 920
Silver Spring, MD 20910
Fax: (301) 588-4629

Position: Research Intern

Department: N/A

No. of Positions Offered Annually: 2

Description: Interns will perform information research on wildlife or plant species and habitat management techniques. Interns will also provide general support for report production, including writing and production of maps and figures. Interns may also assist with clerical and administrative work.

Qualifications: Candidates should be working towards a degree in Wildlife Biology, Natural Resources Management, or related field. Excellent writing skills and experience with word processing and database software a must.

Salary: Unpaid

Position Dates: Winter Break and Summer

Position Location: Silver Spring, MD

Average No. of Applicants Annually: 10-20

Potential for Job Placement: Fair

Application Process: Send cover letter, résumé, and three references.

Deadline: Rolling

Contact: Intern Search Committee

Woodberry Forest Summer School

P.O. Box 354
Woodberry Forest, VA 22989
Phone: (540) 672-6047
Fax: (540) 672-9076

Position: Teaching Intern

Department: N/A

No. of Positions Offered Annually: 21

Description: Summer teaching internships are available for rising college juniors, seniors, and recent graduates to work with a variety of mathematics, science, and English courses. Interns work directly with faculty members and are involved with classroom instruction and working with students on an individual basis. Additional responsibilities involve dormitory supervision, supervising afternoon athletics, drama or music programs, and some weekend chaperoning duties. Room and board are provided.

Qualifications: College junior, seniors, or recent graduates.

Salary: $1,300

Position Dates: Summer

Position Location: Woodberry Forest, VA

Average No. of Applicants Annually: 250

Potential for Job Placement: N/A

Application Process: Send résumé transcript, and a letter of recommendation.

Deadline: March 1

Contact: Jeffery J. Davidsson, Director

Interning Abroad

by Nicole Itano

A generation ago, some college students on summer break filled their backpacks with the essentials of life and trekked off to see the world. They spent the hot summer months hitchhiking from wonder to wonder, swept up in the tides of students exploring the world. Sometimes a few months turned into longer, and they never came home.

Although the era of the backpacking young American has not entirely vanished, many students today are looking for a more productive alternative to aimless wandering. New study-abroad and foreign language programs have popped up in countries around the world, providing opportunities to experience other cultures while gaining course credit. Likewise, foreign internships give students the chance to see a little bit of the world and gain valuable professional experience at the same time. Compared to study-abroad programs, however, international internships usually have more extensive requirements, especially in language proficiency.

Securing an internship in a foreign country requires determination, persistence, and planning. There aren't a lot of established programs, so searching for the right internship can take a while, especially with the problem of overseas communication to overcome. Expect to make a few phone calls in the very late or very early hours in order to call your intended destination during its business hours. An international internship, once attained, can also be an expensive endeavor. Few international internships pay, and the costs of travel and living abroad pile up quickly.

Get an Early Start

The key to success, according to both students and university internship advisors, is an early start. International red tape can take months; imagine having to miss out on a great internship abroad because you haven't received your tourist visa. University advisors recommend getting to work as soon as school gets back in session, or even before if possible. It's never too soon to start putting together a list of potential internship sponsors or thinking about organizations that might need a bright, American college student in their office for a few months. Don't expect to pull everything together in less than six or seven months, especially if you want a good internship and don't want to spend the summer filing papers for a portable bathroom company somewhere in Japan.

The first step in an international internship search is to come up with a general idea of where you want to go and what kind of work you want to do. Although it's important to be open to any great, unexpected opportunities that might pop up during your internship search, blindly looking for an internship somewhere in the world is an overwhelming task. Decide whether location or type of work is the most important factor. Would you rather work in Budapest, or intern for a company that deals specifically with water-rights issues in emerging democracies? Your answer to such a question will affect the way you go about your search. While the best-case scenario would be to find a position that nicely meets both needs, narrowing your search too much may leave you flipping burgers this summer instead of hiking though the Andes mountains.

Consider Your Skills and Needs

When trying to decide how to start your internship search, you should consider both your specific skills and needs. If you have relatives abroad that would put you up for the summer, or if you are fluent in a particular country's language, your best bet might be to tailor your search to that specific country. If on the other hand, your main interest is to work for a multinational corporation, and you speak Spanish, it might be best to start looking for internships offered by multinational corporations that have branches in South or Central America. To narrow your search a little more, if you have a background in trade negotiation, you might look for a position that allows you to work in the company's negotiation division.

The Power of Nagging

**This summer I wanted to work abroad. Unfortunately, internship
programs abroad are not nearly as structured as those in the United
States. Even American-based companies with very formal domestic
programs pretty much leave their international offices alone. I was
interested in working in journalism, so I got the addresses of foreign
bureaus of all the major news networks and sent off résumés and
cover letters. A couple of weeks later, I called each bureau (which is
a pain because of the time difference) and, in most cases, talked to
someone who had no idea what I was talking about. Some had not
heard of internships while others had serious misconceptions about
what they entail. In any case, my options dwindled pretty quickly.
At places where there appeared to be any kind of hope, however, I
continued to call and nag the producers as much as possible.
Finally, a producer at CNN-Rome actually read my résumé and
called me! At first, she invited me to "stop by" if I was going to be
in Rome and "maybe" they would have something for me to do. A
couple of phone calls later, however, we had arranged a formal
internship for six weeks.**

—Yale sophomore

Many international internship programs are not very structured, so you may
have to convince a company that it needs you around for the summer.
Consider what skills you have that will make you attractive to a potential
employer. In some cases, simply being an American college student with an
excellent grasp of English might be enough. But most of the time, as with
any internship search, you'll have to have specific skills that would make you
an asset. Your academic major and experience are big factors. For example, a
big corporation may favor an economics major over a history major. An
American newspaper with an office in Hong Kong will probably care more
about a student's journalism experience than a student's major.

One warning: language proficiency prior to the internship is a must. Don't
show up in Japan without a solid grasp of Japanese and expect to have a
successful internship experience. If your goal is to learn a new language,
stick with a homestay or language program. Although speaking English
will often be an asset, if not a necessity, not speaking the native language

will be a liability, even in an American company abroad. "I would strongly, strongly discourage a student from trying to learn a language during an internship," one college career advisor said. "It just doesn't make for a very successful experience."

Where to Look

Once you have an idea about what you're looking for, it's time to start the search. Few places have well-advertised programs, so it will take some digging to find an internship that meets your needs. There are several ways of going about this.

University Programs

Due to the high level of student demand, many universities now offer internships as one of their study-abroad options. The university places students in an internship abroad that is related to their major field of study. These seldom are paid positions but students receive course credit. Tuition, fees, and room and board for these programs, however, might be quite hefty. In addition to the internship, students must also complete assigned course work, which almost always includes writing a paper and usually also involves assigned readings and seminars.

Check with the international programs office at your school. If your school doesn't have a program you are interested in, you can research the internship offerings of the study-abroad programs of other schools. Two schools with extensive overseas internship programs are Boston University and Syracuse University. Both of these universities attract program participants from schools across the country who then transfer the credit to their own schools.

- Boston University, International Programs, 232 Bay State Road, Boston, MA 02215, (617) 353-5403. E-mail: abroad@bu.edu. Internet site: http://www.bu.bdu/abroad.

- Syracuse University, Division of International Programs Abroad, 119 Euclid Avenue, Syracuse, NY 13244, (315) 443-3471. E-mail: suabroad@syr.edu. Internet site: http://www.sumwed.syr.edu/dipa.

Cyber Searching

For online help in locating an international internship, check out studyabroad.com (http://www.studyabroad.com), which focuses on all kinds of study experiences overseas, including internships.

If you are interested in exploring internships in international relations and foreign policy, check out the embassy site at http://www.embpage.org. It contains links to hundreds of other sites for foreign and U.S. embassies.

Exchange Organizations

There are several international exchange organizations that will arrange internships abroad for a fee. Here are a few of these organizations:

AIESEC—US

The International Association of Students in Economics and Commerce (know by its French initials AIESEC) is a worldwide association of students that offers opportunities for working abroad through a reciprocal internship exchange program in a variety of business and related fields. Internships are offered in 74 member countries lasting six weeks to 18 months. Living expenses are covered by the hosting firm. The programs are restricted to undergraduate and graduate students active in local AIESEC chapters at 70 U.S. colleges and universities. Contact AIESEC at 135 West 50th Street, 20th Floor, New York, NY 10020, (212) 757-3774.

Council on International Educational Exchange

Council's Work Exchange Program eliminates red tape and allows students to obtain short-term work permits in Australia, Britain, Canada, Costa Rica, France, Germany, Ireland, and New Zealand. You must find your own job/internship; however, the organization does provide job listings and help with job placement. Most students work in low-level jobs but with persistence and good leads, some students obtain excellent jobs/internships in their field of study. The fee is $225. Contact Council at 205 East 42nd Street, New York, NY 10017, (800) 2-COUNCIL. Internet site: http://www.ciee.org.

IAESTE Trainee Program

The International Association for the Exchange of Students for Technical Experience provides on-the-job training for students in engineering, architecture, mathematics, computer sciences, and the natural and physical sciences in 60 countries around the world. Juniors, seniors, and graduate students enrolled in an accredited college or university are eligible. Each trainee is paid a maintenance allowance to cover living expenses abroad. Fluency in the language is required for most countries. Fee: $800. Contact IAESTE courtesy of Association for International Practical Training, 10 Corporate Center, Suite 250, 10400 Little Patuxent Parkway, Columbia, MD 21044-3510, (410) 997-2200.

Internships International

Internships of six weeks to six months are available in London, Paris, Dublin, Stuttgart, Florence, Madrid, Mexico City, Santiago, Budapest, and Melbourne. Applicants must have graduated from college and must have a strong command of the language spoken in the city in which they want to intern. The fee is $500. Contact II at 116 Cowper Drive, Raleigh, NC 27608, (919) 832-1575, fax: (919) 834-7170. E-mail: intintl@aol.com. Internet site: http://www.rtpnet.org/intintl/home.htm.

People to People International

In collaboration with the University of Missouri–Kansas City, People to People sponsors two-month summer internship programs in Australia, Britain, Denmark, Germany, Ireland, Kenya, Russia, and Spain. Placements are arranged based on the applicant's background and interests. Six hours of credit may be obtained from the University of Missouri; noncredit participation is also available. The fee is $1,675 (includes tuition). Contact the group at Collegiate and Professional Studies Programs, 501 East Armour Boulevard, Kansas City, MO 64109, (816) 531-4701. E-mail: internships@ptpi.org.

Worldwide Internships and Service Education

Unpaid internships, varying in length from six weeks to six months, are available in London, England, and Toulouse, France. A new program in Germany is being organized as well. Fees start at $1,550. For more information, contact this organization at 303 South Craig Street, Pittsburgh, PA 15213, (412) 681-8120, fax (412) 681-8187.

Seeing Through London's Fog
with Internships International

A former intern tells of his experience at a museum in London:

"After graduating from college, I was faced with the BIG QUESTION: "So what are you going to do now?" I felt the pressure to be productive, get a job, and step out into the real world. There was only one problem. A part of me was reluctant to settle down so quickly. I wanted my last bit of excitement before the perceived doldrums of life as a graduate. A friend approached me with the idea of living in London, England—a once-in-a-lifetime opportunity to get a six-month work permit and explore another culture. I just needed a job—a résumé bolster, some professional experience.

"That's where Internships International came in to play. I decided on an internship in a museum, specifically one dealing with science. Director Judy Tilson immediately contacted her colleague in London, and in less than three weeks I had an internship with the National Science Museum in London. Somewhat to my surprise, I was assigned a good deal of responsibility. I had heard nightmare stories about copy-machine internships—lots of administrative work, no experience. This was completely the opposite. I had interesting projects, wonderful co-workers, and a great working environment. To top it all off, after my three-month stint was over they offered me a full-time, paying job for the remainder of my stay in England."

There are a few organizations that help place students with sponsors in particular geographic regions, but often these programs charge for their services and are not usually connected to big American corporations. These organizations are a good bet if you're looking to work for a foreign company. Two of these organizations are:

- The Visitor Exchange Department of the French-American Chamber of Commerce, (212) 765-4598
- The American-Scandinavian Defense Foundation, (212) 879-9779

Government

Another route is to look for a position with either the U.S. government or the government of a foreign country. These internships are usually highly competitive, nonpaying, and extremely structured. They also usually have early deadlines. "You have to think about it way ahead of time," says a Yale student who received a position in the American embassy in Uruguay. "The advantage though, is that you hear back early."

The State Department is probably the biggest federal government source of summer internships. It sends students to work at consulates around the world, and sometimes even arranges for living quarters. What the State Department doesn't do is cover any costs. Interns are responsible for all of their living expenses and airfare. The deadline for these coveted positions is November 1, but the application process is not too painful, and you can apply to work at up to two different bureaus. The process does require a security clearance, and the federal government asks for biographical information, a one-page essay, and a transcript. No references are required.

To find out more about summer internships contact: Intern Coordinator, U.S. Department of State, PER/RER, Room 7802, 1800 North Kent Street, Arlington, VA 22219. The State Department Web site contains information and applications: http://www.state.gov/www/careers.index.html. Remember, the deadline is November 1.

International Business

If none of the above options appeal to you, you'll have to dig a little harder. Think of international companies or institutions for whom you'd like to work. If you are interested in humanitarian efforts, consider the Red Cross. If international banking is more your style, how about J.P. Morgan? If you're interested in working for a big multinational company, you've picked an opportune time. More and more companies are starting up internship programs in their international offices, and many of them are paid. The best ones have decent stipends, reimburse interns for airfare, and even arrange for housing in company facilities. Some of these programs will be advertised through school career services offices, but a lot of them are still in their fledgling stages. The best way to find out about these programs is to contact the company directly. Start early, because deadlines may be early, and it may take some time for your requests to filter down to the right people. Be aware,

Making the Most of
Your Time Abroad

Last summer I had a fellowship through the Guggenheim Museum based in New York City. I worked at the Peggy Guggenheim collection in Venice, Italy. It was a fantastic experience. I worked four days a week and traveled on weekends with a Eurorail pass. I recommend this (paid) internship to anyone interested in combining art history with Italian studies. It was a really exceptional experience to live in Venice and really get to know this exotic city.

Prior language experience was optional—I personally had never taken Italian. This year I started to take it because I fell in love with the language and culture. The program had an interesting housing solution. Several apartments around Venice (which is a very small city) were rented to the fellows, and when one group vacated their apartment, the next group would move in. We sort of had to fend for ourselves, but by talking to the interns who had just finished their program, we were able to find housing. All the rents were regulated, too, very cheap! In terms of international stuff, all I needed was a passport, no visa. To live in Venice, one needs a *permesso di sogiorno*—something I never got! I guess that's just bureaucratic red tape.

—Yale art history major

however, that these programs are meant for training the next generation of corporate CEOs for the international job market. These companies are generally looking for business-minded students. "I think they were a little apprehensive that I was a history major," says a student who worked in Korea for Samsung Corporation in a new program that takes about 40 people every year.

Make a list, and then start sending off résumés and cover letters inquiring about summer internships abroad. (Check out the Web sites of these groups, too. Internships are often listed there.) Follow up letters with a phone calls. And remember, even if an organization doesn't have an established internship program, that doesn't mean it won't accept you. It just may take a little convincing. "Most companies have pretty established internship programs in their American offices, but aren't used to having American college students come work for them [abroad] in the summer. There's definitely a lot more legwork involved because you have to contact everyone personally," said Lia Dean, a Yale sophomore who nabbed a position in CNN's Italian bureau. "I knew I wanted an internship in journalism, so I sent off letters and résumés to every major bureau. If I could speak the language, I sent off a letter."

Be persistent, and don't be afraid to use personal connections to help you secure a position. If your neighbor works for an international company, ask her whom to contact and what kinds of programs are available for students. Ask where the company has branches and how to get in touch with them. You may send out a lot of requests for information and not receive many replies, but keep at it. Convince them that you'll be a useful person to have in the office for the summer. (Of course, they might be easier to convince if you're willing to work for free.) Beware, however, of companies that ask you to sell them your soul. You want a balance of work and play that gives you a chance to enjoy the country in which you're working.

Dealing with Red Tape

Landing a position isn't the only hurdle involved in interning abroad. You also have to get the permission of the host country to stay there for an extended period of time and special permission to work. These visas can sometimes be difficult to attain. Many countries dislike giving work permits to foreigners because they feel that these foreigners are taking away jobs from citizens. Because of this, many corporations won't pay interns even if they can afford to. It's too difficult. "No one will give me a paid job," says a Yale student looking for a summer internship in China. "They can't even get permission for me to come then." She knew she wanted to work in China for the summer, and she was willing to work either in a bank or in journalism. She was offered two internships for the summer—one in CNN's Beijing office and one at a Chinese bureau of the *Wall Street Journal*—but neither one came with a stipend because of Chinese labor laws

There are ways to get around the red tape. Some countries allow employers to give stipends to students who are also receiving college credit for their work. This is not an option for everyone, since many schools don't give credit for internships. Sometimes even big companies will find a way to bend the rules, perhaps through scholarships or reimbursements for expenses. Even if you don't need a work permit, you might need a visa, especially for extended stays. To apply for a visa, contact the country's nearest consulate office. These are usually located in major cities. If you aren't close to a major city and have to apply by mail, the process may take time, so get the ball rolling early.

Interning Abroad

If you are having trouble getting your visa approved, the Bureau of Consular Affairs in Washington, D.C., can help you find out what the problems is, though they can't force another country to give you a visa. Don't forget to apply for a passport too! This usually takes six weeks, and you need a passport to get a visa, so you should probably apply as soon as you decide you want to leave the country for the summer.

Housing and Expenses

Finding housing in another country can be difficult, especially if the organization you're working for won't help. Some students deal with the problem by staying with family or friends. Renting is always a possibility, but staying in special student facilities is usually more fun and more cost effective. One solution is to enroll in a program, such as a language program or summer school program, that offers housing to students. Sometimes this is expensive, but it's not necessarily more expensive than paying rent for an apartment—and you get classes, too. On the other hand, you may not have time to take classes while working. Check, too, with a local university. Even if the university itself doesn't offer summer housing, it might be able to point you in the right direction. Also, the country's tourism office may be able to help you find special student housing. Some American organizations exist for the sole purpose of finding housing for American students going abroad. These programs are not specifically for students going abroad for internships, but they might work (depending on where you're going). Check with study-abroad programs and even homestay programs.

Funding these international excursions is always a headache. Because few international internships pay, students have to either absorb the cost of the summer, or find creative ways of paying for things. See what scholarships and grants your school offers for students going abroad. Even if they won't help pay specifically for an internship, sometimes you can combine research for a paper, senior project, or professor with your work. Some national organizations provide funding for students going abroad, though this funding is often earmarked for students doing volunteer work, for individuals of a particular ancestry, or for students training in certain fields. To root out such scholarships, check out fastWEB at http://www.fastweb.com, and contact organizations you or your family belong to, as well as organizations in the field or country you want to visit.

Foreign Entry Requirements and Consular Offices

AUSTRALIA

Passport and visa required. (The visa requirement was scheduled to have changed as of mid-1997, no longer being required for U.S. tourists staying 90 days or less.) A minor not accompanied by a parent needs a notarized copy of his/her birth certificate and notarized written parental consent from both parents. Departure tax $20 (Australian). For more information contact the Embassy of Australia, 1601 Massachusetts Ave. NW, Washington, D.C. 20036 (800) 242-2878, (202) 797-3145 or the nearest Consulate General: California (213) 469-4300 or (415) 362-6160, Hawaii (808) 524-5050, New York (212) 245-4000, or Texas (713) 629-9131.

COSTA RICA

Passport or original U.S. birth certificate and photo I.D. required. Tourist card issued upon arrival at airport upon presentation of aforementioned documents for approximately $20. U.S. citizens must have onward/return ticket. For stays over 90 days, you must apply for an extension (within the first week of visit) with Costa Rican Immigration and, after 90 days, obtain an exit visa and possess a valid passport. For more information contact the Consular Section of the Embassy of Costa Rica, 2112 S St. NW, Washington, D.C. 20008 (202) 328-6628 or nearest Consulate General: California (415) 392-8488, Georgia (404) 951-7025, Florida (305) 371-7485, Illinois (312) 263-2772, Louisiana (504) 887-8131, New York (212) 425-2620, or Texas (713) 266-1527.

FRANCE

Passport required to visit France, Andorra, Monaco, Corsica, and French Polynesia. Visa not required for tourist/business stay up to three months in France, Andorra, Monaco, and Corsica, and one month in French Polynesia. Journalists on assignment, ship or plane crew members, and students are required to obtain a visa in advance. For more information contact the Consular Section of the Embassy of France, 4101 Reservoir Rd. NW, Washington, D.C. 20007 (202) 944-6200 or nearest Consulate: California (310) 235-3200 or (415) 397-4330, Florida (305) 372-9798, Georgia (404) 522-4226, Hawaii (808) 599-4458, Illinois (312) 787-5359, Louisiana (504) 523-5772, Massachusetts (617) 542-7374, New York (212) 606-3644, or Texas (713) 528-2181.

GERMANY

Passport required. Tourist/business visa not required for stay up to three months. For longer stays (e.g., for work, for school) obtain temporary residence permit upon arrival. Applicants of residence permits staying over 90 days may be asked to undergo a medical examination. Every foreign national entering Germany is required to provide proof of sufficient health insurance and funds. For more information contact the Embassy of the Federal Republic of Germany, 4645 Reservoir Rd. NW, Washington, D.C. 20007 (202) 298-4000 or nearest Consulate General: California (415) 775-1061, (213) 930-2703, Florida (305) 358-0290, Georgia (404) 659-4760, Illinois (312) 580-1199, Massachusetts (617) 536-4414), Michigan (313) 962-6526, New York (212) 308-8700, Texas (713) 627-7770, or Washington (206) 682-4312.

ISRAEL

Passport, onward/return ticket, and proof of sufficient funds required. Tourist visa issued upon arrival, valid for three months, requires two application forms and two photos. For more information contact the Embassy of Israel, 3514 International Dr. NW, Washington, D.C. 20008 (202) 364-5500 or nearest Consulate General: California (213) 852-5500 and (415) 398-8885, Florida (305) 358-8111, Georgia (404) 875-7851, Illinois (312) 565-3300, Massachusetts (617) 542-0041, New York (212) 499-5300, Pennsylvania (215) 546-5556 or Texas (713) 627-3780.

JAPAN

Passport and onward/return ticket required. Visa not required for tourist/business stay up to 90 days. Passenger service facilities charge $20–$26 (2,0002,600 yen) paid at airport. For more information contact the Embassy of Japan, 2520 Massachusetts Ave.

NW, Washington, D.C. 20008 (202) 939-6800 or nearest Consulate: Alaska (907) 279-8428, California (213) 617-6700 or (415) 777-3533, Florida (305) 530-9090, Georgia (404) 892-2700, Guam (671) 646-1290, Hawaii (808) 536-2226, Illinois (312) 280-0400, Louisiana (504) 529-2101, Massachusetts (617) 973-9772, Michigan (313) 567-0120, Missouri (816) 471-0111, New York (212) 371-8222, Oregon (503) 221-1811, Texas (713) 652-2977, or Washington (206) 682-9107.

KOREA, REPUBLIC OF (South Korea)
Passport required. Visa not required for a tourist stay up to 15 days. For longer stays and other types of travel, visa must be obtained in advance, $20 fee. Tourist visa requires passport, one application form, and one photo. Business visa requires one application form, one photo, and company letter. Fine imposed for overstaying visa and for long-term visa holders not registered within 60 days after entry. If applying by mail, enclose SASE or prepaid air bill. Vaccination certificate required within 14 days of arrival in Korea if coming from infected area. For more information contact the Embassy of the Republic of Korea (Consular Division), 2320 Massachusetts Ave. NW, Washington, D.C. 20008 (202) 939-5663 or nearest Consulate General: California (213) 385-9300 and (415) 921-2251, Florida (305) 372-1555, Georgia (404) 522-1611, Guam (671) 472-6109, Hawaii (808) 595-6109, Illinois (312) 822-9485, Massachusetts (617) 348-3660, New York (212) 752-1700, Texas (713) 961-0186, or Washington (206) 441-1011.

SOUTH AFRICA
Passport required. Tourist or business visa not required for stay up to 90 days. Yellow fever immunization needed if arriving from infected area. Malarial suppressants are recommended. For more information contact the Embassy of South Africa, Consular Office, 3201 New Mexico Ave. NW, Washington, D.C. 20016 (202) 966-1650 or nearest consulate in California (310) 657-9200, Illinois (312) 939-7929, or New York (212) 213-4880.

Information on the entrance requirements of other countries can be acquired by sending a self-addressed, stamped envelope to The Office of Overseas Citizens, Bureau of Consular Affairs, Room 4811, U.S. Department of State, Washington D.C. 20520-4818, or at the bureau's Internet site, http://travel.state.gov

15

How to Make the Most of Your Internship

by Stacy Atlas

While an intern is an employee in a sense, specific responsibilities are not always clear. The agreement is that you'll provide support in exchange for practical experience in the field. The issue of compensation (or the lack thereof) further complicates things. I have held three nonpaying internships; since I wasn't being paid, I felt all the more unjustly abused when I was sent to make photocopies, send faxes, or go on long errands to other states in a car alone.

Interns need to prove they are responsible by starting at the bottom, but there is a fine line between paying dues and proving oneself as a permanent pushover. I needed three tries before I found a satisfactory—not perfect— internship. I hope that you can take my experiences, and those of other college interns, and learn to make the most of your internship.

Get Started on the Right Foot

Once you receive an internship offer, you'll know that you must have made a good first impression. Keep this up and continue to impress—make your employers feel lucky to have such a terrific intern working for them. Be on your best new-job behavior. Arrive early, dress appropriately, be courteous, friendly, enthusiastic, attentive, and interested in everything happening around the office. The intern's job is to make the boss' job easier. The boss should not have to remind the intern of this fact.

Hopefully, the terms of your internship will have been negotiated prior to your acceptance. Yale student Sarah Silverman set the terms of her internship in the opera division of Columbia Artists Management, Inc. "I told them that I would be willing to do whatever it was that they needed, but only if it was useful work," Sarah says. "Since I was willing to work for no money, I made it clear that I didn't want to work for them if I was just answering phones or [photocopying]. . . . It was a great arrangement because we all set our expectations from the start."

It is important to take this initiative to show that you want to get something useful out of your experience. Ask specifically what your responsibilities will entail. Will you have independent projects or parts of larger projects? Will you have a mix of busywork and worthwhile work, instead of a never-ending list of survey phone calls and data entry? You need to know exactly what is expected of you in order to fulfill these expectations. You also should establish a relationship with your supervisor in which you will feel comfortable to speak freely with each other.

In a best-case scenario, your coordinator will be someone to whom you can easily relate and who will agree to work with you on setting your responsibilities. But it's possible that your coordinator or supervisor will have very little contact with you. While any company that hires interns should be prepared to work with their students, this situation does occur. Trevor Uhl, a Yale University student from Lexington, Massachusetts, encountered this type of independence when working with the Yale Astronomy Department to create a new telescope. "Often the people I worked with were too busy to be always checking in on me and making sure I had stuff to do," Uhl says.

The least positive scenario is one in which your supervisor is closed to suggestions and sets out a tedious list of tasks, guaranteed to make any self-respecting person miserable. Then you are faced with the difficult decision of whether—and at what point—to voice your concerns and needs. Remember that a poorly handled disagreement can have serious consequences. But being miserable to the point that it affects your work is not a better option, especially if you are working for free. In some instances, waiting for more experience, respect, and your supervisor's change of heart seems reasonable. But Jill Botwick, a student from the University of Pennsylvania, says she waited too long before taking action. "I should have taken [a more aggressive] attitude from day one instead of waiting to be labeled "fax girl' and only then trying to change perceptions," Jill says of her experience interning for a marketing firm in Philadelphia.

Show Initiative

No matter how things start off, a strong intern goes above and beyond what is asked. First, fulfill all of the responsibilities allocated to you. Then look for more—you won't learn anything by sitting around E-mailing all day. Ask what else you could do that would be helpful. Stay attuned to the office and its issues.

"Be self-directed," one former intern advises. "Find things that you want to do, and find out what you need to know to do them. Don't expect someone to come up with a job for you and drop it in your lap. Give yourself an ambitious program, and follow it."

The more specific and innovative you are on your own, the more impressive you are. "The thing that I do is not just ask for more work, but to pinpoint a specific project and approach my supervisor with my ideas and my potential contributions to the project," say a former intern. "It is much easier for them to tell me 'okay,' than for them to think up something themselves."

I personally had to suggest a great deal of my internship work at *Connecticut* magazine. Before my experience, the editors never allowed interns to help edit the articles that circulated around the editorial department. Since the articles came back to the intern's desk to be picked up and initialized by various readers, I asked permission to glance through them myself in my spare time. Not only did I learn from this task, but I also gained the respect of the editors who repeatedly told me they appreciated my comments on the pieces. In addition, I pushed the magazine to let me write one article, however small, so that I could be published as well. These opportunities do not always happen without the intern's effort; you'll never know if you don't try.

The Art of Schmoozing,
Part Two

So does the schmoozing stop once you get the internship? No. An internship is an ideal networking vehicle. After all, eventually you will be in the job market looking for full-time employment. Maybe you'll want to work for the company where you interned. Or maybe you'll just stay in the same industry. So get to know your co-workers and what they do. Communicate with employees in other divisions if you have the opportunity. Say you work at an ACLU office in Texas but frequently send correspondence to the Los Angeles office. Make sure the people in the L.A. office know who you are. In a few years, you might find yourself still interested in civil liberties but also interested in heading out west. E-mail and interoffice mail are great ways to spread your influence beyond the walls of your own cubicle.

In your own office, try to make more than a cursory acquaintance with your co-workers. This may mean scheduling time to talk with co-workers and supervisors about special projects, about what you would like to accomplish, or about evaluating the work you have already completed. It is important that they see you as more than just "the summer intern." You want to distinguish yourself and be recognized for your work. You also want to give a comprehensive picture of yourself so that in years to come, your supervisors can give references and write recommendations that reflect various aspects of your talents and abilities.

If you do envision yourself trying to get a full-time job with the company in the future, of course you should try to meet as many people as possible and get to know what they do. Also find out about the decision-making processes. The person who hires full-time staff may be different from the person who selects interns. Make it your goal to meet all the people who would be involved in hiring you. If you see yourself staying in the same field but with another company, try to attend conventions or seminars at which you can meet other people in the industry.

Don't Forget to Follow Up

Making an impression is important in the world of networking. Even if you meet with someone at a company, that person may forget about you after a period of time. Or you may talk to someone in July about an internship for the next summer. Chances are by the time you start applying in the fall, that person will need a refresher course on who you are and what you are interested in.

You don't want to be forgotten, and you do want to be taken seriously. Letters, phone calls, and E-mail are great ways to make sure you reinforce the connections you make. Of course, you don't want to harass people so that they try to avoid your calls. But a note every now and then to let them know what you're doing is perfectly acceptable. One journalism intern made it a practice to keep in touch with the intern coordinators he had interviewed with the previous year. Many of these coordinators had not offered him an internship the first year he applied. But by keeping them up-to-date on the work he was doing, he helped lay the groundwork for his application the following year.

Keep the Lines of Communication Open

Communication is key. Effective communication is one of the most valuable skills you can pick during an internship experience. In addition to laying out your expectations at the start, get feedback every step of the way. Make sure that your supervisor is satisfied with your work and that you try to implement any suggestions given. Take criticism in stride and use it to your advantage. Even though you might be used to taking charge of an organization, you cannot always be at the top. Working as part of a team is educational and can be rewarding.

Learn from Those Higher Up

Take advantage of the fact that you are working for experts in your prospective field of interest. Establishing a relationship with your supervisors not only allows for a better experience, but also for connections to future job opportunities. One Massachusetts Institute of Technology student says of her internship with a consulting company, "I worked hard and talked to my bosses a lot. They were the best part of the job. They have such interesting perspectives on the job and on life . . . and about my field in general."

These experts most likely will enjoy sharing their knowledge (if they are not too stressed out and frantically busy). "[Interns] need to take a lot of initiative and not be afraid to ask questions," says University of Pennsylvania student Esther Luh, who interned at the New Haven branch of Merrill Lynch. "People are busy, but they will take the time to answer your questions."

Interns also have much to gain from educational programs, featuring speakers and workshops, that are sometimes provided for them. One Yale student took advantage of these opportunities during the course of her internship at the Children's Defense Fund in Washington, D.C. Although she spent much of her time on secretarial duties, she says, "my knowledge (about the Children's Defense Fund and child advocacy) came largely from weekly intern events and opportunities outside the day-to-day work than from what I was actually doing."

Leave with Something to Show

While all interns gain some type of knowledge from their experiences, it's sometimes difficult to prove this to future employers. The most common way to prove your worth is by asking for a letter of recommendation from your internship supervisor. In some cases, supervisors are accustomed to writing recommendations and even offer them to interns.

Don't be shy or think that writing a recommendation is too great of an inconvenience. You have given your time and energy and deserve to be recognized in this manner. If your supervisor does not seem experienced in this process, either meet to discuss the recommendation or give your supervisor a list of the accomplishments that you believe should be included in the recommendation.

However, there are ways to demonstrate your work other than through recommendations. Document your work right from the beginning. Such records can be beneficial to your employer, can provide good references for a recommendation, can act as notes for your own future use, and will provide something to show future potential employers.

When Things Go Wrong

After reading the advice in this book, you should be ready for internship success. But if problems arise:

Dilemma #1: You're in a bad working environment, stuck in a tiny cubicle isolated away from the hubbub of the office. There's not all that much you can do to solve this dilemma. Realize that intern office space is not a top priority for most companies, but that they do want interns to be happy. Work quietly in your corner, but reach out to people so you don't feel alone. Even ask your coordinator if you could assist someone who works in a busier area after you have completed your responsibilities. You might also suggest weekly intern meetings in order to get to know the other interns.

Dilemma #2: You don't like your co-workers. This could be a big problem. You have made a commitment to this internship and you should try to stick it out. Do your best not to offend others and treat them the way you want to be treated. Always be respectful. Hopefully, things will get better and you can form a good working relationship. If not, step back from the situation and have an outsider evaluate the problem before you do anything drastic. Turn to a neutral intern coordinator, if possible.

Dilemma #3: You're not doing what you expected, whether or not your responsibilities were agreed to beforehand. You're working overtime to the point of exhaustion, or you're bored out of your wits. Try to approach your supervisor in a respectful way. Keep in mind that it's easier to add more interesting work than to eliminate your assigned tasks altogether. Explain the situation, and ask if after you finish your assignment you can also do something more interesting (make a specific suggestion). In fact, your supervisor might actually welcome such a suggestion. If the load is too heavy, try to schedule break times or break it up with easier tasks to help maintain your sanity.

Dilemma #4: Your bosses are not giving you the bacon. The grant didn't come through or your previously agreed-to salary has been forgotten. Approaching an intern coordinator before your immediate advisor is advisable. Money is a touchy issue, so be respectful and polite. However, you have the right to inform your employer of the problem. And don't threaten to quit unless you're willing to do it.

REMEMBER: Interns are cheap if not free labor. So in turn for your hard work and respect, you deserve to be treated with the same respect. Stand up for yourself.

Not only should you document your own work, but you should also try to have your bosses document and publish your work when applicable. Having clips from newspaper or journal articles with your byline attached will be invaluable down the line. Yale student Tara Doyle regrets not coming away from her experience at the Natural Resources Research Institute without completing her individual project mandated by a Research Experience of Undergraduates Grant. "The research I did was publishable and I should have gotten a paper out of it. However, they never gave me the time to analyze all the data and research the background in a manner that would have allowed me to write a paper," she says. "In retrospect, I would have told them that my project needed to come first and theirs second, but I didn't realize I could do this at the time."

I personally checked continually to make sure my name was not forgotten on the masthead credits or on my articles or compiled listings. I now have various pieces of evidence to support my experience and make myself more marketable.

Have Fun . . .

Most of all, enjoy yourself. This experience is something you sought as an interesting way to spend your time—don't forget that. Instead of freaking out and working yourself to the bone, have fun. Be friendly to the other interns and people in the office. Start conversations, reach out, and make lunch dates. One former intern says she should have made a better effort to get to know people. "I didn't really know anyone, so I was kind of isolated. I was also the youngest person on the site, so I felt out of place and didn't talk much, which made lunch pretty dull."

You can also learn a lot from the other interns. Speak with them about their own projects and experiences. If together you are given a particularly tough workload, split it up accordingly. Work as a united team and form a support system for each other. It is much easier to work together than to compete against each other for attention and recognition. Being the favored intern whom the other interns resent (even if you haven't asked for this honor) loses its appeal quickly.

. . . But Not Too Much Fun!

Take your position and responsibilities seriously. Make your internship your first priority, even if it cuts into social time. One former intern looks back on his internship and says, "I would have gotten more sleep over the summer. Most people think of the summer as another excuse to party while making a couple of bucks and getting some career experience. But there is as much to be learned on the job as in the class during term."

Another former intern agrees, adding that too much partying can lead to embarrassment on the job. "Once I fell asleep and the client walked in—yikes!" she says. "On my last day, too. I felt really guilty for my bosses (and) I hope the client didn't care too much. Hopefully the work I did for that internship mitigated all the *faux pas* I made."

Indexes

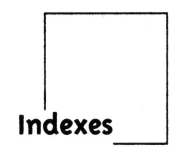

Indexes

Index of Companies Offering Internships

Internship information on the following companies can be found in the listings at the back of the chapters as noted.

A

A.E. Schwartz and Associates, Chapter 6

Accuracy in Media, Chapter 12

Actors Theatre of Louisville, Chapter 8

Aigner Associates, Chapter 5

American-Arab Anti-Discrimination Committee, Chapter 12

American Association of Advertising Agencies, Chapter 5

American Cancer Society, Chapter 7

American Committee on Africa, Chapter 13

American Conservatory Theater, Chapter 8

American Israel Public Affairs Committee (AIPAC), Chapter 12

American Management Association, Chapter 5

American Red Cross, Chapter 13

American Repertory Theatre, Chapter 8

American Rivers, Chapter 12

American Society of International Law, Chapter 5

American Woman's Economic Development Corporation (AWED), Chapter 13

Anchorage Daily News, Chapter 3

Aperture Foundation, Chapter 3

Archive Films, Inc., Chapter 10

Arms Control Association, Chapter 12

Assistant Directors Training Program, Chapter 10

B

Barney's New York, Chapter 5

Beacon Press, Chapter 3

Benetton USA, Chapter 5

Berkeley Repertory Theatre, Chapter 8

Bermuda Biological Station for Research, Inc., Chapter 7

Best Buddies International, Chapter 13

Bet Tzedek Legal Services, Chapter 13

Birmingham News, Chapter 3

The Blade, Chapter 3

Boston University Sargent Camp, Chapter 13

Bozell Public Relations, Chapter 5

Bozell Worldwide Public Relations, Chapter 5

Breckenridge Outdoor Education Center, Chapter 13

Brethren Volunteer Service, Chapter 13

Brookfield Zoo, Chapter 7

Brookings Institution, Chapter 11

Buffalo Bill Historical Center, Chapter 9

The Bulletin, Chapter 3

C

C. Paul Luongo Company, Chapter 5

Camp Courageous of Iowa, Chapter 13

Camp Fire Boys and Girls, Inc.—Georgia
Council, Chapter 13

Carter Center, Chapter 11

Catholic Charities, Diocese of Metuchen,
Chapter 13

CBS News, Chapter 4

Center for California Studies, California State
University, Chapter 11

Center for Campus Organizing (CCO),
Chapter 12

Center for Investigative Reporting, Chapter 3

Central Newspapers, Inc., Chapter 3

Century City Partners, Chapter 5

Charlesbridge Publishing, Chapter 3

Charlie Rose, Chapter 10

Children's Television Workshop, Chapter 4

Chilton, Chapter 3

Chrysalis, a Center for Women, Chapter 13

CIGNA, Chapter 5

City of Cambridge, Chapter 13

CityArts, Inc., Chapter 13

The Cloisters, Chapter 9

CNN, Chapter 4

College Connections, Chapter 5

College Light Opera Company, Chapter 8

Comedy Central, Chapter 10

Connecticut Judicial Volunteer Program,
Chapter 11

Connecticut Magazine, Chapter 3

Coro Fellows Program in Public Affairs,
Chapter 13

Council on Economic Priorities, Chapter 12

Creede Repertory Theater, Chapter 8

Criminal Justice Clinic, Georgetown
University Law Center, Chapter 13

Crow Canyon Archaeological Center,
Chapter 7

Crown Capital, Chapter 5

D

David R. Godine, Publisher, Chapter 3

DC Rape Crisis Center, Chapter 13

Denver Art Museum, Chapter 9

Denver Post, Chapter 3

DesignTech International, Inc., Chapter 6

Detroit Free Press, Chapter 3

Dow Jones Newspaper Fund, Chapter 3

Dye Van Mol and Lawrence, Chapter 5

E

Earle Palmer Brown, Chapter 5

Eisner, Petrou and Associates, Chapter 5

Elite Model Management, Inc., Chapter 5

Elkman Advertising and Public Relations,
Chapter 5

F

Faber and Faber, Inc., Chapter 3

Federal Reserve Bank of New York, Chapter 5

The Feminist Majority, Chapter 12

Fenton Communications, Chapter 5

Fight Crime: Invest in Kids, Chapter 13

Florida Times-Union, Chapter 3

Fortune Public Relations, Chapter 5

Fourth World Movement, Chapter 13

Franklin Advertising Associates, Inc.,
Chapter 5

Frontier Nursing Service, Chapter 7

G

General Mills, Chapter 5

Gould Farm, Chapter 13

Greater Media Cable, Chapter 4

H

Harper's Magazine, Chapter 3

Hearst Book Group, Chapter 3

Heritage Foundation, Chapter 12

Hermitage Association, Chapter 9

Hewlett Packard, Chapter 6

Hill, Holiday, Chapter 5

Houghton Mifflin, Chapter 3

Human Service Alliance, Chapter 13

I

Illinois Legislative Staff Intern Program, Chapter 11

Immigrant Workers' Resource Center, Chapter 13

Inroads, Inc., Chapter 5

Institute for Policy Studies, Chapter 11

Insurance Services Office, Chapter 5

Interlocken Center for Experimental Learning, Chapter 13

International Management Group, Chapter 5

International Partnership for Service-Learning, Chapter 13

Internships International, Chapter 14

Intertec Publishing, Chapter 3

J

J. Paul Getty Trust, Chapter 9

Jacob's Pillow Dance Festival, Chapter 8

Japanese Exchange Teaching Program (JET Program), Chapter 13

John F. Kennedy Center for the Performing Arts, Chapter 8

Journal Star, Chapter 3

K

Ketchum Public Relations, Chapter 5

KGO-TV/Channel 7: San Francisco, San Jose, Oakland, Chapter 4

Korean American Coalition, Chapter 12

KQED-FM, Chapter 4

L

Late Show with David Letterman, Chapter 10

Liggett-Stashower Public Relations, Chapter 5

Lobsenz-Stevens, Inc., Chapter 5

Los Angeles Municipal Art Gallery, Chapter 9

Lucasfilm Ltd., Chapter 10

Lunar and Planetary Institute (LPI), Chapter 7

M

Maine State Music Theatre, Chapter 8

Manhattan Theatre Club, Chapter 8

Massachusetts Public Interest Research Group (MASSPIRG), Chapter 13

Metro-Goldwyn-Mayer/United Artists, Chapter 10

Miami Herald, Chapter 3

Middle Earth, Inc., Chapter 13

Millennium Multi-Media, Chapter 4

Milwaukee Journal Sentinel, Chapter 3

Mitch Schneider Organization, Chapter 10

Moline Dispatch Publishing Company, Chapter 3

Mote Marine Laboratory, Chapter 7

Museum of Contemporary Art, Chapter 9

Museum of Modern Art, Chapter 9

N

The Nation, Chapter 3

National Aquarium in Baltimore, Chapter 7

National Asian Pacific American Legal Consortium, Chapter 12

National Journalism Center, Chapter 3

National Public Radio, Chapter 4

National Wildlife Federation, Chapter 12

NBC, Chapter 4

New Breed Entertainment, Chapter 10

New Dramatists, Chapter 8

New Republic, Chapter 3

New York City Fellowship Programs, Chapter 11

New York Hospital, Cornell Medical Center, Westchester Div., Chapter 7

New York State Bar Association, Chapter 5

Newsweek, Chapter 3

Nike, Inc., Chapter 5

North Carolina Botanical Garden, Chapter 7

NYU Medical Center, Chapter 7

O

Ocean City Advertising Agency, Chapter 5

Oklahoma City 89ers, Chapter 5

Ore-Ida Foods, Chapter 5

Organization of Chinese Americans, Inc. (OCA), Chapter 13

Outdoors Wisconsin Leadership School, Chapter 13

P

Peace Action Education Fund, Chapter 13

Peace Corps, Chapter 13

Penguin Books, Chapter 3

Performance Research, Chapter 5

Philadelphia Magazine, Chapter 3

Pittsburgh Post-Gazette, Chapter 3

The Plain Dealer, Chapter 3

Playhouse on the Square, Chapter 8

PolyGram, Chapter 10

The Population Institute, Chapter 12

Pro-Found Software, Inc., Chapter 6

Public Defender Service for D.C., Chapter 11

Q

Qually and Company, Chapter 8

R

Rock Creek Foundation, Chapter 13

Roll Call Newspaper, Chapter 3

Ruder Finn, Chapter 5

S

Schuylkill Center for Environmental Education, Chapter 13

Science News, Chapter 3

SDV/ACCI, Chapter 5

Seattle Times, Chapter 3

Securities and Exchange Commission (SEC), Chapter 11

Skadden, Arps, Slate, Meagher and Flom, LLP, Chapter 5

Smithsonian Institution, Chapter 9

Society of Professional Journalists, Chapter 3

Solomon R. Guggenheim Museum, Chapter 9

Southface Energy Institute, Chapter 13

St. Vincent's Hospital, Chapter 13

Starlight Foundation, Chapter 13

Student Conservation Association, Chapter 7

Supreme Court of the United States, Chapter 11

T

Training Consortium, Chapter 6

20/20 Vision, Chapter 12

U

United States Chamber of Commerce, Chapter 11

University of Illinois for Illinois General Assembly, Chapter 11

V

Vibe Magazine, Chapter 3

The Village Voice, Chapter 3

W

Wall Street Music, Chapter 10

Washington Center, Chapter 5

Washington Center for Politics and Journalism, Chapter 3

Washington Monthly, Chapter 3

Washington Post, Chapter 3

Washingtonian, Chapter 3

Wediko Children's Services, Chapter 13

Widmeyer-Baker Group, Inc., Chapter 5

Wildlife Habitat Council, Chapter 13

Williamstown Theatre Festival, Chapter 8

Women's International League for Peace and Freedom, Chapter 12

Women's Legal Defense Fund, Chapter 12

Women's Sports Foundation, Chapter 12

Woodberry Forest Summer School, Chapter 13

Woodrow Wilson International Center for Scholars, Chapter 11

World Federalist Association, Chapter 12

Worldwide Internships and Service Education, Chapter 16

WXRK, Chapter 4

Geographic Index

Internship information on the following companies can be found in the listings at the back of the chapters as noted.

UNITED STATES

Alabama

Birmingham

Birmingham News, Chapter 3

St. Vincent's Hospital, Chapter 13

Alaska

Anchorage

Anchorage Daily News, Chapter 3

Arizona

Phoenix

Central Newspapers, Inc., Chapter 3

California

Berkeley

Berkeley Repertory Theatre, Chapter 8

Fortune Public Relations, Chapter 5

Beverly Hills

Century City Partners, Chapter 5

Elite Model Management, Inc., Chapter 5

Cupertino

Hewlett Packard, Chapter 6

Encino

Assistant Directors Training Program, Chapter 10

Hayward

SDV/ACCI, Chapter 5

Laguna Beach

Millennium Multi-Media, Chapter 4

Los Angeles

American Israel Public Affairs Committee (AIPAC), Chapter 12

Bet Tzedek Legal Services, Chapter 13

Coro Fellows Program in Public Affairs, Chapter 13

Korean American Coalition, Chapter 12

Los Angeles Municipal Art Gallery, Chapter 9

Mountain View

Hewlett Packard, Chapter 6

Palo Alto

Hewlett Packard, Chapter 6

Sacramento

Center for California Studies, California State University, Chapter 11

San Francisco

American Conservatory Theater, Chapter 8

American Israel Public Affairs Committee (AIPAC), Chapter 12

Center for Investigative Reporting, Chapter 3

Coro Fellows Program in Public Affairs, Chapter 13

Crown Capital, Chapter 5

Hewlett Packard, Chapter 6

KGO-TV/Channel 7: San Francisco, San Jose, Oakland, Chapter 4

KQED-FM, Chapter 4

San Jose

Hewlett Packard, Chapter 6

San Rafael

Lucasfilm Ltd., Chapter 10

Santa Clara

Hewlett Packard, Chapter 6

Santa Monica

J. Paul Getty Trust, Chapter 9

Sherman Oaks

Mitch Schneider Organization, Chapter 10

Sunnyvale

Hewlett Packard, Chapter 6

Colorado

Breckenridge

Breckenridge Outdoor Education Center, Chapter 13

Cortez

Crow Canyon Archaeological Center, Chapter 7

Creede

Creede Repertory Theater, Chapter 8

Denver

Denver Art Museum, Chapter 9

Denver Post, Chapter 3

Connecticut

Bridgeport

Connecticut Magazine, Chapter 3

Hartford

CIGNA, Chapter 5

Rocky Hill

Connecticut Judicial Volunteer Program, Chapter 11

District of Columbia

Accuracy in Media, Chapter 12

American Israel Public Affairs Committee (AIPAC), Chapter 12

American Red Cross, Chapter 13

American Rivers, Chapter 12

American Society of International Law, Chapter 5

American-Arab Anti-Discrimination Committee, Chapter 12

Arms Control Association, Chapter 12

Brookings Institution, Chapter 11

Criminal Justice Clinic, Georgetown University Law Center, Chapter 13

DC Rape Crisis Center, Chapter 13

Eisner, Petrou and Associates, Chapter 5

Fenton Communications, Chapter 5

Fight Crime: Invest in Kids, Chapter 13

Heritage Foundation, Chapter 12

Institute for Policy Studies, Chapter 11

John F. Kennedy Center for the Performing Arts, Chapter 8

The Nation, Chapter 3

National Asian Pacific American
Legal Consortium, Chapter 12

National Journalism Center,
Chapter 3

National Public Radio, Chapter 4

National Wildlife Federation,
Chapter 12

New Republic, Chapter 3

Organization of Chinese Americans,
Inc. (OCA), Chapter 13

Peace Action Education Fund,
Chapter 13

The Population Institute, Chapter 12

Public Defender Service for D.C.,
Chapter 11

Roll Call Newspaper, Chapter 3

Science News, Chapter 3

Securities and Exchange
Commission (SEC), Chapter 11

Smithsonian Institution, Chapter 9

Society of Professional Journalists,
Chapter 3

Supreme Court of the United States,
Chapter 11

20/20 Vision, Chapter 12

United States Chamber of
Commerce, Chapter 11

Washington Center, Chapter 5

Washington Center for Politics and
Journalism, Chapter 3

Washington Monthly, Chapter 3

Washington Post, Chapter 3

Washingtonian, Chapter 3

Widmeyer-Baker Group, Inc.,
Chapter 5

Women's Legal Defense Fund,
Chapter 12

Woodrow Wilson International
Center for Scholars, Chapter 11

World Federalist Association,
Chapter 12

Florida

Jacksonville

Florida Times-Union, Chapter 3

Miami

Best Buddies International,
Chapter 13

Miami Herald, Chapter 3

Sarasota

Mote Marine Laboratory, Chapter 7

Georgia

Atlanta

Camp Fire Boys and Girls, Inc.—
Georgia Council, Chapter 13

Carter Center, Chapter 11

CNN, Chapter 4

Southface Energy Institute,
Chapter 13

Idaho

Boise

Ore-Ida Foods, Chapter 5

Illinois

Brookfield

Brookfield Zoo, Chapter 7

Carol Stream

Chilton, Chapter 3

Chicago

American Israel Public Affairs
Committee (AIPAC), Chapter 12

Museum of Contemporary Art,
Chapter 9

Evanston

Qually and Company, Chapter 8

Moline

Moline Dispatch Publishing
Company, Chapter 3

Peoria

Journal Star, Chapter 3

Springfield

Illinois Legislative Staff Intern
Program, Chapter 11

University of Illinois for Illinois
General Assembly, Chapter 11

Indiana

Greencastle

Society of Professional Journalists,
Chapter 3

Indianapolis

Central Newspapers, Inc., Chapter 3

Iowa

Monticello

Camp Courageous of Iowa,
Chapter 13

Kentucky

Louisville

Actors Theatre of Louisville, Chapter
8

Wendover

Frontier Nursing Service, Chapter 7

Maine

Brunswick

Maine State Music Theatre, Chapter
8

Maryland

Baltimore

National Aquarium in Baltimore,
Chapter 7

Landover

Fourth World Movement, Chapter 13

Ocean City

Ocean City Advertising Agency,
Chapter 5

Silver Spring

Rock Creek Foundation, Chapter 13

Wildlife Habitat Council, Chapter 13

Massachusetts

Belmont

Aigner Associates, Chapter 5

Boston

Beacon Press, Chapter 3

C. Paul Luongo Company, Chapter 5

Hill, Holiday, Chapter 5

Houghton Mifflin, Chapter 3

Immigrant Workers' Resource
Center, Chapter 13

Massachusetts Public Interest
Research Group (MASSPIRG),
Chapter 13

Smithsonian Institution, Chapter 9

Cambridge

American Repertory Theatre,
Chapter 8

Center for Campus Organizing
(CCO), Chapter 12

City of Cambridge, Chapter 13

Falmouth

College Light Opera Company,
Chapter 8

Framingham

American Cancer Society, Chapter 7

Lee

Jacob's Pillow Dance Festival,
Chapter 8

Lincoln

David R. Godine, Publisher,
Chapter 3

Monterey

Gould Farm, Chapter 13

Newton

Franklin Advertising Associates,
Inc., Chapter 5

Watertown

Charlesbridge Publishing, Chapter 3

Waverley

A.E. Schwartz and Associates,
Chapter 6

Training Consortium, Chapter 6

Williamstown

Williamstown Theatre Festival,
Chapter 8

Winchester

Faber and Faber, Inc., Chapter 3

Worcester

Greater Media Cable, Chapter 4

Michigan

Birmingham

Wall Street Music, Chapter 10

Detroit

Detroit Free Press, Chapter 3

Minnesota

Minneapolis

Chrysalis, a Center for Women,
Chapter 13

General Mills, Chapter 5

Missouri

St. Louis

Coro Fellows Program in Public
Affairs, Chapter 13

Nebraska

Omaha

Bozell Worldwide Public Relations,
Chapter 5

New Hampshire

Hancock

Boston University Sargent Camp,
Chapter 13

Hillsboro

Interlocken Center for Experimental
Learning, Chapter 13

Wediko Children's Services,
Chapter 13

New Jersey

East Brunswick

Catholic Charities, Diocese of
Metuchen, Chapter 13

Teaneck

Pro-Found Software, Inc., Chapter 6

New York

Albany

New York State Bar Association,
Chapter 5

East Meadow

Women's Sports Foundation,
Chapter 12

Millerton

Aperture Foundation, Chapter 3

New York

American Committee on Africa,
Chapter 13

American Management Association,
Chapter 5

American Woman's Economic
Development Corporation (AWED),
Chapter 13

Aperture Foundation, Chapter 3

Archive Films, Inc., Chapter 10

Barney's New York, Chapter 5

Benetton USA, Chapter 5

Bozell Public Relations, Chapter 5

CBS News, Chapter 4

Charlie Rose, Chapter 10

Children's Television Workshop,
Chapter 4

Chilton, Chapter 3

CityArts, Inc., Chapter 13

The Cloisters, Chapter 9

College Connections, Chapter 5

Comedy Central, Chapter 10

Coro Fellows Program in Public
Affairs, Chapter 13

Council on Economic Priorities,
Chapter 12

Federal Reserve Bank of New York,
Chapter 5

Harper's Magazine, Chapter 3

Hearst Book Group, Chapter 3

Insurance Services Office, Chapter 5

International Management Group,
Chapter 5

Intertec Publishing, Chapter 3

Ketchum Public Relations, Chapter 5

Late Show With David Letterman,
Chapter 10

Lobsenz-Stevens, Inc., Chapter 5

Manhattan Theatre Club, Chapter 8

Metro-Goldwyn-Mayer/United
Artists, Chapter 10

Museum of Modern Art, Chapter 9

The Nation, Chapter 3

NBC, Chapter 4

New Breed Entertainment, Chapter
10

New Dramatists, Chapter 8

New York City Fellowship Programs,
Chapter 11

Newsweek, Chapter 3

NYU Medical Center, Chapter 7

Peace Corps, Chapter 13

Penguin Books, Chapter 3

PolyGram, Chapter 10

Ruder Finn, Chapter 5

Skadden, Arps, Slate, Meagher and
Flom, LLP, Chapter 5

Smithsonian Institution, Chapter 9

Solomon R. Guggenheim Museum,
Chapter 9

Starlight Foundation, Chapter 13

Vibe Magazine, Chapter 3

The Village Voice, Chapter 3

Women's International League for
Peace and Freedom, Chapter 12

WXRK, Chapter 4

White Plains

New York Hospital, Cornell Medical
Center, Westchester Div., Chapter
7

North Carolina

Chapel Hill

North Carolina Botanical Garden,
Chapter 7

Winston-Salem

Human Service Alliance, Chapter 13

Ohio

Cleveland

International Management Group,
Chapter 5

Liggett-Stashower Public Relations,
Chapter 5

The Plain Dealer, Chapter 3

Toledo

The Blade, Chapter 3

Oklahoma

Oklahoma City

Oklahoma City 89ers, Chapter 5

Oregon

Beaverton

Nike, Inc., Chapter 5

Bend

The Bulletin, Chapter 3

Pennsylvania

Bala Cynwyd

Elkman Advertising and Public
Relations, Chapter 5

Philadelphia

CIGNA, Chapter 5

Earle Palmer Brown, Chapter 5

Philadelphia Magazine, Chapter 3

Schuylkill Center for Environmental
Education, Chapter 13

Pittsburgh

Pittsburgh Post-Gazette, Chapter 3

Radnor

Chilton, Chapter 3

Warmister

Middle Earth, Inc., Chapter 13

Rhode Island

Newport

Performance Research, Chapter 5

Tennesee

Hermitage

Hermitage Association, Chapter 9

Memphis

Playhouse on the Square, Chapter 8

Nashville

Dye Van Mol and Lawrence,
Chapter 5

Texas

Houston

Lunar and Planetary Institute (LPI),
Chapter 7

Virginia

Arlington

The Feminist Majority, Chapter 12

Springfield

DesignTech International, Inc.,
Chapter 6

Woodberry Forest

Woodberry Forest Summer School,
Chapter 13

Washington

Seattle

American Israel Public Affairs
Committee (AIPAC), Chapter 12

Seattle Times, Chapter 3

Wisconsin

Milwaukee

Milwaukee Journal Sentinel,
Chapter 3

Williams Bay

Outdoors Wisconsin Leadership
School, Chapter 13

Wyoming

Cody

Buffalo Bill Historical Center,
Chapter 9

NATIONWIDE

American Association of
Advertising Agencies, Chapter 5

American Red Cross, Chapter 13

Brethren Volunteer Service,
Chapter 13

CIGNA, Chapter 5

Dow Jones Newspaper Fund,
Chapter 3

Inroads, Inc., Chapter 5

Ketchum Public Relations, Chapter 5

Nike, Inc., Chapter 5

Student Conservation Association,
Chapter 7

INTERNATIONAL

Bermuda

Bermuda Biological Station for
Research, Inc., Chapter 7

Budapest

Internships International,
Chapter 14

Canada

Student Conservation Association,
Chapter 7

Dublin

Internships International,
Chapter 14

Florence

Internships International,
Chapter 14

Jamaica

International Partnership for
Service-Learning, Chapter 13

Japan

Japanese Exchange Teaching
Program (JET Program), Chapter 13

Jerusalem

American Israel Public Affairs
Committee (AIPAC), Chapter 12

London

Internships International,
Chapter 14

Madrid

Internships International,
Chapter 14

Melbourne

Internships International,
Chapter 14

Mexico City

Inroads, Inc., Chapter 5

Internships International,
Chapter 14

Panama

Smithsonian Institution, Chapter 9

Paris

Internships International,
Chapter 14

Santiago

Internships International,
Chapter 14

Stuttgart

Internships International,
Chapter 14

Worldwide

Brethren Volunteer Service,
Chapter 13

Worldwide Internships and Service
Education, Chapter 14

A Special Note for

International Students

About a quarter million international students pursued advanced academic degrees at the master's or Ph.D. level at U.S. universities during the 1995–1996 academic year, according to the Institute of International Education's "Open Doors" report. This trend of pursuing higher education in the United States, particularly at the graduate level, is expected to continue well into the next century. Business, management, engineering, and the physical and life sciences are particularly popular majors for students coming to the United States from other countries. Along with these academic options, international students are also taking advantage of opportunities for research grants, teaching assistantships, and practical training or work experience in U.S. graduate departments.

If you are not from the United States, but are considering attending a graduate program at a U.S. university, here's what you'll need to get started.

- If English is not your first language, start there. You'll probably need to take the Test of English as a Foreign Language (TOEFL) or show some other evidence that you are proficient in English. Graduate programs will vary on what is an acceptable TOEFL score. For degrees in business, journalism, management or the humanities, a minimum TOEFL score of 600 or better is expected. For the hard sciences and computer technology, a TOEFL score between 500 and 550 may be acceptable.

- You may also need to take the Graduate Record Exam (GRE).

- Since admission to many graduate programs is quite competitive, you may also want to select three or four programs and complete applications for each school.

- Selecting the correct graduate school is very different from selecting a suitable undergraduate institution. You should especially look at the qualifications and interests of the faculty teaching and/or doing research in your chosen field. Look for professors who share your specialty.

- You need to begin the application process at least a year in advance. Be aware that many programs will have September start dates only. Find out application deadlines and plan accordingly.

- Finally, you will need to obtain an I-20 Certificate of Eligibility in order to obtain an F-1 Student Visa to study in the United States.

For details about the admissions requirements, curriculum, and other vital information on top graduate schools in a variety of popular fields, see Kaplan's guide to United States graduate programs, *Getting into Graduate School.*

Access America

Kaplan's Access America™ Program offers international students English language training for academic and professional purposes, university and graduate college admissions counseling, advice on obtaining internships while studying, and programs for acquiring professional certification.

Whether you want to work and study in the United States or in your home country, Access America's unique approach to understanding the American system can assist you. The guidelines in this book will help you find an internship that will give you the kind of experience you need to find the right job when you finish your educaton. For more information on job hunting once you complete your degree, see *Access America's Guide to Studying in the U.S.A.*

Here's a brief description of some of the programs available at Kaplan centers through Access America:

The TOEFL Plus Program

At the heart of the Access America program is the intensive TOEFL Plus Academic English program. This comprehensive English course prepares students to achieve a high level of proficiency in English in order to complete an academic degree successfully. The TOEFL Plus course combines personalized instruction with guided self-study to help students gain this proficiency in a short period of time. Certificates of Achievement in English are awarded to certify each student's level of proficiency.

Graduate School/GRE Preparation

If your goal is to enter a master's or Ph.D. program in the United States, Kaplan will help you prepare for the GRE, while helping you understand how to choose a graduate degree program in your field.

Preparation for Other Entrance Exams

If you are interested in attending business school, medical school, or law school in the United States, you will probably have to take a standardized entrance exam. Admission to these programs is very competitive and exam scores are an important criteria.

Graduate Management Admissions Test (GMAT) Preparation. If you are interested in attending business school, you will probably need to take the GMAT. Kaplan can help you prepare for the GMAT, while helping you understand how to choose a graduate management program that's right for you.

Law School Admissions Test (LSAT) Preparation. If you plan to enter a law school in the United States, Kaplan will help you determine whether you need to take the LSAT while helping you to choose an appropriate law program.

Medical College Admissions Test (MCAT) Preparation. If you plan to enter a medical school in the United States, Kaplan can help you prepare for the MCAT. Kaplan also offers professional counseling and advice to help you gain a greater understanding of the American education system. We can help you with every step in the admissions process, from choosing the right medical school, to writing your application, to preparing for the interview.

United States Medical Licensing Exam (USMLE) and Other Medical Licensing. If you are a medical graduate who would like to be FCMFMG certified and obtain a residency in a U.S. hospital, Kaplan can help you prepare for all three steps of the USMLE.

If you are a nurse who wishes to practice in the United States, Kaplan can help you prepare for the Nursing Certification and Licensing Exam (NCLEX) or Commission on Graduates of Foreign Nursing Schools (CGFNS) exam. Kaplan will also prepare you with the English and cross-cultural knowledge that will help you become an effective nurse.

Business Accounting/CPA (Certified Public Accounting). If you are an accountant who would like to be certified to do business in the United States, Kaplan can help you prepare for the CPA exam and assist you in understanding the differences in accounting procedures in the United States.

Applying to Access America

To get more information, or to apply for admission to any of Kaplan's programs for international students or professionals, you can write to us at:

> Kaplan Educational Centers, International Admissions Department
> 888 Seventh Avenue, New York, NY 10106

Or call us at 1-800-522-7770 from within the United States, or at 01-212-262-4980 outside the United States. Our fax number is 01-212-957-1654. Our E-mail address is world@kaplan.com. You can also get more information or even apply through the Internet at http://www.kaplan.com/intl. Good luck with your internship.

come to us for
the best prep

about
KAPLAN

EDUCATIONAL CENTERS

"How can you help me?"

From childhood to adulthood, there are points in life when you need to reach an important goal. Whether you want an academic edge, a high score on a critical test, admission to a competitive college, funding for school, or career success, Kaplan is the best source to help get you there. One of the nation's premier educational companies, Kaplan has already helped millions of students get ahead through our legendary courses and expanding catalog of products and services.

"I have to ace this test!"

The world leader in test preparation, Kaplan will help you get a higher score on standardized tests such as the SSAT and ISEE for secondary school, PSAT, SAT, and ACT for college, the LSAT, MCAT, GMAT, and GRE for graduate school, professional licensing exams for medicine, nursing, dentistry, and accounting, and specialized exams for international students and professionals.

Kaplan's courses are recognized worldwide for their high-quality instruction, state-of-the-art study tools and up-to-date, comprehensive information. Kaplan enrolls more than 150,000 students annually in its live courses at 1,200 locations worldwide.

"How can I pay my way?"

As the price of higher education continues to skyrocket, it's vital to get your share of financial aid and figure out how you're going to pay for school. Kaplan's financial aid resources simplify the often bewildering application process and show you how you can afford to attend the college or graduate school of your choice.

KapLoan, The Kaplan Student Loan Information Program,* helps students get key information and advice about educational loans for college and graduate school. Through an affiliation with one of the nation's largest student loan providers, you can access valuable information and guidance on federally insured parent and student loans. Kaplan directs you to the financing you need to reach your educational goals.

"Can you help me find a good school?"

Through its admissions consulting program, Kaplan offers expert advice on selecting a college, graduate school, or professional school. We can also show you how to maximize your chances of acceptance at the school of your choice.

"But then I have to get a great job!"

Whether you're a student or a grad, we can help you find a job that matches your interests. Kaplan can assist you by providing helpful assessment tests, job and employment data, recruiting services, and expert advice on how to land the right job. Crimson & Brown Associates, a division of Kaplan, is the leading collegiate diversity recruiting firm helping top-tier companies attract hard-to-find candidates.

Kaplan has the tools!

For students of every age, Kaplan offers the best-written, easiest-to-use **books.** Our growing library of titles includes guides for academic enrichment, test preparation, school selection, admissions, financial aid, and career and life skills.

Kaplan sets the standard for educational **software** with award-winning, innovative products for building study skills, preparing for entrance exams, choosing and paying for a school, pursuing a career, and more.

Helpful **videos** demystify college admissions and the SAT by leading the viewer on entertaining and irreverent "road trips" across America. Hitch a ride with Kaplan's *Secrets to College Admission* and *Secrets to SAT Success.*

Kaplan offers a variety of services **online** through sites on the Internet and America Online. Students can access information on achieving academic goals; testing, admissions, and financial aid; careers; fun contests and special promotions; live events; bulletin boards; links to helpful sites; and plenty of downloadable files, games, and software. Kaplan Online is the ultimate student resource.

KAPLAN®

Want more information about our services, products, or the nearest Kaplan educational center?

HERE

Call our nationwide toll-free numbers:

1–800–KAP–TEST
(for information on our live courses, private tutoring and admissions consulting)

1–800–KAP–ITEM
(for information on our products)

1–888–KAP–LOAN*
(for information on student loans)

Connect with us in cyberspace:
On **AOL**, keyword **"Kaplan"**
On the Internet's World Wide Web, open **"http://www.kaplan.com"**
Via E-mail, **"info@kaplan.com"**

Write to:
Kaplan Educational Centers
888 Seventh Avenue
New York, NY 10106

Feeling Left Out?

If your organization's internship program wasn't listed here and you'd like it to appear in the next edition, please send the following information to the *Yale Daily News*:

- Company address, phone and fax numbers, and E-mail address
- Title of the internship position
- Department
- Number of positions offered annually
- Description of the position
- Qualifications
- Salary/compensation
- Dates/length of the position
- Location of the position
- Average number of applicants annually
- Potential for job placement
- Application process
- Deadline
- Who to contact

Send by January 31 to:

**Editor
Guide to Internships
Yale Daily News
P.O. Box 209007
New Haven, CT 06520-9007
(203) 432-2414 / fax (203) 432-7425**